Enhancing Enterprise and Service–Oriented Architectures with Advanced Web Portal Technologies

Greg Adamson
University of Melbourne, Australia

Jana Polgar
Dialog IT, Australia

Information Science
REFERENCE

Managing Director:	Lindsay Johnston
Senior Editorial Director:	Heather Probst
Book Production Manager:	Sean Woznicki
Development Manager:	Joel Gamon
Development Editor:	Heather Probst
Acquisitions Editor:	Erika Gallagher
Typesetters:	Devvin Earnest, Deanna Jo Zombro
Cover Design:	Nick Newcomer, Lisandro Gonzalez

Published in the United States of America by
Information Science Reference (an imprint of IGI Global)
701 E. Chocolate Avenue
Hershey PA 17033
Tel: 717-533-8845
Fax: 717-533-8661
E-mail: cust@igi-global.com
Web site: http://www.igi-global.com

Library of Congress Cataloging-in-Publication Data

Enhancing enterprise and service-oriented architectures with advanced web portal technologies / Greg Adamson and Jana Polgar, editors.
     p. cm.
  Includes bibliographical references and index.
  Summary: "This book offers the latest research and development within the field, filled with case studies, research, methodologies and frameworks from contributors around the world and addressing a wide range of subject matters, levels of technical expertise and development, and new technological advances within the field"--Provided by publisher.
  ISBN 978-1-4666-0336-3 (hardcover) -- ISBN 978-1-4666-0337-0 (ebook) -- ISBN 978-1-4666-0338-7 (print & perpetual access) 1. Web portals. 2. Information technology. I. Adamson, Greg, 1954- II. Polgar, Jana, 1945-
  HD30.37.E54 2012
  025.042'2--dc23
                          2011045046

British Cataloguing in Publication Data
A Cataloguing in Publication record for this book is available from the British Library.

All work contributed to this book is new, previously-unpublished material. The views expressed in this book are those of the authors, but not necessarily of the publisher.

Table of Contents

Section 2
Security, Architecture and Mobility in Portals

Section 3
Practical Experiences of Business Today

Detailed Table of Contents

Section 1
Portal Technology

Chapter 1

    Jana Polgar, NextDigital, Australia

Today the Web is used as a means to allow people and business to use services, get information and conduct transactions. Businesses today depend upon their visibility in their respective marketplaces and provision of e-services to customers. The Internet has become an important delivery mechanism of business visibility. Internet also significantly extends businesses capabilities to sell and buy worldwide. Therefore, the company website plays important role in maintaining and extending the business opportunities over the Internet. One of delivery tools are Content Servers (CMS). The paper discusses the issues and reasons why companies should use CMS to enhance their visibility.

Chapter 2

    Jun-Jang Jeng, IBM, USA
    Ajay Mohindra, IBM, USA
    Jeaha Yang, IBM, USA
    Henry Chang, IBM, USA

Application services entail multi-billion dollars of market in IT industry. However, to construct an application service is a labour- intensive and error-prone process. Application services developed through traditional development methods expose the same pitfalls that are witnessed in most development processes of enterprise applications such as late delivery, over budget, unpredictable quality, lack of reuse and so on. The paper investigates the process of leveraging clouds in developing application services within the context of large corporate with the magnitude of thousands of application services being built, delivered and used. Instead of using cloud simply for a better runtime engine, it is being used as the development platform to accelerate and optimize the solution development process based on large scale application services.

Jerh. O'Connor, IBM, Ireland
Ronan Dalton, IBM, Ireland
Don Naro, IBM, Ireland

Human Resources departments are often burdened with administrative tasks performed on behalf of employees who lack the tools necessary to complete these tasks themselves. A software approach known as self-service aims to streamline HR processes by providing employees with access and control of their personal information. Different approaches to self-service have been developed, including solutions offered by SAP, Sage Software, and IBM. This paper examines the approach taken by IBM Lotus Workforce Management, which is a self-service solution for IBM WebSphere Portal.

Jana Polgar, Next Digital, Australia

Portlets based on JSR168 and JSR 286 specifications are used in portal applications. Web Services for Remote Portlets (WSRP)provide the way to use light weight SOA integration. This paper examines the relationship of WSRP specifications (1.0 ans 2.0) with the portlet specifications JSR 168 and JSR 286 and evaluates some shortcomings of WSRP specification 1.0. The paper also discusses the impact of WSRP 2.0 and the portlet specification JSR 286 on "on glass" integration paradigm.

Tony Polgar, Dialog IT, Australia

Currently, there is a demand for integration using web services in a portal and it is expected that other business partners would connect to these services in the Service Oriented Architecture (SOA) fashion. Such web services have to be published in the repository accessible to all partners such as UDDI. Web Services for Remote Portlets (WSRP) attempt to provide solution for implementation of lightweight SOA. UDDI extension for WSRP enables the discovery and access to user facing web services provided by business partners while eliminating the need to design local user facing portlets. Most importantly, the remote portlets can be updated by the web service providers from their own servers. Remote portlet Consumers are not required to make any changes in their portals to accommodate updated remote portlets. This approach results in easier team development, upgrades, administration, low cost development and usage of shared resources. Furthermore, with the growing interest in SOA, WSRP should cooperate with service bus (ESB).

Jana Polgar, Dialog IT, Australia

Web analytics are typically branded as a tool for measuring website traffic. They can be equally well used as a tool for business research, results of advertising campaigns and market research. Web analytics provides data on the number of visitors, page views, measure a visitor's journey on a website, etc. This collection of data is typically compared against key performance indicators, and used to improve a web site or marketing campaign's audience response. Tracking portal visits is important in order to obtain better understanding which parts of the portal are delivering value. However, portals have unique attributes associated with the page composition techniques which pose specific challenges, and offer new opportunities to gain insights about portal usage and user behaviour. Portals are inherently multidimensional, and effective tool to monitor and analyse portal data usage must be able to support multidimensional analysis.

Chapter 7

Modern web applications and servers such as Portal require adequate support for integration of search services. The primary reasons being user focused information delivery and user interaction, as well as new technologies used to render such information for the user. An example being the two fundamental problems that web crawlers in the past already had to deal with: dynamic content and Javascript generated content. Even today the solution is simple: ignore such web pages. In order to enable 'search' in Portals, a different 'crawling' paradigm is required to allow for search engines to gather and consume information. WebSphere Portal provides a framework which propagates content and information through so-called 'Seedlists' - comparable to HTML based sitemaps, but richer in terms of features. Of course it mandates that information or content delivering applications need to be 'search engine aware' - it requires them to enable services and seedlists for fast, efficient and complete delivery of content and information. This would be the main integration point for search engines into the portal for Portal site search services with rich and user focused search experience. The apaper also discusses the options of how such technologies can also allow for more efficient crawling of public Portal sites by the prominent Internet search engines as well as discussing some myths around search engine optimization.

Chapter 8

While Portals are very good at aggregating and integrating applications "at the glass" on desktop PCs and laptop browsers, more and more users expect to access Portals on their mobile devices. The challenge to support multiple devices is a difficult one. Standard HTML web pages cannot be delivered to most mobile devices. These devices have different capabilities such as screen sizes, image formats, input methods, etc. With thousands of devices in the marketplace and the frequent introduction of new devices, how can a Portal support the many types of mobile devices that want to connect to the Portal's many applications? The focus of this paper is to discuss the issues and solutions to this many-to-many relationship. The solution is seen in the IBM Mobile Portal Accelerator which provides multiple device support from a Portal by using a version of XHTML called XDIME as the content markup and a multi-channel component coupled with a device repository to provide the proper device specific view. As a result, the page that is sent to the device is appropriate for that specific device and its capabilities, where no horizontal scrolling is required, all the information fits on the screen, the forms work, and all images are rendered properly creating a positive user experience.

Section 2
Security, Architecture and Mobility in Portals

The paper deals with the security issues specifically proposed hybrid identity fusion model at decision level for our Simultaneous Threat Detection Systems. The hybrid model is comprised of mathematical and statistical data fusion engines; Dempster Shafer, Extended Dempster and Generalized Evidential Processing (GEP). The Simultaneous Threat Detection Systems improves threat detection rate by 39%. In terms of an efficiency & performance, the comparison of 3 inference engines of the Simultaneous Threat Detection Systems showed that GEP is the better data fusion model as compared to Dempster Shafer and Extended Dempster Shafer. GEP increased precision of threat detection from 56% to 95%.

Tracking the behaviour of users of online learning systems is an important issue, but current techniques have not been able to give deep views on what users do with Web-based learning systems. This paper shows how use of Ajax can provide a richer model of how users / learners interact with Web systems. A case study is discussed and results analysed.

Average Revenue Per User (ARPU) is a measure of the revenue generated by Users of a particular business service. It is a term most commonly used by consumer communications and networking businesses. For mobile devices, they try to generate ARPU through network and content services (value-added services) that they make accessible to the User. It seems that the more accessible these services are, the greater the ARPU generated - the harder something is to find, the less likely someone is to use it. This paper explores the potential Continuum between ARPU and service discoverability for mobile services by comparing and contrasting various technologies with respect to development, user experience, security, and commercialisation.

Chapter 12

Sofien Khemakhem, CNRS and University of Toulouse, France, & University of Sfax, Tunisia
Khalil Drira, CNRS and University of Toulouse, France
Mohamed Jmaiel, University of Sfax, Tunisia

Software components composition can improve the efficiency of knowledge management by composing individual components together for complex distributed application. There are two main research in knowledge representation for component composition: the syntactic based approach and the semantic-based approach. . In this work, we propose an integrated ontology-supported software component composition, which provides a solution to knowledge management. Our novel search engine(SEC++) provides dual modes to perform component composition. Ontologies are employed to enrich semantics at both the component description and composition. SEC++ is an efficient search engine which helps developer to select components by considering two different contexts: single QoS-based component discovery and QoS-based optimization of component composition.

Chapter 13

Amit Goel, RMIT University, Australia

Computer Software Intensive systems have become ingrained in our daily life. Apart from obvious scientific and business applications, various embedded devices from cars to iPhones to washing machines, are empowered with computer software. Such a diverse application of Computer Software has led to inherent complexity in building such systems. As civilizations moved forward, the concept of architectural thinking and practice was introduced to grapple with the complexity and other challenges of creating buildings, skyscrapers, townships and cities. The Practice of Software Architecture is an attempt to understand and handle similar challenges in Software Intensive Systems. The paper introduces software architecture and the underlying philosophy thereof. The paper also provokes a discussion around the present and future of Software Architecture. This paper also discusses skills and role of Software Architect.

Section 3
Practical Experiences of Business Today

Chapter 14

Manish Gupta, State University of New York, Buffalo, USA
Raj Sharman, State University of New York, Buffalo, USA

Despite so much research done on benefits of web portals to companies, no research exists that looks into impact of adoption of web-portals on company's market valuation. This paper looks into impact of web-portal announcements on company's stock prices (market value). Using event-study methodology, we provide empirical evidence on the effect of announcements of web portals on the market valuation of the company for a sample of 25 publicly traded companies in year 2008. The study examines stock data to access investors and shareholders' reactions to web portal announcements. Published results indicate that web portal announcements does significantly positively influence investors' perceptions about the financial worth and future prospects of the company. The authors discuss these findings in detail and present implications for both research and practice. The findings of this study offer insights that can be used by managers and executives in understanding the role and effect of such announcements on companies' market value.

Chapter 15

Portals, and Service Oriented Architecture in general, simplify the process of delivering services to users. But this doesn't represent a fundamental change to the user experience. Changing the user experience depends on business intent, and while Web 2.0 functionality is available for users today, corporate and government department practices are often not ready to embrace it. In fact the most effective uptake of new technologies may not be the company intranet at all, but an external company community hosted on MySpace or FaceBook. This case study examines the experiences of delivering both strategy and implementations to Fortune 500-type companies and Australian government departments. It compares the experience of delivering web and pre-web services, and notes the impact of the global financial crisis on innovation, concluding with the observation that in this changing climate SOA remains part of the industry practitioner's toolkit.

Chapter 16

Not-for-profit organisations make extensive use of portal technology for public outreach and service delivery. While lacking the resources of the commercial sector, their needs may be similarly complex if they are relying on a portal for service delivery to a vulnerable client sector, or for the protection of medical records. This case study looks at the challenges of a resource-poor sector and how it meets often sophisticated requirements. The study is based on the experience of industry practitioner Rick Noble, who has worked with not-for-profits in a technology development, support and management capacity for eleven years. He is interviewed by Greg Adamson.

Chapter 17

E-learning promises to improve the learning process through application of technology including portal technology. Portals can provide personalisation and interactivity functionality that e-learning requires. However, the long held promise that technology will improve learning has often failed to deliver. This paper looks at technology promise, and compares the specific demands of e-learning to the actual capability of portals and the underpinning Internet and World Wide Web. It then identifies four 'costs' of using technology for e-learning, and points to existing project management tools that may minimise the effect of these 'costs'.

Like the internet, a decade later Service Oriented Architecture is challenging many aspects of project management methodology. Having emerged from many years of speculation there is, perhaps, a mixed blessing with SOAs: while solving one type of problem, it merely serves to create an alternative set. But for the business objective focused professional who manages the risk-reward balance for an organisation, success is found in determining which set of problems is more manageable - on the assumptions that (i) we recognise the varying problem sets (ii) we can define them correctly and rigorously and (iii) we can deliver on that promise! And it is in the failure to validate these relatively simplistic but necessary assumptions (at the very start of any projects work) that I focus because we are still not getting the message!

The portal is a point of convergence for many uses and users. Along with the Internet itself, the portal crosses or combines many traditionally separate areas of research, each with its own perspective or perspectives. Such a combination creates a challenge for researchers: how to combine these various perspectives in examining portal and Internet use. This paper looks at the methodological challenge by combining five perspectives: historical, technical, media, regulatory and business theory. The paper provides examples of the misunderstanding found regarding concepts that are fundamental and widely understood within a single field, but unknown or misunderstood outside of that field. This misunderstanding between business, technologists, media theorists and regulators contributed to the gulf between Internet investment expectation and the 2000 to 2001 results, the US$4 trillion 'tech wreck'. Avoiding them will be important to the effective implementation of portal-based business solutions.

This article defines the standardized elements used in the building blocks portal design framework in detail. This article explains the (simple) rules and relationships for combining Containers and Connectors into portal structures. This article shares best practices, examples, and guidelines for effectively using the building blocks framework during portal design efforts.

Chapter 21

Portals gather and present content from a wide variety of sources, making the assembled items and streams more valuable for users by reducing the costs of content discovery and acquisition. By placing diverse content into close proximity, specialized forms of portals such as the dashboard support knowledge workers in creative and interpretive activities including synthesis, strategy formulation, decision making, collaboration, knowledge production, and multi-dimensional analysis.

Chapter 22

This article is a case study exploring the use of the Building Blocks portal design framework over a series of enterprise portal projects spanning several years. This article describes the business contexts that shaped each portal as it was designed, showing the use and reuse of design and development elements based on the Building Blocks. This article discusses the changes and adaptations that shaped the elements of the Building Blocks design framework over time.

Preface

INTRODUCTION

Since their origins in the 1990s as purpose built software applications catering for individual on-line users, portals have taken a central place in the web landscape of the 21st century. This is the second book in a series describing the evolving character of the Portal, and in particular its implementation using another typically 21st century technology, Service Oriented Architecture (SOA). Since the release of the first collection of writings on the subject, New Generation of Portal Software and Engineering: Emerging Technologies, the trends we wrote about then have become even clearer. The promise of SOA to simplify information technology development in a cost effective way, and the expectation of individuals that they would be able to access information tailored to them via their phone, laptop, or increasingly rarely their desktop, continue to drive portal technology adoption forward.

This second volume explains and reflects this trend in detail. As in the first it continues the approach of combining academic research and industry experience. The chapters here were originally published in an earlier format in the quarterly International Journal of Web Portals (IJWP). The approach we have followed in IJWP, and described in the preface to the first book in this series, remains true: 'First, a strong understanding of Portals, SOA, and the published research in these fields. In these areas IJWP sought to build on previous research. Second was an enterprise-based experience of factors that challenge implementation of Portal and SOA projects in practice. This brought in not just the practical challenges of such a project, but an enterprise customer view of the customer-vendor relationship in a field which requires large investment by both customer and vendor, and in its current phase a risk about the future of Portals and SOA shared by both customers and vendors. By combining these perspectives, IJWP provided a unique approach to research in the field.'

By 2010, when the originals of the chapters here were first published, the impact of the Global Financial Crisis on long-term technology investment was entrenched. Understanding the benefits of a Portal is easy. But for many reasons, quantifying them at the outset of a project is difficult. This has often been the case in the introduction of new technologies. The introduction of the US system of federal highways is an often quoted example. It is impossible to doubt the commercial benefit which has been achieved in the past half century from this project. But to have asked planners in the 1950s to identify what uses would be made of the road system even two decades later would have been a silly. Portals share the same characteristics of infrastructure projects. They provide the basis for services and applications that cannot be imagined, and certainly not quantified, at the outset. Those who build them expect to reap the rewards. However, 'I don't know what it will be used for' doesn't sit well in a business case. Even, 'Everyone else is doing it and we can't afford to miss out' sounds weak at a time when investments can only be made if they promise significant return in a short timeframe such as 18 months. This can lead to a gulf between investment need and investment appetite.

Where practical evidence is required, this calls for practical research. The chapters in this book lend themselves to this purpose. Practitioners describing and reflecting on their experiences of practical challenges, and theoreticians looking at the next generation of purposes and approaches in the use of Portals. We hope you find this a useful approach, and that it assists you in meeting the challenge of determining next steps in an ever-changing technical and business environment.

In this volume we have once again grouped contributions by topic, rather than chronologically, as follows:

- Portal Technology section: new developments in Portals, featuring, in particular, IBM extensive research in SOA, cloud middleware and portal search tools
- Section on Security, Architecture and Mobility in Portals contains several chapters dedicated to the research in portal security, portal architectures and portal mobile clients
- Practical experiences of business today: a review of the experiences of users of portal and SOA technology.
- Learning for future implementations: experiences today that assist us in contributing to the success of future implementations.

This book is structured around these four areas, and each of these is now examined in detail.

PORTAL TECHNOLOGY

Today the Web is used as a means to enable people and business access to information, services, and to execute financial transactions. Businesses need the worldwide visibility in their respective marketplaces. They also have to provide reliable provision of e-services to customers in order to maintain be successful. The Internet has become an important delivery mechanism of business visibility. Web portals with well designed services significantly extend businesses capabilities to sell and buy worldwide. The company website and its useability plays an important role in maintaining and extending business opportunities over the Internet.

What is a portal and a portlet? Different rendering and selection mechanisms are required for different kinds of information or applications, but all of them rely on the portal's infrastructure and operate on data or resources owned by the portal, like user profile information, persistent storage or access to managed content. Consequently, most of today's portal implementations provide a component model that allows plugging components referred to as Portlets into the portal infrastructure. Portlets are user-facing, interactive web application components rendering markup fragments to be aggregated and displayed by the portal.

There are a number of key conditions which make the web experience for all users as if it were custom fit for them incorporating their preferences, devices, location, social networks, and behaviours. Businesses need to meaningfully interact with, and listen to customers. On the other hand, customers must transform their online experience to two-way information sharing. This means that integration and service provision must be easy. To create interactive, context-aware Web applications, the application must be able to easily leverage and extend existing data sources such as CRM systems, social media sites, and back-end applications, as well as cloud-based services. However, developing application services through the traditional development cycle is a labour intensive and error prone process.

Content Management Systems (CMS) provide the way of achieving visibility and maintaining currency of content. A brief discussion of CMS by J Polgar ("*Do You Need a Content Management System?*") provides a perspective on CMS design development issues. Usually the CMS software provides authoring tools designed to allow users with little or no knowledge of programming languages or markup languages to create and manage content with relative ease of use. These tools represent an advantage as the development cost can be low and the content can easily be maintained by the users. However, the customization of content presentation is often required. A typical CMS would provide a presentation layer displaying the content to regular Web-site visitors based on a set of templates. The templates are sometimes XLST files. The content and presentation designer can opt for a web site created fully by the custom code, use CMS with embedded custom code, or keep CMS and portal code separately. Some CMS vendors have developed highly complex products that are often too complex for smaller organizations, and the design and management of such web sites can be a very frustrating task.

Vendors often deliver so called cloud applications (also known as *software as a service*, or SaaS) that actually are only one of the models of cloud applications. Real cloud applications are capable of providing benefits if they are designed to be cloud applications, and delivered in a cloud model. In general, cloud application are characterized among others by multi-tenancy in cloud space, seamless integration on demand including business driven configurability, fast deployment, provision of full control to the owner organization, and supports application scaling. The cloud provider is responsible for maintaining sustainable IT infrastructure as well as negotiated SLAs.

The chapter by Jun-Jang, et. al titled '*A Cloud Portal Architecture for Large Scale Application Service*' provides the cloud development framework called Cogito-C . The framework deals with application services development within the context of large corporate applications with thousands of application services being built and delivered. The framework enables real cloud application services to be developed and delivered. This framework is not using cloud simply as a better runtime engine. Rather, it is used as the development platform to accelerate and optimize the solution development process based on large scale application services.

One of the important features of portal application services is self service. Self service is utilized in many Human Resources applications such as SAP, Sage Software and IBM Lotus Workforce Management. In majority of applications, the self-service capabilities are designed as 'out-of-the-box' service with only a few options to customize. The chapter by O'Connor, et. al. titled 'Lotus Workforce Management' discusses the approach taken by Lotus Workforce Management software to HR self-service solution. The application focuses on providing three key features that allow organizations more choice and control over the implementation of a self-service solution. These features are extensibility, customization, and ease of integration which are implemented with one of the widely used portal engines such as IBM's WebSphere Portal, currently v7. Extensibility is provided through the WebSphere Portal framework that lets users add or remove components and functionality and determine the structure of communication between portal resources. Integration with IBM WebSphere Portlet Factory gives developers the ability to customize and design a solution that is tailored to the user's needs. WebSphere Portlet Factory is a very powerful and flexible tool for fast portlet building. It sits on top of a Service Oriented Architecture (SOA) and developers can easily use and deploy core assets and automatically assemble them into custom portlets.

Recently, we witnessed appearance of new portal standards such as WSRP 2.0 and JSR 286. Both standards greatly contributed to the portal capabilities. For example, inter-portlet communication in JSR 168 could only be achieved with great effort. Typical implementations would include vendor-specific extensions placed on top of the portlet. This solution often resulted in breaking inter-operability. Some solutions focused on portlets using a shared store to exchange data, such as the session context or a database. All of these workarounds typically required unstructured effort. Furthermore, the portals render and aggregate information into composite pages to provide information to users in a compact and easily consumed form. Among typical sources of information are web services. Traditional data-oriented web services require aggregating applications and provision of specific presentation logic for each of these web services. This approach is not suitable for dynamic integration of multiple business applications and content without using integration middleware such as Enterprise Service Bus (ESB) or similar middleware.

The chapter by J Polgar titled '*Using WSRP 2.0 with JSR 168 and 286 Portlets*' examines the relationship of WSRP specification with the portlet specification JSR 168 and evaluates some shortcomings of WSRP specification 1.0. The conclusion postulates that a clear architectural approach combining usage of WSRP and AJAX is required to enable creation of standards based, customizable, and dynamically generated reusable portlets that have required interactivity, response time and usability. The chapter also discusses the principles of building web services using the Web Services for Remote Portlets (WSRP) specification. The specification builds on current standard technologies, such as WSDL (Web Services Definition Language), UDDI (Universal Description, Discovery and Integration), and SOAP (Simple Object Access Protocol). It aims to solve the problem of traditional data oriented web services which required the applications to be aggregated before any specific presentation logic could be applied for presenting the content. The portlet standard (JSR 168) complements the WSRP mechanism by defining a common platform and APIs for developing a UI in the form of portlets. WSRP enables reuse of an entire user interface. One of the advantages is that only one generic proxy is required to establish the connection.

The demand for integration using traditional (WSDL) web services in a portal forces other business partners to connect to these services in the Service Oriented Architecture (SOA) fashion. Such web services have to be published in the repository accessible to all partners such as UDDI. In addition, all published services would have to be maintained by business partners including their presentation logic. Web Services for Remote Portlets (WSRP) attempt to provide a solution for implementation of lightweight Service Oriented Architecture (SOA). The UDDI extension for WSRP enables discovery and access to user facing web services provided by business partners while eliminating the need to design user facing portlets locally. Most importantly, the remote portlets can be updated by web service providers from their own servers. Remote portlet Consumers are not required to make any changes in their portals to accommodate updated remote portlets. This approach results in easier maintenance, administration, low cost development and usage of shared resources. Furthermore, with the growing interest in SOA, WSRP should cooperate with ESB.

The chapter by T Polgar titled '*WSRP, SOA and UDDI*' deals with the technical underpinning of the UDDI extensions for WSRP and their role in web service sharing among business partners. A brief description of the architectural view of using WSRP in enterprise integration tasks and the role Enterprise Service Bus (ESB) is presented to outline the importance of remote portlets in the integration process. Leveraging web services through portals by means of the Java Portlet and WSRP standards gives companies a relatively easy way to begin implementing an SOA. Most portals have built-in support for the

Java Portlet API and WSRP in the Portal Server which makes implementing a portal-based SOA even easier and cheaper. Portal support for the WSRP standard allows companies to easily create and offer SOA-style services and publish them in order to be accessed by other Consumers. The Consumers can combine several of these user facing services from diverse sources and portals to form the visual equivalent of composite applications. This approach delivers entire services to the other Consumer in a fashion which enables them to conveniently consume the services and use them without any programming effort. Furthermore, the Enterprise Service Bus (ESB) can be used to create a controlled messaging environment, thus enabling lightweight connectivity. Using WSRP and UDDI extensions for remote portlets makes the end-user completely shielded from the technical details of WSRP. In contrast to the standard use of data-oriented web services, any changes to the web service structure are implemented within the remote portlet and the *Consumer* is not affected by these changes.

Web analytics are typically branded as a tool for measuring website traffic. They can be equally well used as a tool for business research, and to measure the results of advertising campaigns and market research. Web analytics provides data on the number of visitors, page views, measure a visitor's navigation through a website, and so on. This collection of data is typically compared against some metrics to indicate whether the web site is delivering expected values, and what improvements should be considered. These metrics are also used to improve a web site or marketing campaign's audience response.

The use of web analytics in portal applications is discussed in chapter by J Polgar titled '*Use of Web Analytics in Portals*'. Tracking portal visits is important in order to obtain better understanding of which parts of the portal are delivering value. However, portals have unique attributes associated with the page composition techniques, page and portlet refresh. Portals always present multiple topics on the same page which pose specific challenges to explore exciting opportunities allowing the web designer to gain insights about portal usage and user behaviour. Furthermore, portals are inherently multidimensional, and an effective tool to monitor and analyse portal data usage must be able to support multidimensional analysis.

Web analytics or site analytics are used to provide data about the number of visitors, page views, show the traffic and popularity trends. Portals are inherently multidimensional web sites. In portal applications, the key to knowing what to track and monitor is understanding how the site is built and how the page URL is formed. In addition, portals are often used in conjunction with Content Management Systems (CMS). The use of site metrics to capture and measure user activity primarily to understand end user needs, behaviours and site usability enable the designers to build better portals and better target the content. It is often expected that a knowledge of user behaviour would lead to increases in revenue with better content targeting and can also impact the cost of automatic tuning. Site Analytics are also know as being a factor in reduction of testing costs with better designs.

In portals, the integration with site analyser tools is often performed by generating reports based on the portal site analyser logs or manually embedding tags into portlets and themes. A well designed portal is expected to provide an environment for the necessary collection of analytics data and offer seamless integration of the web analytics engine with the portal. Web Analytics are typically gathered in one of following ways: server-side log analysis, active page tagging, and click analytics.

In many well performing organizations, analytics has replaced intuition as the best way to answer questions about what markets to pursue, how to configure and price offerings, and how to identify where operations can be made more efficient in response to cost and environmental constraints. Yet, as much as business leaders are eager to capture the benefits of new intelligence, they need to take analytics the full distance. Top performers are enacting their business analytics and optimization (BAO) vision, making it possible to make decisions operational and optimize business performance across the enterprise. To do this, they are using the most effective toolsets, governance and change management practices.

Modern web applications and servers such as a Portal require adequate support for integration of search services. The primary reasons are user focused information delivery and user interaction, as well as new technologies used to render such information for the user. Web crawlers in the past already had to deal with dynamic content and JavaScript generated content. The solution very often resulted in ignoring such web pages.

Portal Search supports the use of seedlists to make crawling websites and their metadata more efficient and to provide content owners fine-grained control over how content and metadata are crawled. WebSphere Portal provides a framework which propagates content and information through so-called 'Seedlists' - comparable to HTML based sitemaps, but richer in terms of features. Of course it mandates that information or content delivering applications need to be 'search engine aware' - it requires them to enable services and seedlists for fast, efficient and complete delivery of content and information. This would be the main integration point for search engines into the portal for Portal site search services with rich and user focused search experience. The chapter by Prokoph titled '*Search Integration with WebSphere Portal: The Options and Challenges*' discusses the options of how such technologies can also allow for more efficient crawling of public Portal sites by the prominent Internet search engines as well as discussing some myths around search engine optimization. He states that it is obvious that it becomes very tedious for crawlers to focus on the core information of a 'web page'. Ideally they should be able to dispose of any ornaments on such pages, like navigation bars, banners, and so on, and then focus on the core information provided on that page. So for any content published to such Portal pages, it would make sense to provide the crawler through a URL with that essential information only. Yet still it should be able to navigate the user via the search result list, to the correct context in which that specific content object is rendered. The Content Provider Framework provides the infrastructure for Seedlists. It defines for an entity within the Seedlist two types of URLs:

- crawler URL – as the name states, for a crawler to pick up the content itself, e.g. the content object from the WCM library which typically would get rendered through the Content Viewer portlet on one or more Portal pages
- display URL – this would be the URL that is given to a user to view that exact same content in the correct context of the Portal

In this way the search engine crawls and analyses the content delivered by the backend service through the crawler URL, whereas later on when searching, the user will be presented with the display URL in the search result list, to ensure that they see the information in the right context of the Portal.

As we already mentioned, portals are very good at aggregating and integrating applications so called at the glass on desktop PCs and laptop browsers. With the current trend of mobile devices, more and more users expect to access Portals on their mobile devices. The challenge to support multiple devices with different sizes of presentation medium is a difficult one. Current technology favours HTML for PCs and other desktops. However, standard HTML web pages cannot be delivered to most mobile devices. These devices have different capabilities such as screen sizes, image formats, input methods, etc. With thousands of devices in the marketplace and the frequent introduction of new devices, a Portal cannot support the many types of mobile devices that want to connect to the Portal's many applications. Fitzgerald and Van Landrum in their chapter titled *'Challenges of Multi Device Support with Portals'* discuss the issues and solutions to this many-to-many relationship. Their solution is seen in the IBM Mobile Portal Accelerator which provides multiple device support from a Portal by using a version of XHTML called XDIME as the content markup and a multi-channel component coupled with a device repository to provide the proper device specific view. As a result, the page that is sent to the device is appropriate for that specific device and its capabilities, where no horizontal scrolling is required, all the information fits on the screen, the forms work, and all images are rendered properly creating a positive user experience.

SECURITY, ARCHITECTURE AND MOBILITY IN PORTALS

Computer security has become critical issue in entire IT industry. Many organizations are facing security threats both from employees and outside intruders. Web portals are not immune to hackers and on many occasions, hackers have broken the existing security barriers and have damaged the IT infrastructure. The chapter by Sultan and Kwan titled *'Generalized Evidential Processing in Multiple Simultaneous Threat Detection in UNIX'* proposes a hybrid identity fusion model at decision level for Simultaneous Threat Detection systems. The hybrid model is comprised of mathematical and statistical data fusion engines: Dempster Shafer, Extended Dempster and Generalized Evidential Processing (GEP). The Simultaneous Threat Detection Systems improve threat detection rate by 39%. In terms of an efficiency & performance, the comparison of 3 inference engines of the Simultaneous Threat Detection Systems showed that GEP is the better data fusion model as compared to Dempster Shafer and Extended Dempster Shafer. GEP increased precision of threat detection from 56% to 95%.

Any producer of web-based material is interested in what users do with the pages they visit: what do they visit, how long do they spend there, and what do they do while there? In the educational domain, knowledge of a user's activities can help to build a better educational experience. The intent is to build up a model of the user and to customise the site to desirable users. Current techniques for tracking behaviour of users in online learning systems have not been able to give deep views and enable user behaviour analysis. The chapter by Newmarch titled *'Using Ajax to Track Student Attention'* shows how use of Ajax can provide a richer model of how users interact with Web systems. The chapter provides the description and results of case study deployed in one of the larger Melbourne teaching institutions. Ajax consists of a JavaScript call that can be made asynchronously to a web server. Typically such a request carries XML data, although this is not prescribed. The browser does not pause, or refresh while such a request is made. If a reply is received, the JavaScript engine may act on this. Some Ajax applications may use JavaScript to manipulate the browser's DOM model, to cause apparently interactive responses. The advantage of Ajax is that it can avoid the fetch-wait-refresh cycle usual in following hyperlinks or submitting forms.

Average Revenue Per User (ARPU) is a measure of the revenue generated by Users of a particular business service. It is a term most commonly used by consumer communications and networking businesses. For mobile devices, they try to generate ARPU through network and content services (value-added services) that they make accessible to the User. It seems that the more accessible these services are, the greater the ARPU generated - the harder something is to find, the less likely someone is to use it.

The chapter by Young and Jessopp titled '*How Thick Is Your Client?*' explores the potential continuum between ARPU and service discoverability for mobile services by comparing and contrasting various technologies with respect to development, user experience, security, and commercialisation. From the discussion presented in this chapter, it seems clear that increasing discoverability of services often involves more complex device integration efforts with the creation of a thin network hosted site accessed through the native device browser being the simplest but hardest to expose and thick native integration (idle screen, home screen) the most complex but highly surfaced. It is apparent that the more obvious the access method to a service is, the more likely a User is to make use of it at least once. The answer to the question, how thick is your client?, then appears to ideally involve facilitating the best User access possible to network services on a device-by-device basis. It is also to offer the User the choice of all possible access mechanisms (web, plug-in, portal, client) supported by their device; 'horses for courses' as it were. The consideration then is what the Business can financially justify to support this approach.

Software components composition can improve the efficiency of knowledge management by composing individual components together for a complex distributed application. There are two main research approaches in knowledge representation for component composition: the syntactic based approach and the semantic-based approach. The chapter by Khemakhem, et. al. titled '*An Integration Ontology for Components Composition*' proposes an integrated ontology-supported software component composition, which provides a solution to knowledge management. The proposed search engine (SEC++) provides dual modes to perform component composition. Ontologies are employed to enrich semantics at both the component description and composition. SEC++ is an efficient search engine which help the developer to select components by considering two different contexts: single QoS-based component discovery and QoS-based optimization of component composition.

PRACTICAL EXPERIENCES OF BUSINESS TODAY

Technology functionality only goes part way to identifying benefits that organizations will achieve from investment in Portals and Service Oriented Architecture. A major theme of the International Journal of Web Portals has been look at the experience of organizations, whether they are corporations, government agencies, smaller enterprises, or the not-for-profit section. Has the promise been met? Have expected benefits eventuated?

The first contribution in this section asks a specific question, does an announcement of intention to implement a Portal affect the market valuation of a company? Gupta and Sharman in '*Impact of Web Portal Announcements on Market Valuations*' identify that while significant research into the provision of electronic services has been undertaken, this relatively obvious metric has not been previously examined. Using the event-study methodology, they look at the impact of Portal announcements on a company's share price, using a sample of 25 publicly traded companies. This looked at share price movement prior to the announcement, and then in the period after the announcement. The cases themselves include various factors including the size of the enterprise. It also looks at two different approaches to the use of Portals foreshadowed in publicly announced plans to create a Portal. The first of these is to expand the range of services that are currently offered to existing customers. In this, a company undertaking such an action is seen to be proactively addressing the changing environment. It can also be viewed as being able to adopt new technologies to assist existing services such as communication, collaboration, information and personalization. The other area is to use the Portal to reach new customers, and a Portal provides a platform on which a company can move into other market segments. The findings of this report were that announcements of plans to implement a Portal provide a significant boost to market value.

The ubiquity of Portals for modern enterprises has in turn led to an expectation that technology service providers will have the necessary skills to advise and implement these solutions for their customers. The second chapter of this section, '*Part of the Tool Kit: SOA and Good Business Practices*' is a case study conducted with Wong from the service provider, e-CentricInnovations. This company focuses on providing services to Fortune 500-type companies and government departments. It specializes in several technologies including SOA, Portals, and collaboration tools. At the time of publication, Web 2.0 technologies including social networking were just beginning to make their impact in the enterprise environment. Wong looks at the experience with Twitter, Facebook, Google and others. Since then these applications have gone on to change many social and corporate environments. This is similar to the way that e-mail had changed practices in the previous decade. The need for an approach to addressing technologies that previously hadn't existed has therefore been born out. One irony described in this interview is the concern of many companies regarding allowing staff to share information via the company intranet. As Wong describes, in many cases the company's de facto intranet has become Facebook. Over-tight internal controls have therefore resulted in a complete loss of company control over the channel. Social media have also exposed a generational divide among corporate executives. For the older ones, they don't get it, but they don't care because they will have retired in five or ten years. On the other hand, a small proportion are beginning to innovate. While the growth of social media has made corporate technology use more complicated, Service Oriented Architecture has the potential to make it more simple. For Wong, there is nothing in SOA that couldn't have been done a decade earlier, with enough money, time, and a large enough team. However, SOA puts this functionality, in a standardized format, into the toolkit of every technology practitioner. It meets the long-held technology promise of reuse, 'invent it once and use it many times'.

While the focus of much of the research described in this book has been for enterprise implementations, both corporate and government, many of the lessons are also applicable to the not-for-profit sector. A case study is provided based on an interview with Noble, an industry practitioner with extensive understanding of and experience in the sector. The key finding of this is that the sector, rather than being less demanding, is actually more demanding. This occurs because some of the challenges facing the sector are more exacting, while the resources available are significantly more limited. For example, in providing harm minimisation services to drug users, perceived privacy is an important feature in gaining the confidence of the client base. Challenges such as these place the not-for-profit sector at the forefront of demands for sophisticated Portal software, yet without the resource base to undertake this through a normal commercial path. While commercial software providers will generally assist by making their software available to the sector at a significant discount, when the sector seeks to access technical support, it is competing for services at the market rate. In contrast to this, a self-help approach between different organisations in the sector using open source software has been a common response. This shared approach has also resulted in the sector being a strong supporter of standardisation in Portal and SOA technologies.

In the last chapter in this section, '*Portals, Technology and e-Learning*', Adamson looks at the benefits that Portals and Internet based technology generally can provide to e-learning. Some of the key attractions of e-learning are: the flexibility of delivery, in time, across geographies, across media formats; the rapid turnaround for changes to content; the inclusivity of the technology, being able to repurpose content for individuals for example with disabilities; the ubiquity of the World Wide Web today; the low cost of delivery; and the reliability of delivery with no single point of failure. These benefits have complex effects which need to be well understood. For example, the means by which educational services are delivered can provide an important aspect of the education itself. The loss of direct contact between a human teacher and a student could be expected to significantly affect the educational experience of a student.

LEARNING FOR FUTURE PORTAL AND SOA IMPLEMENTATIONS

The previous section examines the experiences of Portal and SOA implementation, and the impact that these have had. This section looks at possible approaches for improving such implementations. Richardson, a UK based practitioner with experience in major enterprise implementations, in '*Improving Our Approach to Internet and SOA Projects*', describes the experience of implementing new technologies using existing tools poorly. His focus is on the project world, where he sees the dominant project management methodologies as a mixed blessing. While methodologies such as Prince2 have provided standardized approaches, the experience of projects based on these remain mixed. He counterposes this to focusing on both the defined project management methods, and the soft skills around people management. Where the hard skills of project management are reduced to a set of product features, and these are presented as a comprehensive approach to the requirements of complex project (the rule rather than the exception for Portal and SOA projects), failure awaits. If practitioners then blame the tools they have missed the point: the tools by themselves were never going to assure reliable project delivery.

The difficulty of learning from past Portal and Internet projects in improving the delivery of future projects is examined in '*Challenges in Researching Portals and the Internet*' by Adamson from an historical perspective. Part of the challenge a decade after the dot-com crash of 200-01 is that with some $4 trillion share market value lost at that time, entire classes of business disappeared. It was impossible for even the best business model with the greatest governance and most competent staff to continue when the entire ecosystem in which they existed vanished. In these circumstances, instead of learning clear lessons from the first generation of e-businesses, we just learned that when a bubble bursts it isn't good place to be. A second difficulty is that Portals cross many boundaries. Is the ability to recognize a customer and provide them with tailored services a marketing function, a service function, or a business development function? Each of these areas of a traditional organization could expect the Portal to be their responsibility. At the same time, wherever it ends up (and some large corporations have been known to establish multiple competing initiatives), that area will have a traditional skill set which will initially fail to appreciate the complexity and detail of the other functions they are now taking on. A third problem has been a misunderstanding of what stays the same and what changes with the Internet. Debates included whether technology mattered, whether traditional business theory was relevant, whether companies had to actually provide a good or service, and whether companies could indefinitely replace profitability with 'first mover advantage'. Looking back many of these theories appear naïve. However, knowing which theories to keep and which to replace continues to be a challenge one decade after the crash. In addition, Portals and other e-business features have blurred the boundary between technology and business to an extraordinary extent. This has led to significant incorrect assumptions, as technology makes assumptions about business that are simply false, and vice versa. For example, the claim that technology provides competitive advantage (as defined by Michael Porter) is incorrect: competitive advantage is achieved by the way technology is applied, not by the technology per se. While a technologist may call that splitting hairs, from a business investment perspective the difference is significant.

An extensive discussion about better ways to create Portals is provided by Lamantia from the Netherlands, in '*Framework for Designing Portals*'. The framework itself has been introduced in the previous volume in this series. In this volume we examine the elements of the framework, how these elements work together, and consider some large enterprises where this framework has been tested. These include the rules and relationships in regard to the basic structural elements of Containers and Connectors. While the comments in the previous paragraph describe the blurring of lines between business and technology from the perspective of understanding investment drivers, this framework considers another cause of blur: the proposal that technology simplification at the highest level will allow business users to directly make use of Portal technology as they wish. The complex side of technology (from programming to testing) will then be done 'under the covers'. Lamantia's proposal works seamlessly across the design framework, information architecture, Portal experience, portlets, technology management and governance, business design, and enterprise architecture.

The second of Lamantia's chapters here looks at the goals that business will be pursuing as it engages more closely with what had previously been technical functions: collaboration, dialog, and support for social networking. The chapter looks at issues such as Portal management and governance. These are terms now shared extensively between business and technology, although it is difficult to determine whether there is a greater shared understanding of these terms than five or ten years ago. For example, on the simplest measure of technology engagement with the business, the relationship between a Chief Information Officer (CIO) and a Chief Operating Officer (COO) there is still no agreement. Strategists continue year after year to argue the merits of the CIO directly reporting to the Chief Executive Officer (CEO), versus the CIO reporting through the COO to the CEO. While this simple question arouses such difference of opinion, we cannot say that business and technology see eye-to-eye. The third of Lamantia's chapters deals with practical experiences of large enterprises which have applied the framework, and the experiences gained from this. He concludes with an approach that combines the technical and business: 'Looking around and ahead, we can see that the decentralized model underlying Web 2.0 reflects (or is driving, or both?) a fundamental structural shift; the information realm is ever more modular and granular. Consequently, the digital world is evolving complex structure at all levels of scale, and across all layers, from the organization of businesses into networks of operating units collaborating within and across corporate boundaries, to the structured data powering so many experiences. In fact, the whole digital / information realm - public, private, commercial, etc. - is rapidly coming to resemble the enterprise environments that encouraged the creation and use of the Building Blocks, and shaped their evolution as a design tool.'

CONCLUSION: IS OUR FUTURE IN THE CLOUDS?

In this book, there are several chapters discussing the difficulties and pitfalls the developers face when building web services, integrating applications, and architecting SOA frameworks. Clouds are next generation infrastructure which applies the mechanism of using virtualization technologies such as virtual machines. Three prime cloud delivery models are *Infrastructure as Service* (IaaS), *Platform as Service*

(PaaS), and *Software as Service* (SaaS). Cloud computing offers a pool of shared resources (applications, processors, storage and databases), on-demand usage of these resources in self-service fashion, elasticity (dynamic procurement), network access, and usage based metering.

It is expected that in the near future there will be millions of users using applications on the cloud. The reason seems to be in fast adoption and subsequent migration of client applications and processes to the new cloud service platform(s) currently being developed and delivered by major software and hardware companies such as IBM, Microsoft and others. It is not a dream to expect that in the future many larger software vendors could build their own cloud platforms and portfolios and sell cloud services. Such cloud platforms would have middleware to support service solutions, appropriate hardware and software for deploying customer cloud based applications, and usage metering services. The platform providers would provide consulting services to modify existing cloud models according to customer needs and administration services. Important administration services would cover management and tracking of business transactions, performance monitoring, data security, and many others currently burdening IT departments.

What should we focus on when considering cloud as new home for company applications?

Horizontal capacity scaling and parallelism: IT services and infrastructures always run out of capacity, and need to add capabilities on demand without investing in new infrastructure, training new personnel, or licensing new software. Cloud computing is typically seen as technology that uses the internet and central remote servers to maintain data and applications, and allows consumers and businesses to use applications without being involved in maintaining the IT infrastructure. In addition, it is believed that cloud resources allow applications scaling horizontally (scale up) with no capacity limits.

Typical applications are designed to be scaled vertically. However, the applications that are intended to be deployed on the cloud should be designed to scale-out (horizontally) rather than having the ability to scale-up. The process of scaling up is understood as adding more processing power by using faster CPUs, more RAM and larger throughput. All of that can be done by upgrading single server. But applications in the cloud need to have the ability to scale horizontally. It means adding more servers without any change in processing power. The design for horizontal scalability or parallel processing is the key to cloud computing architectures. The benefit of executing in parallel is that the same task can be completed faster using multiple servers. One of the key design principles is to ensure that the application is composed of loosely coupled processes, preferably based on SOA principles. This does not mean that the cloud enabled application would use a multi-threaded architecture (meaning resource sharing through mutexes works in monolithic applications). Clearly, multithreaded architecture does not provide any real advantage when there are multiple instances of the same application running on different servers.

How do we maintain consistency of the shared resource across these instances when application is not design for utilizing parallelism?

There are currently several suggestions as well as implementation in the research community. One method is using queues. The solution architects should aim at thread-safe the application which uses queues that cloud provides as means of sharing across instances. The application does not share resources any other way. However, queues are known for their negative impact on the performance of the system.

Many large applications use the '*Memcached*' algorithm which is caching technology (http://mem-cached.org/, Brad Fitzpatrick (2004), Chris Bunch, Navraj Chohan, Chandra Krintz, Jovan Chohan, Jonathan Kupferman, Puneet Lakhina, Yiming Li, Yoshihide Nomura (2010)). This is a high-performance, distributed memory object caching system, which is intended for use in speeding up dynamic web applications by managing database load and session management. '*Memcached*' allows configuring page snapshots at certain time intervals, avoiding the need to assemble together the same page over and over again thus saving some processing power of the underlying hardware. If a page is heavily based on DB reads with low sensitivity to time, the server load is reduced and the site becomes significantly more responsive. '*Memcached*' is currently used on high-traffic sites such as Wikipedia and others.

Another method is to use the *MapReduce* algorithm (D. Thain, C. Moretti, and J. Hemmes. Chirp (2009), D. Thain, T. Tannenbaum, and M. Livny (2005), P. Pantel, E. Crestan, A. Borkovsky, A. Popescu, V. Vyas (2009), Brad Fitzpatrick (2004)) where the variables across instances are handled by 'map,' and the 'reduce' part handles the consistency across instances. *MapReduce* is a programming model and an associated implementation is typically used for processing and generating large data sets. Users specify a map function that processes a key/value pair to generate a set of intermediate key/value pairs, and a reduce function that merges all intermediate values which are associated with the same intermediate key. Programs written in this functional style are automatically parallelized and executed on a large cluster of commodity machines. In addition, grouping the results of like keys (i.e., gathering all the intermediate key/values for a given word) is handled by Apache Hadoop (http://hadoop.apache.org/) in the background. The Apache Hadoop software library is a framework that allows for the distributed processing of large data sets across clusters of computers using a simple programming model. It is designed to scale up from single servers to thousands of machines, each offering local computation and storage. Delivering high-availability does not depend on hardware only, the library itself is designed to detect and handle failures at the application layer. This allows programmers without any experience with parallel and distributed systems to easily utilize the resources of a large distributed system.

As the solution for handling parallelism and distribution by applications is research in progress with many already successful implementations, there are still some areas where the cloud-enabled software is not readily available.

IDE: Applications have to be developed with parallelism in mind. It means there are some development platforms allowing the developers to write the code and test it. Cloud based applications have to be developed using appropriate IDEs. Ideally, these IDE would offer specific Cloud testing, performance testing, deployment options, plug-ins for multiple cloud providers, or embedded virtual cloud test environments.

Middleware: There is also important development in middleware. So far, middleware products are being used on dedicated physical servers. The advantage cloud utility model (pay-per-use) provides cannot be applied to applications and application platforms which are not designed to scale up or down based on SLAs. Therefore, a new generation of application servers, such as GigaSpaces XAP ((http://www.gigaspaces.com/files/InsideXAP.pdf) and Appistry and their CloudIQ middleware, are gaining popularity among cloud users. GigaSpaces eXtreme Application Platform (XAP) is an application server with XAP middleware enabling to build scalable and highly performing enterprise applications in Java and .Net. Scalable, on-demand middleware is also an appealing solution for large enterprises which want to avoid bottlenecks by outsourcing parts of the middleware infrastructure into a SOA-Cloud. Appistry CloudIQ middleware simplified the process of deploying applications on to the cloud and between the clouds to simple drag and drop.

Administration: It is also envisaged that professional services focusing of system administration, configuration and network management will undergo significant innovation or more likely these services will have to be automated. The cloud-based middleware will provide administrative tools to manage space, distribution, and performance using an automated approach across multiple clouds.

All the above areas would have to be considered when designing applications living in the cloud. We would like to mention that this discussion does not cover many other issues associated with cloud computing such as security issues; this is just a brief peek into cloud computing landscape.

Greg Adamson
University of Melbourne, Australia

Jana Polgar
Dialog IT, Australia

REFERENCES

Bunch, C., Chohan, N., Krintz, C., Chohan, J., Kupferman, J., Lakhina, P., et al. (2010). An Evaluation of Distributed Datastores Using the AppScale Cloud Platform. In *IEEE 3rd International Conference on Cloud Computing*, (pp. 305-312). ISBN: 978-0-7695-4130-3

Fitzpatrick, B. (2004). Distributed caching with memcached. *Journal Linux, 2004*(124).

Thain, D., Moretti, C., & Hemmes, J. (2009). Chirp: A practical global file system for cluster and grid computing. *Journal of Grid Computing, 7*(1), 51–72. doi:10.1007/s10723-008-9100-5

Thain, D., Tannenbaum, T. & Livny, M. (2005). Distributed computing in practice: The condor experience. *Concurrent Computing – Practical Experience, 17*(2-4), 323 -356.

Pantel, P., Crestan, E., Borkovsky, A., Popescu, A., & Vyas, V. (2009). Web-Scale Distributional Similarity and Entity Set Expansion. In *Proceedings of the 2009 Conference on Empirical Methods in Natural Language Processing*, (pp. 938–947). Singapore: ACL and AFNLP.

Section 1
Portal Technology

Chapter 1
Do You Need a Content Management System?

Jana Polgar
NextDigital, Australia

ABSTRACT

Today the Web is used as a means to allow people and business to use services, get information and conduct transactions. Businesses today depend upon their visibility in their respective marketplaces and provision of e-services to customers. The Internet has become an important delivery mechanism of business visibility. Internet also significantly extends businesses capabilities to sell and buy worldwide. Therefore, the company website plays important role in maintaining and extending the business opportunities over the Internet.

BUSINESS AND VISIBILITY

The goal of a web site for a company is to provide up-to-date information and content for a broad audience, with the ability to rapidly update and modify this information to reflect the latest company position, products etc. In this agile world, business moves rapidly, new promotions are introduced, prices change, and product features change. A successful web site ensures that the latest and most relevant information is shared with

customers. Such rapid move typically results in growing not only content volume (numbers of items) but content types (documents, images, streaming media, instant messages, mobile portals, e-mail and so on). In order to comply with such requirement some kind of Content Management System (CMS) must be used. The roots of the CMS software are in the necessity to have a tool to help in structuring large amount of data and content types, managing the site and the most importantly delivering the web site in a short period of time.

Well designed web site provides information and services, not just data, it is well organized,

DOI: 10.4018/978-1-4666-0336-3.ch001

and easily navigable. Over the years, the Content Management Systems have become integral part of the web sites. In past years we have observed a rapid growth in both content volume and content types which requires not only more powerful hardware but also significant improvement in the management capabilities of the CMSs and capability to meet users' expectations.

Delivering a Web site (Internet or intranet) that is successfully presented to its target audience is a challenging task. The problem or challenge can be attributed to a growing number of users who expect often more from a web site than the authors ever intended to deliver. Successful websites are expected to deliver more than just static information that is poorly laid out, with unclear navigation paradigm, and difficult to find. The successful website presents well navigable content and services matching customer requirements for information, good performance, and stability. In additions, businesses often use portals to support faster access to information, people, knowledge and education as well as provide the access to multiple services on single site.

The CMS and custom developed service delivery attached to the CMS typically present a variety of information:

- Information and services are dynamically published from back-end databases.
- Map-based displays
- Services such as booking systems, buy / sell transactional services
- Variety of dashboards often allowing personalization
- Front end business applications are often served via customized CMS
- Collaborative tools and wikis
- In Intranets, some functionality is delivered by HR or finance systems which need to be incorporated to the CMS.

Many of the above information and services are supported by some custom code in order to deliver required functionality and sophistication. The ultimate aim is to provide the web site to match customer expectations but at the same time maintain the currency of the information and keep the site maintenance within the budget brackets.

WEB SITES DESIGN FOR SUCCESS

We all have some experience with web sites and portals failing. The reasons are mostly because organizations do not understand the target audience, and their expectations. The designers of the successful web site should adhere to the rules outlined below:

- **Focus on organization objectives**: Organization has to have clear view of their objectives and the businesses requirements. A web site or portal must meet the objectives of the business and needs of its target audience..
- **Design and content balance**: This is mandatory requirement for a web site to be successful. Too much in either direction might mean that the Web site is perceived as difficult to use. Content and design are key elements for ensuring that the initial experience with the Web site is good and then repeated consumer visits can be expected. Since the evaluations are often subjective and difficult to measure objectively the usability experts together with web analytics software might be the best sources of success measures.
- **Importance of content updates**: Any type of content (textual, applications, video, and audio) is important as long as it delivers required information and pleasing experience for the consumer. However, consumers who revisit a web site expect some new content to be presented as often as possible,. A consumer can stop visiting the web site when the content is out of date or no longer relevant. Therefore, the maintenance of the web site is vital to the success and should

be planned and budgeted for as part of the project.

- **Understanding the audience**: To anticipate the usage patterns and number of visitors visiting the web site at any peak time is be difficult., but it is important for web site success. If the site is designed to accommodate hundreds of users in a peak hour, when actual numbers are in the ten thousands, this can lead to the Web site being slow and unresponsive. If more users are staying on the Web site longer, perhaps reading or watching video, then this can mean that total visitor concurrency numbers are higher than expected. Therefore, the experience for the visitor might become unpredictable. Understanding who the audience is, what they will be doing, and how they might be doing it is key to ensuring that a Web site does not fail.

VISION FOR CONTENT MANAGEMENT SYSTEMS

Usually the CMS software provides authoring (and other) tools designed to allow users with little or no knowledge of programming languages or markup languages to create and manage content with relative ease of use. Some CMS vendors developed highly complex products that are often too complex for smaller organizations, and the design and management of such web sites can be a very frustrating task.

The typical CMS would provide a presentation layer displaying the content to regular Web-site visitors based on a set of templates. The templates are sometimes XLST files. Most systems also use some form of server side caching which enables a better of performance. Administration is typically done through browser-based interfaces, but some systems require the use of a fat client (often the mobile CMS). In summary, a CMS are intended to support the following features:

- Identification of all key users and their content management roles.
- The ability to assign roles and responsibilities to different content categories or types.
- Definition of workflow tasks for collaborative creation, often coupled with event messaging so that content managers are alerted to changes in content. (For example, a content creator submits a story, which is published only after the copy editor revises it and the editor-in-chief approves it.)
- The ability to track and manage multiple versions of a single instance of content.
- The ability to capture content (e.g., scanning).
- The ability to publish the content to a repository to support access to the content. (Increasingly, the repository is an inherent part of the system, and incorporates enterprise search and retrieval.) so material can be refactored for new uses (e.g., use the same base content in different ways for desktop browsers, mobile browsers, and print output).

For the purpose of this paper we distinguish three main categories of CMS:

- **Enterprise CMS** refers to the technologies, strategies, methods and tools used to capture, manage, store, preserve, and deliver content and documents related to an organization business processes. It is often combined with a portal to allow the management of organization's information. It will often run on the Intranet.
- **Web CMS** is typically a web application which facilitates creation, content control, editing, and many essential maintenance functions. Most systems use database to store the metadata and pointers to the actual content.
- **Mobile CMS** is capable of storing and delivering content and services to mobile devices, such as mobile phones, smart phones, and

PDAs. Mobile content management systems often exist as add-ons of larger content management systems capable of multi-channel content delivery. Mobile content delivery deals with specific constraints including widely variable device capacities, small screen size, limited wireless bandwidth, small storage capacity, and weak device processors. As an example, WebSphere Everyplace Mobile Portal Enable extends business services by delivering content to mobile employees. It is a mobile portal solution which enables mobile Web applications to be delivered to mobile phones users and provides an environment that simplifies integration and deployment for developers.

One of the open source CMS is **UMBRACO** project with roots back to year 2000. It was released as open source in 2004: Umbraco is based on Microsoft's ASP.NET. Prior to that it was founder Niels Hartvig's home-grown weapon of choice for working as a freelancer. Today it is among the top fifteen most popular open source.NET applications and in May 2008 reported 50.000 installed and active websites. We will bring more details on UMBRACO in our next issue.

Another example of the Enterprise Content Management System is **Documentum**: It contains comprehensive suite of services for managing all types of content. Digital Asset Management is vital for storing, finding, accessing, and modifying rich media assets within a centralized repository. It support management of a wide range of assets, including photographs, design graphics, streaming video, Flash animations, Microsoft PowerPoint presentations, documents, and marketing collateral. Content Server uses an e object oriented model to store content and metadata in the repository. The metadata for each object is stored in tables in the underlying RDBMS. Content files associated with an object can be stored in file systems, in the underlying RDBMS, in content-addressed storage systems, or on external

storage devices. The variety of content types is supported by special services for examlle Media Transformation Services to handle digital media content such as audio and video files and thumbnail renditions. Metadata retrieval is supported by a special version of SQL called Document Query Language (DQL).

FatWire is another CMAs used by many large organisations. The FatWire architecture is composed of three layers: front end presentation, business logic layer, and back-end layer. Content Server sits on top of a database and an application server, and the rest of the FatWire content applications sit on top of Content Server. Each application utilizes and builds upon the capabilities of the ones below it in the stack.. One of the important features of FatWire is the capability to separate the format of the web pages from their content. This is accomplished by well structured metadata and through modular page design, where web pages are composed of blocks of code called elements. Another concept common to other CMS are assets. An asset is a Java object that allows managing the content and organize web site.

IBM Lotus Web Content Management provides a Web content management tool and platform that supports the delivery and management of business information. One of the features is collaborative approach to content creation. It allows standard CMS and Document Management functionality such as approval of processes, management, and assets. Lotus Web Content Management is well integrated with IBM Portal Server and other IBM tools..

CMS AND PORTAL BASED WEB SITES

Portals are often "complemented" by a sophisticated CMS. As CMSs have become richer in their functionality and capabilities, supporting large amount of publishing so called "out-of-the-box" they are often used as development platform to support customization of the web site or portal. The decision how much of custom code is reasonable to use and how to control the spread of customization and its growing sophistication while being able to maintain the web site and keep the cost within the budget.

We all know that some evaluation has to be done in order to make sound decision on what CMS would fit to the organisation. James Robertson is one of our regular contributors. He outlined well the approach to the CMS selection process in his paper (http://www.steptwo.com.au/papers/kmc_evaluate). His guideline evolve around a set of assumptions such as size of the organisation, complexity and type of the web pages, business requirements, CMS processing and structuring requirements and many others. His recommendations are worthwhile to look at even if you are not in the CMS evaluation process.

The customization usually intended to improve customer experience and provide richer services is often achieved by some custom code which is attached to the back-end database. Robertson in his paper identified three approaches (Robertson, 2009).

- **Published site is entirely created by custom code**. This approach typically provide good solution to meet the organisation objectives. Definite advantage to the organization is complete control over the site. The drawback is the possibility of exceeding the allocated budget boundaries. Such an web site typically sit on the top of a portal server and it is delivered via a custom java or .NET code. The integration with other back-end systems is very tight and any changes/content updates require new code to be written and integrated into the site. Furthermore, any application server upgrades and bug fixes would require additional budget and resources. It is usually extensive development project which could take longer than what is acceptable for fast content and service delivery. Finally, the

company can become locked in a vendor tool sets in order to reduce complexity of integration. Some vendors such as IBM provide tools supporting and speeding up the development (IBM Rational Application Developer, modelling tool and Portlet Factory). These tools not only reduce the time required for coding but they often reduce the complexity of development. However, the experienced developers who know the tools are needed and they cost money.

- **Portion of custom code is delivered via the CMS**. CMS and portals often complement each other. They pledge to reduce the development cost, complexity and integration effort. They enable functionality reuse, personalisation via a set of APIs, and simplify the development. However, downside is the tight coupling of portal and CMS which typically means hiring experienced developers and deal with the difficulties to implement more sophisticated customizations which are not included in the core functionality of portal or CMS. The developers must "bend the rules" and this often lead to maintenance problems. In addition, the integration with back-end applications can prove to be complex.
- **CMS and portal code are kept separate**. This solution provide more freedom in selecting the portal or CMS. The main advantage is often seen in reduced complexity of the development process. However, the functionality provided by the CMS as well as portal server are often not fully utilized. Full the integration between CMS and portal is often very difficult task. At the end the decoupling of portal and CMS may not result in expected simplification of the development process, meeting budget s and the delivery time constraints. Furthermore, significant developers expertise is required and the company may find itself to be dependent on the experts provided by consulting

companies "who know the applications" and become unreplaceable.

WEB SITE PERFORMANCE AND WEB ANALYTICS

Web site performance measurement are something called Web Analytics. To measure the quality and performance of a web site is typically subjective measure which does not fit to all situations. What may be a good measurement indicator to one website may not be adequate for another. The focus of web analytics is to obtain insights into the company website traffic and marketing effectiveness. Some software currently used for web analytics provides powerful, flexible and easy-to-use features to analyse the traffic data in an entirely new way. For example with Google Analytics, the company can utilize the measurements and prepare better-targeted adds, strengthen marketing initiatives and create web site better fitting to the company objectives. Eric Peterson states (2004):

Web Analytics is the assessment of a variety of data, including Web traffic, Web-based transactions, Web server performance, usability studies, user submitted information and related sources to help create a generalized understanding of the visitor experience.

Web Analytics are even hotter topic on mobile phones. Smartphones like the iPhone and Palm provide the ability to get any information while person is on the move. Measuring mobile web efficiency is not easy task considering the diversity of technologies involved and the rapid evolution of the mobile technology leading to large amount of different handsets, communication protocols, and presentation requirements (Young, in press).

Because the mobile opportunity (WAP Mobiles, 2009) is growing each day the company called Web Analytics Demystified started taking a closer look at measurement earlier this year (Peterson, 2009). The paper discusses the delivery issues to mobile customers (browsers, screen constraints, etc). Inaccuracy in mobile analytics is often sited as reason to justify lack of measuring effort. The paper also provides interesting discussion what is and what is not possible in order to obtain information about mobile web access. The comprehensive list of questions for the vendor who provides analytics applications provides good guidance for buyers.

REFERENCES

Mobiles, W. A. P. (2009). *WAP review*. Retrieved from http://wapreview.com/?id=134

Peterson, E. (2004). *Web analytics demystified: A marketer's guide to understanding how your web site affects your business*. Portland, OR: Celilo Group Media and CafePress.

Peterson, E. (2009). *The truth about mobile analytics*. Retrieved from http://www.nedstat.com/white-paper/uk.html

Robertson, J. (2009). *Custom code, CMS and portals*. Retrieved from http://www.steptwo.com.au/papers/kmc_customcode/index.html

Young, A. (in press). Mobilizing the enterprise. *International Journal of Web Portals*.

This work was previously published in the International Journal of Web Portals 2(1), edited by Greg Adamson and Jana Polgar, pp. 1-6, copyright 2010 by Information Science Publishing (an imprint of IGI Global).

Chapter 2
A Cloud Portal Architecture for Large-Scale Application Services

Jun-Jang Jeng
IBM, USA

Ajay Mohindra
IBM, USA

Jeaha Yang
IBM, USA

Henry Chang
IBM, USA

ABSTRACT

Application services entail multi-billion dollars of market in IT industry. However, to construct an application service is a labor- intensive and error-prone process. Application services developed through traditional development methods expose the same pitfalls witnessed in most development processes of enterprise applications such as late delivery, over budget, unpredictable quality, lack of reuse and so forth. We have leveraged clouds in developing application services within the context of large corporate with the magnitude of thousands of application services being built, delivered and used. Instead of using cloud simply for a better runtime engine, it is being used as the development platform to accelerate and optimize the solution development process based on large scale application services. This paper will focus on the portal architecture of this framework—coined as Cogito-C that contains four spaces: (a) infrastructure space; (b) application space; (c) business space; and (d) presentation space. This paper illustrates Cogito-C by scrutinizing the models in the aforementioned spaces. This paper will focus on the descriptive models of this framework. Examples are used to explain how this framework is organized and exploited for large-scale application services.

DOI: 10.4018/978-1-4666-0336-3.ch002

1 INTRODUCTION

Application services entail multi-billion dollars of market in IT industry. As such, application service providers and consumers continue investing considerable amount of time and efforts to develop application services-based solutions. Prepackaged business applications such as enterprise resource planning and customer relationship management offer significant benefits for businesses and are critical for business success. In this direction, leading package application ser-vice providers such as HP, IBM and SAP (IBM, 2009a), exploit domain-specific skills to help their clients excel competitors through cost reduction and risk mitigation. However, current approach is quickly encountering its very own limitation. First, the project planning and implementation for application services are still time-consuming and costly. It usually requires a variety of skills and expertise that many companies do not possess. There are also high cost associated with the ongoing management and maintenance of these applications. Second, because packaged applications are often tightly integrated with existing systems, the clients typically require a broad range of technical expertise to run them, which is usually hard or expensive to obtain from other parties. Third, with major concern about cost, both service providers and consumers fall into the vicious cycle—more cost reduction leads to more efficiencies which raise the expectation of more cost reduction. Consequently, no one is the winner because service quality is overlooked in this cycle. No room is left in the delivery process for considering quality—not to mention to improve it.

Application services pertain richer functionality and content than normal specialized services. They scale up the concepts of service-oriented computing to business-level so that service-oriented computing concepts became more receptive to business professionals. Technically, application services can be composed and configured to different but similar domains. An application service hides the implementation detail from its users and, by itself, can be also a composite of other services. To construct an application service is a labor-intensive and error-prone process. Moreover, application services developed through traditional development methods expose the same pitfalls that are witnessed in most development processes of enterprise applications such as late delivery, over budget, unpredictable quality, lack of reuse and so on.

Clouds are the next generation of infrastructure, bestowing the mechanism of virtualization technologies such as virtual machines. Clouds are able to dynamically provision services on demand as a personalized resource collection to meet a specific service requirement, which is established through negotiation and accessible as a service via network (Herssens, Faulkner, & Jureta, 2008a, 2008b). We have leveraged clouds in developing application services within the context of large corporate with the magnitude of thousands of application services being built, delivered and used. Instead of using cloud simply for a better runtime engine, it is being used as the development platform to accelerate and optimize the solution development process based on large scale application services. This paper will focus on the portal architecture of this framework - coined as *Cogito-C* that contains four spaces: (a) infrastructure space; (b) application space; (c) business space; and (d) presentation space. This paper illustrates *Cogito-C* by scrutinizing the models in the aforementioned spaces. This paper will focus on the descriptive models of this framework. Examples are used to explain how this framework is organized and exploited for large-scale application services.

The rest of this paper is organized as follows. Section 2 presents the overall architecture of *Cogito-C* with emphasis on market viewpoint. Section 3 presents briefly the cloud platform being used for realizing *Cogito-C*. Section 4 shows how applications are provisioned and deployed to *Cogito-C* and made ready for use by users. Section 5 describes the space that provides business services to service consumers. Section 7 contains related research efforts. Section 8 concludes this paper with future work of *Cogito-C*.

2 CLOUD SERVICE ARCHITECTURE

Cloud computing is claimed by many to be the next generation of computing paradigm. Cloud computing is more a style of computing than a set if disruptive technologies. Cloud computing comes into prime time when most information systems need a new way of increasing capacity, adding capabilities dynamically without investing in new infrastructure, training new knowledge-intensive staff, and/or licensing new software. Cloud computing also covers the capabilities of utility computing such as subscription-based or pay-per-use service that, in real time over the Internet, to extend IT's existing capabilities (Knorr & Gruman, 2009). On the surface, Clouds appear to be the combination of old concepts Grid, SOA, network, storage, dynamic resource management, modular design etc. Nevertheless, cloud computing enables a new service market for service providers, service consumers and service brokers. This idea is derived from the concept of market-oriented programming (Wellman, 1994; Mullen & Wellman, 1995) which is aimed to solve a distributed resource allocation problem by formulating a computational economy and finding its competitive equilibrium.

Service consumer relies on the cloud to provide services as an alternative for their technology/ information system's platform. Cloud is a viable solution compared with former generation of similar platforms since cloud allows service consumers performs decisions at the economic level without being concerned how underlying technologies support their businesses. Therefore, to sustain and optimize their business operations, service consumers chose clouds to mandate the quality of services they will receive based on mutual agreements e.g. SLAs. For a service

consumer, the cloud platform materializes the concepts of utility computing (Yeo & Buyya, 2006) that promote pay-per-use pricing similar to electricity and gas. With this, service consumers reduce their infrastructure risks and potential sunk cost due to initial investment.

On the other hand, clouds are viewed by service providers as the next generation of data centers, which are virtualized through hypervisor technologies such as virtual machines. Resources can be dynamically provisioned on the fly as context-sensitive resource bundles to comply with consumer-desired quality of services that are established through negotiation and accessible as network services. Clouds allow service providers be equipped with new deployment mechanism with focus beyond traditional system resource management architecture and incorporating resources from everywhere in the marketplace. There are more incentives for service providers to share resources and to make efforts to differentiate services based on various quality-of-services requirements (Buyya et al., 2009). For service brokers, clouds provide new opportunities of mediating the interactions among different parties in the cloud marketplace. Service brokers grant service consumers the access to distributed resources by discovering suitable cloud services for given requests, deploying and monitoring execution on the cloud services, accessing data from private or public cloud, collating and delivering results to service consumers. The service broker features a standards-compliant service, to allow access to most of the features of the broker through well-defined service interfaces (Venugopal, Buyya, & Winton, 2004).

Figure 1 shows the cloud service architecture for supporting package application service-oriented development and production. Mainly, this architecture provides the foundation of service-oriented cloud management by differentiating the functions into cloud spaces: infrastructure space, application space, business space and presentation space. The infrastructure space contains the services that supply infrastructure-level resources and related functions to service requestors. The application space provides applications as resources to the requestors. Business space contains all the services for provisioning services and allocating resources accordingly. Examples of business services include provisioning services, resource allocation services, metering services for gauging cost and other measurements, monitoring services and so on. Business space also contains services enabling the functions managing service demands such as SLA services for managing SLAs,

account services for managing accounts, billing service, pricing services and profiling services for describing preferences and constraints. The aforementioned spaces are described in detail in following sections.

Corgito-C promotes Quality-of-Service resource allocation mechanism to dif- ferentiate service requests based on *utility* values. *Corgito-C* as a framework manages the relationships and transactions in the cloud whereby different parties can exchange services, resources and monetary currencies. Demand agents and supply agents

Figure 1. Cloud service architecture

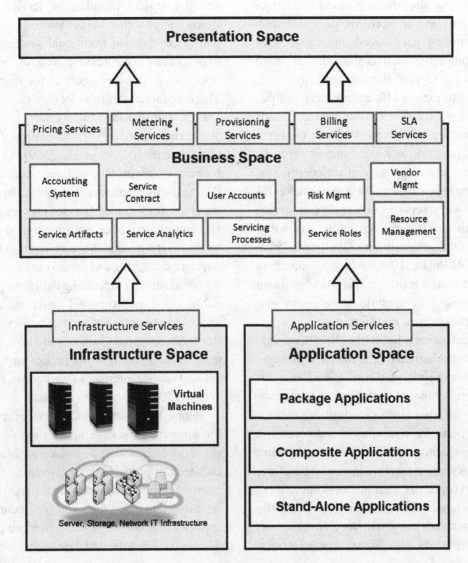

represent the parties on the demand and supply sides, respectively, to participate in the transactions occurring in the cloud market managed by *Corgito-C*. This framework is positioned to play the keystone role in the ecosystem of cloud services as well as to facilitate the cloud parties as integrated components of the cloud market. Each exchange through this framework is a transaction. All the activities enabled by *Corgito-C* have impacts on the prices in the cloud ecosystem, in terms of either monetary or non-monetary values (e.g. quality, risks etc) that are associated with exchanged resources and services. The ecosystem enabled by *Corgito-C* observes and captures data generated by the transactions endowed by the cloud parties. Thus, business models can be derived or depicted by exploitation the data capturing and analysis provided by the cloud marketplace. Such business model, however, is beyond the scope of this paper and will be presented in future publications.

3 INFRASTRUCTURE SPACE

The infrastructure space provides the environment of virtualization and pro- visioning for application services in *Cogito-C*. Both physical and virtual re- sources are comprehensively managed in the infrastructure space. The technology adopted in this space has been developed and deployed to the research community at International Business Machines Corp, coined as Research Compute Cloud (RC2) (IBM 2009b). The RC2 initiative seeks to integrate many of research technologies and products into a virtual data center and harness the value of Re- search's "living lab" for high growth client driven value, with future plans for a highly distributed, globally accessible set of computing cloud resources. RC2 has been given early access to validate the existing capabilities and garner insight for future cloud computing models. Images and data are handled by accompanied Research Storage Cloud—with separation of concerns between runtime and data processing. The storage cloud is meant to be an environment for providing durable images with zero effect by the runtime and, in the meantime, it will support multi-tenancy for service consumers. As such, the infrastructure space is able to harness consolidated computing resources and then parcel them out via an automated life cycle management request process.

Enterprises run their package applications in their back-office systems. Most of time, those applications are not considered to be ported to other contexts. The usual case to have a new requirement from either corporate or clients, a new set of applications with the newest functions will be ordered and installed into similar environment. It can be easily imagined that much has been wasted in this paradigm. First, the knowledge that has been created in the environment that host existing applications is essentially lost. The new applications have to be installed, deployed and configured in an unavoidable way of *déjà vu*. Second, the capabilities of applications are unlikely fully utilized as more similar applications are installed in similar contexts. Third, the effort of managing applications in traditional environment is proportional with the number of copies running in the system. Therefore, the managerial effort is increased with no help of previous experiences. An approach of deployment and configuration using virtualization resolves all the above issues. Virtualization technology like Hypervisor captures not only physical instances into images but also the knowledge and experi- ences carried by the target application instances. Through provisioning images into another context, the captured knowledge including configuration and best practices are literally resurrected into new lives. Of course, customization is still needed for newly provisioned instances but the purpose of reuse can be achieved effectively via clouds.

Two main subsystems in this space are *image management subsystem* and *provisioning subsystem*.

- The former provides an efficient way to manage storage and provenance of virtual images and manages the lifecycle of images and appliances from birth to demise.
- The latter provides a provisioning abstraction layer to support a multiple target virtualization technologies and allocates resources for provisioning application services in response to service requests.

An appliance is an image with metadata. Here is a sample of appliance definition where both software requirements are recorded to mandate the resources to be provisioned to this specific appliance, and the software resource template definition (SRTDefinition) describes the configuration parameters that need to be instantiated when an instance is being provisioned or after provisioning:

```
<appliance-def>
<device-model name="AI_EContract_
Ofbiz_VMWare_2Host_DeviceModel"
category="VirtualAppliance"/>
<software-module name="AI_EContract_
Ofbiz_VMWare_2Host_SoftwareModule"
version="all" description="VMWare ESX
with 2 Guests: EContract on Windows
2003,
OfBiz on RHEL5u2" vendor="IBM" mod-
ule-type="SOFTWARE" title="AI_ECon-
tract_Ofbiz_VMWare_2Host">
<software-category
name="VirtualAppliance"/>
</software-module>
<!-- VMWareGuest Linux SRTDefinition
-->
<srt-definition name="AI_EContract_
Ofbiz_VMWare_2Host_Host1_HostSRTDefi-
nition" description="AI_EContract_Of-
biz_VMWare_2Host_Host1_HostSRTDefini-
tion"
software-resource-type="INSTALLATION"
software-resource-device-model="AI_
EContract_Ofbiz_VMWare_2Host_Devic-
```

```
eModel">
<software-requirement name="os.fam-
ily" type="OS">
<software-requirement-value
value="VMWare"/>
</software-requirement>
<srt-definition-param
name="deploymentType"
description="deploymentType"
parameter-type="String" multiplic-
ity-type="One" is-hidden="false"
is-changeable="false" is-
encrypted="false">
<srt-definition-param-value
value="Guest"/>
</srt-definition-param>
...
<!-- Appliance SRT Definition -->
</appliance-def>
```

Figure 2 shows a simple scenario supported by the infrastructure space. On the top, package applications are captured by the image management subsystem into raw images which will be consequently enhanced to be virtual appliances.

Note that virtual appliances can be composed into application service template as indicated on the right-hand side of the diagram. The infrastructure space also manages physical resources such as servers, storages and networks. Mainly, such functions are defined as the process of identifying demands, matching resources to service requests, allocating those resources, and scheduling and monitoring resources over time (Nabrzyski, Schoof, & Weglarz, 2003). *Cogito-C* incorporates resource management as necessary but not the central concern of the framework in general. Instead, *Cogito-C* is more geared for enabling business-driven resource management with the concerns deduced from cloud market in mind.

Figure 2. A scenario of infrastructure space

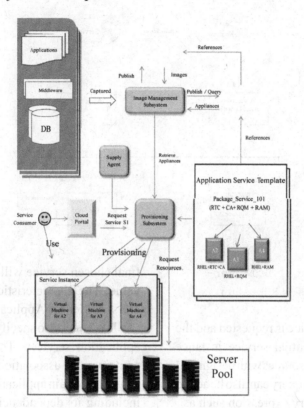

4 APPLICATION SPACE

Application space provides applications such as the "resources" that are delivered to the service consumers through either humans or software agents. Application services serve as the building blocks for IT-enabled enterprise functions. A service provider provides a service specification for an application that supports a specific set of business functions. A service consumer discovers and invokes multiple application services that are necessary to support business solutions. Referring to the scenario in Figure 2, the service requestor in this case was the provisioning subsystem being part of the infrastructure space.

Cogito-C promotes reuse at all levels of software stack: operating system, middleware, databases, applications, contents, interfaces and so on. Unless absolute necessity, a new requirement should not render full-scale development

as before. Instead, the project manager or solution architect of a project should participate in the cloud ecosystem or marketplace enabled to make queries of desired applications services and, subsequently, they should be able to manage to find appropriate application services. In *Cogito-C*, application services are formally specified and stored in service catalog waiting for queries issued by service consumers. When a service query arises as a service requirement, it can be addressed by provisioning a new instance in the infrastructure space with customization. By customization of application services, we mean the workflow by which the behavior of existing application services can be modified to meet the service demands.

Figure 3 shows a model for the application space. Service requests come from users or automated agents. A service request can be as simple as keyword-based query such as

Figure 3. A simple model of application space

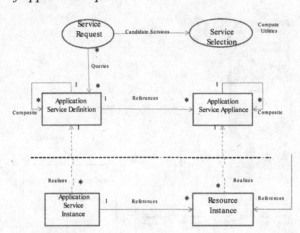

```
Rational Team Concert 1.0.1+ Web-
SPhere 6.1 + DB2 9.2 + RUEL 5u3
```

where an application service is requested and the configuration of the eventual service instance should be running on the resources with designated resource configurations. A query can also be added more formalized into query expression such as

```
ApplicationService(ServiceInstanc
eID,ServicePrice):- application(
ServiceInstanceID,'Rational Team
Concert 1.0.1'), appServer(Serv
iceInstanceID,'WebSPhere 6.1'),
database(ServiceInstanceID,'DB2
9.2'),
os(ServiceInstanceID, 'RHEL 5u3'), pr
icing((ServiceInstanceID,priceVal),
priceVal<5.
```

This case provides a formal query expression to specify the characteristics of the requested service, e.g., the price of returned service has to be under $5 per unit of time. Again, the query can be sent by a user or an agent. The response to the query will contain a set of candidate services.

The function *Service Selection* will run on-demand analysis to calculate utility values for each returned service (Degabriele & Pym, 2007). The final chosen service will have the highest utility value. The characteristics of a service instance are specified in Application Service Definition (ASD), which also specify the relationship among application services. The relationships include containment, association, and dependency. For example, certain application may have constraints including its dependencies on the specific platform, the number of licenses that can be used at a time, the upper limit of service cost, and access control constraints.

The dependency information tells configuration workflow when and what to configure to guarantee the the service to be functioning in a new environment. This is generally the problem of customization. This problem is tackled by for- malizing both the impact rules among appli-cations and the variability points that are associated with the resources (Metzger & Pohl, 2007). The following rules are similar to those used in Mazzoleni and Srivastava (2008). They show the ideas of using impact rules to define configuration dependencies among application services (AS), application service definitions (ASD), appliances and resources:

```
Rule#1: % If a Resource X changes
than all resource depending from X
should change changeResource(Y):-
```

```
resourceDependsOnResource(Y,X),
changeResource(X)
% Application Service Rules
Rule#2: % If an AS X changes,
all ASs referenced by X might
change changeAppService(Y):-
asReferencesToAs(Y,X),
changeAppService(X)
Rule#3: % If an Appliance X changes,
all ASs realizing the AS Definitions
that reference X should change
changeAppService(Z):-
changeAppliance(X),
asdReferencesAppliance(Y,X),
asRealizesASD(Z,Y)
```

5 BUSINESS SPACE

The business space embedded in *Cogito-C* serves as the coordinator among busi- ness functions in specific business context. Before designing good business ser- vices in the cloud, a service designer needs to understand the business context of the service design (Glushko, 2009). We believe that context impacts the behavior of all par- ties in the cloud ecosystem or marketplace at least in three different ways. First, recognizing the business context assists the service designers to set the service parameters and suggesting which objectives are achievable and what types are applications will be likely to achieve the goals. For example, a business goal of high performance data transactions implies more resources (network bandwidth, disk space) need to be assigned to specific appliance.

Second, business context helps the agents in the ecosystem or marketplace to be more focused on fulfilling essential business goals (Turner, 1993). For example, sup- ply agents deal with multiple service requests the same time. In many possible scenarios, some of the requests contradict one another due to the fact of limited resources. Business contexts provide the business goals to help supply agents to make decision as to what to be provisioned to whom at what time. Sometimes, rapid availability of application services is critical since the service consumer needs to get on board quickly. In other situation, however, she can wait for more ample and appropriate resources ready before being granted the service instances as requested.

Third, business context determines how cloud exceptions should be handled by the underlying processes. Exceptions can be of many types in including quality-of-service exceptions such as *low responsiveness*, or system-level exceptions such as *denial of access*. Each exception can have various causes and takes different effort to be resolved. Even we adopt the mechanism autonomic management (Herssens, Faulkner, & Jureta, 2008a; Brandic, in press), an automated exception-handling agent would take resources itself. With the help of business contexts, an exception handling agent would be able to pri- oritize the exceptions and use them as guidelines to resolve the issues e.g. resolving the exception itself versus delegating the task to another agent which has the expertise.

Figure 4 shows a context-based model for the business space. This model pro- vides the foundation of managing cloud resources and relevant processes such as provisioning and exception handling. *Business Objectives* say why an application service is needed, based on the business conditions, which may be internal processes or an external market.

A business objective describes what service characteristics will satisfy this context. It will also say what conditions have to be met or avoided when designated services are provisioned into service consumer's environment. A typical ex- ample of business objective is shown as follows:

```
% The cost of whole opera-
tion of year 2009 should be less
than 90% of year 2008. BO#1:
assert(BO(less(Cost(2009), 0.9 *
Cost(2008)))).
```

Figure 4. A context-based business space model

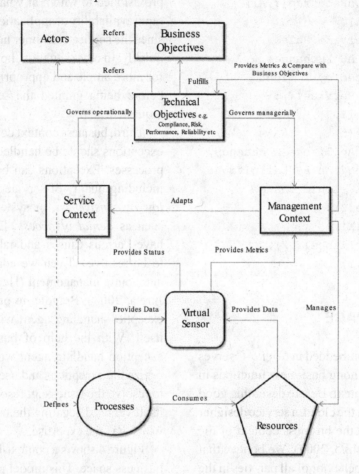

```
% The income of whole operation of
year 2009 should increase 10% com-
pared with year 2008. BO#2: assert(BO
(greater(Revenue(2009), 1.10 * Rev-
enue(2008)))).
```

Technical Objectives are the counter part of business objectives but said in technical terms. An example of technical objective is shown as follows:

```
% The number of transactions to be
handled in year 2009 should increase
10%. TO#1: assert(TO(greater(#Tra
nsactions(2009), 1.10 * Transac-
tions(2008)))).
% The turnaround time of handling
```

```
exceptions should be less than 30min.
TO#2: assert(TO(less(ExceptionHandlin
gTime,30min))).
```

The mapping between business objectives and technical objectives has to exist so the continuity from business to technical spaces can be maintained. However, it is beyond the scope of this paper to discuss the mapping mechanism. A context is a concrete, identifiable, self-describing chunk of information that can be used by a business person to actually manage processes in his/her business, which is similar to the concepts of *business artifacts* (Nigam & Caswell, 2003). A context is a set of records that are suitable for most actors in the cloud marketplace. In order to make context to be useful for the actual running of the marketplace, as opposed to an abstract model for analysis, contexts have to be recognizable; that is, they have to contain information in one place because information has to be available before a process can be managed in a meaningful manner. Our ultimate goal is to make the Business Space to be efficiently and effectively managed by either technical of business leaders. There are two types of contexts: *Service Context* and *Management Context*. Service context captures the essential information that has been used for enabling cloud market operations. An example of service context for an appliance is shown as follows:

```
ContextID: ServiceC1011
ApplianceID: AI_EContract_Ofbiz_
VMWare_2Host_DeviceModel
CPU: 4GB MEMORY: 8GB DISK: 100GB
OS: LINUX_RHEL_5u3
MIDDLEWARE: WAS_6_1_1
DB: DB2_9_2
APP[] = {RTC_1_0_1, RQM_1_0, SAP_Sol-
MAN} ParentImageID: AI_EContract
Created: 13:26 04/17/1998
Owner: JoeSmith
```

The above example shows the service context of an appliance containing resource requirements, which are important when this appliance is being provisioned to the infrastructure space. A management context corresponding to the above service context is shown as follows:

```
ContextID: ManageC7837
ApplianceID: AI_EContract_Ofbiz_
VMWare_2Host_DeviceModel
Measurements {ProvisioningStatus,
DiskConsumptionRate, Provisioning-
Cost} Rule#1 {
Condition{ProvisioningCost>2K} Action
{SendAlert(ProvisioningCost);
TriggerCostAnalysis(ProvisioningCo
st)}}
Rule#2
```

```
Condition{ProvisioningException} Acti
on{TiggerExceptionHandlingProcess(Pro
visioningException)}}
```

This example shows measurements associated with the target appliance and simple management rules for handling exceptions, where one is involved cost and another provisioning. With the management rules, problems associated with the appliance process will be handled either autonomically by supply agents or resolved responsively by human staff. Either way is much better than no action. The measurements are collected by virtual sensors that are deployed into the data sources such as resources, services, applications, or processes.

6 PRESENTATION SPACE

Cogito-C has been developed and deployed to world-wide operations supporting consultants working on the domain of package application services. Specifically, the framework is being used and extended to enhance the ERP service offerings. As the first phase of this project, much effort has been dedicated to infrastructure space and application space. As the project progresses, other spaces will be developed to fulfill the vision of cloud ecosystem and marketplace.

Figure 5 shows the components of the presentation space in the cloud portal. The Cloud Repository contains persistent cloud assets such as application ser- vices, images, instances and business-related data. The Cloud Agent provides programmatical interfaces of retrieving data from the cloud platforms, persisting data into the Cloud Repository, and providing data to the portal. The Cloud Controller serves as the coordinator among the Portal, the Cloud Platform, and Cloud Repository. It receives the commands issued from the Portal and forwards those commands to the back-end cloud platform and services, and also helps the data agent to obtain the latest data items from the platform. On the other hand, the

Figure 5. Cloud portal components

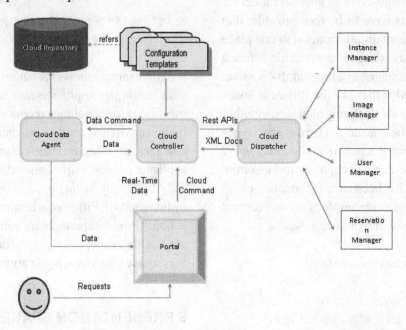

Cloud Dispatcheris exploited as the facade of the cloud services in the back-end cloud platform by receiving Rest calls and issuing system-level commands to the back-end cloud platform. The Configuration Templates describe the relationship among application services and physical instance. In current implementation, such information is captured in the data model which will be described in this section.

Figure 6 shows a high-level data model designed for the presentation space of the cloud portal architecture. At the center of this data model are two tables: Image and Instance where the former stores the information about images and later about the physical instances i.e. virtual machines provisioned from designated images. An application service contains one or more instances where the relationship between images and services are defined through the table Service Definition. Similarly, a service instance may contain multiple physical instances as stated by the tables Instance and Service Instance. Business-related information is captured in the tables Domain, Client, and Project. The data maintained

by these tables are geared for the use of rendering content in the cloud portal. The data is updated based on the portal configurations, which can be synchronized based on predefined schedules or only when the portal is accessed and new data items are requested from the servers.

Figure 7 shows an example of the cloud portal for service consumers. Service consumers tend not to be technical and are proficient more in business than technology. This sample portal enables service consumers to request application service instances in the cloud via simple wizards. On the top, the user is prompted by five choices of application services definitions. Without knowing the technical detail, she would make decisions with business concerns. After selecting the type of application service to be provisioned, the framework would kick off the provisioning process as discussed in Section 3. When the service instance is ready, the detail of provisioned appliances that were defined as part of selected application service would be displayed as shown at the lower screen shot of Figure 7.

Figure 6. Data model for the presentation space

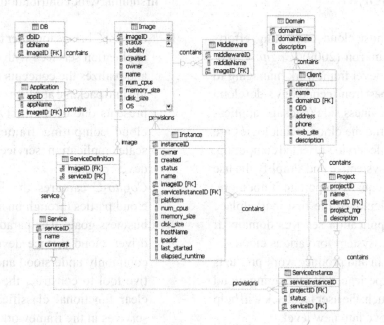

Figure 7. An example of cloud portal

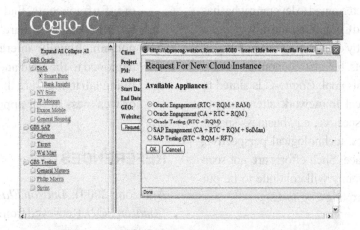

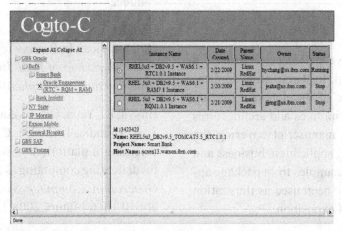

7 RELATED WORK

Compared with most cloud computing efforts (Google, 2009; Amazon (2009), *Cogito-C* represents a business level framework managing to bring together the best from technology side (cloud computing) and business side (package application services). While the cloud technologies are critical in large-scale service-oriented computing, making efforts to systemize and simplify the use of technologies is equally important if not more. We've built and deployed the first marketplace architecture for application services domain. It provides fertile ecosystem for various cloud actors to participate in and produce work products with first hand experiences of leveraging cloud technologies. As such, the user feedback will help the technology move into new level.

Market-based resource allocation has been explored for many years especially in the area of Grid Computing. We are determined to leverage what has been performed in Grid Computing and move *Cogito* to allocate resources by considering not just physical goods and IT assets, but also economics values. In order to achieve this goal, *Cogito-C* is aimed to produce a symmetrical framework attempting to balance business perspective, e.g. business spaces vs. application spaces, technological perspective, e.g. infrastructure space. Such efforts are not seen in literatures but certainly will continue to be our main strategy of improving *Cogito-C*.

8 CONCLUSION

In this paper, we have presented *Cogito-C*, a cloud portal framework for large- scale application services in terms of development, testing and deployment. The motives and architectures are accounted in the manuscript covering the spaces - infrastructure, application, business and presentation spaces. Examples from package application services have been used as illustration tool for the purpose of exposition.

In summary, the contributions of this paper are:

1. *Cogito-C* brings together the business-level application services with cloud computing and realizes the concepts of cloud computing into package application services. It also presents one of the first industry-strength cloud computing framework for large-scale application services-based solution development.
2. *Cogito-C* captures the intentions of the cloud parties through business context and business goals. The paradigm of business-driven cloud service development can be commonly understood and becomes effective tool to construct the framework with clear functional classification among the services in the framework.
3. *Cogito-C* presents itself as a research framework which covers many areas and proof-of-concepts that can be leveraged to embark new research endeavors in this domain. Equally interesting, *Cogito-C* is deployed to the field and will be used as the living lab to measure the effectiveness and/or weakness of our approaches.

REFERENCES

Amazon. (2009). *Amazon Elastic Compute Cloud (Amazon EC2)*. Retrieved from http://aws.amazon.com/ec2/

Brandic, I. (in press). Towards self-manageable cloud services. In *Proceedings of Second International Workshop of Real-Time Service-Oriented Arachitecture and Applications*.

Buyya, R., Yeoa, C. S., Venugopala, S., Broberg, J., & Brandic, I. (2009). Cloud computing and emerging it platforms: Vision, hype, and reality for delivering computing as the 5th utility. *Future Generation Computer Systems*, 25, 599–616. doi:10.1016/j.future.2008.12.001

Degabriele, J. P., & Pym, D. (2007). *Economic aspects of a utility computing service* (Tech. Rep. HPL-2007-101). Palo Alto, CA: HP Laboratories.

Glushko, R. J. (2009). Seven Contexts for Service System Design. In *Handbook of Service*.

Google. (2009). *Google App Engine*. Retrieved from http://code.google.com/appengine/

Herssens, C., Faulkner, S., & Jureta, I. (2008a). Context-driven autonomic adaptation of sla. In Bouguettaya, A., Krger, I., Margaria, T., eds. IC-SOC. Volume 5364 of Lecture Notes in Computer Science. 362–377

Herssens, C., Faulkner, S., & Jureta, I. (2008b, June 23-26). Cloud computing: Issues, research and implementations. In *Proceedings of Information Technology Interfaces* (pp. 31-40).

IBM. (2009a). *IBM Application Services for SAP*. Retrieved from http://www-935.ibm.com/services/us/index.wss/offerfamily/gbs/a1030831

IBM. (2009b). *IBM Perspective on Cloud Computing*. Retrieved from http://www.ibm.com/cloud/

Knorr, E., & Gruman, G. (2009). *What cloud computing really means*. Retrieved from http://www-935.ibm.com/services/us/index.wss/offerfamily/gbs/a1030831

Mazzoleni, P., & Srivastava, B. (2008). Business driven SOA customization. In A. Bouguetaya, I. Krger, & T. Margaria (Eds.), *Proceedings of International Conference on Service-Oriented Computing (ICSOC)* (LNCS 5364, pp. 286-301).

Metzger, A., & Pohl, K. (2007, May 20-26). M variability management in software product line engineering. In *Proceedings of 29th International Conference on Software Engineering* (pp. 186-187).

Mullen, T., & Wellman, M. P. (1995, June). A simple computational market for network information services. In *Proceedings of the First International Conference on Multiagent Systems* (pp. 283-289). Washington, DC: IEEE Computer Society.

Nabrzyski, J., Schoof, J. M., & Weglarz, J. (Eds.). (2003). *Grid Resource Management: State of the Art and Future Trends*. Dordrecht, The Netherlands: Kluwer Academic Publishers.

Nigam, A., & Caswell, N. S. (2003). Business artifacts: An approach to operational specification. *IBM Systems Journal*, *3*, 428–445.

Turner, R. M. (1993). Context-sensitive reasoning for autonomous agents and cooperative distributed problem solving. In *Proceedings of the IJCAI Workshop on Using Knowledge in its Context* (pp. 141-151).

Venugopal, S., Buyya, R., & Winton, L. J. (2004). A grid service broker for scheduling dis- tributed data-oriented applications on global grids. In *Proceedings of the 2nd Wordshop on Middleware for Grid Computing* (pp. 75-80).

Wellman, M. P. (1994). Market-Oriented Programming: Some Early Lessons. In *Market- Based Control: A Paradigm for Distributed Resource Allocation* (pp. 74-95).

Yeo, C. S., & Buyya, R. (2006). A taxonomy of market-based resource management systems for utility-driven cluster computing. *Software, Practice & Experience*, *36*(13), 1381–1419. doi:10.1002/spe.725

This work was previously published in the International Journal of Web Portals 2(1), edited by Greg Adamson and Jana Polgar, pp. 7-21, copyright 2010 by Information Science Publishing (an imprint of IGI Global).

Chapter 3

Lotus Workforce Management:
Streamlining Human Resource Management

Jerh. O'Connor
IBM, Ireland

Ronan Dalton
IBM, Ireland

Don Naro
IBM, Ireland

ABSTRACT

Human Resources departments are often burdened with administrative tasks performed on behalf of employees who lack the tools necessary to complete these tasks themselves. A software approach known as self-service aims to streamline HR processes by providing employees with access and control of their personal information. Different approaches to self-service have been developed, including solutions offered by SAP, Sage Software, and IBM®. This paper examines the approach taken by IBM Lotus® Workforce Management, which is a self-service solution for IBM WebSphere® Portal. Most of the self-service solutions available in the marketplace do provide HR capabilities for an organization's workforce, however, these solutions are usually designed as "out-of-the-box" software that require an organization to adopt a particular approach and a specific set of functionality. Lotus Workforce Management, on the other hand, focuses on providing three key features that allow organizations more choice and control over the implementation of a self-service solution. These features are extensibility, customization, and ease of integration. Extensibility is provided through the WebSphere Portal framework that lets users add or remove components and functionality and determine the structure of communication between portal resources. Integration with IBM WebSphere Portlet Factory gives users the ability to customize and design a solution that is tailored to their needs. Finally, ease of integration with HR resources that reside in a back end system is important as most organizations would be reluctant to change or make complex configurations to that system. For this reason, Lotus Workforce Management uses existing components for SAP ERP systems and provides functional code for rapid and simple integration without extensive configuration.

DOI: 10.4018/978-1-4666-0336-3.ch003

1. INTRODUCTION

This paper describes an approach taken to develop a solution that streamlines Human Resource Management tasks with an emphasis on openness and flexibility to focus on the work performed by employees, managers and HR staff.

Interaction with Human Resource departments is not without problems. These issues affect all participants from average employees to managers to customer service representatives. All these users stand to benefit from a solution that streamlines their tasks and processes and removes or reduces pain points. In this paper we share our experiences and insight gained during the design and development of Lotus® Workforce Management, a framework solution built on WebSphere® Portal. This framework provides a foundation to create flexible, extensible, and readily customisable HR self-service applications.

This paper begins with a description of the Human Resources Management space, the major players within this space, and the issues and ideas that led to the creation of the Lotus Workforce Management framework. This paper then describes the main components of the framework and explains how these components collaborate to fulfil the solution requirements. The paper closes with a summary of what we have learned about the technical challenges in the HR self-service domain from our customers as well as some plans for the future.

1.1 Human Resource Management

Human Resource Management (HRM) is the professional practice and academic theory that relates to the structure and management of a workforce. In nearly every major organization today, there exists a Human Resources (HR) department. Regardless or whether public or private, profit or non-profit, organizations rely on HR departments to ensure that they not only attract a talented and competent workforce, but that the individuals who make up that workforce gain a sense of personal fulfilment and are encouraged to improve their skills and professional abilities, thereby assuring the organization's retention of the workforce.

As HR evolved, the level of associated administrative duties increased proportionally. Research suggests that as much as 70% of the time spent by the personnel of many HR departments was performing administrative tasks (Barron, 2002). These tasks were largely manual, paper-based, and focused on maintaining employee records. Information was often difficult to locate and changing it was a time-consuming affair. Data inaccuracy was common. Correcting mistakes diverted even more time and effort away from business-related activities.

However, HR departments have increasingly been able to make use of software systems that streamline these administrative processes. In turn, HR departments have been able to gain back valuable time to focus on strategic goals such as the recruitment and training of employees, the development of specific business practices and policies, and all the other functions that focus on the efficiency and effectiveness of an organization's workforce.

Numerous HRM systems have been developed and implemented, all with varying degrees of success. For the most part, though, currently available HRM systems fail to deliver true value to HR departments. The failures of these software systems stem from a single cause; employees are unable to take control of their own information and must ultimately depend on the HR department to complete common tasks. Whether because their information was spread over multiple systems, requiring multiple passwords, or because they were unable to access their information at the time when they needed to, employees often find HRM systems problematic and end up contacting their HR department to either enter the required information or to verify that the information was entered correctly. This failure has two effects: the first is that employees feel frustrated and dissatisfied; the second is that HR departments become weighed down in unnecessary administrative work.

A software approach known as self-service has taken shape to deal with the failures of previous HRM systems and not only give HR departments the ability to focus on their strategic objectives, but also to deliver a solution that is truly of benefit to a workforce.

1.2 Self Service

In the context of HRM, self-service is the ability of employees to manage their own HR information easily and at any time. Research has shown that HR departments benefit from self-service solutions, whether ESS (Employee Self-Service) or MSS (Manager Self-Service). Such benefits include gaining back time that would have been spent processing information and reducing data inaccuracy.

In one case study of a public sector organization in Australia, SAP's HR/Payroll module (4.0b), which included the ESS module and SAP's Workflow tool, was used to replace the existing system (Hawking, Stein, & Foster, 2004). In this study, the ESS module was shown to provide a number of benefits to the HR department such as an reduction of time spent processing payroll, an improvement in productivity, and an increase in strategic focus, while overcoming initial resistance from the workforce who were adapted to the previous system. The view taken by Hawking et al. was that the adoption of the ESS solution led to increased satisfaction among the workforce.

However, studies do suggest that the adoption of a self-service solution depends largely upon a positive reception by the workforce. Furthermore that the success of the self-service solution depends upon an intuitive user interface and verification of transactions (Marler & Dulebohn, 2005). Additional research indicates that employee satisfaction with self-service was also influenced by a single authentication mechanism and prompt access to HR information (Rahim, 2006).

Taking into account the conclusions drawn from such research, Web portals can be seen to offer much value to self-service applications as users can access portals through Web browsers, which presents a familiar and comfortable environment for users. Users do not need to learn how to use an entirely new client application and are familiar with entering data through Web forms and views. Additionally, when the Web interface to HR management systems are rendered through a Web portal, value can be added by connecting other Web applications and integrating more closely with the work environment. This integration makes the transition to self-service a much more seamless and cohesive experience for the workforce.

2 LOTUS WORKFORCE MANAGEMENT

IBM® Lotus® Workforce Management is a self-service accelerator for IBM WebSphere® Portal that improves employee productivity and performance by streamlining employee and manager-related activities. Lotus Workforce Management provides employees with personalised, online views into the specific content, self-service transactions, company intranet applications and third-party applications and services they require to operate more efficiently.

Lotus Workforce Management consists of a number of high-level components that collaborate to expose a wealth of Human Resource information and processes that are not traditionally accessible in a user friendly fashion.

The two Lotus Workforce Management components that users interact with most frequently are two portlets known as the checklist framework and the unified task list, UTL. Working together, these two components provide a means of launching and completing profiled events and activities in a uniform way even though individual activities may, and frequently do, occur on disparate back-end systems.

Lotus Workforce Management also provides specific pages and portlets that give managers a dynamic overview of the timesheets, leave requests, and general calendar-related activities for their employees.

The other components that give the checklists and UTL functionality are:

- an innovative approach to SAP data access
- a dynamic and flexible authentication framework
- IBM WebSphere Portlet Factory
- IBM WebSphere Portal and all its various features

The following diagram shows how all the UX and other components collaborate at run-time (Figure 1). The sections that follow the diagram describe the illustrated components in more detail.

2.1 IBM WebSphere Portal

IBM WebSphere Portal provides the runtime environment for the Lotus Workforce Management application. As well as a JSR compliant portlet container there are a number of specific components for both Portal and the underlying IBM WebSphere

Application Server, which make the resulting Lotus Workforce Management application more extensible and robust. This section provides a list of the most important of these components along with a brief description of what they do and which parts of Lotus Workforce Management use them.

2.1.1 Application extension registry

WebSphere Application Server has enabled the Eclipse™ extension framework that applications can use. Applications are extensible when they contain a defined extension point and provide the extension processing code for the extensible area of the application.

An application can be plugged in to another extensible application by defining an extension that adheres to what the target extension point requires. The extension point can find the newly added extension dynamically and the new function is seamlessly integrated in the existing application. It works on a cross Java™ 2 Platform, Enterprise Edition (J2EE) module basis. The application extension registry uses the Eclipse plug-in descriptor format and application programming interfaces

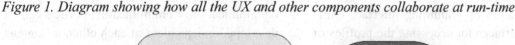

Figure 1. Diagram showing how all the UX and other components collaborate at run-time

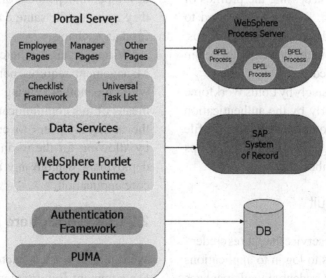

(APIs) as the standard extensibility mechanism for WebSphere applications. Developers can use WebSphere Application Server extensions to implement their functionality to an extensible application, which defines an extension point. This is done through the application extension registry mechanism.

The architecture of extensible J2EE applications follows a modular design to add new functional modules or to replace existing modules, particularly by those outside of the core development team. Each module is a pluggable unit, or plug-in, that is either deployed into the portal or removed from the J2EE application using a deployment tool that is based upon standard J2EE and portal Web module deployment tooling. A plug-in module describes where it is extensible and what capability it provides to other plug-ins in the plugin.xml file.

The Lotus Workforce Management authentication and checklist frameworks both rely on the application extension registry to provide their dynamic extensibility.

2.1.2 PUMA

The Portal User Management Architecture (PUMA) System programming interface (SPI) provides interfaces for accessing the profiles of a portal User or Group. PUMA SPI is used to find, create, modify and delete users and groups. Profile information about the currently logged in user can also be retrieved.

PUMA is used extensively by Lotus Workforce Management, particularly by the authentication framework and in all components which profile content based on the logged in users and the groups to which users are members.

2.1.3 Credential Vault

The Credential Vault is a service that stores credentials and allows portlets to log in to applications on behalf of a user. The Credential Vault manages multiple identities for portlets and users. Using the Credential Vault, a portlet can retrieve a user's authentication identity and pass the information to a backend application.

The Credential Vault is a mature and easily used component which is core to the default authentication implementation that the Lotus Workforce Management authentication framework provides.

2.1.4 Portlet Wires

Portlet Wires are used to direct the information flow between portlets that communicate with one another using portlet events.

A wire connects a publishing event to a processing event of another portlet. When the source portlet fires an event source event has outgoing wires, the information is propagated to the target portlet(s). At the same time the corresponding handler code is invoked. Conversely, if an event is produced that is not wired to any targets, the event is simply discarded.

Creating wires is a part of page administration and requires appropriate access permissions. It is separated from the portlet development or deployment process, so that the portlet developer does not need to know the actual structure of inter-portlet communication. Communicating portlets can be developed independent of each other, as long as they agree on the same data type and semantics for data exchange.

Wiring is used wherever Lotus Workforce Management requires portlets to communicate with one another. Wiring not only provides the means of this communication but also enhances the ability of users to customise the solution by allowing for the wiring to be changed after deployment without any need to redevelop the core application.

2.2 IBM WebSphere Portlet Factory

WebSphere Portlet Factory is an Integrated Development Environment (IDE) and run-time environment for developing Java Web applications and portlets. While WebSphere Portlet Factory has many different capabilities and can run on various platforms, we used WebSphere Portlet Factory to create solutions hosted on IBM WebSphere Portal. Most of the components of the Lotus Workforce Management solution are developed on WebSphere Portlet Factory as it provides foundational artefacts that deliver the functionality that Lotus Workforce Management required much faster.

WebSphere Portlet Factory has a design time component and a run-time component. The WebSphere Portlet Factory designer is an Eclipse plug-in that provides the IDE for developing with WebSphere Portlet Factory. To develop applications in WebSphere Portlet Factory, developers assemble builders into models and then build portlets from the models. Models are XML documents that define the order in which builders are called and what parameters are passed to the builders. Builders themselves are snippets of Java code that can do many things from generating a simple piece of HTML to retrieving data from a remote service. The builders assembled into a model are used to generate the contents of a Web application and a model is usually either consumed by other models or deployed as a portlet. Taken all together the models and builders in a WebSphere Portlet Factory project within the designer result in a web application for deployment on a portal server.

At run-time time the automation engine (a servlet) handles incoming requests and in conjunction with the WebSphere Portlet Factory profiling functionality provides dynamically profiled content.

2.3 SAP

SAP is a leading European software provider that is based in Germany. SAP products primarily focus on Enterprise Resource Planning (ERP). The company's main product is called SAP ERP. The current version is SAP ERP 6.0, which forms part of the SAP Business Suite. The previous version was R/3 and is still in widespread use.

SAP ERP is one of five enterprise applications in SAP's Business Suite. The other four applications are:

- Customer Relationship Management (CRM)
  - Helps companies acquire and retain customers as well as gain marketing and customer insight
- Product Lifecycle Management (PLM)
  - Helps manufacturers with product-related information
- Supply Chain Management (SCM)
  - Helps companies with the process of resourcing manufacturing and service processes
- Supplier Relationship Management (SRM)
  - Enables companies to procure from suppliers

2.3.1 SAP in HRM

SAP HRM or HCM (Human Capital Management) is also a part of SAP ERP and it is the part in which we are most interested as SAP is one of the leading providers of HCM solutions. Given SAP's dominance in the marketplace, engaged customers, and pre-existing software artefacts, SAP was chosen as the first system of record that Lotus Workforce Management would support.

The other driving force behind the decision to support SAP initially was the general dissatisfaction amongst customers with the user experience when interacting with SAP. This is especially true with regard to the older versions. To move to a more modern interface was not a simple upgrade when staying within the SAP product suite, which remains to be true today. The Lotus Workforce Management solution offers an attractive, non-proprietary, and complementary route to enhanced data interaction as well as the potential for integration with multiple other systems by leveraging the underlying capabilities of the WebSphere Portal and Application Server products.

2.3.2 SAP Integration

As discussed in the preceding section, SAP provides Enterprise Resource Planning software. Lotus Workforce Management leverages SAP's HR component as a system of record for its Employee and Manager Self Service functionality. Integration with SAP from Lotus Workforce Management is achieved by the use of SAP's Java Connector library. This Java Connector library, the SAP JCo, allows applications developed using the Java programming language access to SAP data via Remote Function Calls (RFCs). These RFCs are essentially remote enabled applications running on a deployed SAP system. SAP provides a suite of RFCs that can be called to perform a variety of operations. These RFCs provided by SAP are known as BAPIs. Lotus Workforce Management interacts with these BAPIs but also provides a set of additional RFCs that are deployed on an SAP system. These Lotus Workforce Management RFCs allow for a greater degree of access to information stored on SAP's HR component.

Data in SAP's HR component is structured as a set of infotypes. Infotypes are logical representations of data as this data exists inside the SAP HR component. The data to which we refer here is essentially employee related information. For example, you'd expect a HR management system to capture data about an employee's address, pay details, emergency contact information and so on. Each of these examples are stored on SAP's HR component as infotypes. Each infotype in turn can have a number of subtypes. As a generic infotype becomes specialised, this specialised infotype is referred to as a subtype. Again, an example may help with the understanding here. Take the address infotype, this address can be of varying types, for example a permanent address, a temporary address, a holiday address and so on. Each of

these specialised types of address is considered a subtype of the address infotype.

SAP's BAPIs, the remote enabled applications we introduced above, provide access to these infotypes and subtypes, but do so in a defined and somewhat restrictive manner. Calling a BAPI to read an instance of an infotype, requires that a defined set of parameters be passed when making the remote call and in turn a defined set of return values are made available. The return values made available when calling a BAPI on SAP do not reflect the entire Infotype data structure. Rather, a limited set of fields are returned, which may not meet the requirement of the calling application. Let us use an example to help illustrate. Let us say for example, we wanted to read an employee's permanent address from an SAP system. When reading a permanent address using a BAPI, we have access to only a subset of the infotype information on SAP. So where a permanent address infotype on SAP may include 50 fields, we have access to only 10 for example.

For this reason, the Lotus Workforce Management application delivers an implementation of an approach to retrieving all infotype data via remote function call. The implementation is delivered as ABAP code (the SAP specific programming language) by Lotus Workforce Management and is a fully functional RFC. By deploying this ABAP code on an SAP system, access is provided to all infotypes and subtypes available on the SAP HR component. This ABAP once deployed and configured as an RFC, can be called by a remote Java application using the SAP JCo connector. In this manner any application developed using the Java programming language has access to all SAP infotypes.

Lotus Workforce Management provides a tight approach to integration with this RFC by delivering a specially designed WebSphere Portlet Factory builder. This builder, called the SAP Infotype builder, leverages the existing SAP builders delivered by WebSphere Portlet Factory to connect with SAP via the SAP JCo Connector library. Having established a connection, the SAP Infotype builder interacts directly with the custom RFC delivered with the Lotus Workforce Management solution, providing services to create, retrieve, update and delete infotypes on SAP.

Using this and other builders as it's foundation, Lotus Workforce Management provides a means of interacting with the SAP system of record that is not possible using the traditional BAPI approach.

2.4 Custom Components

The following components are those we developed specifically to resolve issues in streamlining the HRM interaction action experience. These components leverage underlying application features as mentioned in previous sections.

2.4.1 Checklist Framework

When we need to do tasks that comprise a number of steps we work from a checklist. We do this in everyday day life when we work from a recipe or use a grocery list. In the content of human resource interaction these lists are for tasks such as hiring a new employee or changing of one's marital status. As we progress through these lists we check off completed items. So put simply a checklist is a list of activities to be carried out to accomplish a particular task. Within Lotus Workforce Management this task, or event, can be anything and comprises a list of activities which can involve interaction with people and applications. An oft used example of a checklist is that of the change address event.

To extend flexibility there are many attributes which activities possess:

- They can be organised into related groups
- They can be mandatory or optional
- They can have a required completion order
- They can integrate with various external systems
- They can exist on various backend repositories

Moreover the containing checklist can:

- Be unique or multiply occurring for the owning user
- Restricted in access particular groups
- Have its status changed based on its age

Both checklist templates and in-flight checklists are represented as xml documents the storage of which is provided and abstracted by a persistence layer. This representation allows for simple manipulation of the checklists as well as enhanced readability of the checklist contents outside of the Lotus Workforce Management application.

2.4.1.1 Presentation

Checklists are presented to the user by one of three portlets.

The My Resources Portlet

The My Resources portlet (Figure 2) provides a profiled and categorised list of checklists to the logged in user. This profiling provides for targeting of function so that a manager can for example exploit resource management events such as promotion which would not be presented to an employee.

The UTL Task List Portlet

The task list portlet of the UTL displays in-flight checklists that are owned by the current logged in user. This is the users' primary means of accessing active checklist instances.

The Checklist Portlet

The checklist portlet is responsible for rendering checklists and presenting the activities to the user. Most of the heavy lifting here is performed by the checklist builder, a custom built WebSphere Portlet Factory artefact.

Figure 2. The My Resources portlet

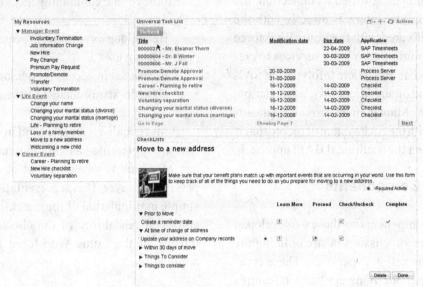

2.4.1.2 Operation

New events are initiated by the user via the My Resources portlet. A user simply selects one of the categorised events and typically a new checklist instance is created and displayed in the checklist portlet. If however the selected event is unique and pre-existing it is the pre-existing instance of the checklist which is presented to the user. An example of one such event is the change marital status event which is unique per user at any given time.

With the checklist available in the checklist portlet the user can proceed with completing the listed activities. Unsequenced activities can be completed in any order and non-mandatory activities can marked complete by the user or simply ignored. At any stage the user may save the state of the checklist and proceed to do other things.

To return to an in-flight checklist the user typically uses the UTL task list portlet. On the selection of the required task from this portlet the checklist portlet restores the previous state of the checklist and work can proceed.

Each individual activity in a checklist delegates its function to an activity handler. Activity handlers can be as simple as URL handlers handling

redirection to another portal page or as complex as a handler to interact with a workflow engine.

Lotus Workforce Management ships with a number of pre-built handlers including those for interacting with WebSphere Portlet Factory models and portal page redirects. Additional handlers can easily and dynamically be added via the implementation of an extension class or statically added with the creation of a new WebSphere Portlet Factory model.

As in real life as time passes the status of incomplete checklist instances changes, the checklist sub-component of the checklist framework runs on a configurable schedule and visits each in-flight checklist in turn. For each instance it compares the current time with the creation time of the checklist and based on a set of customer configurable values it changes the status of the checklist and/or sends email alerts to specified parties.

2.4.2 Unified Task List

The UTL task list portlet aggregates tasks and activities from multiple systems into a single user interface. WebSphere Portal users access the unified task list portlet to complete these tasks and activities in order to advance workflows.

2.4.2.1 Presentation

The UTL presents a simple and easily understood interface to the business user as well as a comprehensive range of configuration options to an administrative level user. As with all the major components used in Lotus Workforce Management the UTL is also flexible and dynamically extensible. Some of its capabilities are listed in the following table by user role (Table 1).

The tasks presented to the user are those the individual task providers decide the user is eligible to see (Figure 3). This may mean simply that the user is the owner of the task as in the case of a checklist task or that the user is one of the potential owners of a WebSphere Process Server hosted process task.

2.4.2.2 Operation

When the task list portlet is loaded it determines the logged in users attributes via PUMA, the Portal User Management Architecture, SPI. The central task dispatcher then passes this information to each of the listed task providers. It is then the individual task provider's responsibility to return a list of relevant tasks to sort and display. In the current version there are task providers for Checklist tasks, IBM WebSphere Process Server tasks, and SAP workflow tasks.

Table 1. UTL capabilities

Role	Task
All	add task list providers at runtime via the portlet configuration view
All	enable the filtering and sorting of the aggregated task list
Administrator	enable or disable caching
Administrator	configure how task pages should be launched

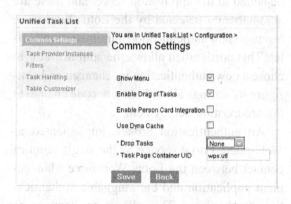

Figure 3. Unified task list

The user can now select any task from the list. Each task type is handled by a task details portlet the launching of which is user configurable. We have already seen that the checklist portlet provides the task details UI for checklist tasks and whilst a generic UI is provided for the out of the box task types the pattern of usage would be that the details portlets would very much be task specific and need to be developed by the customer of a case by case basis.

2.4.3 Authentication

The Lotus Workforce Management authentication solution was designed to provide a dynamic and extensible framework for single sign-on between the portal resident Lotus Workforce Management application and the HR repository of choice at the backend. It has a generic approach to authentication which allows for the dynamic alteration of authentication mechanism with no observable impact on the end user. The framework comprises largely WebSphere Portal server artefacts with companion WebSphere Portlet Factory client artefacts to allow for its use in portlet factory base applications.

The framework leverages WebSphere Application Server's implementation of the Eclipse extension framework and it is this which allows for the flexibility and extensibility of the solution. Additional authentication mechanisms can be added to the application server and these are automatically detected by the Lotus Workforce Management authentication administration portlet. This portlet then allows the administrator to chose a new authentication mechanism and configure its settings all without any code change to the pre-existing deployment.

An authentication broker, implemented as WebSphere Portal service, is the single point of contact between the Lotus Workforce Management application and the pluggable authentication mechanisms. This allows applications to be developed without being tied to a particular authentication mechanism.

2.4.3.1 Identities

There are three main artefacts when it comes to authentication and identification between the Lotus Workforce Management application and the HR backend. These are the credentials used to authenticate with the portal system, the credentials used to authenticate with that backend, and the employee's identifier in the HR backend.

The following sections describe each of these artefacts in turn and explain how they interoperate to surface information to the Lotus Workforce Management user.

2.4.3.2 Portal Authentication

By default WebSphere Portal uses the Custom Form-based Authentication mechanism of IBM WebSphere Application Server to prompt users for identity. Users type their user ID and password in the login portlet or the login screen of the portal. It has support for many other types including SSL, custom forms, and third party authentication with Tivoli® Access Manager for example.

2.4.3.3 SAP Personnel Number

In SAP employees are identified but their personnel number, a system wide unique string which is used in most interactions with the SAP backend system. The personnel number supplied to the

backend ensures that the employee information specific to that personnel number is returned to the requestor. For example a call to get an address will only return address information for the personnel number passed to the get address call. There are temporal and other standard parameters that also affect the information returned but for the purposes of this section we are only interested in the personnel number.

2.4.3.4 Backend Authentication

Obviously before one can retrieve information from the HR system the request must be authenticated. As our solution is Java based we use the SAP Java Connector to connect to the SAP backend. The connection methods of the java connector require credentials to authenticate requests and subsequently return information. The Java Connector supports SSO with username and password credentials and logon tickets. It also supports x509 certificates. Whilst the Lotus Workforce Management authentication framework is flexible enough to accommodate all there, and more, the out of the box authentication implementation uses the common username and password credential combination. The username has no relation to the personnel number. It is used purely to authenticate with the backend and determine authorisation rights. Depending on the rights of the username, information on more than one personnel number may be retrieved or altered.

2.4.3.5 Interoperation

WebSphere Portal stores information about it's users in a user registry and access to this registry is provided programmatically via PUMA, the Portal User Management Architecture, SPI. Our solution leverages the WebSphere Portal user registry and its credential vault component to provide a single sign-on mechanism between the Lotus Workforce Management application and the HR backend.

We map the SAP personnel number to an attribute in the Portal user registry. This provides the linkage between the user's identity in Portal and their identity in SAP. Independently if this link we store the SAP logon credentials in Portal's credential vault. The credentials stored are determined by the mapping type chosen by the portal administrator. The default mapping is n-1 where multiple portal users logon to SAP with the same shared credential. The other mapping supported by the username and password authentication mechanism is a 1-1 mapping where each portal user has their own SAP credential in the vault.

These mappings provide two distinct runtime paths on initial logon to the Lotus Workforce Management application:

- n-1 mapping
  - There is no credential challenge as only the administrator can set the password. If the password is set and valid the user notices nothing. If the password is invalid (unset or expired for example) the user is presented with a customisable error message.
- 1-1 mapping
  - If a valid credential exists in the vault for the user they seamlessly go to the Lotus Workforce Management application. If the password is invalid the user is presented with a challenge. On successful completion of the challenge the new valid credential is persisted to the vault and the user continues to the Lotus Workforce Management application.

The challenge is determined by the authentication mechanism in use and in the case of the default username and password implementation the challenge is the familiar dual text entry field for username and password. The framework allows for any type of challenge as long as the accompanying authentication mechanism can handle the returned credential.

2.4.4 Builders

A set of WebSphere Portlet Factory builders we developed and released with the Lotus Workforce Management solution. These builders were designed to provide rapid application development capabilities for the Portlet Factory developer creating HR portlets in particular. The builders themselves are broken into three broad categories:

1. Base builders
2. SAP builders
3. Checklist builders

The Checklist builders form part of the previously discussed checklist framework and provide a solution for lightweight workflow type applications running on WebSphere Portal. SAP builders and Base builders are designed specifically to build HR portlets using data from SAP. The sections that follow discuss each category in more detail.

2.4.4.1 Base Builders

The Base builders delivered with Lotus Workforce Management provide essentially two core services for the SAP builders. Firstly the Base builders operate as a point of integration with the Authentication Framework. Tightly coupled with services provided by the Authentication Framework, the Lotus Workforce Management Credential builder will determine whether a user has already supplied valid credentials to access SAP. If no valid credentials are present, the user will be asked to enter a user name and password for SAP. Once these credentials are verified, the builder will then store these values in WebSphere Portal's credential vault. Secondly, the Lotus Workforce Management Base builder will provide access to a range a valuable data from SAP to a Portlet Factory model developed using the Lotus Workforce Management SAP builders. This data is core information about the logged in user that may be required numerous times in the life of the application. This Lotus Workforce Management Base builder will retrieve relevant information via a one time call to SAP, store the information in local variables and make this information available via a set of public methods that can be called by other builders in the model.

2.4.4.2 SAP Builders

The SAP builders delivered with Lotus Workforce Management aim to abstract away from the complexity of calling Remote Function Calls on SAP. Five builders are included in this category of builders with specialised functions to

- Read table data on SAP
- Perform create, retrieve, update and delete (CRUD) operations on HR data on SAP
- Provide a presentation layer for the data access functions listed above

The SAP Infotype builder is one of the foundational builders in this category. Responsible for performing the CRUD operations on HR data mentioned above, this builder is designed for use by the business analyst that has no specific knowledge of working with SAP APIs known as BAPIs. Creating a web application or portlet that interacts with SAP as a HRM system would typically require expert knowledge of SAP's BAPIs. Clever logic inside the SAP Infotype builder removes this onus from the developer, empowering the business analyst to develop SAP HR portlets in just minutes.

This category of SAP builder should not be confused with the SAP builders delivered with the WebSphere Portlet Factory product itself. WebSphere Portlet Factory's SAP builders are raw data access builders that require the user be skilled in working with SAP's BAPIs when developing a web application. These builders certainly have a place in the SAP web application development space but the Lotus Workforce Management SAP builders are of particular value when leveraging

SAP as a Human Resources Management System. Technically, the Lotus Workforce Management SAP builders have a dependency on the WebSphere Portlet Factory SAP builder and in fact leverage the SAP Function Call builder delivered with WebSphere Portlet Factory. This dependency is of course by design, leveraging the connection pooling already implemented by Portlet Factory.

3 CONCLUSION

In this paper we described the motivations behind the development of the Lotus Workforce Management solution; the desire for a customisable solution, the need for ease of integration, and the requirement for extensibility. We showed how each of these goals were met and what technologies and assets were used to create Lotus Workforce Management. During the course of the project we strove to reuse as much as possible of the underlying stack components. Both WebSphere Portal and WebSphere Portlet Factory provided us with a significant amount of functionality out of the box, for example, the user management feature of Portal and the SAP feature set in Portlet Factory. WebSphere Portal and WebSphere Portlet Factory also provided the ability to customise and extend Lotus Workforce Management. The Eclipse extension framework in Portal and the builder/model architecture in Portlet Factory are perhaps the most pertinent examples of the capacity for customising and extending Lotus Workforce Management.

The following sections enumerate some of the experiences of the team during this project and provide a view on the future direction of work on Lotus Workforce Management.

3.1 Lessons Learned

The development of the Lotus Workforce Management solution involved a relatively large team of developers, some with experience of Java, some with SAP, and some more with Portal. During the course of the project we encountered the usual issues development teams hit as well as some more specific ones. This section aims to share a synopsis of those issues.

3.1.1 Knowledge Acquisition

Throughout this project we had SAP domain experience in two key areas of SAP; the functional area of human resources within SAP and the development of Advanced Business Application Programming, ABAP, the COBOL like language used to develop on SAP.

These skills enabled us to develop the SAP resident functionality we required and administer the SAP systems we used for test. However, even with such expertise onboard there was still much effort involved in determining the information we required to interact with SAP at the level we wanted to. The experience of our SAP resources allowed us the mine this information more quickly but knowledge acquisition was still something that took longer than originally anticipated.

3.1.2 User Experience

The main purpose of this project was to streamline access to HR data. The presentation of such data to the end user, as well as the paths to access this data, is one of the most important means of achieving this streamlining. With the use of the Universal Task List, the My Resources portlet and its companion the checklist framework, as well as the themed portal pages we feel we successfully achieved this user experience goal.

As always some things slip through however and in our case the most obvious of these is the need for a user to specifically save a checklist to persist state. It would be better if activities could be auto-saved on completion. So doing would prevent users losing state if they were to forget to manually save a checklist before moving on.

The lesson here is that experienced UX resource involvement at all stages of the project and most especially at the beginning and end is invaluable.

3.1.3 Testing

As we have shown the Lotus Workforce Management solution comprises a number of collaborating components used at both design time and run-time. Both of these types of components presented their own challenges from a test point of view.

The design time builders had to be tested for integration with the rest of the WebSphere Portlet Factory artefacts and also for integration with the WebSphere Portlet Factory builders on which some of them are built.

The run-time components, both those produced via WebSphere Portlet Factory and the authentication framework, naturally had to be system and performance tested as a whole. The development of a test harness and the allocation of unearthed defects proved to be the most troublesome aspects here due to the number of moving parts.

When going through a similar project in future planning and implementation effort will be expended to system and performance the larger components in isolation before the whole solution is subjected to these tests.

REFERENCES

Barron, M. (2002). *Retail web-based self-serve isn't just for customers, it's for employees*. Chicago: Internet Retailer.

Hawking, P., Stein, A., & Foster, S. (2004). e-HR and Employee Self Service: A Case Study of a Victorian Public Sector Organisation. *Issues in Informing Science and Information Technology, 1*.

Lotus®, is a trademark or registered trademark of IBM Corporation and/or Lotus Development Corporation in the United States, other countries, or both.

Marler, J. H., & Dulebohn, J. H. (2005). A Model of Employee Self-Service Technology Acceptance. *Research in Personnel and Human Resources Management, 24*, 137–180. doi:10.1016/S0742-7301(05)24004-5

Rahim, M. M. (2006). *Understanding Apdotion and Impact of B2E E-Business Systems: Lessons Learned from the experience of an Australian University.* Melbourne, Victoria, Australia: Monash Univesity. 5 Trademarks Trademark information is provided to identify terms that are exclusively reserved for use by the owner.

Tivoli®, and WebSphere®, are trademarks of the IBM Corporation in the United States, other countries, or both.

This work was previously published in the International Journal of Web Portals 2(1), edited by Greg Adamson and Jana Polgar, pp. 22-36, copyright 2010 by Information Science Publishing (an imprint of IGI Global).

Chapter 4
Using WSRP 2.0 with JSR 168 and 286 Portlets

Jana Polgar
Next Digital, Australia

ABSTRACT

WSRP—Web Services for Remote Portlets—specification builds on current standard technologies, such as WSDL (Web Services Definition Language), UDDI (Universal Description, Discovery and Integration), and SOAP (Simple Object Access Protocol). It aims to solve the problem of traditional data oriented web services which required the applications to be aggregated prior to any specific presentation logic could be applied for presenting the content. Portlet standard (Java Community Process, 2005) complements WSRP mechanism by defining a common platform and APIs for developing UI in the form of portlets. WSRP enables reuse of an entire user interface. One of the advantages is that only one generic proxy is required to establish the connection. At present, portlets based on JSR 168 (Java Community Process, 2005) as well as JSR 286 (Java Community Process, 2008) specification are often used in portal applications. This paper examines the relationship of WSRP specification with the portlet specification JSR 168 and evaluate some and shortcomings of WSRP specification 1.0 (OASIS, 2003). We discuss the impact of WSRP 2.0 (OASIS, 2009) and portlet specification JSR 286 (Java Community Process, 2008) on "on glass" integration paradigm.

INTRODUCING WSRP SPECIFICATIONS

The WSRP specification (*WSRP specification version 1* introduced two complimentary the concepts of *Producer* and *Consumer*. The WSRP 1.0 (*WSRP specification version 1* specification

DOI: 10.4018/978-1-4666-0336-3.ch004

requires that every *producer* implements two required interfaces, and allows optional implementation of two others:

1. **Service Description Interface (required):** This interface allows a WSRP *producer* to advertise services and its capabilities to consumers. A WSRP *consumer* can use this

interface to query a *producer* to discover what user-facing services the *producer* offers. Furthermore, the description also contains additional metadata and technical capabilities of the producer. The producer's metadata might include information about whether the *producer* requires registration or cookie initialization before a *consumer* can interact with any of the remote portlets. For the *consumer*, this interface can be used as a discovery means to determine and localize the set of offered remote portlets.

2. **Markup Interface (required):** This interface allows a *consumer* to interact with a remotely running portlet supplied by the *producer*. For example, a *consumer* would use this interface to perform some interaction when an end-user submits a form from the portal page. Since this interface supports the notion of the state, the portal might obtain the latest markup based on the current state of the portlet (for example when the user clicks *refresh* button or interaction with another portlet on the same page takes place).

3. **Registration Interface (optional):** This interface serves as a mechanism for opening a dialogue between the *producer* and *consumer* so that they can exchange information about each others' technical capabilities. The registration interface allows a *producer* to ask *consumers* to provide additional information before they start interaction with the service through the service description interface and markup interfaces. This mechanism enables a producer to customize its interaction with a specific type of *consumer*. For example, a *producer* may use a filter and reduce the number of offered portlets for a particular *consumer*.

4. **Portlet Management Interface (optional):** This interface gives the *consumer* control over the life cycle methods of the remote portlet. A *consumer* acquires the ability to customize a portlet's behaviour, or destroy

an instance of a remote portlet using this interface.

Processing user interaction When the user clicks on a link or submits form data, the *consumer* application controls the processing and invokes the performInteraction() method (). When the *producer* receives this call, it processes the action and returns the updated state. To redraw the complete page, the *consumer* then invokes the getMarkup() call to receive the latest markup fragment. Because the state of the *producer* has changed since the previous getMarkup() call, the markup fragment returned is typically different from the one previously returned. The end user can then perform another action, which starts a new interaction cycle. (See Figure 1)

Handling customization and initialization: In a typical interaction a single centrally hosted services are used by multiple consumer applications and/or multiple individual users. The WSRP protocol supports multiple configurations of a single service. Good example is a lookup in a remote list of the course offerings and subjects offered within a particular course to international students. The list can be configured to display different offerings per semester, different currencies for subject fees or both depending on the *consumer* country and language prerequisites.

The WSRP protocol provides a set of function calls which allow *producers* to expose multiple versions of the same service each with different preconfigured interface. Furthermore, *consumers* can create and manage additional configurations of the same service, and end users can customize their configurations. However, such configurations are static (predefined) only in the current version of WSRP 1.0 (*WSRP specification version 1*.

SERVICE DESCRIPTION INTERFACE

Service Description interface enables the *consumer* to determine what services are available

Figure 1. Remote portlet interaction in view and action modes

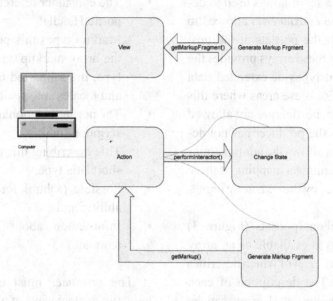

and also provides information about the service capabilities. The services can be discovered through UDDI or other public registry. The access to the *producer* metadata is provided through getServiceDescription()method. All *producers* must provide the service description. This is important because it affects the decision whether the portal can display the markup, cookies handling, registration requirements, etc. In addition, the service description also includes the access to the information about portlet capabilities – supported portlet modes, window states and list of locales the portlet supports. The service description structure supports also an extension field. This is an Array of objects that allow both client and server to support custom features. The ServiceDescription object contains useful information for the *consumer* such as whether the registration is required, list of offered portlets, need to initialize cookies and list of resources. The list of allowed types for ServiceDescription structure is in Figure 2:

Figure 2. ServiceDescription structure

```
ServiceDescription type (structure) details:
       boolean requiresRegistration
       PortletDescription offeredPortlets[]
       ItemDescription userCategoryDescriptions[]
       ItemDescription customUserProfileItemDescriptions[]
       ItemDescription customWindowState Descriptions[] 20
       ItemDescription customModeDescriptions[]
       CookieProtocol requiresInitCookie
       ModelDescription registrationPropertyDescription
       String locales[]
       ResourceList resourceList
Extension extensions[]
```

ItemDescription is a set of arrays used to describe custom items the *consumer* is allowed to use in interaction with the portlets at the *producer* location. Each of these arrays provides the description of different types of extended data (e.g. custom modes). For those areas where this information is provided, portlets are not allowed to use extended values the producer has not described. This restriction allows the administrator of the consumer to determine a mapping of these values to those supported by the *consumer* implementation.

The information about portlets (Figure 3) that the *producer* hosts is available as an array of PortletDescription(s), each of which describes single offered portlet. The description of each portlet listed in offeredPortlets[] array can be obtained by invoking getPortletDescription() method. This interface allows the *consumer* access to the following information:

- The consumer references this portlet using portletHandle;
- Markup types this portlet can generate in the array markupTypes. For each markup type, the supported modes, window states and locales are specified;
- The portlet functionality is stored in the description field;
- Title describing this portlet is stored in the shortTitle type;
- Possible (x)html forms generation availability; and
- Information about the usage of URL templates.

The *producer* must expose one or more logically distinct ways of generating markup and handling interaction with this markup (Figure 3).

The boolean field usesMethodGet was added to this metadata due to the difficulties introduced by means in which browsers handle query string

Figure 3. Portlet description structure

```
PortletDescription type (structure) details:
    Handle portletHandle
    MarkupType markupTypes[]
    ID groupID
    LocalizedString description
    LocalizedString shortTitle
    LocalizedString title
    LocalizedString displayName
    LocalizedString keywords[]
    string userCategories[]
    string userProfileItems[]
    boolean usesMethodGet
    boolean defaultMarkupSecure
    boolean onlySecure
    boolean userContextStoredInSession
    boolean templatesStoredInSession
    boolean hasUserSpecificState
    boolean doesUrlTemplateProcessing
    Extension extensions[]
```

in GET request method. It suggests that the portlet will or will not generate any (x)html forms using GET methods to submit the input data. The query string is the part of the URL following the question mark. The browsers tend to drop any query string on the URL to be submitted before generating a query string reflecting the *consumer* input data in the form's fields. Many *consumers* may prefer to encode information such as which portlet is to receive this information within the query string as well as the knowledge whether or not the portlet should be handled in a special manner. While there are many options available to *consumers* for handling these types of portlets, typically some form of encoding this information into the path of submitted URL is required.

MARKUPTYPE STRUCTURE DETAILS

The MarkupType structure is used to carry portlet metadata of mime type. The important members of this structure are portlet modes and window-States which reflect the same structures in portlet specification (Java Community Process, 2005). Portlet renders different content and performs different activities depending on its state and the operation currently being process. Part of basic responsibilities of any portal container is support portlet interactions and correctly handle portlet modes. Portlets may request mode changes or some modes may not be supported by the portlet. During two operations - getMarkup() and perform-BlockingInteraction() the *consumer* indicates to the portlet its current mode.

Portlet modes are properties of the *producer's* portal presentation model. Portlet modes allow the portlet to display a different "face" depending on its usage. There are four modes supported by the WSRP protocol:

1. VIEW (wsrp:view) mode is to render markup reflecting the current state of the portlet.

2. HELP (wsrp:help) mode supports the help mode, and a help page can be displayed for the user.

3. EDIT (wsrp:edit) mode produces markup to enable the user to configure the portlet for their personal use.

4. PREVIEW (wsrp:preview) mode renders its standard view mode content as a sample of current configuration.

5. The Extension array provides some space for additional custom modes.

Portlet window states (windowStates) are specified in PortletDescription data structure mentioned previously. They determine how the portlet is displayed in the portal during the aggregation stage. The *consumer* has to inform the *producer* about window states used in the aggregated portal pages. Four states of a portlet (to be precise the portlet window states) are:

1. Normal (wsrp:normal): The portlet is displayed in its initial state and size as defined when it was installed.

2. Maximized (wsrp:maximized): The portlet view is maximized and takes over the entire body of the portal, replacing all the other portal views.

3. Minimized (wsrp:minimized): The portlet should not render visible data.

4. Solo (wsrp:solo) indicates that the portlet is the only portlet being rendered in the aggregated page. Note that not all portal vendors support this mode.

The portlet modes and window states are accessible from the portlet window title bar. As with local portlets, clicking on these icons can change the portlet's mode.

REGISTRATION INTERFACE

The Registration Interface (Figure 4) is used by the *producers* to allow *in-band* registration of *consumers* to provide all necessary information during the registration process (Figure 4). The *producers* can also offer *out-of-band* processes to register a *consumer*. Both processes provide the unique handle - registrationHandle – which refers to the remote portlet context (Registration-Context). It is returned by the register() operation during the establishment of *consumer - producer* relationship. The registration can be modified using modifyRegistration(). The relationship between *consumer* and *producer* ends when one of them successfully invokes deregister() operation.

It is important to understand the difference between *in-band* and *out-of-band* registration. The consumer can register through the WSRP registration port type[1] using register() call. The *consumer* provides all required information to the *producer* before any service invocation is carried out. In *out-of-band* registration the consumer's administrator must manually obtain the registration handle from the producer's administrator. The *out-of-band* registration is not standardized in WSRP.

Figure 4. Optional registration interface

```
RegistrationData:
    String consumerName
    String consumerAgent
    boolean methodGetSupported
    String consumerModes[] 20
    String consumerWindowStates[]
    String consumerUserScopes[]
    String customUserProfileData[]
    Property registrationProperties[]
    Extension extensions[]
```

MARKUP INTERFACE

The Markup Interface must be implemented by all interactive user-facing interfaces to comply with WSRP standard. The operations defined by this interface allow the *consumer* to request the generation of markup as well as processing of interactions with his markup. The Markup Interface structures contain important information for handling sessions, runtime and portlet modes.

The *consumer* requests the markup for rendering the current state of a portlet by invoking the getMarkup() method and in return it receives the structure called MarkupResponse. The MarkupResponse is a structure containing various information about markup context and session needed to render valid markup (Figure 5).

The format of the call getMarkup() is below:

```
MarkupResponse =
getMarkup(RegistrationContext,
PortletContext, RuntimeContext, User-
Context, MarkupParams);
```

The SessionContext contains information about sessionID and its expiration time. The sessionID enables the consumer to maintain the consumer portlet state as if it was the local portlet. The RuntimeContext defines a collection of data

Figure 5. Markup response structure

```
MarkupResponse:
    MarkupContext markupContext
    SessionContext sessionContext
    Extension extensions[]
```

required for end user authentication: userAuthentication (password information), portletInstanceKey (reference to the RegistrationContext), namespacePrefix, templates used to generate the URL pointing back to the requesting application, and sessionID. The PortletContext structure is used to supply the portlet information relevant to the consumer using this portlet. It also contains portlet state thus providing portlet state required persistency.

HANDLING URLS IN REMOTE PORTLETS

URLs need to point back to the *consumer* so that the *consumer* can supply any stateful data needed for interacting with the clone portlet. The *consumer* has to direct the interaction to the original *producer* portlet. This interaction pattern results in the scenario where the original portlet knows the details needed for this particular URL while the *consumer* controls the overall format and target of such URLs. WSRP provides two solutions for this problem: URL rewriting at the *consumer* site, and URL templates.

Consumer URL rewriting uses a specification defined format for URLs that allows the *consumer* to find (for example by parsing) and replace the URL. All portlets' URLs are demarcated in the markup by the start tag <wsrp_rewrite> and end tag </wsrp_rewrite>. All value/pair data are placed within these tags.

Producer URL rewriting is made simpler by the WSRP specification which introduces URL templates. The portlet has to specify whether or

not it is willing to do template processing as the means to generate proper URLs. This effectively means that the *consumer* delegates the need to parse the markup to the *producer*.

Another aspect of generating proper URL is related to the action the *consumer* should activate when the URL is activated. WSRP specification defines a portlet url parameter called wsrp-urlType to carry this information. This parameter must be specified first when using the *consumer* URL rewriting template. The wsrp-urlType can have several values. We mention only the following three value but for more details you can consult the WSRP specification (*WSRP specification version 1.*

1. wsrp_urlType = blockingAction is the information for the *consumer* that this interaction is a logical update of the portlet's state and it must invoke performBlockingInteraction() method.
2. wsrp_urlType = render informs the *consumer* that this is the request to render new page from the portlet and it must invoke the getMarkup() operation.
3. wsrp_urlType = resource tells the *consumer* that it is acting as a proxy to get the resource (e.g. a gif picture). The *consumer* receives the actual URL for the resource including any query string parameters.

Remote portlets can handle end user interaction as well as update the persistent portlet state. The operation performBlockingInteraction() has been designed to support the situations in which the interaction may change the navigationalState attribute or shared data (e.g. database content). This is transient state and it is only passed to the original invocation and not when the markup is being regenerated (for example when the page is refreshed and portlets pass through the page aggregation stage).

The navigationalState attribute is used by portlets which need to store the transient data needed to generate current markup. It roughly corresponds to the concept of the URL for a web page. Furthermore, a stateless *consumer* can store the navigationalState for all aggregated portlets by returning them to the client, for example using URL to encode navigationalState. This information then can be used for handling of the next interactions.

JSR 168 ALIGNMENT WITH WSRP 1.0.

In order for the *consumer* and *producer* successfully exchange the information in the form of remote portlets, both parties has to adhere to one or more standards. The WSRP and JSR 168 (Java Community Process, 2005) are already aligned in many aspects (*producer* or *consumer*). Similarities and differences are discussed below (Hepper, 2004):

1. URL encoding and creating URLs pointing to the portlet corresponds to both the *consumer* and *producer*.
2. The state of a portlet fragment is supported in WSRP under the term of navigational state and in JSR 168 with the render parameters. The portlet rendering parameters can map to WSRP's navigational state.
3. Storing persistent state to personalize portlet's rendering is realized in WSRP through the properties of arbitrary types, whereas JSR 168 (Java Community Process, 2005) supports only preferences of type *string* or *string array*. This means that WSRP *pro-*

ducers based on JSR 168 (Java Community Process, 2005) use only a subset of the WSRP functionality.
4. Information about the portal calling the portlet is called RegistrationData in WSRP, and it is the equivalent to PortalContext object in JSR 168 (Java Community Process, 2005).

As evident from the above list, the portlets adhering to JSR 168 (Java Community Process, 2005) specification can be exposed and accessed via WSRP as remote services. In Table 1 we provide information about important concept realization in both WSRP and local portlet space.

WSRP 2.0 BRIEF OVERVIEW OF ADDITIONAL FUNCTIONALITY

Recently, WSRP 2.0 (OASIS, 2009) and JSR 286 (Java Community Process. (2008). *JSR 286* have been introduced. WSRP 2.0 responds to the shortcoming of its predecessor—WSRP 1.0. Java Portlet Specification JSR 286 (Java Community Process. (2008). *JSR 286* introduces several new features, such as coordination between portlets (a feature IBM portlets always supported by Inter Portlet Communication - IPC), serving resources, portlet filters, and AJAX support. The aim is still the same: provide the ability to publish remote Java portlets and create proxy Java portlets that can be used as remote portlets within portals.

Resource rendering and resource serving additions are some of a few missing features of the WSRP 1.0 (OASIS, 2003) and JSR 168 (Java Community Process. (2008). *JSR 286*. The ResourceServingPortlet lifecycle interface has the method serveResource(), that can be triggered by a ResourceURL. The portlet can create this URL via the PortletResponse.createResourceURL() method. In another words, the resource serving lifecycle interface also enables *asynchronous rendering of markup fragments* without coordination with the portal simply by using the standard

Table 1. Comparison WSRP and JSR 168

Concept	WSRP	JSR 168	Comment
Portlet Mode: indicates portlet in what mode to operate for a given request	View, Edit, Help + custom modes	View, Edit, Help + custom modes	full support
Window State: the state of the window in which the portlet output will be displayed	Minimized, Normal, Maximized, Solo + custom window states	Minimized, Normal, Maximized, Solo + custom window states	"Solo" is missing in the JSR, but can be implemented as a custom state;
URL encoding to allow re-writing URLs created by the portlet	Defines how to create URLs to allow re-writing of the URLs either on *consumer* or *producer* side	Encapsulates URL creation via a Java object	Fully compliant
Namespace encoding to avoid that several portlets on a page conflicting with each other	Defines namespace prefixes for *consumer* and *producer* side namespacing	Provides a Java method to namespace a String	Fully compliant
User – portlet interaction operations	*performBlockingInteraction*: blocking action processing *getMarkup*: render the markup	*action*: blocking action processing *render*: render the makup	Fully compliant
View state that allows the current portlet fragment to be correctly displayed in sub-sequent render calls	Navigational state	Render parameter	Fully compliant (WSRP navigational state maps to JSR render parameters)
Storing transient state across request	Session state concept implemented via a *sessionID*	Utilizes the HTTP web application session	Fully compliant
Storing persistent state to personalize the rendering of the portlet	Allows to have *properties* of arbitrary types	Provides String-based *preferences*	Full alignment
Information about the portal calling the portlet	*RegistrationData* provide information of the *consumer* to the *producer*	*PortalContext* provide a Java interface to access information about the portal calling the portlet	Full alignment

XMLHttpRequest. This approach supports some of the basic AJAX code for portlets. The portlet can leverage all the information in the portlet context, like portlet mode, window state, render parameters, or portlet preferences. However, some limitations apply, for example, any of the previously mentioned state information cannot be changed in such a call.

To align JSR 286 and the WSRP version 2.0 specification, the additional functionality is defined as categorised below:

- **Coordination (Eventing)**: The Portlet 2.0 specification (JSR 286) (Java Community Process. (2008). *JSR 286* enables the communication among portlets using events. Events allow portlets to respond to user

actions or state changes that might not be directly related to user actions. The WSRP version 2.0 (OASIS, 2009) specification complements this mechanism by extending these events to portlets that are published or consumed via the WSRP thus providing a mechanism by which a consumer can coordinate events between portlets.

- **Coordination (Shared/Public Render Parameters)**: Because public render parameters are encoded in the URL, the restrictions of the URL are applied to the types of objects that can be shared between two portlets. In eventing it is possible for two portlets to share a complex data types thus avoiding the restrictions of URL. Another coordination mechanism that is introduced in WSRP 2.0 (OASIS, 2009) are public navigational parameters. The JSR 286 (Java Community Process. (2008). *JSR 286* specification calls it public render parameters. The public render parameters work like events; the only difference is that the state is encoded in the URL and then shared across portlets. Public render parameters are lightweight coordination mechanisms where the coordination happens over the parameters that are encoded in the URL.

- **Caching**: There are two kinds of caching defined by WSRP specifications:
  - *Markup caching*: the WSRP consumer caches the content generated by the render call of a portlet.
  - *Resource caching*: the WSRP consumer facilitates caching of the content/resource generated by the serveResource call of a portlet.
- **Leasing**: is defines as the concept of scheduled suspension and destruction of items such as Registration Handle and Portlet Handle. In a nutshell, after the lease period expires, the artefact is made unavailable. This feature is particularly useful when the user wants the registration or the portlet handles to be valid only for a specific period.
- **Resource Serving**: The resource serving portlet lifecycle enables a portlet to serve a resource. The JSR 286 specification (Java Community Process. (2008). *JSR 286* supports two ways of resource serving for portlets: through direct links to the resource (efficient for static resources that are the same for all portlet states), or by serving the resource through a servlet. Direct links are insufficient in situations where the information from the portlet context is needed such as rendering different resources based on the portlet mode, window state, current render parameters, or portlet pref-

erences. Another benefit of rendering resources directly through the portlet is that, the resource is accessed through the portal, and thus protected through the portal access control. Portlets can create two kinds of resource links to serve requests:

- **Direct links to the resources in the same portlet application.** Direct links are not guaranteed to pass through the portal server and do not have portlet context available. So a direct link should be used in cases where access to the portlet context and access through the portal server is not needed.
- **Resource URL links that point back to the portlet.** These links call the serveResource() method of the ResourceServingPortlet. This way, the portlet can serve a resource that is protected by the portal security and can utilize the information embedded in the portlet context. The portlet container does not render any output in addition to the content returned by the serveResource call. Thus, the serveResource() method provides more flexibility to you by giving access to modify the response object, whereas the portal server acts only as a proxy.

One of the committee members for WSRP 2.0 is IBM. Therefore, as we expected, IBM WSRP 2.0 Producer for IBM WebSphere Application Server has already been announced as light weight producer which exposes JSR 268 (Java Community Process. (2008). *JSR 286* as well as JSR 168 (Java Community Process. (2008). *JSR 286* portlets deployed on IBM WebSphere Application Server Version 7.0 as WSRP services. The Producer will be completely stateless (with the exception of session data) and will push portlet customization to the WSRP Consumer.

WSRP and AJAX (Asynchronous JavaScript and XML) are two technologies which complement each other in terms of reducing the effort of sharing of aggregated content and better usability of such content. WSRP provides standards based interfaces for creation of presentation oriented services using web services technology. However, any WSRP based remote portlet needs to be refreshed every time when even a single data element changes in the portlet. AJAX also allow for content aggregation and asynchronous data retrieval. The advantage of AJAX is that only the required control needs to be refreshed, whenever data changes. In AJAX, each aggregator has to include AJAX control accessing the same back end service which leads to significant replication of effort.

NOTES ON WSRP 1.0 AND ITS SHORTCOMINGS

There are some additional issues which in our opinion outweigh the advantages of WSRP. Firstly, we would like to present some thoughts on security issues. WSRP does not provide any standardisation for security. It only relies on the lower-level protocols. Secured transmission depends on HTTPS. In a web application, servlets execute in neutral environment and are responsible for validating the user's authenticity and authority to make a specific request. Portlets operate only in the context of the portal server and cannot be called directly. The portal server is responsible for authentication and for authorizing all user access. The authentication and authorization is performed prior to the portlet's execution. However, the portlets may perform some authorization in order to associate content with a specific user or role. Therefore, authentication is a daily concern of servlet developers, but it is optional for portlet developers. In WSRP, *producers* are responsible for authentication and authorisation. Remember that threats to web services represent threats to

the host system, host applications and the entire network infrastructure.

In WSRP 2.0, the portal now provides improved WS-Security support for the WSRP Consumer. WS-Security is configurable for individual WSRP Producers by using the portal administrative portlets or the XML configuration interface by selecting a security profile. The portal provides three default WSRP security profiles and allows y additional custom security profiles to be included. Additionally, there is an option to dynamically set whether requests to a Producer use HTTP, HTTPS, or, if the Producer can handle both. For the WSRP Producer for example, the IBM WebSphere Portal 6.1 provides three sample WS-Security configurations that correspond to the default security profiles on the Consumer side and allow a faster setup.

Secondly, load balancing in WSRP is a part of the *producer* environment. The difficulties are associated with session maintenance. Some portal servers (e.g WebLogic or WebSphere Portal 5) provide the environment for clustering. In such situation it is required that the *consumer* supports load-balancing, replication, and fail-over to functions. The initCookie operation allows the *producer* to initialize cookies and return those over the HTTP response underlying the SOAP response. When a user views a page containing a remote portlet for the first time, the *consumer* sends an initCookie request. The underlying HTTP response contains a Set-Cookie response header. The consumer is supposed to supply this cookie with all future requests to the *producer*. To enable clustering at the *producer*, *consumers* are required to send an initCookie request once per user per *consumer*. Furthermore, the *consumer* is supposed to keep track of any returned cookies and supply those cookies with subsequent requests. Typically, consumer stores these cookies in its user's HTTPSession which travels with the HTTPRequest object. The *consumer* then is highly dependent on transport mechanism, number of cookies in HTTP.

In WSRP 2.0, handling of cookies has been improved. The portal WSRP Consumer handles all cookies that are set by remote portlets. These are either cookies for the session context that are set during session initialization, or, for JSR 286 portlets (Java Community Process. (2008). *JSR 286*, cookies set by the portlet itself. The portal also handles cookies set by resources that are served by the WSRP Consumer as a proxy. Cookies that the Consumer receives are stored in the Consumer session. They are later forwarded in requests to remote portlets and resources served by the WSRP Consumer as a proxy according to the standard cookie matching and expiry rules.

JSR 286 (Java Community Process. (2008). *JSR 286* also contributes significantly handling the cookies. JSR 286 (Java Community Process. (2008). *JSR 286* adds API methods for reading and writing cookie properties to portlet request and response, but leaves it open to portal implementations about how these cookies are stored and handled. For example, WebSphere Portal 6.1 translates cookie properties into actual HTTP cookies. Cookies are not within a namespace. They can be shared between portlets and / or shared with other Web applications. Cookies therefore provide an alternative mechanism for coordination between portlets. New cookies that have been set by a portlet are visible to all portlets in subsequent life-cycle phases of the same client request, and also in later requests unless the client decides to discard them.

Finally, there is also problem in WSRP 1.0 (Java Community Process. (2008). *JSR 286* with fault tolerance and application reliability. The *producer* detects the fault and displays an error in the portlet. Alternatively, the error is not properly detected and forwarded to the consumer's portlet thus resulting in the situation that portlet cannot be displayed. Developers know that such portlet behaviour does not constitute adequate error handling but it can result in a non-recoverable problem consequently taking down entire portal. It would be better if the *producers* adhere to some fault handling standard so if the *producer* falls over, the portal page at the *consumer* site still renders correctly.

CONCLUSION

Traditional data based web services require the application to provide specific presentation logic for each web service. The motivation for WSRP and WSIA stems out of the fact that the current approach to web services is not suitable for remote portals. Therefore, the WSRP is intended for use with WSIA (Web Services for Interactive Applications), which is also being developed by the OASIS committee (OASIS, 2005). WSIA provides well-defined interfaces and contracts on top of the generic ones to remedy the problems pose by common presentation logic in WSRP.

The portal event handling style, inter-portlet and cross portal application communications have direct relevance to processing remote portlets. The inter-portlet communication between remote portlets is not expected to happen at the *consumer* portal. Furthermore, the WSRP 1.0 (OASIS, 2003) specification does not provide any details concerning communication between remote and local portlet. It is assumed that the remote web services represent entire application (business process) which is contextually separated from any local processing and therefore there is no requirement to exchange messages relevant to inter-application communication.

One of the new features introduced in WSRP 2.0 (OASIS, 2009) and JSR 286 (Java Community Process. (2008). *JSR 286* is the mechanism for cross-portlet communication. This mechanism will allow portlets to broadcast event information to other portlets spread across multiple producers. The key issue is the ability of portlets to post their contextual information about their interaction (state) so the other portlets than can adjust their content information accordingly and generate appropriate markup.

There is no easy answer to the ever growing requirement to dynamically generate user facing content from variety of sources, customize the content and share aggregated content together with portlets state information with remote consumers. It seems that there is no single technology to fulfil this requirements. We believe that clear architectural approach combining usage of WSRP, AJAX is required to enable creation of standards based, customizable, and dynamically generated reusable portlets that have required interactivity, response time and usability.

KEY TERMS AND DEFINITIONS

Portlet: A Web application that displays some content in a portlet window. A portlet is developed, deployed, managed and displayed independently of all other portlets. Portlets may have multiple states and view modes. They also can communicate with other portlets by sending messages.

Portal: A Web application which contains and runs the portlet environment, such as Application Server(s), and portlet deployment characteristics.

Web Services: A set of standards that define programmatic interfaces for application-to-application communication over a network

Web Services for Remote Portlets: Presentation oriented Web services.

REFERENCES

Hepper, S. (2003). Comparing the JSR 168 Java Portlet Specification with the IBM Portlet API. Retrieved May 11, 2005, from http://www-128. ibm.com/developerworks/websphere/library/ techarticles/0312_hepper/hepper.html

Hepper, S. (2004). *Portlet API Comparison white paper: JSR 168 Java Portlet Specification compared to the IBM Portlet API.* Retrieved May 11, 2005, from http://www-128.ibm. com/developerworks/websphere/library/techarticles/0406_hepper/0406_hepper.html

Hepper, S., & Hesmer, S. (2003). *Introducing the Portlet Specification, JavaWorld.* Retrieved from http://www-106.ibm.com/developerworks/ websphere/library/techarticles/0312_hepper/ hepper.html

Java Community Process. (2004). *JSR-000154 Java servlets specification 2.4.* Retrieved from http:// www.jcp.org/aboutJava/communityprocess/final/ jsr154

Java Community Process. (2005). *JSR 168. Portlet specification.* Retrieved from http://www.jcp. org/en/jsr/detail?id=168

Java Community Process. (2008). *JSR 286 JSR-000286 portlet specification 2.0.* http://jcp. org/aboutJava/communityprocess/final/jsr286/ index.html

OASIS. (2003). *WSRP specification version 1.* Retrieved from http://www.oasis-open.org/ committees/download.php/3343/oasis-200304-wsrp-specification-1.0.pdf

OASIS. (2005). *Web Services for Interactive Applications specification – WSIA.* Retrieved from http://www.oasis-open.org/committees/wsia

OASIS. (2009). *Web Services for Remote Portlets Specification v2.0.* Retrieved from http://docs. oasis-open.org/wsrp/v2/wsrp-2.0-spec.html

ENDNOTE

[1] This port is used in WSDL description of the remote service. It is discussed further in this paper.

This work was previously published in the International Journal of Web Portals 2(1), edited by Greg Adamson and Jana Polgar, pp. 45-57, copyright 2010 by Information Science Publishing (an imprint of IGI Global).

Chapter 5
WSRP, SOA and UDDI

Tony Polgar
Dialog IT, Australia

ABSTRACT

Web Services for Remote Portlets (WSRP) provide solutions for implementation of lightweight Service Oriented Architecture (SOA). UDDI extension for WSRP enables the discovery and access to user facing web services provided by business partners while eliminating the need to design local user facing portlets. Most importantly, the remote portlets can be updated by web service providers from their own servers. Remote portlet consumers are not required to make any changes in their portals to accommodate updated remote portlets. This approach results in easier team development, upgrades, administration, low cost development and usage of shared resources. Furthermore, with the growing interest in SOA, WSRP should cooperate with service bus (ESB).In this paper, the author examines the technical underpinning of the UDDI extensions for WSRP (user facing remote web services) and their role in service sharing among business partners. The author also briefly outlines the architectural view of using WSRP in enterprise integration tasks and the role Enterprise Service Bus (ESB).

INTRODUCTION

Leveraging web services through portals by means of the Java Portlet and WSRP standards gives companies a relatively easy way to begin implementing an SOA. Most portals have built-in support for the Java Portlet API and WSRP in the Portal Server which makes implementing a portal-based SOA even easier and cheaper. Portal support for the WSRP standard allows companies to easily create and offer SOA-style services and publish them in order to be accessed by other Consumers. The Consumers can combine several of these user facing services from diverse sources and portals to form the visual equivalent of composite applications. This approach delivers entire services to the other Consumer in a fashion which enables conveniently consume the services and use them

DOI: 10.4018/978-1-4666-0336-3.ch005

without any programming effort. Furthermore, Enterprise Service Bus (ESB) can be used to create controlled messaging environment, thus enabling lightweight connectivity.

During the architectural design involving WSRP we have to consider several design issues associated with usage of currently web technologies:

- Cookies handling, cookies protocol
- URL rewriting rules
- Ajax and security handling

In the following section we will discuss each of these topics and where possible, suggest the solution approach and highlight architectural points which would need special attention in the design.

COOKIES HANDLING

Cookies are commonly used in any web application. WSRP standard does not prescribe strictly how cookies should be handled thus introducing possible "disagreement" between the WSRP Consumer and Producer. These discrepancies are handled by WSRP extensions (WSRP 2.0 Portlet Specification, 2006). There have been several different approaches taken by Consumer implementations of how cookies sent to the Consumer are stored and distributed. The key difference is the distribution scope of a cookie set via a Set-Cookie response header during a markup operation other than initCookie() (getMarkup(), performBlockingInteraction(), handleEvents(), getResource()) (Polgar Jana, 2009). The WSRP extension enables the Producer to discover the method the Consumer uses to handle cookies (the actual protocol) and may allow the Producer to amend its behavior accordingly. In IBM WebSphere Portal Server cookies that the Consumer receives are stored in the Consumer session. They are later forwarded in requests to remote portlets. The portal also handles cookies set by resources that are served by

the WSRP Consumer as a proxy. They are served by the WSRP Consumer as a proxy according to the standard cookie matching and expiry rules.

The two distribution schemes have been proposed:

- RFC2109 - Cookies are sent to any Producer (and its portlets) that matches the domain and path attributes of the Set-Cookie header (http://www.ietf.org/rfc/rfc2109.txt)
- Use of Producer Cookie Protocol which restricts who can receive the cookies (rule is that Cookies are only sent to the originating Producer and portlets which match the Producer's Cookie Protocol in the service description. (http://docs.oasis-open.org/wsrp/v2/wsrp-2.0-spec-os-01.html#_CookieProtocol)

The proposal in the WSRP extension so far suggests to tie portlet cookies to the transport level similar to Producer managed cookies as a plain HTTP state mechanism. Cookies should be transferred and managed at the transport level. This approach has already been introduced in the earlier specification 1.0 and does not require any need for a change.

URL REWRITING

This WSRP extension provides a means of constructing a URL to a resource, which may be rewritten (or partially composed) by client-side scripting. The specification allows URL rewriting for commonly used means of URL rewriting, in particular, standard techniques of path manipulation and parameter additions, deletions, and updates must be enabled. However, due to the nature of a resource URL and security concerns there are some limitations placed on what can be rewritten. The resource URL cannot be rewritten for the following reasons: The resource-ID and/or wsrp-url are encoded, the location of these fields are determined by Consumer; the Consumer may totally rewrite or secure the URL thus making rewriting impossible.

As in the IBM Portals, the URL may refer to either a proxy or resource. The Producer must chose whether to serve the resource via a SOAP operation or via a HTTP proxy. This is because, the client can only easily rewrite either the URL or the resource-ID, but not both.

In the case where the resource is a proxy, it must be composed of the host, port, any part of the path the Producer chooses to make non-rewritable, or any additional state the Producer chooses to encode.

In the case where the resource is being served, the composition must include the resource's state, or any part of the path the Producer chooses to make non-rewritable.

AJAX AND WSRP

Ajax introduces the capability to create very responsive interactive web interfaces. Web applications can retrieve data from the server in asynchronous manner in the background without interfering with the display and behaviour of the existing page. However, one of the key flaws of Ajax is security. As it uses mainly client side interaction, the website could be easily attacked since codes could be easily injected to the application. That code will refer the application to website where the hacker code could launch an attack to extract information. The result is unwanted cross site scripting which could lead to data loss and enable some access to sensitive user information. This is only one of the security problems of Ajax that developers would have to face when they plan to build an Ajax based application.

A good solution for addressing the security problems in Ajax is by integrating it with WSRP (Web Services for Remote Portlets). Developers can build Ajax in a regular manner but the client

and the server side communication is done through WSRP. By using WSRP, the communication protocol and security rules are established between the client and the server. Remote portlets can also provide better customization for security by introducing the security rules for example, a single portlet will only allow a number of users. There are also other development option for introducing strict screening for the communication between Producers and Consumers which are out of scope of this paper.

WSRP could be the source of slower response because the direct communication of client to server is replaced by more complex protocol between the Producer and Consumer. Intensive screening especially for secured websites is typically very slow since secured websites often have more portlet security implemented.

PRINCIPLES REGISTRATION OF WEB SERVICES IN UDDI

Portlets (JSR 168, 2005) provide user interface to data delivered from web services. Before we explain the remote portlet publishing and discovery process in UDDI, we need to refresh the concept of publishing and discovering the web services in UDDI (Haas, Moreau, Orchard, Schlimmer, & Weerawarana, 2004). Web services expose their interfaces by registering in UDDI (UDDI Specifications, 2005). The web service Consumer must find the service, bind to it and invoke the service. The basic mechanism for publishing and discovering Web services is in Figure 1.

Regardless of whether the web service will be accessible to a single enterprise or to other companies (public access), the details about the service (its interface, parameters, location, etc.) must be made available to *Consumers*. This is accomplished with a WSDL description of the Web service and a Web service directory where the details of the Web service are published (refer to Web Services Description Language (WSDL)).

Figure 1. Publish-find-bind mechanism in UDDI

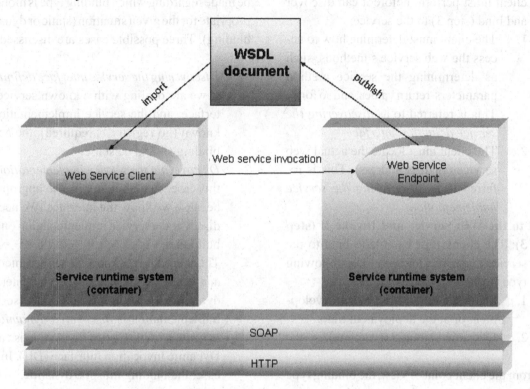

There are three steps which have to be performed in order to discover and use a web service published in the UDDI:

Publishing Web Service (step 1): In order to be accessible to interested parties, the web service is published in a Registry or web service directory. There are several choices regarding where to publish a web service:

1. If the web service is intended for the general public then a well-known registry is recommended. Consequently the WSDL description together with any XML schemas referenced by this description is made public.

2. The web service intended for enterprise use over an intranet should be published in a corporate registry only. No public access from the outside of the firewall is required.

3. Finally, providing all clients are dedicated partners in business, and there is an existing agreement on usage of this service, the web service can be published on a well-known location on the company server - with proper security access protection. Such a server would be placed on the public side of the company firewall but it would allow limited access, similar to a B2B Web server.

4. Web services directories are made up of a repository and the taxonomies (classification of registered entities for easier search) associated with them. There are no restrictions on publishing the web service in multiple registries, or in multiple categories.

Discovery of Web Service (step 2): Registry implementations can differ but there are some common steps, outlined below, that the client must perform before it can discover and bind (step 3) to the service:

1. The client must determine how to access the web service's methods, such as determining the service method parameters, return values, and so forth. This is referred to as *discovering the service definition interface*.

2. The client must locate the actual web service (find its address). This is referred to as *discovering the service implementation*.

Bind to the Web Service and Invoke It (step 3): The client must be able to bind to the service's specific location. The following types of binding may occur:

1. Static binding during client development or at the deployment time.

2. Dynamic binding (at runtime).

From the client point of view, the binding type and time play important roles in possible scenarios relevant to the client's usage of the web service. The following situations are typical:

1. A web service (WSDL and XML schemas) is published in well-known locations. The developers of the application that use the service know the service, its location, and the interface. The client (which is a process running on a host) can bypass the registry and use the service interfaces directly. Alternatively, the client knows the location and can statically bind to the service at the deployment time.

2. The web service expects its clients to be able to easily find the interface at build time. These clients are often generic clients. Such clients can dynamically find the specific implementation at runtime using the registry. Dynamic runtime binding is required.

Development of web service clients requires some rules to be applied and design decisions to be made regarding which binding type is more appropriate for the given situation (static or dynamic binding). Three possible cases are discussed:

1. *Discovering the service interface definition*: If we are dealing with a known service interface, and the service implementation is known (no registry is required), the actual binding should be static.

2. *Discovering the service implementation*: In this case, static binding is also appropriate because we know the interface. We need to discover the service implementation only at build time.

3. The client does not know the service interface and needs to discover the service interface dynamically at build time. The service implementation is *discovered dynamically at runtime*. This type of invocation is called Dynamic Invocation Interface (DII). In this case, the binding must be dynamic.

Each WSDL description of the service published in UDDI must contain the following six elements: definitions, types, message, portType, binding, and service. The main elements of the UDDI data model are listed below (Figure 2):

- businessEntity represents the physical company which registered the services with UDDI;

- businessService represents a specific service offered by a company;

- bindingTemplate contains instructions for service invocation;

- publisherAssertion structure allows businesses to publish relationships between businessEntities within the company; and

- tModel is a structure similar to a database table. It contains the following information about an entity: the name, description, URL, and the unique key.

Figure 2. UDDI model composition

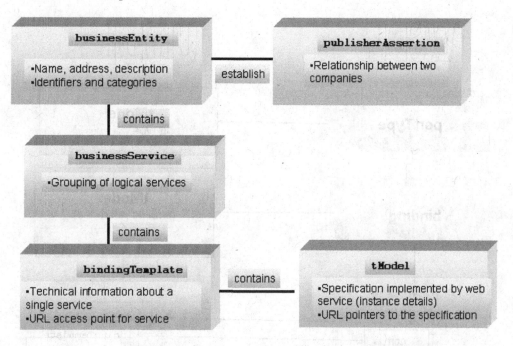

The relationships between the description and actual registered structures are outlined in Figure 3. The portType is represented by a UDDI structure called tModel. This tModel is categorized using unified *Category System* and the WSDL Entity-Type structure. The relevant *Category System* is known as WSDL portType tModel category and distinguishes it from other types of tModels with which the service might be associated.

A WSDL binding is also represented by a tModel structure. This is the binding tModel structure. This kind of categorization uses the same *Category System* as the portType tModel, but with a different key value to differentiate a binding tModel from a portType tModel.

The WSDL may represent a web service interface for an existing service. However, there may be an existing UDDI businessService that is suitable, and WSDL information can be just added to that existing service. If there is no suitable existing service found in the UDDI registry, a new businessService must be created. Finally, the WSDL binding port is represented by UDDI bindingTemplate. A WSDL service may contain multiple ports. These ports are exactly mirrored by the containment relationship in a UDDI businessService and its bindingTemplates.

REGISTERING WSRP SERVICES AS REMOTE PORTLETS IN UDDI

WSRP *Producer* is considered as a web service on its own, exposing multiple Bindings and Port-Types. It is described through the WSRP WSDL services description and some additional portlet types. Portlets are not fully fledged services, they are only HTML fragments. Therefore, they do not expose PortType, binding template and access points. The portlet is exposed by its *Producer* and the *Consumer* interacts indirectly with remote portlets using the *Producer's* infrastructure. The remote portlet is addressed by a portletHandle defined within the *Producer's* scope.

Figure 4 shows an example how a portal finds and integrates a remote portlet published in the UDDI. Content or application providers (known as WSRP *Producers*) implement their service as

Figure 3. Mapping from WSDL to UDDI

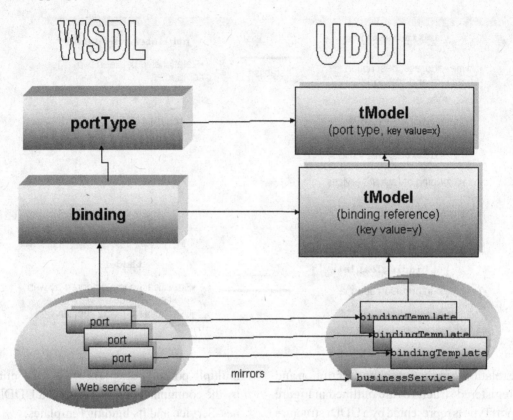

WSRP service and publish it in a globally accessible directory. *Producer's* WSDL description provides the necessary information about remote service actual end-points. The directory lets the *Consumers* easily find the required service. Directory entries, published in WSDL format, briefly describe the WSRP components and offer access to details about the services. The portal administrator uses the portal's published functions to create remote portlet web service entries in the portal local registry. Furthermore, the portlet proxy binds to the WSRP component through SOAP, and the remote portlet invocation (RPI) protocol ensures the proper interaction between both parties.

Typical discovery and binding steps are summarized below:

• A provider offers a set of portlets and makes them available by setting up a

WSRP *Producer* and exposing them as remote portlets. These portlets are then made available to other businesses by publishing them in a UDDI registry. The provider may perform the publishing task either through a custom built user interface or through the interface provided by a UDDI Server.

• End-user wants to add a portlet to his own portal. Using the tools provided by his portal (for example portal administrative interface or a custom-written XML interface[1]), he/she searches for remote portlets. After finding the suitable remote portlet, these portlets can be added to the portal pages. Alternatively, a portal administrator could search the UDDI registry for portlets and make them available to end-users by adding them to the portal's internal database.

Figure 4. Publishing and locating remote portlets with the UDDI

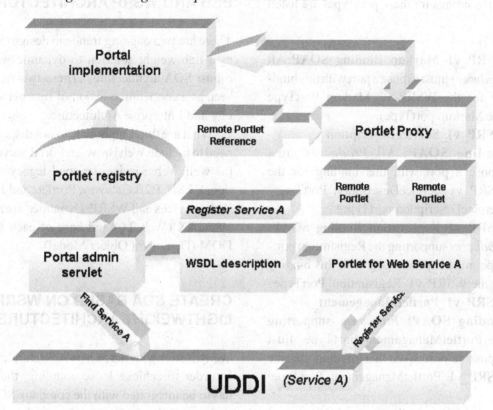

- The user can now access the page containing newly added and running remote portlets. Behind the scenes, the portal is making a web service call to the remote *Producer*, and the *Producer* is returning a markup fragment with the required data for the portal to render on the portal page.

In order to provide necessary information about remote portlets, WSRP extended the definition of the bind namespace for portTypes and SOAP binding. The following extensions are defined (WSRP specification version 1, 2003). This WSDL defines the following portTypes (normative definitions):

- **WSRP_v1_Markup_PortType:** This is the port on which the Markup Interface can be accessed. All *Producers* must expose this portType.

- **WSRP_v1_ServiceDescription_ PortType:** This is the port on which the Service Description Interface can be accessed. All *Producers* must expose this portType.

- **WSRP_v1_Registration_PortType:** This is the port on which the Registration Interface can be accessed. Only *Producers* supporting in-band registration of *Consumers* need expose this portType.

- **WSRP_v1_PortletManagement_ PortType:** This is the port on which the Management Interface can be accessed. *Producers* supporting the portlet management interface expose this portType. If this portType is not exposed, the portlets of the service cannot be configured by Consumers.

SOAP bindings for these portTypes are listed below:

1. **WSRP_v1_Markup_Binding_SOAP:** All *Producers* must expose a port with this binding for the WSRP_v1_Markup_PortType (the Markup portType).
2. **WSRP_v1_ServiceDescription_ Binding_SOAP:** All *Producers* must expose a port with this binding for the WSRP_v1_ServiceDescription_PortType (ServiceDescription portType).
3. **WSRP_v1_Registration_Binding_SOAP:** *Producers* supporting the Registration port-Type must expose a port with this binding for the WSRP_v1_Registration_PortType.
4. **WSRP_v1_PortletManagement_ Binding_SOAP:** *Producers* supporting the PortletManagement portType must expose a port with this binding for the WSRP_v1_PortletManagement_PortType.

Web service is typically represented by several remote portlets and relevant WSDL description (Figure 5) which contains pointers to all required and optional WSRP portlet interfaces (e.g., registration interface, service description, etc.) in the form of a portType.

In essence, WSRP *Producers* are web services. They expose PortTypes and bindings which the *Consumers* can use to access and interact with. It means that the process of publishing a *Producer* corresponds to publishing a web services together with associated portlet metadata. Besides the portletHandle, the Portlet Title and textual description, all further portlet metadata are missing in the UDDI. These remaining metadata must be retrieved from the respective ports (Service-Description portType or PortletManagement portType).

ESB AND WSRP ARCHITECTURE

There are two ongoing trends in design: Web 2.0 as a lightweight solution to dynamic web and. robust SOA architectures. These two trends are seen as a cooperative fusion of Internet technology and Enterprise Architecture.

What are the components to our disposal? We need to include Web Browser, Portal Server, SOA (as well Web Service wrapped legacy applications), ESB, B2B Gateway, Portlets and JSR286, Web Services and WSRP. Dynamics are realized by AJAX (Web 2.0) and base of each browser DOM (Document Object Model).

CREATE SOA BASED ON WSRP – LIGHTWEIGHT ARCHITECTURE

We will start with the SOA –WSRP architecture. In order to achieve loose coupling, the portlet has to be integrated with the company SOA. The architecture has to avoid tight coupling between the portlet and the specific service implementation context (technology, geography). The technology and geography independence is the basic requirements in this architecture and it can be achieved only by using web services. Web services are the standards based interfaces to expose application functions. The other requirements is associated with the presentation logic independence. The aim is to avoid maintenance of the application specific logic in portal server and a SOA based implementation. This approach would be beneficial for accessing the SOA from multiple portals, each of which would have an instance of the portlet implemented with the application specific logic. Therefore, the portlet implementation will have two parts: a generic part (at the portal side) and an application specific part (at the SOA-side). The generic part facilitates UI logic such as presenting personalization, house-style decoration and other mock-up. The application specific part holds the application state. The application specific part is

Figure 5. WSDL definition for WSRP example

```
<?xml version="1.0" encoding="UTF-8"?>
<wsdl:definitions
xmlns:urn="urn:oasis:names:tc:wsrp:v1:bind"
    xmlns:wsdl="http://schemas.xmlsoap.org/wsdl/"
    targetNamespace="urn:myProducer:wsdl">
    <wsdl:import
namespace="urn:oasis:names:tc:wsrp:v1:bind"
    location="http://www.oasis-
open.org/committees/wsrp/
    specifications/version1/wsrp_v1_bindings.wsdl"/>
    <wsdl:service name="WSRPService">
    <wsdl:port name="WSRPBaseService"
    binding="urn:WSRP_v1_Markup_Binding_SOAP">
    <soap:address
xmlns:soap="http://schemas.xmlsoap.org/wsdl/soap/"
    location="http://myProducer.com:9098/portal/Produ
cer"/>
    </wsdl:port>
    <wsdl:port name="WSRPServiceDescriptionService"
    binding="urn:WSRP_v1_ServiceDescription_Binding_S
OAP">
    <soap:address
xmlns:soap="http://schemas.xmlsoap.org/wsdl/soap/"
    location="http://myProducer.com:9098/portal/Produ
cer"/>
    </wsdl:port>
    <wsdl:port name="WSRPRegistrationService"
    binding="urn:WSRP_v1_Registration_Binding_SOAP">
    <soap:address
xmlns:soap="http://schemas.xmlsoap.org/wsdl/soap/"
    location="http://myProducer.com:9098/portal/Produ
cer"/>
    </wsdl:port>
    <wsdl:port name="WSRPPortletManagementService"
    binding="urn:WSRP_v1_PortletManagement_Binding_SO
AP">
    <soap:address
xmlns:soap="http://schemas.xmlsoap.org/wsdl/soap/"
    location="http://myProducer.com:9098/portal/Produ
cer"/>
    </wsdl:port>
    </wsdl:service>
</wsdl:definitions>
```

often coupled with presentation logic which is conventionally implemented by a portlet. This component does not have to run in a portlet container of a portal server. We only need to expose the presentation as an addressable presentation service which would form the user interaction point of the SOA. WSRP can be used for the interaction between the two portlet portions.

CREATE MESSAGING INFRASTRUCTURE

The ESB is the enterprise's web services platform. The ESB-infrastructure is used to pass the WSRP-messages. In this way we obtain a level control for most of the non-functional requirements such as security, identity, reliability, performance as well as robustness of the design.

AJAX AND ESB

To answer the problem of security in WSRP and AJAX, it is suggested to change the general architecture of the application using Enterprise Service Bus (ESB). With ESB, the middleware components provide useful way for directly bridging the server to the client. ESB is an event driven middleware which aims at optimizing the server engine messaging. The ESB also handles features such as security and caching and acts like a single-point proxy for WSRP Producers and the Web Services there by addressing any browser-side restriction. The portlet will be connected to ESB; the ESB provides the required communication bridge and portlet responsiveness will not be affected by the speed of the UI operations. The ESB manages UI customization based on a user profile by transforming a markup fragment generated from the WSRP Producer. AJAX controls are used to do partial updates of remote portlets by making a direct call to the ESB instead of routing the call from the browser to the WSRP Producer via the WSRP Consumer. This approach results in significant performance benefits and a rich user experience.

These strategies which need aggregation and customization of reusable UI components along with value-added features of rich user interface and security could benefit from using components such as ESB, AJAX and WSRP.

DISCUSSION

The lightweight SOA can be formed using WSRP, portals and ESB. Portal engine is one of the most important components in the proposed architecture. Several portal offerings for WSRP from key players in the market have been analysed by (Das, Chaudhuri, & Chawla, 2006). They selected the following parameters for comparison of vendor portal server products and their capability of handling WSRP:-

- Session Management as means of communications between portlets, between browser sessions and inter-portlet communications.
- Markup Generation and use.
- Security from the perspective of the supported standards and its integration with portal application.
- Interoperability between portal and different technologies.
- The extent of available customization and difficulties in customisation.

Although the findings presented in (Table 1) provide valuable information, we would like mention that some of the tested products are now superseded with higher versions and the information may lose its full relevance.

ESB plays the role of the communication bridge. There are also numerous open source products as well as commercial implementations such as IBM's WebSphere Process Server (WPS).

CONCLUSION

Portlet displaying web service's raw data arriving from a UDDI businessService structure (web service) reflects the infrastructure of the web service and needs to bind to the service. This is an undesirably tight coupling of user interface and service raw data which often cause problems to the *Consumer* in time of any changes to web service raw data. This problem is typically resolved by the *Producer* providing relevant libraries.

Using WSRP and UDDI extension for remote portlets, makes the end-user completely shielded from the technical details of WSRP. In contrast to the standard use of data-oriented web services, any changes to web service structure are implemented within the remote portlet and the *Consumer* is not affected by these changes.

UDDI version 1.1 allows the *Producers* to describe its presence together with each of the

Table 1. Comparison of portal server products (adapted from Das, Chaudhuri, & Chawla, 2006)

Parameters	Weblogic Portal 8.1 SP3	WebSphere Portal 5.1	MS SharePoint Portal Server 2003	Sun ONE Portal Server
Session Management	The Producer-Consumer session is tied to the user session.	Session data is lost for each request. An additional request to the Producer is submitted to establish a session.	Allows Web Parts to interchange information and objects within a browser session.	HTTP Session easily configurable
Markup Generation	URLs may be written by the Producer or the Consumer. Consumer supplies URL templates for Producer rewriting. Producer inserts markers in the markup for Consumer rewriting.	Submitting data to a portlet through forms changes state of the portlet. It prevents the submission of form data through render requests. Portlets that use render URLs to submit form data don't work remotely.	SharePoint Products and Technologies now use Web Part Pages and Web Parts based on the.NET Framework and ASP.NET.	Applets and frames
Security	Although, Weblogic supports various open standards, WSRP security is not that well matured.	Complies with the JSR-109 standard, can use WS-security features. WSRP Consumer and Producer can be configured to use Lightweight Third-Party Authentication (LTPA). The WSRP Portal may configure Secure Socket Layer (SSL) with Client Certificate Authentication.	Uses Windows authentication or Web-based authentication depending on the user registration. Single sign on.	Uses Secure Remote Access to provide highly secure remote access portals. Single sign on.
Interoperability	Tested with Consumers that use IBM, Oracle and Citrix Producers.	Tested with numerous Consumers.	WSRP-complaint Web parts deployable.	Tested with numerous Consumers.
Customization	The settings like WSRP SOAP Ports, Proxy Settings not easily customizable.	The WSRP SOAP Ports, Proxy Settings, Parallel Port Rendering, Switching Catching Off and On easily configurable.	Provides own custom style sheet.	Provides good customization facilities.

services it offers. The most important feature planned for higher versions of UDDI specification (specifically version 2 and higher) is the provision of cross portlet communication. Portlets should be able to broadcast their event information to other portlets spread across multiple *Producers* if necessary. This feature allows other portlets to tailor their generated content according to broadcasted events.

So far, there is seemingly no need to publish remaining portlet metadata. However, we envisage that the concept of semantic web and web service matchmaking as outlined in Akkiraju, Goodwin, Doshi, & Roeder, (2003) will require better annotation of available remote portlets functionalities to be published in a public registry. In such case, searching for portlets defining certain metadata values in UDDI will become the necessity.

SOA seems to be now widely adopted architectural approach to flexible integration. SOA implementation at the user interface layer using WSRP is the latest in the SOA solution trends. SOA has been implemented in a number of flavors such as AJAX based rich user interface (e.g., Google Maps), provisioning value-added services by using mashUps to combine data from multiple sources (e.g., chicagocrime.org), social communication-based on peer-to-peer interactions (e.g., Facebook and Flickr), and creating collective knowledge base (e.g., Digg and del.icio.us).

In the lightweight SOA architecture which combines the rich UI (AJAX), WSRP would support scenarios where a user needs to access the data from more than one portlet from different WSRP Producers. The user credentials are validated only once which is the feature provided by using WSRP Security. Features like the selective access of portlets to certain users, message encryption, digital signatures, and SSO/secure access to enterprise services from browser-based AJAX controls is provided by the middleware (ESB). Using WSRP and AJAX along with an ESB is a viable proposition in the real-world scenarios that need to share a dynamically customized UI based on Consumer profiles and support rich UI, while the security requirements are not compromised.

REFERENCES

Akkiraju, R., Goodwin, R., Doshi, P., & Roeder, S. (2003, August). A Method for Semantically Enhancing the Service Discovery Capabilities of UDDI. *In Proceedings of the IJCAI Information Integration on the Web Workshop*, Acapulco, Mexico. Retrieved from www.isi.edu/info-agents/workshops/ijcai03/papers/Akkiraju-SemanticUDDI-IJCA%202003.pdf

Das, A. S., Chaudhuri, A. P., & Chawla, M. (2006). *Point of view for WSRP compliant portal technologies*. Retrieved from http://searchsoa.techtarget.com/tip/0,289483,sid26_gci1186223,00.html

Haas, H. P. L. H., Moreau, J.-J., Orchard, D., Schlimmer, J., & Weerawarana, S. (2004). *Web Services Description Language (WSDL) Version 2.0 Part 3: Bindings. W3C.* Retrieved from http://www.w3.org/TR/2004/WD-wsdl20-bindings-20040803

http://www.oasis-open.org/committees/download.php/3343/oasis-200304-wsrp-specification-1.0.pdf

JSR 168. (2005). *Portlet Specification*. Retrieved from http://www.jcp.org/en/jsr/detail?id=168

Polgar, J. (2009). Using WSRP 2.0 with JSR 168 and 286 Portlets. *International Journal of Web Portals, 2*(2).

Servlets Specification 2.4. (2004). Retrieved November 2005 from http://www.jcp.org/aboutJava/communityprocess/final/jsr154

Specifications, U. D. D. I. (2005). *Universal Description, Discovery and Integration v2 and v3.* Retrieved November 2005, from http://www.uddi.org/specification.html

Web Services Description Language (WSDL). An Intuitive View. (n.d.). Retrieved from http://java.sun.com/dev/evangcentral/totallytech/wsdl.html

WSRP 2.0 Portlet Specification. (2006). Retrieved November 2009 from http://www.oasis-open.org/committees/download.php/18617/wsrp-2.0-spec-pr-01.html

WSRP specification version 1. (2003). *Web Services for Remote Portlets, OASIS*. Retrieved in 2005 from

ENDNOTE

[1]   In IBM WebSphere Portal 5.1, this activity is supported via the configuration portlets or XML configuration interface

This work was previously published in the International Journal of Web Portals 2(2), edited by Greg Adamson and Jana Polgar, pp. 38-50, copyright 2010 by Information Science Publishing (an imprint of IGI Global).

Chapter 6
Use of Web Analytics in Portals

Jana Polgar
Dialog IT, Australia

ABSTRACT

Web analytics are typically branded as a tool for measuring website traffic. They can be equally used as a tool for business research, results of advertising campaigns, and market research. Web analytics provide data on the number of visitors, page views, measure a visitor's navigation through a website, etc. This collection of data is typically compared against some metrics to indicate whether the web site is delivering expected values, what improvements should be considered, and so on. These metrics are also used to improve a web site or marketing campaign's audience response. Tracking portal visits are important in order to obtain a better understanding of which parts of the portal are delivering value. However, portals have unique attributes associated with the page composition techniques, page, and portlet refresh. Portal always presents multiple topics on the same page, which pose specific challenges to explore exciting opportunities allowing the web designer to gain insights about portal usage and user behaviour. Furthermore, portals are inherently multidimensional, and effective tools to monitor and analyse portal data usage must be able to support multidimensional analysis.

WHAT ARE WEB ANALYTICS?

Web analytics (Eric Patterson, 2004) or site analytics are used to provide data about the number of visitors, page views, show the traffic and popularity trends. In portal applications, the key to knowing what to track and monitor is understanding how the site is built and how the

page URL is formed. In addition, portals are often used in conjunction with Content Management Systems (CMS). The use of site metrics to capture and measure user activity primarily to understand end user needs, behaviours and site usability enable the designers to build better portals and better target the content. It is often expected that the knowledge of user behaviour would lead to increases in revenue with better content targeting and can also impact the cost of automatic tuning.

DOI: 10.4018/978-1-4666-0336-3.ch006

Site Analytics are also know as being a factor in reduction of testing costs with better designs. In portals, the integration with site analyser tools is often performed by generating reports based on the portal site analyzer logs or manually embedding tags into portlets (JSR 168, 2005) and themes. Well designed portal is expected to provide environment for the necessary collection of analytics data and offer seamless integration of web analytics engine with the portal. Web Analytics are typically gathered in one of following ways:

1. **Server-side log analysis**: It's a fine-grained resource usage reporting method. Web servers record some of their transactions in logfiles. A typical server-side site analytics architecture is based on user interactions and metadata are written to server logfiles hosted on the Portal server. However, analytics engines are often not part of the Portal product.

2. **Active page tagging**: It is a client side script-based real-time reporting method, which collects cached content as well. This concept evolved to include certain information about the page and the visitor. Ajax enables to implement a call back to the server from the rendered page. When the page is rendered on the web browser, AJAX call-back code would call back to the server and pass the information about the visitor. This approach can become a problem considering browser restrictions on the servers which can be contacted with this protocol (XmlHttpRequest objects).

3. **Click analytics**: is a special type of web analytics reporting technique that gives special attention to clicks. The click analytics focuses on on-site analytics. A designer of a web site uses click analytics to determine the performance of the site, with regards to the number of clicks and their position on the web site.

With Web 2.0 the tracking of events has become even more important. The page / portlet designer must determine ahead in time what events are worse while to track and how to track them. However, if the site is using AJAX technology then the tracking of views is not providing expected results (Typically defined as the number of times a page was viewed). In a traditional web page, every click of a link or a button results in a trip to the web server and a reloading of a new page view. In an AJAX enabled web page or portlet refresh these server trips are replaced by the call-back calls, so instead of having several page views, we obtain only single view even though the data is changing constantly. In a site that is built using AJAX or another Web 2.0 technology, the only way to obtain consistent information about the visitor is to track all events.

Google Analytics (GATC) use the method of page tagging technology (Google Analytics Official Site - http://www.google.com/analytics/). It is based on a hidden snippet of Java Script that the user adds on every page. The purpose is to collect private visitor data and send it back to Google data collection servers for processing. In essence, GATC loads a large file from the Google web server, sets the variables and associates them with the user account. GATS also uses cookies on each visitor computer to track anonymous information such as returning visitor, timestamp, where from the site is being accessed.

There are of course disadvantages in using cookies. Many browser provide ad filtering extensions and can block GATC. In addition, the privacy networks such as Tor can mask the user's actual location and therefore provide distorted data. Furthermore, cookies can be deleted or blocked which results in loss of data and inaccurate reports. GATC technology is also facing some difficulty with mobile phones due to the usage of cookies and tags.

PORTALS ARE DIFFERENT FROM TRADITIONAL WEB SITES

Portals are inherently multidimensional web sites. One dimension are users. Portals are typically deployed to a defined user community. In company context, they could be used in B2B or B2E portals, or social sites like company twitter. In either case, the user has to log into the portal and authenticate herself by submitting her user name and password and session is tight to the user's identity. This property makes the portal and a portal session different from most traditional web-site sessions in a significant way.

Second dimension deals with the page composition. Unlike web sites, which consist of discrete HTML pages, portal pages are comprised of dynamically arranged independent portlets. Due to portal customization capabilities, these portlets can form different initial web pages for different users. Therefore, the experience of one user is unlikely to be identical to that of user another user.

Third dimension is the content shown in user-portlet-portal context. Many portal are linked to CMS and they serve documents. CMS technology may introduce some noise in the usage data. As an example, a portal taxonomy may include a document link in more than one category, each pointing to the same document. When a user clicks on that document link, that action records two events: the document-read event, and the appropriate taxonomy folder navigation event. Caching content is very common way to improve portal performance. Interaction with cached content typically is not recorded on the portal logs. Therefore, it is difficult to effectively track events associated with cached documents.

Several other dimensions refer to the technology used to compose and display portal page. Some portal engines facilitate portlet wiring or inter-portlet communication (Behl, Hesmer, Koch, & Steinbach, 2006). For example, if we want to communicate data to other portlets, we have several option to do so: using the portlet coordination feature that enables sending events to other portlets using the Property Broker infrastructure, or create render URLs to other portlets or pages using URL generation API. These and similar technologies create confusion in data collections. The page view does not change, and the inter-portlet communication is not clearly bound to the user action.

WEB ANALYTICS, AJAX, WSRP AND SECURITY

Ajax introduces the capability to create very responsive interactive web interfaces. Web applications can retrieve data from the server asynchronously in the background without need to refresh the existing page. Ajax is also used in conjunction with web analytics engines. However, one of the key flaws of Ajax is security. As it uses mainly client side interaction, the website could be easily attacked by injecting malicious codes to the application. That code will hijack the application to website where the hacker code could launch an attack. The result is unwanted cross site scripting which could lead to data loss and enable some access to sensitive user information. This is only one of the security problems of Ajax that developers would have to face when they plan to build an Ajax based application.

One of the solutions which addresses the security problems in Ajax is by using WSRP (Web Services for Remote Portlets) (WSRP 2.0 Portlet Specification, 2006) in client-server context rather than outward facing portal. Developers can build Ajax in a regular manner but the client and the server side communication would be accomplished through WSRP. The communication protocol and security rules would be established between the client and the server (typically SSL type of security, digital signature). In addition, the remote portlets can also provide better customization for security by introducing additional security rules such as, a single portlet will only allow predefined number of users. There are also other development option for introducing strict screening for the communication between Producers and Consumers which are out of scope of this paper.

The question how to secure Ajax code used with web analytics is still outstanding. Active page tagging and Ajax call-backs implies that website would be the subject to cross-site request forgery (XSRF). There are several strategies how to secure Ajax scripts. However, we have not found anything specifically designed to be deployed with web analytics tooling.

WEBSPHERE PORTAL AND WEB ANALYTICS BRIEF OVERVIEW

In previous papers (Polgar, 2009; J. Polgar & T. Polgar, 2009), we have examined how the portal works and how the portlets are rendered. In portal page, AJAX is embedded in the portlet and it is used to fetch portlet-only relevant information. The tracking code is typically placed within events that occur within a page. It means that page view has not changed but the portlet content has. This information would not be recorded. Each portlet is responsible for its own content only, and it is unaware of any other portlets on the page.

The servlet and portlets may share the session. ID attributes are not only used in site analytics but they are often used in Ajax to quickly update a portion of the page (Bishop & Phillips, 2006). Because ID attributes within any HTML tag are global to the DOM, they must be unique. If for some reasons there are duplicate ID attributes, then results are unpredictable and may lead to incorrect data collections.

In a portal environment, Ajax is also used to refresh the page or more often just a portlet. This operation is more problematic than in a simple Web application because of the fact that multiple portlets are on a page. It is envisaged that active page tagging may not produce clear results with regards to page / portlet statistics.

WebSphere Portal 6.x provides mostly server site loggers and enables logging of events for each portlet that is rendered, regardless the page which contains the portlet (Liesche & Uhlig, 2006). Typical architecture is shown in Figure 1.

There are several loggers available: SiteAnalyzerPageLogger, SiteAnalyzerPortletLogger, SiteAnalyzerPortletActionLogger and SiteAnalyzerErrorLogger. The information available for collection contains unique object ID of the portlet, portlet name, portlet mode (View, Edit, Configure, Help) and state (Normal, Minimized, Maximized). Switching on all loggers may result in multiple log records for single page.

Figure 1. Typical architecture of server side analytics in WebSphere Portal 6.x

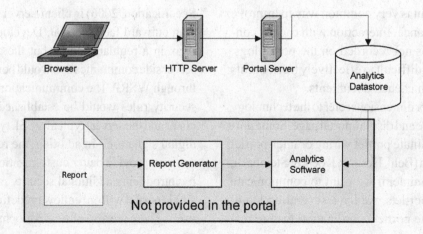

CONCLUSION

Tracking portal visits and collecting data about portlets usage is important in order to obtain better understanding which parts of the portal are delivering value. In addition, web analytics enable to gain insights about portal usage and user behavior. However, unlike traditional websites, portals have unique attributes associated with portlet delivery and refresh which pose specific challenges when applying web analytics and extracting the reports. Web site tracking tools rely predominantly on web server logs or page tags. By parsing the web logs, these tools provide a picture of portal events, listing where an IP addresses came from, portlet name and action and also the information relevant to the portlet navigation (where it went and possibly how long it stayed on any specific portlet). Because of the inherently multidimensional nature of portals, an effective tool to monitor and analyse portal data usage must be able to support multidimensional analysis. Multidimensional analytic tools should be able provide more information than standard log parsing tools. These analysers could include the information about the most popular documents on the portal, what are the most used portlets, who are the most active users, how often is the "Edit" mode used, how often the portlet was refreshed, etc. As already mentioned, the nature of portal technology and usage of logs to analyse data introduces significant noise in the data collections.

REFERENCES

Behl, S., & Hesmer, S. (2007). *Refreshing individual portlets and preferences using Single Portlet Refresh in WebSphere Portal V6.0.1.* Retrieved from http://www.ibm.com/developerworks/websphere/library/techarticles/0712_behl/0712_behl.html

Behl, S., Hesmer, S., Koch, S., & Steinbach, D. (2006). *Leveraging WebSphere Portal V6 programming model: Part 2. Advanced URL generation in themes and portlets.* Retrieved from http://www.ibm.com/developerworks/websphere/library/techarticles/0612_behl/0612_behl.html

Bishop, K., & Phillips, D. (2006). *Using Ajax with WebSphere Portal.* Retrieved from http://www.ibm.com/developerworks/websphere/library/techarticles/0606_bishop/0606_bishop.html

Google Analytics Official Site. (n.d.). Retrieved from http://www.google.com/analytics/

JSR 168. (2005). *Portlet Specification.* Retrieved from http://www.jcp.org/en/jsr/detail?id=168

Liesche, S., & Uhlig, S. (2006). *IBM WebSphere Developer Technical Journal: Using portal analytics with open-source reporting tools.* Retrieved from http://www.ibm.com/developerworks/websphere/techjournal/0609_liesche/0609_liesche.html

Patterson, E. (2004). *Web Analytics Demystified: A Marketer's Guide to Understanding How Your Web Site Affects Your Business.* New York: Celilo Group media and Cafe Press.

Polgar, J. (2009). Using WSRP 2.0 with JSR 168 and 286 Portlets. *International Journal of Web Portals, 2*(2).

Polgar, J., & Polgar, T. (2009). Building Portal Applications. *International Journal of Web Portals, 1*(1), 47–67.

Servlets Specification 2.4. (2004). Retrieved from http://www.jcp.org/aboutJava/communityprocess/final/jsr154

WSRP 2.0 Portlet Specification. (2006). Retrieved from http://www.oasisopen.org/committees/download.php/18617/wsrp-2.0-spec-pr-01.html

Zakas, N. C., McPeak, J., & Fawcett, J. (2006). *Professional Ajax.* New York: Willey Publishing.

This work was previously published in the International Journal of Web Portals 2(4), edited by Greg Adamson and Jana Polgar, pp. 40-44, copyright 2010 by Information Science Publishing (an imprint of IGI Global).

Chapter 7
Search Integration with WebSphere Portal:
The Options and Challenges

Andreas Prokoph
IBM, Germany

ABSTRACT

Modern web applications and servers like Portal require adequate support for integration of search services due to user focused information delivery and user interaction, as well as new technologies used to render such information, which is exemplified by two fundamental problems that have long plagued web crawlers: dynamic content and Javascript generated content. Today, the solution is simple: ignore such web pages. To enable "search" in Portals, a different "crawling" paradigm is required to search engines to gather and consume information. WebSphere Portal provides a framework that propagates content and information through "Seedlists"—comparable to HTML based sitemaps but richer in terms of features. This mandates that information and content delivering applications must be "search engine aware", requiring them to enable services and seedlists for fast, efficient and complete delivery of content and information. This is the main integration point for search engines into the portal for Portal site search services for a rich and user focused search experience. This article discusses how such technologies can allow for more efficient crawling of public Portal sites by prominent Internet search engines as well as myths surrounding search engine optimization.

1. PORTAL SITES AND TRADITIONAL WEB SEARCH ENGINES

WebSphere Portal allows people to interact with applications, processes, other people, documents and content in a personalized and role-based fashion. In a day and age when information overload has become commonplace, Portal allows context-relevant resources to be presented via common Web browsers, placing what people need to complete the job at hand at their fingertips, regardless of where they are.

DOI: 10.4018/978-1-4666-0336-3.ch007

Figure 1. Portal and application integration overview

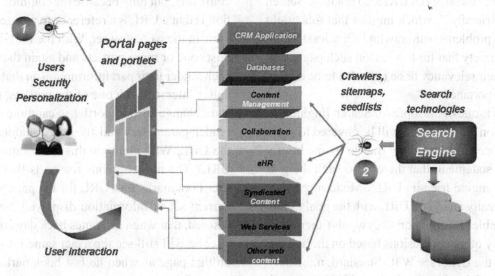

Figure 1 shows the range of applications and services that integrate with Portal, as well as how that information and content is visualized to the end user.

Figure 1 also shows on a very high level how a search engine can integrate with the Portal:

1.   Traditionally a regular web crawler starts with the homepage and then follows all links to capture all information provided by the portal site. What options are available to optimize this process will be described in this article. We will also discuss the restrictions and limitations. as well as options to resolve some of these

2.   We will show how a new crawling technique can be enabled on the application level, which no longer requires the crawler to communicate and explore applications and repositories (pull technique). The application will rather send the crawler on request the list of what information the crawler is requested to fetch and process (push technique). Technical details as well as advantages of doing so foremost in a Portal environment is also discussed in more depth throughout this article

1.1 Content Centric Portal - Just Like "Any Other Website"

The simplest case to look at first is a Portal site which delivers static content through its pages and portlets. Portal provides a rich user experience in terms of consistent navigation, appearance and information delivery.

Crawling such a Portal site is a matter of pointing the crawler either at the homepage, a sitemap, or a site-directory. The crawler will then identify and record all links to referenced pages of that site, fetch their content and then send it for final processing to the indexing service. And once stored in the index, the user will then be able to perform his search requests.

That said: this is "business as usual" for the web-crawler, no real difference compared to crawling a standard web-server delivering more or less static HTML content.

1.2 What About the URLs?

We just started to look at a portal site and it being crawled by a web-crawler like for example the Google-Bot. To some this might already ring a bell. If not or in addition: others might then ask the question: "those portal URLs do not look 'search engine friendly'", which implies that this might result in problems with crawling. Or at least feeIng some anxiety that for this reason such pages will loose their relevancy or be regarded to be of very little importance.

This is one of the topics of Search Engine Optimization (SEO) which will be covered to some extent later in this article. But do let me briefly make a statement, that there is no such thing as 'search engine friendly URL'. Modern crawlers do not really analyze a URL with the goal to find 'searchable' information (keywords) therein or draw any other conclusions based on the appearance of the URL (see W3C Standard, n.d.).

To explain a bit why the Portal URLs are built the way they are, we'll take a closer look at such a portal URL, like for example:

```
https://www.whereami.com/wps/portal/
our-site/!ut/p/c5/04_SB8K8xLLM9MS-
SzPy8xBz9CPOos3gLI28zT0tvA0t3N2MT-
A08LR-dATxMTYwNXc_1wkA6zeDenEA_fkGB-
jA3ezYBcDozA_U0NjfzMDA38ziLwBDuBooO_
nkZ-bql-QnZ3m6KioCACQuFn1/dl3/d3/
L0lDUmlTUSEhL3dHa0FKRnNBL1lCUmZ3QSE-
hL2Vu
```

This portal URL contains (encoded) information such as:

*   What page to navigate to
*   What language is used
*   Render-parameter information for individual portlets
*   Navigational state information – for example what portal page the user navigated from (which is e.g. required for 'back button' support of the browser)

With this in mind, we will understand that there is no single and unique URL pointing to a portal page, but that rather multiple URLs can point to that same physical portal page. This might sound confusing, but only because the common perception is that a URL is a reference to a page that we view in the web browser. With the Portal, a page hosts one or more portlets and again the portlets each render their part information on that page. If a user interacts with one of the portlets, then the state change of that portlet is captured through render parameters and these are maintained in the URL. Why maintain this information in the URL? The most obvious reason is that when a user bookmarks that URL for the page with the current set of information displayed, he can be assured, that when he comes back days or weeks later he will still see the exact same information on that page as when he last bookmarked it (of cause if the contents has been altered or deleted, etc. this might not be that case).

On the other hand: web crawlers assume that a URL for every page in unique and more specifically: the URL is a "primary key" for a web page in its search index. So we need to understand there is a conflict here. However: since the crawler does not behave like a regular user, and its expectation level around URLs is quite low, there are options available in the Portal to handle such conflicts. The technicalities will be explained in more detail in "Public Portal sites".

1.2.1 Web Crawler History – Truncating or Avoiding Too Long URLs

Another one of such misconception has to do with the problems that crawlers had in the past with "dynamic" content delivery. This included initial techniques of spoofing the crawler, by feeding it one flavor of information, opposed to a regular user that gets the other flavor of information – an typically what each of the two got to see was totally different.

This describes the darker side of false content delivery, however similar techniques were used to generate dynamic content for users based on their preferences and navigational information (e.g. stored in cookies), like coming from page 'Y' and now on page 'Z'.

Such logic had been encode within URLs by adding parameters which had been delimited by question marks '?' or ampersands '&'. The strategy of web crawlers back then ('back then' is at least going back 5-8 years) was to assume that if such parameters are stripped off the URL, that for one thing the 'normalized' URL is still valid, and secondly it will output the default content on that page.

Today however we see the world has changed. Many web applications require more complex URLs and the URLs can not easily be manipulated any longer hoping that after truncation that they are still valid and point to some (default) resource hosted on that specified server. With that in mind, crawlers largely (have to) accept URLs as they are.

Note: to some extent 'URL normalization' where meaningful is still applied, e.g. removing fragment components (relative address within a given portal page), and the like (see Wikipedia, n.d.).

2. PUBLIC PORTAL SITES

Now in order to dive a bit deeper into the world of portals and web crawlers, we'll take a closer look at first at 'public' portal sites and how search engines deal with them. 'Public' portal sites are to be honest easier for search engines to deal with. The main capabilities that a portal delivers, such as security, personalization, and dynamic content through extensive user interaction, is not at all or only very little exploited and thus imposes no real challenges to web crawlers.

Now not to say one cannot accomplish a great user experience by providing personalized content, where the user information is taken from a cookie, and thus the returning user is greeted by name and based on his known preferences, personalized information is presented in addition

to the regular information shown to other visitors of that portal site as well.

It is also important to understand that web crawlers do not behave the exact same way as a human user does. Some distinguishing characteristics between the two are:

- The most obvious – and in early years too often misused – is its web-agent ID. Which is unique for the crawler ("Googlebot/2.1" for example is as the name suggests that of Google's web crawler)
- Next: web crawlers do not typically state what their 'preferred language' is, thus anticipating to see the information presented in the default language of the portal or web site it is visiting
- And then third on the list – but not the last, more to come later – is that such crawlers do not handle Javascript. Which essentially means as trivial examples, that any content or URLs generated through Javascript will not be picked up and processed by the crawler

2.1 Out-of-the-Box Crawlability Support

In the first section we talked about Portal's URLs and why they are as they are. It was also hinted at the fact, that the URLs are not unique for any given Portal page, but the content of the URL varies dependent for example from which Portal page a user has navigated to the other. It is also again obvious for what reason Portal generates URLs as it does: "bookmark-ability" and browser 'Back' button support. Meaning: when a user interacts with Portal pages and portlets, this will certainly cause portlets on that page to show specific content and possibly also that one portlet vanishes and another appears in its place. Once a user stores the URL of that pages as a bookmark, he will of course expect that when he visits that portal page via his bookmark a couple of weeks later, that the page and portlet still show that same information compared to the point in time when he had bookmarked the page.

Now this URL related functionality of the Portal was introduced a couple of years ago with Version 5.1 of WebSphere Portal. Unfortunately this collided with the fact that some of the Portal customers prepared to "go public" with their Portal site. With that, once gone public, web crawlers started to hit that portal site.

But! What then happened was the unexpected and either of two things:

- Worst case was that only the homepage made it into the search engine's search index and thus was the only page that could be searched for and returned in the search result list
- In many cases: only few and high level pages made it into the search index

What has happened? The crawler as the automated 'click on everything user' started to fetch the Portal site's pages. And since having clicked on all links on every page, it also navigated from different other pages to that same page. As more and more pages are queued by the crawler, the more and more it gets confused. The confusion war simply, that apparently duplicate pages with different URLs where queued up and the list could not be refined by applying standard URL normalization techniques. In the end a decision is made by the robot to either stop crawling and then keep the pages it has fetched so far in its search index, or because of the many duplicate pages detected to just keep the homepage in its search index. This is of course a problem for every site owner – not having his web pages properly available in an Internet search engine's search index. "If the page cannot be found in Google, then it doesn't exist!"

2.1.1 Solution for Web-Crawlers on Public Portal Pages

Portal V6.0 introduced a new feature dubbed 'crawlability feature' which addresses the issues that web crawlers ran into, when fetching content from a Portal site. This feature has been designed and implemented to allow web crawlers to now safely and efficiently crawl public portal pages. Note the explicit mentioning of '*public*' portal pages and not portal pages in general. The reason is that the logic that was introduced is not applicable for secured portal pages. This means that for secured portal pages a different approach would need to be taken. More details around this in "Time for change – inverting the crawling process".

In short how this feature works is the following: Portal checks the client's agent ID and if it matches one of those in the list (includes name patterns) of web crawlers, it will then initiate that Portal URL generation will only encode that information into the URL which is mandatory for a web crawler to navigate from one Portal page to the other. Including of course the need to be able to identify if a page link it has detected has been discovered before already. This is essentially all what the web crawler wants to do. And last: it also needs to be ensured, that when later on a user clicks on such a URL from within the search result list, that this URL will be valid for a 'regular' user as well.

Such a URL we call a Portal 'normalized URL'. The component within Portal which handles navigational state is the 'State Manager Service'. The relevant configuration parameter for this service is called 'com.ibm.wps.state.outputmediators. OutputMediatorFactory.normalization_xsl_file' and it accepts as value an XSL style sheet file that contains the specifics for the URL transformation. The default XSL file specified is 'UrlNormalization_MIN.xsl' and it contains the states for 'selection' and 'locale' in the normalized URL. All other states included in the URL if listed will be removed.

Box 1.

```
<root>
<state type="navigational">
<selection selection-node="6_CGAH47L00066C02B566R9A3861">
<mapping src="6_CGAH47L00066C02B566R9A30I2" dst="6_CGAH47L0085GA02B56D1CN1GS3"/>
<mapping src="6_CGAH47L00066C02B566R9A3G30" dst="6_CGAH47L00066C02B566R9A3861"/>
<mapping src="6_CGAH47L00066C02B566R9A3GT3" dst="6_CGAH47L00066C02B566R9A3861"/>
</selection>
<expansions>
<node id="6_CGAH47L00066C02B566R9A30I2"/>
<node id="6_00000000000000000000000A0"/>
<node id="6_CGAH47L00066C02B566R9A3G30"/>
<node id="6_CGAH47L00066C02B566R9A3GT3"/>
</expansions>
<theme-template>Home</theme-template>
<portlet id="7_CGAH47L00066C02B566R9A38M0" portlet-type="legacy"/>
</state>
<target portlet-type="legacy" portlet-id="7_CGAH47L00066C02B566R9A38M0" id="JaUDW14">
<target-type>action</target-type>
<action-ref>sa.ActionManageSearchables</action-ref>
</target>
</root>
```

Note that the online product documentation might still list additional states, like 'portlet-mode' and 'window-mode', but this will be corrected soon (see InfoCenter, 2010).

Examples of such two flavors of Portal URLs:

This URL is available to a user after having navigated through 3 pages and interacted with one portlet:

```
http://localhost:10040/wps/
myportal/!ut/p/c5/04_SB-
8K8xLLM9MSSzPy8xBz9CP0os3hnd-
0cPE3MfAwMDMzNnAyMnUzOzIEtHY-
wszQ6B8JE55A08jFN0Wpu6OYFkXQ2c_Q_
dgY7y63Y0NKLDbPcSYgO5wkF_xux0k-
b4ADOBrg1Q92PT55oPv8PPJzU_
Uj9aPMcbrT10A_Mic1PTG5Ur8gNzQ-
0wiDTU9fNUREAtSvaJw!!/dl3/d3/
L0lJSklna21DU1EhIS9JRGpBQU15QUJ-
FUkNKRXFnLzRGR2dzbzBWdnphOUlBOW9JQSE-
hLzdfQ0dBSDQ3TDAwMDY2QzAyQjU2N1I5QTM
4TTAvSmFVRFcxNC9zYS5BY3Rpb25NYW5hZ-
2VTZWFyY2hhbYmxlcw!!/
```

in its decoded version (see box 1).

As a crawler (GoogleBot in this case) it receives the following Portal URL:

```
http://localhost:10040/wps/
portal/!ut/p/c4/04_SB8K8xLLM9MSSzPy8x-
Bz9CP0os3hnd0cPE3MfAwMLU3dHAyMnUzMXQ2
c_Q_dgA_2CbEdFAO_RsWg!/
```

and the decoded version of the URL is as follows (see box 2):

Note: decoding of Portal URLs can be accomplished by using the following published API:

Box 2.

```
<root>
<state type="navigational">
<selection selection-node="6_CGAH47L-
00066C02B566R9A3861"/>
</state>
</root>
```

```
http://hostname>:<port>/wps/
contenthandler?uri=state:<the portal
URL goes here>
```

The result of the API call is the XML output of the navigational state encoded within the URL as shown in the two examples above.

More technical information on the topic of Portal URLs can be found in the Portal Wiki in the article "What you always wanted to know about URIs in WebSphere Portal v6 – or more than that …" (Leue, 2009).

2.2 Action Required: Portlet Interaction Causes Content to Change – Example Based on a WCM Usage Scenario

There are some cases where the default configuration of the State Manager Service does require the attention and action of the Portal administrator. An example would be: one of the typical usage scenarios with WCM and Portal is to deploy a content rendering portlet on a portal page, which as a default view shows a list of news article with some abstract text for every news article entry plus a link to the full article. Now when a user clicks on such a link to see the details of the selected article, he will technically seen remain on that same portal page, however the content rendering portlet will now present to the user the full news article he had selected.

The problem in this case that gets surfaced, is that when a web crawler gets navigated to this page and selects or follows the link to such a news article within the "News" portlet, is that the page and portlet content is returned in that exact same view the crawler had received it at its first visit. This essentially means that the web crawler will never be able to process the full news articles on that page within the 'News" portlet.

It needs to emphasized here that this behavior could also be intentional, in that interaction with a portlet and the information its returns is really just for the eyes of a regular user, thus not meant to be picked up by a web crawler. As and example: a Calendar portlet which displays events on a monthly basis and in addition allows to add a new Event or to comment a selected event. This should not be enabled for the web crawler.

Note: usually such actions would be enabled as 'POST' requests and one of the reasons doing so is also because web crawlers only process 'GET' requests, but such guidelines are not always followed or simply overseen.

2.2.1 Solution: Configure Portal State Manager Add 'Render Parameters' to a Normalized URL

To deal with this 'problem' shows the strengths of Portal: the 'State Manager Service' can be configured to change the behavior of URL transformation for specific agent IDs. We mentioned above the parameter 'com.ibm.wps.state.outputmediators. OutputMediatorFactory.normalization_xsl_file' and the XSL stylesheet file that it uses to generate the URL for a web crawler. What needs to be done is either update the existing 'UrlNormalization_MIN.xsl' file or add a new XSL file to now include next to the states for 'selection' and 'locale' now also 'renderparameters' in the normalized URL.

The result of this modification to the style sheet is that in the content delivery scenario outlined above, the web crawler will now be able to get at the full news article displayed within the content rendering portlet and the URL will still be unique for the purpose of web crawling.

Still: when applying such a change to the behavior of the Portal and the way it generates its URLs, care must be taken to make sure this does not result in unexpected or not anticipated behavior in conjunction with other types of portlet applications as this configuration modification affects all deployed portlets.

2.3 If Requested – 'User' Friendly URLs Can Be Configured As Well

Let's at first emphasize the fact, that there is no such thing as 'search engine friendly' URLs.

As stated previously, years ago crawlers tried to manipulate URLs (or even drop them completely) if they looked like they would deliver dynamic content. However today as web applications grow more complex – so do their URLs. And this fact is being acknowledged by web crawlers as well.

Portal Server however does allow to provide more 'human readable' URLs (Figure 2), meaning that if presented to a end user, he then could make sense of what type of information such a URL is pointing to, by just looking at the keywords used in the relative path of the URL. This is an important aspect for example when URLs are used for campaigns and sent via Emails. We can all anticipate, that we a URL is short and contains meaningful terms (such as: ".../our/campaign/2010/gold_customers") that the likelihood

of the addressee actually clicking on such a URL will increase compared to when the URL would be a very long string of meaningless combination of alpha-numerics.

3. "OLD SEARCH AND NEW PORTAL"

Admittedly the title of this section is intended to be a bit of a teaser. It is not intended to make search technology look bad and Portal on the other hand look bright. It is more about how the pace of requirements and implementation differ comparing Portal development with search technology development.

3.1 Portal Pages

Portal distinguishes between three different types of pages:

Figure 2. WebSphere Portal's 'user friendly URLs'

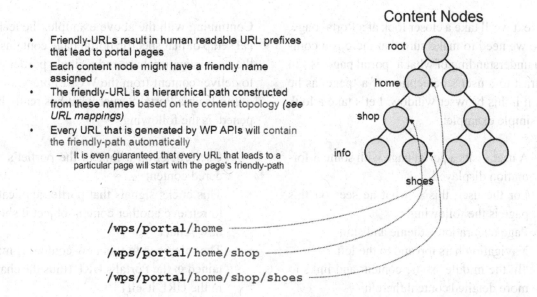

Friendly-URLs

- Friendly-URLs result in human readable URL prefixes that lead to portal pages
- Each content node might have a friendly name assigned
- The friendly-URL is a hierarchical path constructed from these names based on the content topology *(see URL mappings)*
- Every URL that is generated by WP APIs will contain the friendly-path automatically
  - It is even guaranteed that every URL that leads to a particular page will start with the page's friendly-path

```
/wps/portal/home
/wps/portal/home/shop
/wps/portal/home/shop/shoes
```

- Standard Portal page – allows for one or more portlets to be deployed. Security can be applied to the whole page, to individual portlets deployed on that page, as is true for personalization and visibility rules
- Content page – a special type of portal page, which is optimized for the purpose of content delivery. In essence it allows for handshaking between Portal and IBM Web Content Management (WCM) by associating a WCM site-area within a library with the chosen portal page. Its importance and relevance for search integration will be explained in short
- Static HTML page – another special version of a Portal page. This type is used in cases when 'regular' HTML page content is to be rendered on that page. This can be done, by either preserving the Portal page's look and feel by still rendering the theme and navigation on that page. The only modification that needs to be done to the HTML source is to just provide the '<body> … </body>'. Or: render the page such that it fills the browser window entirely – achieved by including the complete HTML source of such a page beginning with the '<html>' tag.

Next we'll take a closer look at a Portal page, since we need to make sure that there is a common understanding of what a 'portal page' is - in contrast to a user's perception of a 'page' as he sees it in his browser window. Let's take a look at a simple example:

- A user visits a portal page with some information displayed
- For the user, this is what he sees on this page is the following:
- Page decoration – theme and skin
- Navigation bars top and to the left
- "In the middle" some content and links to more detailed content therein

Now when the user clicks on one of the available links within the content, e.g. to get more details on a subject that is only briefly explained on that current page, the user then gets the following impression:

- The displayed information (in the portlet) has changed
- Theme and navigation remain largely the same
- The URL has changed somewhat
- His conclusion (if asked): this is a new page he has been navigated to
- The proof: clicking on the 'Back' button will bring him to the previous 'page'

However what happened technically speaking was that he still remained on that same Portal page and what has changed was only the content that was rendered in the same portlet. This state change of the portlet is stored in the Portal URL. Clicking on the 'Back' button will still have the user on that same page, only the state of the portlet will revert back to its state it have before.

3.1.1 Portal Pages Are Not Static Content May Change on That 'Same Page'

Continuing with the above example, the technical setup of that specific portal page contains the theme, navigation bars and a single portlet used to deliver content from the WCM library.

So from a Portal Server what has really happened, is the following:

- User clicks on a link in the portlet's rendered content
- This clicks signals that portlet application to retrieve another content object it should now render
- The reference to this new content is maintained in the Portal's URL (thus the change in the URL itself)

- The new content is rendered in the portlet on the same page

All of this happens transparently to any user or visitor of the Portal Site. However this fact needs to be considered and understood when looking at the Portal site with the eyes of a search engine – and to primarily acknowledge why those URLs need to be the way they are.

3.2 Selective Display of Information on a Page

One of the important objectives of Portal is to allow to show (or not to show) specific information to a known user. A user is 'known' either due to the fact that he has logged in to the Portal site, or because he is a returning visitor and had accepted a cookie from his last visit.

There are two basic types of techniques available which allow determining what a user gets to see. And for both of these we need to make an important distinction:

- **Personalization** is used to promote information to a user. It does not prohibit him from seeing other type of information.
- **Security** on the other hand explicitly makes sure that users only get such information to which they have been granted access.

Example: a site publishes three articles on a specific topic – article-A, article-B and article-C. All of the articles are anonymously accessible.

From a personalization perspective: user 'X' matches best to article-B and so this is what he gets to see first on that specific page. However: either through navigation means or by modification of the URL (though a Portal URL here would certainly be a challenge) nothing will prevent him from having the other two articles rendered either in that same portlet or on another page. Same example with security enforced on those three articles: user 'X' has only access to article-B. No links to the other

two are available and manipulating the URL to point to the others will also not work.

3.3 Javascript and Ajax Based Portlets

The decision making of what to selectively display to a specific user can also be done using technologies such as Javascript or Ajax. In any case: the rules of what to show to which user can be programmed with Javascript.

It needs to be stated, that web crawlers do not interpret Javascript. Not because they couldn't do so, but rather because it is not something meaningful for a crawler to do. One of the obvious reasons being, that it potentially opens the door for spoofing of information.

That said: if Javascript is used for good reason, one has to take note, that any information produced by Javascript will not be available to a web crawler. A prominent example of the past has been anchor links that were generated through Javascript, e.g. to generate flashy navigation menus with drop-down selections. Those links however were never picked up by most web crawlers. Thus, if no other means were available for the crawler to get to other linked pages (like a site directory or sitemap) it was not possible to get past that initial web page. Of course if links from other external sites referenced that site's pages, then the crawler could also "get in through the back door".

3.4 Crawling Secured Portal Pages, Portlets and Content

Security is another reason why page-based (web) crawling will not work – or work only with certain limitations. As an example we'll take a look at a "company performance dashboard" page which shows to entitled users how well the company, its divisions and products are performing. Such a page might include three portlets: one for the overall performance of the company, next that of the user's division and last not least a portlet which shows the 5 top performing and 5 worst performing products. Now for a limited group of users (executive level) a forth portlet would be rendered to show additional, highly confidential information such as level of expenses per division, incentives paid to leading sales people, etc..

Now: how should a web-crawler be able to capture all of that information?

An option would be to do the following:

1. Have one crawler per representative user group crawl the intranet portal. The implication would be to create and maintain a potentially large number of crawlers
2. Sub-optimal: have one crawler to represent an authenticated user in general and another to cover the executive information available. This might leave out a subset of important information for specific user groups

More questions? Would each of the crawlers feed into the same search index? It would be likely to then have a large set of redundant information in that search index. Next is the question how to deal with security? The trivial option would be: before presenting the result to the user, it is first required to take all references in the search result list and challenge them against the respective server. This will definitely lead to performance degradation and for that reason is not acceptable by the vast majority of the user community. Not even diving into details about the worst case: the top 1000 result returned only 4 qualify, thus requiring searching for even more, so that at least the first 10 hits can be shown on the first search results page.

Next option: capture the security information (users and groups) for every page? This is unlikely to work reliably given above scenarios around security enforced on individual portlets.

3.4.1 Crawlability Feature Cannot Be Enabled for Secured Portal Pages

The crawlability feature available with WebSphere Portal for public pages cannot be enabled in a secured portal environment for technical reasons. Thus it was required to look into alternative ways to enable integration of search engines with Portal. Read on what the solution is in the next section.

4. TIME FOR CHANGE: INVERTING THE CRAWLER PROCESS

"Time for change" has come for the one prominent reason: in today's world, more and more users are expecting that information and content they require for various purposes of daily work can be easily searched for. Having a search box available on every page of the Portal site allows users to make use of the search service(s) provided at any point in time and to get at the information fast.

Now this is often still ideal thinking – not all applications or services can be integrated seamlessly for convenient searching. Reality still is, that users would need to know what application or web-page to navigate to, in order to find relevant information using the local search provided by that application or service. Given the importance of search as the fastest means for navigating to relevant information, it should be mandatory for applications to allow for convenient promotion of their content and information for the purpose of being captured and processed by a search engine of choice.

The burden for search engines today still is, that accomplishing the task of discovering and fetching information in an enterprise still lies mostly in the hands of the providers of search technology. Above all this comes with the "penalty" of having to write the interface code (crawlers) between their search engine and the applications hosting the content. In the case of IBM OmniFind Enterprise Edition for example, this means to support more than 40 applications and repositories with a large set of unique crawlers. In addition it requires continuous development efforts to make sure that newer versions of existing applications remain supported by the crawlers as well as develop new ones needed to support new sources of content and information. And not only getting at the content, but also all metadata as well as security related information for more optimal security filtering of search results.

The approach which IBM is taking with Portal and Lotus applications (based on the Portal platform right now) requires only the use of a single crawler type to support Portal, WCM, Quickr Document libraries and Lotus Connections resources. The key to streamlining crawling is "Seedlists" (Shapiro, 2009).

4.1 Search Engine Integration via Seedlists

Seedlists are in essence an extension of the idea around "Sitemaps". A HTML based Sitemap is essentially a list of HTML anchor links pointing to a site's web pages. A sitemap allows for some level of control as to which pages can be fetched (those listed) and others not to be fetched are 'marked' using the appropriate robot directives. The Sitemap idea has been around for a long time and was actually promoted by Internet search engines as a way to optimize the crawlers task of retrieving web pages of a specific web site as well as to reduced the possible extra load that web crawlers might add to a web server often significantly. The latest incarnation of the 'Sitemaps' idea is a protocol supported by Google, Yahoo! and Microsoft – called the "Sitemaps 0.90 protocol" (Prokoph, 2007).

Seedlists are similar, however much more capable and extensible compared to traditional Sitemaps and even the Sitemaps 0.90 protocol. They are standards based: Atom syndication format (RFC-4287).

4.1.1 Features of the IBM Seedlist Protocol

One of the most important new features of the Seedlists is the notion of defining two URLs for accessing the content/information. Some background information regarding the rational behind this idea: looking at today's web applications, it is obvious that it becomes very tedious for crawlers to focus on the core information of a "web page". Meaning ideally be to be able to dispose any ornaments on such pages, like navigation bars, banners, and so on, and then focus really on the core information provided on that page.

So for any content published to such Portal pages, it would make sense to provide the crawler through a URL with that essential information only. Yet still be able to navigate the user via the search result list, to the correct context in which that specific content object is rendered.

The Content Provider Framework provides the infrastructure for Seedlists. It defines for an entity within the Seedlist two types or URLs:

- **Crawler URL** – as the name states for a crawler to pick up the content itself, e.g. the content object from the WCM library which typically would get rendered through the Content Viewer portlet on one or more Portal pages
- **Display URL** – this would be the URL that is given to a user to view that exact same content in the correct context of the Portal

This way the search engine crawls and analyzes the content delivered by the backend service through the crawler URL, whereas later on when searching, the user will be presented with the display URL in the search result list, to ensure that he sees the information in the right context of the Portal.

Supporting life cycle management by providing 'Actions' for each of the objects in the seedlist. Keeping search indexes in sync with the content has always been a challenge for web crawlers. Pages moved or deleted in most cases needed to be determined through crawler statistics, thus introducing a certain degree of latency until such pages were actually removed from the search index. Seedlists allow to provide 'Actions' with the entities: so to specifically point out whether a piece of content has been newly created, updated or deleted.

Metadata – not always part of the content. Metadata is often not part of the content itself, e.g. that it is not available with the HTML source managed by a web content management system, but might be maintained separately in a repository and associated with the content objects (HTML). The Seedlist allows publishing metadata specifically as entities with the Seedlist associated with a specific content item entry. This has another big benefit of not requiring to publish metadata in the HTML file and thus potentially could be seen by users as well (when viewing the HTML source).

Enabling to support for security - Access Control information. Security is and has always been a challenge for search engines. Often because of the penalty that has to be paid for to perform security filtering. Historically in order to guarantee real-time security filtering on search results, search engines used "post-filtering" mechanisms on search results, which often resulted in processing overhead: consulting the respective applications for an access check on each result item. Better performing is the approach to store the ACL information in the search index, and to perform security filtering as part of the regular search execution process. Comparable to a fielded search request, where the field is the security field that has the ACL information stored, and the values are the group memberships and user IDs of the respective users that have access permissions to such resources. When a user performs a search request, then all that needs to be done, is ask the security service what user groups that specific user is member of, adds the filter constraint to the user's query and performs the search. This technique is thus called "pre-filtering". For best possible security filtering a combination with post-filtering will pair fast query processing with runtime verification of the user's entitlements.

Performance and Scalability through pagination of seedlists. Sitemaps can potentially grow to huge sizes, which will quite often result in truncation of such files. "Truncation" of documents or content is an often used technique by search engines to ensure that their processing does not result in too much system resource consumption. For that reason, the Seedlist can include pagination by providing the "Previous" and "Next" URLs to get to the previous or next Seedlist page.

Incremental updates. An important feature which allows for very efficient crawling. This is accomplished by allowing the crawler to specify when it had last retrieved the Seedlist, so that in this request only the changes in the respective repository are published in the new Seedlist.

4.2 Example: IBM WCM and Seedlists

With WebSphere Portal V6.1.0.2 and above, integration between WCM and Portal has become even tighter (Figure 3). As explained previously, it is possible to create a Portal page and declare it to be of type 'content'. When doing, so the administrator can then select from a list of known WCM libraries, sites and siteareas, which sitearea to associate with that page (Portal Catalog, 2009).

This wiring now allows identification of each content object stored in WCM, given the sitearea they are stored in, on which page in the Portal site that piece of content can be rendered in.

Figure 3. Binding between Portal pages and WCM libraries/siteareas

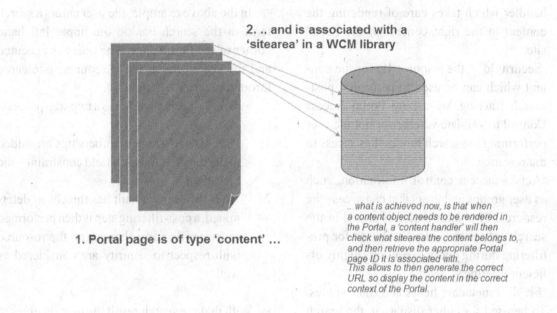

Wiring of WCM content with the Portal site infrastructure ....

2. .. and is associated with a 'sitearea' in a WCM library

1. Portal page is of type 'content' ...

.. what is achieved now, is that when a content object needs to be rendered in the Portal, a 'content handler' will then check what sitearea the content belongs to, and then retrieve the appropriate Portal page ID it is associated with. This allows to then generate the correct URL so display the content in the correct context of the Portal.

When we now take a look at the Seedlist that WCM outputs (Figure 4) we can see the following major entities:

- 'Content' – this is the link that is used by the crawler to retrieve the content object and prepare for indexing

Figure 4. WCM Seedlist – sample entry for a content object

```
- <atom:entry>
   <atom:id>bf12ce804fb7a9bf9e3bbf2ea12b4e16</atom:id>
   <atom:link href="/wps/mypoc/!ut/p/digest!kBPnnxBbpt7kA1hCNetfqg/wcm/path%3a%252FCountries%252FWorld%252FEurope%252FUK"
   rel="via" title="UK"/>
   <atom:content src="/wps/wcm/myconnect/Countries/World/Europe/UK"/>
- <wplc:securityId>
     6QReDe2JP23PCC53E03QOC2RD2MS8C6BEAMP8C2JP4JI5CHHC46QKCHHD0
   </wplc:securityId>
- <atom:author>
      <atom:name>uid=wpsadmin,o=defaultWIMFileBasedRealm</atom:name>
   </atom:author>
   <atom:category term="Country" scheme="com.ibm.wplc.taxonomy://wcmretriever_taxonomy" label="Country"/>
   <atom:title>UK</atom:title>
   <atom:updated>2009-09-27T19:55:58+02:00</atom:updated>
   <wplc:action do="insert"/>
- <wplc:acls>
      <wplc:acl>uid=wpsadmin,o=defaultwimfilebasedrealm</wplc:acl>
      <wplc:acl>cn=wpsadmins,o=defaultwimfilebasedrealm</wplc:acl>
   </wplc:acls>
   <wplc:fieldInfo id="LASTMODIFIER" name="LASTMODIFIER" description="This field shows the last modifier of an item" type="string"
   contentSearchable="true" fieldSearchable="true" parametric="false" returnable="true" sortable="false" supportsExactMatch="false"/>
   <wplc:fieldInfo id="KEYWORDS" name="keywords" description="Keywords authors have added to tag the content" type="string"
   contentSearchable="true" fieldSearchable="true" parametric="false" returnable="true" sortable="false" supportsExactMatch="false"/>
   <wplc:fieldInfo id="EFFECTIVEDATE" name="EFFECTIVEDATE" description="This field shows when an item became effective" type="string"
   contentSearchable="true" fieldSearchable="true" parametric="false" returnable="true" sortable="false" supportsExactMatch="false"/>
   <wplc:field id="LASTMODIFIER">uid=wpsadmin,o=defaultWIMFileBasedRealm</wplc:field>
   <wplc:field id="KEYWORDS">UK</wplc:field>
   <wplc:field id="EFFECTIVEDATE">Mon May 25 20:32:09 CEST 2009</wplc:field>
   <atom:published>2009-05-25T20:32:48+02:00</atom:published>
   </atom:entry>
```

- 'Link' – the URL is identified by 'poc' or 'mypoc' in the relative path. 'poc' stands for 'piece of content' and references the handler which takes care of rendering the content in the right context of the Portal site.
- 'SecurityId' – the resource ID for the content which can be used to perform a post-search filtering, by asking Portal Access Control to validate whether or not the user performing the search request has access to the resource.
- 'Acls' – access control information, such as user groups and users that can access the resource. This information is stored in the search collection (index) and used for pre-filtering during query execution (highly efficient filtering)
- 'Field' – metadata fields and their values. To be used for either display in the search result and/or searching purposes. The 'fieldinfo' specifies in detail the exact usage of the respective field.

Now let's take a look at a sample search based on the above described WCM indexing scenario (Figure 5).

In the above example, the user enters a search term in the search bar on the upper left hand corner of the Portal page. The query is executed and the search result list if required is cleared through security.

Security filtering is done as a two step process:

1. User ID and group memberships are added to the query as a search field constraint – the 'acl' field.
2. After the search result has thus been determined, a post-filtering step is then performed to ensure that any changes on the resource with respect to security are considered as well

With that the search result the user receives in his browser window, contains only those items he can access. Note that in the example above, the information of the various countries presented above, are all rendered on that same portal page.

Figure 5. Searching for WCM content

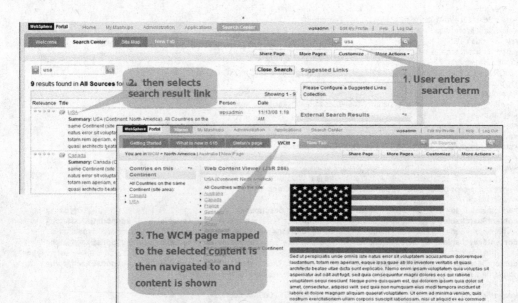

The content objects are all stored in the same sitearea 'Countries' which has been associated with that Portal page.

The links in the search result list all go through the 'poc' handler which takes care of navigating the user to the correct portal page that renders that content.

The benefits of the Seedlist framework can thus be summarized as follows:

- Allows selective publishing of metadata
- Allows to specify how metadata is used – for searching or display in the search result or both
- Security information can be provided to the search engine to enable efficient security filtering
- URLs for fetching the content is optimized for two types of 'readers':
  - The crawler gets the content rendered exclusively, meaning outside of the context of the portal page. This allows to focus its processing solely on the content itself
  - A 'display URL' is provided for the end user to allow him to see the content in the correct context of the Portal site
- When new content is published to a sitearea, it will automatically be associated with the portal page that 'is wired' with that sitearea

The following applications and servers that integrate with WebSphere Portal provide 'Seedlist support':

- WebSphere Portal – for portal site crawling
- IBM Web Content Management
- Lotus Quickr
- Lotus Connections

Seedlists are supported by Portal Search Engine, IBM OmniFind Enterprise Edition and Autonomy through IBM Seedlist connector.

5. A BRIEF LOOK INTO IMPROVING THE USER SEARCH EXPERIENCE

Once the search service and search indices (search collections) have been setup and now ready for search, it is important to have designed and implemented the end-user search experience. This subject has the same and even higher priority to deliver best quality to users. The reason is simple: if the users do not accept and turn away from 'search' then this results in "money badly spent" setting it up in the first case.

For that reason, the following sections briefly touch this subject and address the main components and options to consider.

5.1 General Aspects of End-User Search

- **Search must be intuitive**. When users perform a search and they then look at the results, they check for quality and if not met, they start to reformulate their search requests until the expected result shows up (or not). That said: it is for acceptance reasons imperative that keywords used in search also appear in the content presented to the user. If for example metadata is injected into web pages which cause certain pages to be listed in the search result, this might leave the user with the impression, that he is being 'hijacked' to pages based on someone else's decision.
- **Do not manipulate – term weights or the like – user will notice**. Often heard, but seldom seen to actually deliver "better quality search results": mingling with terms weights. The reason simply being, that usually one tweaks and tests with

those search requests and keywords that are critical for a specific purpose. However the potential is there that the majority of the queries executed will rather see a decrease in the quality of search results. Main reason is that for determining the correct weight factors it would be required to have the knowledge of the overall heuristics captured in the search index and understand their relationship amongst themselves as well. Since this is seldom the case, it would be more of a coincidence to find the right weight factors. And even if found: dependent on the update frequency of information in the corpus: the heuristics will over time change as well thus asking for constant adjustments.

- **Allow user to filter search results – Search scopes in the Portal Search Center**. It is definitely the case, that one will see two users using the exact same set of keywords in his query, with the intention of finding different types of information. This is not a problem that search technology can easily solve. The easiest and most obvious for a user would be to present him at first with the complete search result, paired with additional means to filter and identify an appropriate subset of that result list. An example would be: the user knows that the information he is seeking is very likely within a PDF document. So he would then ask to only show PDF documents in the search result list. Portal Search and its Search Center allows to setup 'Search Scopes', which allow to define one or more search constraints, such as what search collection(s) to search within, what content delivered by which crawler(s) and query constraints such as: "return web-pages which contain keyword 'xyz' in the title".
- **Advanced search.** Often asked for but rather seldom used (less than 5% of the us-

ers) is finer granular search. Which allows for more control over the search query, like search within metadata fields such as date field, as well as making use of more complex (Boolean type) queries. Portal provides the Search and Browse portlet for such purposes. However the caveats are: it can only search against one search collection and the built-in list of metadata fields it can search within is pre-defined. Of course a source code version is provided that allows to programmatically make adjustments as required. In addition: the Search Center allows only for 'simple' queries, however there is a developerWorks article, which explains how to change or add such capability to the Search Center (Shapiro & Ben-Nahum, 2008).

5.2 Search in Parallel Using Additional Search Services

The more search services gain popularity on the Internet, the more users might want to tap into those. The search scenario could be to couple the Intranet search service with a "look-aside search" provided by a news service.

Given the widespread of published web interfaces (REST APIs) that allow to do so, this task is fairly easy to accomplish. One note to take is that requesting all information gathered (internal and external search) to be presented in a unified search result, is doomed to fail.

The reason is quite simple: typically search results are shown in the order of descending relevance. And the relevance score is what is not comparable between the various search services. Thus a simple join and then sort will always promote the results delivered by one search engine over those of the other.

Portal provides the "External Results" portlet to show results of a specific search service side-by-side with the organic search results delivered by Portal Search on the Search Center page. The query that is sent to the external search service is the same that was sent to Portal Search via the Search Center. The note to be taken here is that it can be configured to work only with such search services that return the search result in RSS or Atom format. HTML data streams can for obvious reasons not be rendered within the portlet.

5.3 "I Want to Add Term Weights to Improve Search Results"

As mentioned already in the introduction of this section: it is not suggested to perform manipulations of any kind to "improve search quality". User will very likely notice or feel manipulations and thus turn away from using such a search service.

If it is found to be important to promote certain pages or content to users based on the keywords used in the query, then the option at hand would be to show a list of additional links to the user separate to the search result. A list of additional links

grouped and titled as "Given the keywords used, we suggest to consider looking at the following pages as well" will be appreciated by the users.

Portal provides the Suggested links portlet, which similarly to the External Results portlet is wired with the Search Center portlet. So that any search request going against Portal Search will also be sent to the Suggested Links portlet. The visualization of the two search results on the portal page will obviously leave it to the user to look at the link suggestions or continue with the organic search results (Figure 6).

5.4 Custom Developed Search Portlet for those Special Needs

For all those cases where the portals and their capabilities are not sufficient to meet specific requirements: the documentation of the IBM Search APIs (SIAPI) also comes with sample code for a search portlet, which essentially maps

Figure 6. Search Center page with External Results and Suggested Links portlets

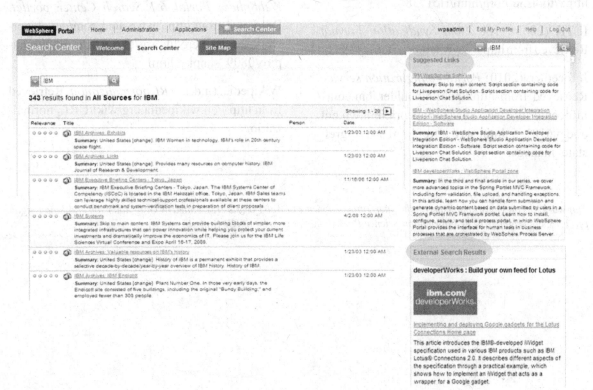

to the Search An Browse portlet that comes out of the box with Portal.

6. SUMMARY

WebSphere Portal provides an infrastructure and service which allow for efficient integration of search engines. The Seedlist framework is mandatory to support in order to meet the challenges of modern web applications.

Internet search engines can safely and effectively crawl and index content and information provided by WebSphere Portal.

The quality of search that Portal Search delivers is excellent and can be paired with additional search utilities to further improve the user search experience.

REFERENCES

W3C. (n.d.). *Standard RFC-1738*. Retrieved from http://tools.ietf.org/html/rfc1738

IETF. (2005). *The Atom Syndication Format.* Retrieved from http://www.ietf.org/rfc/rfc4287.txt

Infocetner. (2010) *Portal configuration service.* Retrieved from http://publib.boulder.ibm.com / infocenter/wpdoc /v6r1/topic/com.ibm.wp.ent. doc_v6101 /admin/srvc fgref.html #srvcfgref_ state_manager

Leue, C. (2009). *What you always wanted to know about URIs in WebSphere Portal v6 – or more than that* .... Retrieved from http://www-10.lotus.com /ldd/portalwiki.nsf/dx /what-you-always-want-ed- to-know-about-uris-in- websphere-portal-%E2%80%93- or-more-than-that-%E2%80%A6

Portal Catalog. (2009). *IBM Lotus Web Content Management Rendering Portlet.* Retrieved from http://www- 01.ibm.com/software/brandcatalog /portal/portal /details?catalog.label=1WP1001S6

Prokoph, A. (2007). *Help Web crawlers efficiently crawl your portal sites and Web sites.* Retrieved from http://www.ibm.com/developerworks/ library/x-sitemaps/

Shapiro, E. (2009). *Making content searchable anywhere using IBM WebSphere Portal's publishing Seedlist Framework.* Retrieved from http:// www.ibm.com/developerworks/websphere/zones /portal/proddoc/dw-w-seedlist/

Shapiro, E., & Ben-Nahum, B. (2008). *Customizing and extending the functionality of the IBM WebSphere Portal 6.1 Search Center portlet.* Retrieved from http://www.ibm.com/developer-works/websphere/library /techarticles/0809_sha-piro/0809_shapiro.html

Wikipedia. (n.d.). *URL normalization.* Retrieved from http://en.wikipedia.org/wiki/URL_normal-ization

This work was previously published in the International Journal of Web Portals 2(3), edited by Greg Adamson and Jana Polgar, pp. 1-18, copyright 2010 by Information Science Publishing (an imprint of IGI Global).

Chapter 8
Challenges of Multi Device Support with Portals

Jaye Fitzgerald
IBM, USA

Van Landrum
IBM, USA

ABSTRACT

Although Portals can aggregate and integrate applications "at the glass" on desktop PCs and laptop browsers, more users expect to access Portals on their mobile devices. The challenges to support multiple devices are difficult. Standard HTML web pages cannot be delivered to most mobile devices, which have different capabilities like screen sizes, image formats, and input methods. With thousands of devices and the frequent introduction of new devices, how can a Portal support the many types of mobile devices connecting to the Portal's many applications? In this paper, the authors discuss the issues and solutions to this many-to-many relationship. IBM Mobile Portal Accelerator provides multiple device support from a Portal by using a version of XHTML called XDIME as the content markup and a multi-channel component coupled with a device repository to provide the proper device specific view. As a result, the page that is sent to the device is appropriate for that specific device and its capabilities, where no horizontal scrolling is required, all information fits on the screen, forms work, and all images are rendered properly, creating a positive user experience.

INTRODUCTION

Portals have been around for some time now, delivering content to standard browsers. A good definition of a Portal is; "A web portal is an entry point to a set of resources that an enterprise wants to make available to the portal's users." (Tran, 2002).

The components of a portal include an aggregator. The aggregator is combining the content, for instance pages and portlets together to fulfill a user's request. The challenge for content authors even in supporting HTML markup is to get a com-

DOI: 10.4018/978-1-4666-0336-3.ch008

Figure 1. The many devices and applications in Portal (Landrum, 2009)

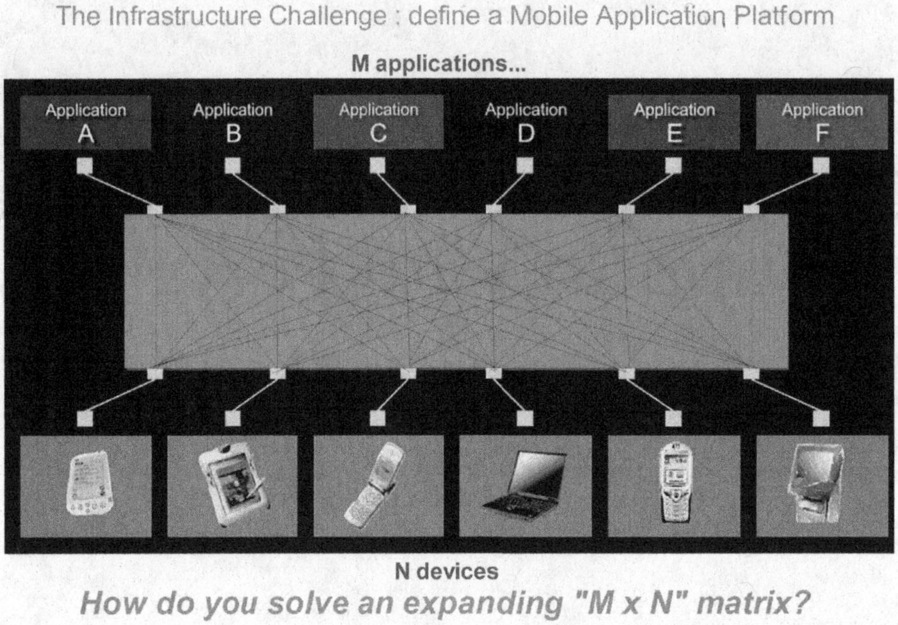

mon solution for each popular browser. Portals will want to support the top market browsers and any that their clients need. Desktop browsers (different js/css/dom, todo:elaborate a bit on IE/FF/Safari/other browser challenges).

The task is daunting when we introduce thousands of devices with several protocols, different markup, different support for css and javascript (Figure 1). Additionally, the device may or may not use color, therefore a content author will want to fallback to a black and white image when necessary.

When building a quality user interface for a mobile device, the obvious challenge is presenting the right UI artifacts in a smaller window. A developer must understand the use case and stick to the essentials. Unlike a desktop screen where some pages have superfluous areas that can be filled, a mobile device does not have that option. Window space is at a premium.

A designer should use the best practice guidelines. A designer will want to "where appropriate, use device capabilities to provide a better user experience on more capable devices." (W3C,

n.d.). The use of color images or color with fonts is common place but what will the fallback be on a basic device? Coding a fallback technique done well will help with maintenance but may not eliminate updates to the code.

It might be suggested by some that a smaller user interface might help performance because there is less content to request, but it is important to note that lesser doesn't necessarily mean improved performance. What the application requests from Portal is the key. The designer must know the expense of the request to the backend that Portal is aggregating for any request, but it is more important to a wireless device crossing it's telecommunications provider network. Supporting mobile device clients requires performance testing of the Portal and appropriate sizing of the server infrastructure. Delays in the backend will magnify the delay at the device due to the nature of the network topology.

The standards for device identification and support are JSR 188 (Java Community Process, n.d.) and W3C Device Description Repository Simple API (W3C, n.d.). Portals using the standards provide the confidence that their technology is extensible and proven technology that has subject matter expert support. Portals deploying applications for mobile devices by building homegrown, non-standard applications with device support logic in their applications are destined to become maintenance drain. Your business does not want their return on investment impacted by poor architecture choices that will have a lasting impact on the deployment.

Good design practices of for a portal architecture include decoupling the application logic from the device attributes to support many devices. A good design will have application code separated from the layout, branding and customized attributes for the markup delivered to a device.

Usability is far and away the priority when developing content for mobile devices. But what is usable for one might not be for another. Short URLs are important on a mobile phone. Standard portal sites can have long URLs that a user on a phone would never tolerate having to type. A goal needs to be short and easy to read and type URLs. Organizing your site content and pages is essential to easy and usable navigation. You want to front load the must have content. Similar to a taxonomy, a designer needs to organize their pages and navigation to manageable and logically organized sections. Once a user gets to the content they are looking for, it needs to be in a format that is usable for a smaller screen. The content should be concise. Generally, users will not want to scroll through pages of content from a mobile device. It is also best to keep scrolling to one direction, either vertical or horizontal. The right balance between too many links and too long navigation path is important. A designer will want to identify the most often used links and make it easy to get to the content. The less frequently used content may require multiple clicks to access it. A good goal is to keep the number of of clicks to three or less. More than that will lead to frustration and users not willing to use the site. Navigation needs to be consistent and optimized for the consumer or organization's patterns of use. Good navigation will support memorization of the site, if done well. For must have links, a shortcut or accelerator should be used.

Along with usability is performance. The request and the content must be rendered in a relatively timely fashion. Consumers need to be warned if a download will be take a long time or if there is an additional cost for the download.

Scrolling is improving now that some smartphones support portrait to landscape orientation changes. This is a small percentage of devices and regardless of this nice feature with the accelerometer, designers want to reduce the amount of scrolling required. There is also the problem that some phones have limits on the page size of content. Depending on your design, this could require multiple downloads. A tactic in practice is to separate styling from content with multiple requests then merge the downloads together for presentation on the client side.

A developer must be aware of memory usage when building an application. Good design for any code, server, client or web demands optimized memory usage. It's particularly noticeable if a mobile device is impacted by poor memory usage that worse case will freeze the device. The central tenant of good design for a mobile device is usability. If memory management is not optimal, then usability will not be good. Along with memory usage is size of the application, sometimes referred to as the footprint. A smaller application footprint affects the network payload and the device heap. Download time increases along with footprint size. The size of the application and how it affects usability is another focus area developers must be mindful about.

Battery use is an important factor in designing a mobile device application, whether it be a device application, hybrid or web application. If the application is running javascript or using native calls to perform background tasks, the battery life will be reduced. This can be compounded if the user isn't aware that their battery is being drawn down.

- Thousands of devices in marketplace with several new devices added weekly.

Today we see introduction of smartphones by wireless providers worldwide. This has everyone's attention. For consumers and business, we all are drawn to the latest and snazziest smartphone and its features. There are accelerometers that allow portrait to landscape orientation change. GPS capable phones allow applications to exploit proximity of the customer. If a marketer wants to show advertisements of their products or services, what better way then to know that you're a block away from their store. Introducing these features improves the consumers life and introduces amazing use cases. Smartphones are still a small percentage of the mobile devices. Feature and regular phones with browsers are the majority. In developing countries the percentage of smartphones is very small. There are multi channel service providers approaching seven thousand (7,000) devices in their repository. In the last six months over six hundred (600) new devices were added. Competition from the manufacturers is intense and the telecommunications providers want to woo you to upgrade to a new phone. The tactic is obvious to sell you a device and sell you services and content. Telecommunications providers are becoming store fronts for personalized ringtones, communities and content. If you're a fan of a soccer club or basketball team, they can sell you a ringtone or a team skin for your phone. The point is that consumer phones are turning over more frequently and it's an issue for content providers to stay current with new devices.

Depending on your age, some consumers are using their phones for many tasks rather than their notebook or desktop computer. "Tweeting" or Facebook updates, checking the balance in your checkbook are a few of the everyday tasks that mobile devices are expected to perform. Perform and be usable. The growing adoption of mobile devices to do these tasks and driven by a younger "net" generation to expect and demand usable applications is the future of multi-channel Portals.

Solutions and Their Advantages and Disadvantages

It is possible to build a mobile portal for certain targeted devices. You can code the application logic to customize to the device. An advantage to this design is your code can customize the user experience to the device. You can exploit a device specific feature and your end users should enjoy an optimal experience. This technique does have risk as the maintenance cost can grow as problems are discovered or device changes are introduced in new versions. This could be the firmware, the browser or a default setting. You will have to customize the code for new devices as they are added. Your code base will grow as you have custom code for each new device. If you are supporting a few devices, maybe 3 or less, this may work for your portal. It's not a plan that will allow growth easily though, for when a client of your portal changes their mobile device and asks for support, you will have to replicate your original custom code for the new phone. As previously mentioned, mobile devices inherently change for consumers as new features and service provider options are offered. It's the nature of the market and continues to be an expectation for device users. Mobile devices grow old rather quickly. If you invest in custom development to support a client on your portal, you'll want that development cost to be well used. We've discussed the fact that hundreds of device attributes that a coder will have to know to exploit in the custom code. If you are unsure that the application will have to support new devices, and that number will grow, you should be designing an application architecture that supports flexibility and extensibility. It's a bad design if you have to support a code base that is replicated for each new phone. Common code can be re-packaged in libraries but the user interface code will not be common. There will be multiple code bases for devices and it's a strategy that will be come unwieldy and unmanageable.

Solutions to support more by custom coding is far too risky as new devices come to market, requiring new code. It's a poor architecture to replicate existing code for new devices. The obvious risk too is the maintenance quagmire that future support will be for the original set of devices and the code.

Another might be to pick a popular mobile device and decide to build custom applications for that device. It's certainly attainable and your code is tailored to the device. You can exploit the device's snazzy new feature. As with a solution where you replicate your portal code to identify and build application logic, the risk of that device being replaced by the next greatest version and the ongoing upkeep of the code is typically not a good and sustainable architecture plan.

Good software engineering design and coding practice, regardless of the client are required. The model-view-controller (MVC) architecture is a well known design that decouples the application layers. Object oriented design has been around for many years and is the foundation for component architecture and design. The standards and use of these practices provide extensibility and reusability of the application code. The positive result these practices is reduced cost and maintenance.

Mobile Portal Accelerator Solution

IBM Mobile Portal Accelerator is one solution that provides multiple device support from a Portal. IBM Mobile Portal Accelerator uses XDIME (XHTML Device Independent Markup Extended) as the content markup and a multichannel component coupled with a device repository to provide the proper device specific view. XDIME and policies are processed by the multichannel component, which identifies the device by its user agent and determines the best way to format the content for the device. As a result, the page that is sent to the device is appropriate for that specific device and

its capabilities, where no horizontal scrolling is required, all the information fits on the screen, the forms work, and all images are rendered properly creating a positive user experience.

Mobile Portal Accelerator portlet designers can "write once and render to many devices" using XDIME and policies.

The M to N dilemma solved with Mobile Portal Accelerator.

The challenge to delivering content to mobile devices lies in the diversity of devices in the marketplace. Standard web pages do not show well on mobile device browsers. The content is often scrambled, the images do not show up and forms do not work. Even using an iPhone browser in which the user can zoom in and out and scroll side to side to view standard web pages, the experience is less than optimal. The end user should not have to adapt to the web page, the web page should adapt to the end user's device.

On the left in Figure 2 is a standard IBM web page on an iPhone browser. The end user only sees about $1/12^{th}$ of the page on the screen of the device. While the user could scroll and zoom to view the content it is not the best way for the user to interact with the site. On the right you see a web page that was formatted for the iPhone. This page is much easier to use. The user does not have to zoom in and out or scroll left and right. All the content shows well on the screen and is easy to read. The web application is adapted to the particular device.

So what is the best way to deliver content to all these devices with different requirements and capabilities? IBM's solution is Mobile Portal Accelerator (MPA). MPA is software that installs into IBM's WebSphere Portal Server and enables it to deliver content to mobile device browsers as well as desktop/laptop browsers (Figure 3).

IBM® WebSphere® Portal Server is the foundation offering of the WebSphere Portal product family, with enterprise portal capabilities that enable you to quickly consolidate applications and content into role-based applications, complete

Figure 2. Standard page compared with that formatted for the iPhone (Landrum, 2009)

with search, personalization, and security capabilities.

Mobile Portal Accelerator uses standard HTTP/HTTPS request response technology familiar to all web programmers. The Mobile Portal server is typically placed into the network in the intranet behind the DMZ (see Figure 4). The HTTP server is in the DMZ and contains a plug-in that connects

Figure 3. WebSphere everyplace mobile portal (Landrum, 2009)

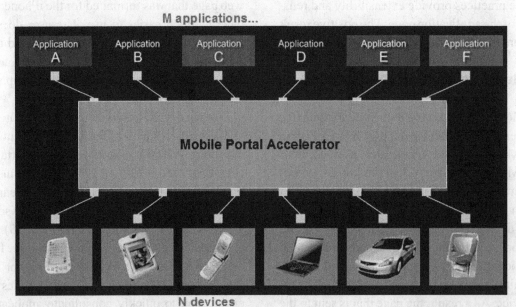

Figure 4. Design of the network (Landrum, 2009)

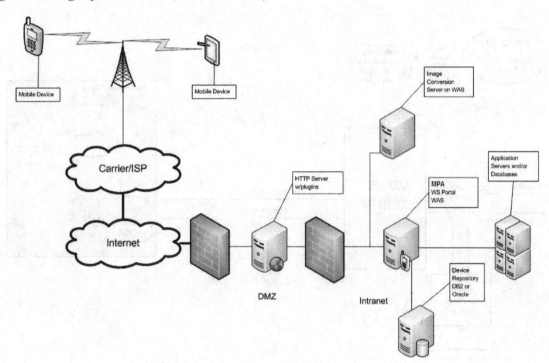

to the Mobile Portal server. In addition to the MPA server there is a Image Conversion Server and a database server.

Paradigm – The main idea behind MPA is to separate the content from the display so that one set of content can be displayed in many ways. In a typical JSP java code is used to get the content and which is then wrapped in HTML. The HTML determines how the content is displayed in the browser. The HTML provides one and only one way to display the content. Mobile Portal JSPs wrap the content in a form of XML called XDIME (XML Device Independent Markup Extension). This markup describes the content but not how to display it. The output from the MPA JSPs is basically an XML document which is handed to the Multi-Channel Server (MCS). The MCS looks up the device that made the request in the database and then applies the correct layout, images, JavaScript, markup, etc and delivers a device specific page back to the requesting device. The end result is a page that fits the browser and the device screen, is easily read, whose forms work and requires no scrolling left or right.

Components – Mobile Portal consists of the Multi-Channel Server (MCS), mobile aggregator, XDIME JSPs, device repository and the Mobile Portal Toolkit. Mobile Portal installs into IBM WebSphere Portal extending the portals capabilities to be able to deliver content to mobile devices (Figure 5).

The process as illustrated in Figure 6.

0. First you create a mobile view of your portlet by adding XDIME JSPs to the portlet and policies to determine layout, images, etc.
1. Then using the administration interface to WebSphere Portal, create the mobile navigation and content model. Next add portlets to the pages and set permissions for the portlets and pages.

Figure 5. Mobile Portal architecture (Landrum, 2009)

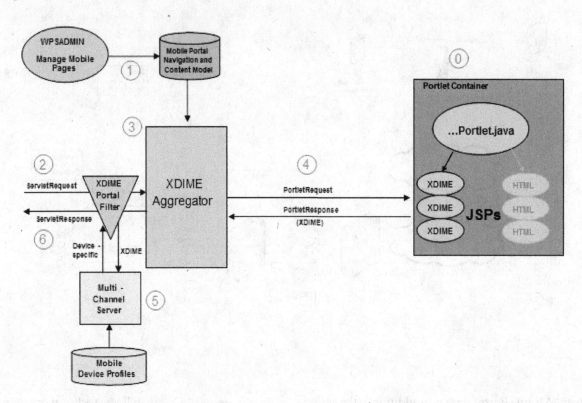

Figure 6. The flow of the content (Landrum, 2009)

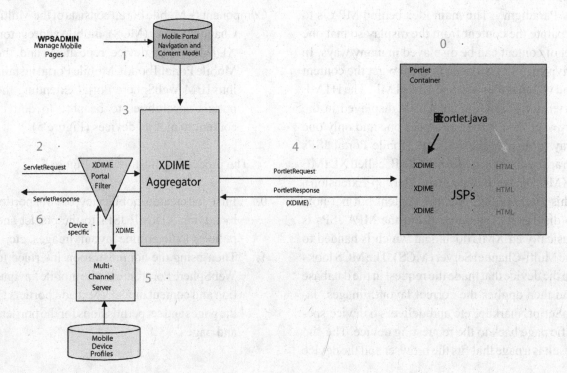

2. When a request comes in it first hits the portal filter. The portal filter determines if the request is coming from a mobile device or a desktop/laptop. If it is coming from a desktop/laptop then the request is handed over to the Portal Server and it is responded to as Portal normally would if MPA was not present.
3. If the request comes from a mobile device the request is handed over to the mobile aggregator.
4. The mobile aggregator builds the page and calls the portlet on the page. The portlet runs the way it normally would except that when it is time to render a page it uses an XDIME JSP instead of an HTML JSP.
5. The XDIME output goes to the MCS engine. The MCS uses the user agent string to find the device in the device repository.
6. The MCS uses the information in the database along with the layout, image, markup, etc.

policies to create a device specific page to return to the requesting device.

Another view of how the MPA server delivers content to both the desktop and mobile device can be illustrated in the following way. Typically in the Portal server the entry point to the portlet is the Portlet.java file. This file contains the processAction and the doView methods among others. The processAction method is called when the user sends input parameters back to the server. This method processes the parameters, retrieves content from backend systems and places the content into the sessionBean. Then the doView method is called. This method runs the proper jsp to render the next page in the browser. In a standard portal, this is an HTML jsp. When the jsp runs, it gets the content from the sessionBean and wraps it in HTML tags and sends the results back to the browser for display (see Figure 7).

Figure 7. Another view of how the MPA server delivers content (Landrum, 2009)

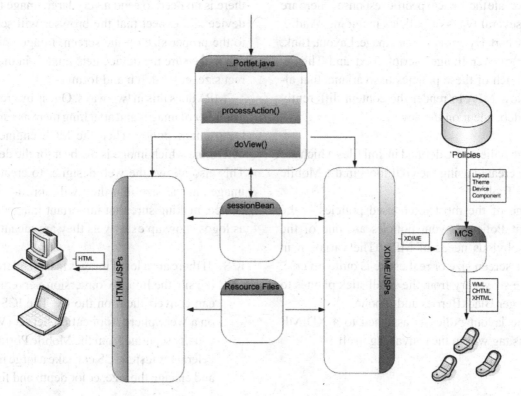

In this figure the blue highlighted items are used to send content to the desktop/laptop standard browsers on the left side of the figure and the red items are used to send content to the mobile devices on the right side. When a mobile device requests a portlet the same Portlet.java file can be called. The processAction method processes any parameters in the same way it would for a desktop browser. It gets the content and places it into the sessionBean. The difference comes when the doView method is called. In the case of a mobile device request the doView calls an XDIME jsp which gets content from the sessionBean and creates an XDIME document which is sent to the MCS engine. The MCS engine uses the policies in the database to create a page that is sent to the device. This figure illustrates how a single MPA portlet can deliver content to desktop and mobile users. MPA can reuse the Portlet.java file, the sessionBean and the resource files when sending content to mobile devices.

Policies: MPA uses policies to determine how to create the device specific response. There are several types of policies including, Audio, Chart, Dynamic Visual, Image, Layout, Link, Rollover Image, Script, Text and Theme. Each of these policies has variants that allow MPA to render the content differently dependent on the device.

The policies are defined in xml files which are easily created using the GUI tools in the Mobile Portal Toolkit.

One of the most often used policies is the Layout Policy. Layout policies are one of the most obvious needs of MPA. The variation in device screen size or real estate is quite diverse. Screen sizes vary from the small stick phones to the larger BlackBerries and iPhone.

The layout policy is assigned to a XDIME canvas tag within the canvas tag itself.

```
<canvas layoutName="/sample_layout.
mlyt" type="portlet">
```

There is only one layout policy for each canvas tag, but each layout policy can contain a number of variants. Each variant can be assigned to a number of devices or groups of devices as seen in Figure 8.

Each layout variant consists of grids and panes that define where the content will go on that device's screen (Figure 9).

The XDIME markup in the JSP labels the content using pane tags with names that correspond to the names of the panes in the layout policy variant (Figures 10 and 11).

Images: Some devices have a preference in what kind of images they can render. For example, a Blackberry can render a PNG image in the background but on an iPhone it must be a JPG image for backgrounds, even though iPhone can render PNG images in the foreground of the page. Size is also an issue. While the bandwidth of mobile device connections is certainly improving, there is no need to send a very large image to the device and expect that the browser will scale it to the proper size on the screen. Image policies can make sure the device gets images in the correct size, color depth and format.

MPA does this in two ways. One is by creating a number of images and attaching them as variants to an image policy. Then the MCS engine will determine which image is the best for the device. This also allows the web designer to create the images in the size that they will appear on the device, making sure that important images such as logos show up exactly as they are meant to.

ICS – If there are a lot of images to be rendered on the site the Image Conversion Server (ICS) can convert them on the fly. The ICS runs on a WebSphere Application Server (WAS) usually separate from the Mobile Portal Accelerator cluster. ICS can take a large image and change the size, color depth and format

Figure 8. Layout policy overview tab (Landrum, 2009)

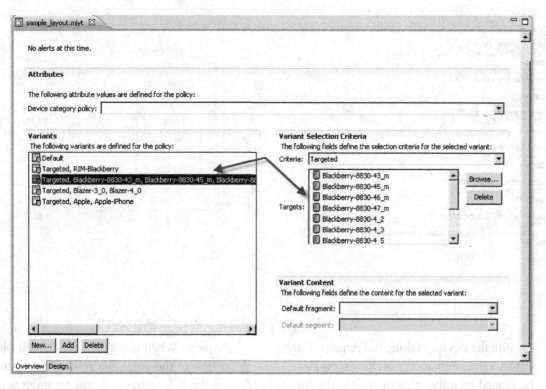

Figure 9. Layout policy design tab (Landrum, 2009)

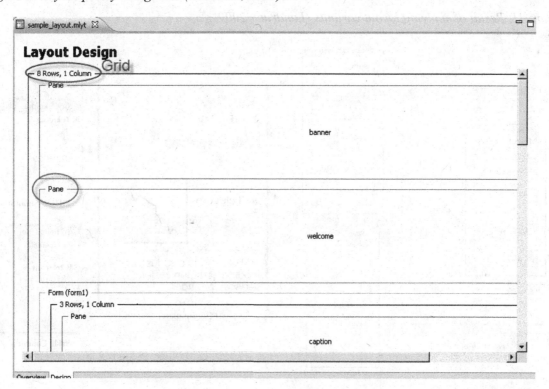

Figure 10. XDIME to Layout Variant Relationship (Landrum, 2009)

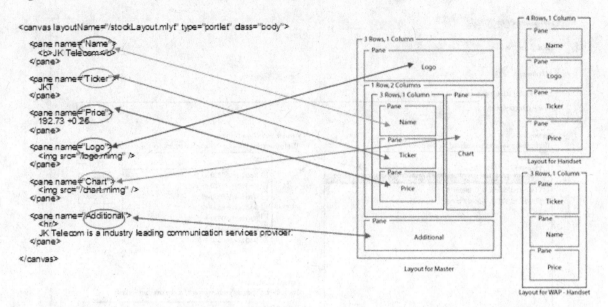

to suite the device making the request. For enhanced performance, a caching server can be placed on either side of ICS so the images do not have to be recreated with each request. When using ICS, MCS will place a link in the page that refers to the image on the ICS server and add parameters that tell ICS what size, color depth and format to

Figure 11. Result of applying layout variants (Landrum, 2009)

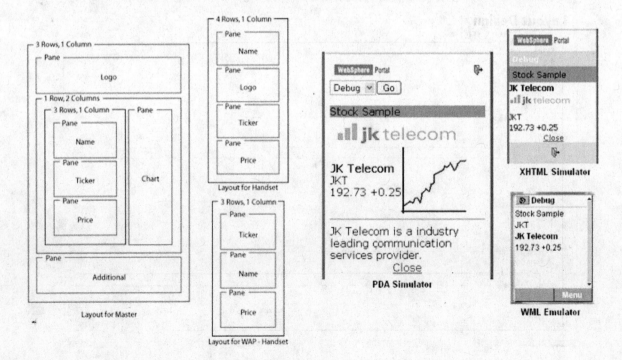

convert the image to so that when the device browser requests the image, ICS can convert the image to the specs requested.

Script – script policies also allow you to deliver the correct JavaScript to the device browser. Not all browsers use the same version of JavaScript. Script policies let you create multiple JavaScript variants and include them in the same script policy assigning them to various devices. When MCS creates the page it will include the correct JavaScript for that device. For example while the Blackberry Curve recognized the JavaScript document.form1.submit(), the iPhone did not recognize the document so the iPhone version uses only form1.submit(). Also, the iPhone has JavaScript event handlers that monitor changes in rotation that can be used to change the layout when the user rotates the phone from portrait to landscape. Other phones do not have this capability and would not need these event handlers in their JavaScript.

Markup – As was previously mentioned, MPA uses a version of XML called XDIME to mark up the content as it moves from the JSP to the MCS. By the way, the life of the XDIME markup ends at the multi-channel server. The MCS digests this markup and creates a page to send to the device in what ever markup that browser requires i.e. wml, html, chtml, xhtml, etc.

XDIME comes in two varieties. XDIME, also called XDIME1, is the original markup that was created before the W3C created a standard. XDIME2 is a newer markup that conforms to the Device Independent Authoring Language (DIAL) W3C standard. Only one version of XDIME may be used between any two canvas tags. However you can use multiple canvas tags on a page and therefore combine versions of XDIME.

XDIME1 and XDIME2 are two sets of markup that have some common characteristics and features but each has features the other does not have. Therefore one is not a superset of the other.

Client Framework – The Client Framework is a number of widgets that can be used on smart phones to control the content on the screen and validate data in a form at the client. There are widgets to bring content onto the screen in many ways like sliding from the left, right, up or down, or fading in and out etc. There are also widgets for date pickers, scrolling text, and other effects. The Client Framework requires XDIME2.

Device Repository – The device repository (Figure 12) is an integral part of the MPA server. The device repository contains information on over 6,600 device makes/models. Each device in the device repository has up to 600+ attributes listed. Everything from the screen size in pixels in the x and y direction, types of files it can download, supported features like rollover images, JavaScript version, right down to the physical size and weight of the device. The device repository is used in a compressed XML file in the development environment and is in a database like DB2, Oracle, or MS SQL in the server environment. Of course the device repository is of no use unless new devices are added as they come into the marketplace. MPA offers a device update service which allows the device database to be updated from the master database on a regular basis, daily, weekly, monthly or on any other schedule that is deemed appropriate for the business environment.

Toolkit - MPA uses the Mobile Portal Toolkit (MPTK) for development. The MPTK is an eclipse plug-in to Rational Application Developer (RAD) or Rational Software Architect (RSA). The MPTK contains wizards to create basic mobile portlets. The MPTK supports JSR 168, JSR 286 and Struts port-

Figure 12. Device repository (Landrum, 2009)

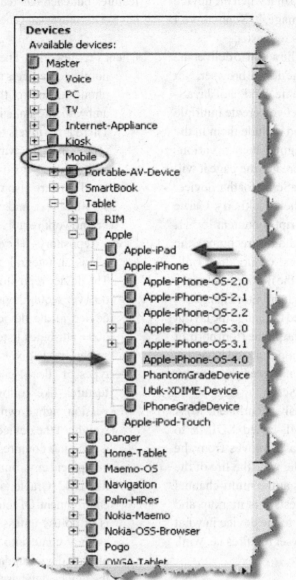

lets. The MPTK also provides GUI interfaces to create policies.

Mobile Portlets can be run and tested on a Portal/MPA server within the development environment. In order to test the portlet a mobile browser or emulator is needed. One good method of testing your portlets is via Device Anywhere. Device Anywhere has real devices strapped to rack mounted servers around the world (Figures 13 and 14). These devices can be accessed via a web browser and can be used to test your web site. Device Anywhere is a subscription service.

Some device manufacturers provide device emulators on their web site for developers. Black-Berry device emulators can be seen at http://www. blackberry.com/developers/downloads/simulators/ (Figure 15). While the iPhone emulator is included in the Apple SDK which only runs on an Apple Computer, there are also other iPhone

Figure 13. Device Anywhere (Landrum, 2009)

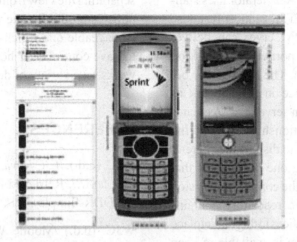

Figure 14. Device Anywhere (Landrum, 2009)

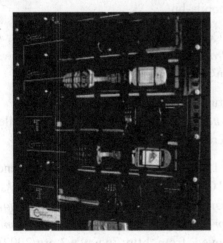

Figure 15. BlackBerry 8330 Simulator (Landrum, 2009)

emulators which run on Windows machines and use the Safari browser dlls. One example of such an emulator is iBBDemo.exe which is available from http://labs.blackbaud.com/NetCommunity/article?artid=662. The Safari browser for Windows can also be used by changing the user agent string to that of an iPhone. It can also be enhanced by going to the following site: http://testiphone.com. A Firefox browser with a user agent switcher plug-in can be used to emulate mobile devices. And of course the best method of testing is to use real devices. You may only need a few devices which represent the different classes of devices you want to support.

Summary - Mobile Portal Accelerator uses standard web HTTP/HTTPS request response technology. An MPA server can deliver content from a single portlet to both desktop and mobile browsers. The MPA server occupies the same place in the network as other web application servers. MPA creates a one-to-many relationship between the content and the ways to display the content. It does this by using one set of JSPs that generically mark up the content in a version of XML. The device repository contains information on the devices in the marketplace and an update service is available to keep the device repository current. The MCS engine uses policies and the device repository to create a device specific page to deliver back to the browser in the requesting device. The Mobile Portal Toolkit is an eclipse plug-in to Rational Application Developer (RAD) or Rational Software Architect (RSA). This toolkit makes it easy to create mobile views of portlets by creating XDIME JSPs and policies for layouts, images, themes etc. Mobile portlets can be run in the development environment and tested with device emulators.

Creating a mobile view into a portal can be a daunting task considering the variation in the many devices in the marketplace. However, by separating the view from the content and applying policies on the fly, the task can be reduced to a manageable one which allows the web designer to have control over how the content looks and works on a variety of devices.

REFERENCES

W3C. (n.d.). *W3C Device Description Repository Simple API.* Retrieved from http://www.w3.org/TR/DDR-Simple-API/

W3C. (n.d.). Mobile Web Best Practices 1.0: Basic Guidelines. Part 5.1.2 Exploit Device Capabilities. Retrieved from http://www.w3.org/TR/mobile-bp/

Java Community Process. (n.d.). *JSR 188: CC/PP Processing.* Retrieved from http://www.jcp.org/en/jsr/summary?id=188

Landrum, V. (2009, October). *Mobile Portal Accelerator.* Paper presented at Portal Excellence Conference, San Diego, CA.

Tran, L. (2002). Authoring Device Independent Portal Content. In *Proceedings of W3C Workshop on Device Independent Authoring Techniques: Authoring Device Independent Portal Content.* Retrieved from http://www.w3.org/2002/07/DIAT/posn/sun-portal.html

Section 2
Security, Architecture and Mobility in Portals

Chapter 9
Generalized Evidential Processing in Multiple Simultaneous Threat Detection in UNIX

Zafar Sultan
University of New England, Australia

Paul Kwan
University of New England, Australia

ABSTRACT

In this paper, a hybrid identity fusion model at decision level is proposed for Simultaneous Threat Detection Systems. The hybrid model is comprised of mathematical and statistical data fusion engines; Dempster Shafer, Extended Dempster and Generalized Evidential Processing (GEP). Simultaneous Threat Detection Systems improve threat detection rate by 39%. In terms of efficiency and performance, the comparison of 3 inference engines of the Simultaneous Threat Detection Systems showed that GEP is the better data fusion model. GEP increased precision of threat detection from 56% to 95%. Furthermore, set cover packing was used as a middle tier data fusion tool to discover the reduced size groups of threat data. Set cover provided significant improvement and reduced threat population from 2272 to 295, which helped in minimizing the processing complexity of evidential processing cost and time in determining the combined probability mass of proposed Multiple Simultaneous Threat Detection System. This technique is particularly relevant to on-line and Internet dependent applications including portals.

1. INTRODUCTION

Computer security has become very critical issue in the IT industry. Almost every organization is facing security threats both from employees and outside intruders. Internet and Web and web portal IT systems are highly vulnerable to hackers and on many occasions, hackers have broken the existing security measures and have stolen million dollar information and damaged the IT infrastructure. The increasing complexity of the web portals

DOI: 10.4018/978-1-4666-0336-3.ch009

and internet architecture has simply widened and opened another area of security challenges for the whole IT industry. In order to protect organizations securities in terms of critical business and personal data, IT industry has to keep on strengthening their efforts to develop intrusion detection system. As a result, organizations need to spent billion of dollar just for securing and smooth run of their business data over the internet. For example Microsoft spent $1.2 billion to stop Sapphire/Slammer worm in 2003 (Ma, 2001; Spafford, 1991).

Business dependence on Internet-based services, and Internet-facing platforms such as enterprise portals, significantly increase the prospect of concerted security attacks. In spite of all these security measures and highly recommended Intrusion Detection Systems, hackers still continuously breaking companies securities, exploiting system weaknesses and perform illegal functions such as stealing important information, business secrets, damaging data or systems etc. etc. The biggest challenges in the security fields are the types of attack, their point of origin and the quantity of damage and of course to identify attack and block it in time is the most demanding aspect for the IT industry (Braun, 2000; Siaterlis & Maglaris, 2004).

Due to complexity of the UNIX applications infrastructure and Network architecture and implementation of multiple monitoring systems, false alarms have really become a big headache for the large companies. Millions of dollars have been spent just to build monitoring infrastructure but there does not seem to be any solution to stop false positive and false negatives. In general most of the Intrusion Detection Systems check the application layer, data layer and network layer data based on pattern matching with the existing situations of the processes and systems attributes. However, it is quite difficult to track an attacker if he / she just penetrate security and then keep steeling business data for months and months until new security updates find this attack but it is then too late. Damage has already been done.

Looking into these facts, it looks a continuous battle between security implementers and hackers. But this is well known fact that an advancement of Intrusion Detection Systems have certainly reduced the number of security violation incidents and it has become more difficult for hackers to penetrate any IT systems that is well protected and secured using advance implementations of fire-walls, intrusion detection system and monitoring systems (Bendjebbour et al., 2001; Hall, 1992).

The emphasis of our research is the experimental evaluation of the simultaneous multiple threat detection system using Multi-sensor data fusion, its various approaches and techniques in UNIX environments. Our research will help in building multiple simultaneous threat detection system for computer security in general and for web based applications, web portals and internet applications of UNIX environments in particular. The main target of this paper is an advance step to use Dempster Shafer, Weighted Dempster Shafer and Generalized Evidential Processing (GEP) theory for Multi-sensor data fusion whilst in our previous research experiment, We used only Dempster Shafer and weighted Dempster Shafer for data fusion. Therefore, in this paper we will provide numerical comparisons between Dempster Shafer, Weighted Dempster Shafer and Generalized Evidential Processing and compare their efficiency and performance.

2. EXISTING THREAT DETECTION APPROACHES IN UNIX

Parametric / non parametric techniques like Bayesian, Dempster Shafer, fuzzy rule and Kalman Filter are the most predominated techniques used for multiple threat detection in UNIX (Braun, 2000; Grocholsky, Makarenko, & Durrant-Whyte, 2003; Wu, Siegel, Stiefelhagen, & Yang, 2002). Theory of Set Cover, Chapman-Kalmogorov prediction model and method of least squares have also been used as an integral model with Bayesian,

Dempster Shafer, Extended Dempster and GEP (Koks & Challa, 2005).

Intrusion Detection Systems fetch data from system network layer, log files and other monitoring files. Data may be sniffer's packets; sys log files, SNMP traces, system messages and other similar activities of the network. The existing IDS monitoring and alarming system provide good security measures against most of the internal and external threats but these systems are not intelligent enough to detect 100% of the threats as they can detect only the threats whose information exist in their databases. The security systems of a large company Langley could not detect threats on their network until their business server crashed (Computer Security Institute, 2002).

Though a few years back UNIX was one of the secure environments from the hackers but in the past few years, intruders have broken many business applications and databases in UNIX network whilst all critical business like credit cards, client profiles and financial transactions are online and need more security ever than before. The current IDS cannot auto track, identify and block all the threats. Therefore, additional research and development is required in the field of multiple sensor data fusion of IDS in UNIX environment (Bendjebbour et al., 2001; Klein, 1999; Rehman, 2003).

2.1 Other Data Fusion Approaches

A real time numerical comparisons and calculations of data fusions models are rare for Bayesian, Dempster Shafer and Extended Dempster Shafer and almost nonexistent for GEP in the UNIX environment. Although there is some valuable literature is available in defense and other related fields. GEP is therefore, a relatively new area to work on. Mostly researches used Bayesian, Dempster Shafer, parametric / non parametric and few others inference engines for Multi-sensor data analysis in their IDS.

Dong and Deborah (2005) commented that hybrid model of Bayesian is the better technique to improve the intrusion detection precision for IDS. They found 19% improvement in threat detection with their hybrid data fusion models (Chatzigiannakis et al., 2002).

Siaterlis and Maglaris (2004) also used hybrid data fusion model based on Bayesian and Dempster Shafer and concluded that hybrid model increased the precision in threat detection. Though there is no numerical comparisons provides in their papers.

Wu, Siegel, Stiefelhagen, and Yang (2002) found a theoretical relationship of Bayesian and Dempster in comparisons with classical probability model. And concluded that the combined inference model of Bayesian and Dempster Shafer will be a promising area for Multi-sensor data analysis in IDS

Habib, Hefeeda, and Bhargava (2003) and Siaterlis and Maglaris (2004) worked only on Bayesian inference and did not use any hybrid model.

Zamboni (2000) used a pattern matching detection model to detect new attacks, however, he did not mention any particular fusion model in his experiment.

Chatzigiannakis et al. (2002) used Principal Component Analysis for Multi-sensor data fusion for intrusion detection and found that their fusion model is more effective than single metric analysis.

Gorodetski, Karsaev, Kotenko, and Khabalov (2002) suggested that combining a decision model is better in threat detection precision than a Meta model in IDS.

Kumar (2000) worked on IDS architecture and found that rule set knowledge, expert systems state models and string match are useful parameters in the development of an advance threat detection model.

Hugh (2005) described mathematical model for their fusion model. They analysed data with hybrid model of Kalman Filter and Bayesian theorem.

Brugger (2004) worked on offline data fusion model, used data mining approach in her IDS.

However, she did not produce any particular model during her experiment.

In the view of all above literature references, it is obvious that in general, there is enough material on Multi-sensor data fusion models of IDS in the field of defense and other related areas. However, very little was reported in the UNIX environment. And almost negligible work was found if we search material or study on numerical calculations or comparisons of the performance & efficiency of the multiple simultaneous threat detection in the field of UNIX.

3 ORIGINAL CONTRIBUTIONS

In this research, we will identify a multiple simultaneous threat detection model. This model will be a hybrid of Bayesian, Dempster Shafer, Extended Dempster Shafer and GEP theory of inferences. Set Cover theory will be used as a middle tier data processing tool. The set cover will help only to provide the reduced set of data to achieve better control in final data fusion and cost savings of the data processing. This hybrid model will increase the precision in threat detection and reduce the volume of false alarms in UNIX environment. The use of the model will assist in decreasing the data security expenses, particularly web based businesses and web portals. Researchers will get also benefit for future IDS developments in UNIX (Burroughs, Wilson, & George, 2002).

The new multiple simultaneous threat detection model will be able to detect more than one threat simultaneously. Another advantage is that the results of this research can be applied in high speed networks like cyberspace. There are also some additional situational parameters that will be generated as a result of this work such as high level architecture of multiple threat detection model, identification of proper Multi-sensor environment based on hybrid model, and identification of middle tiers of the research.

This research, in fact, is a step forward of our previous research results on Multiple Simultaneous Threat Detection to address the additional precision in multiple threat detection process as compared to the existing threat detection approaches in UNIX and it is different in many ways from other's work in Multi-sensor data fusion in IDS development.

3.1 Set Cover

Set Cover is a branch of mathematics and in this research we deal with sets, subsets and their interaction sets. Set Cover is the basic system of mathematics. Simple facts of set union and its subsets are used in cover sets of multiple simultaneous threat detection system that is a basic branch of mathematics (Aickelin, 2002).

In multiple simultaneous threat detection system the total numbers of elements were 2274 (Derived in section 5.1) denoted by:

$$\bigcup = \sum_{i=1}^{n} u_i \qquad (1)$$

Where $\bigcup$ is the universal set and $\sum_{i=1}^{n} u_i$ is sum of all the elements in the universal set

In the experiment, the types of threats represented by subsets

$S_1, S_2, S_3, \ldots, S_j \subseteq \bigcup$ And the cost of each set is $C_1, C_2, C_3, \ldots, C_k$.

In our case threat(s) are present in different data substrings from any of the 4 different intrusion detection systems of a distributed Unix Network. The target is to find the sets P = {1, 2,..., l} that must contain minimum number of strings having threats so that each set have all the relevant strings of data and summation of sets will have all the strings of the inputs. Cover set using greedy algorithm also provides minimum cost represented by Q.

$$Q = \sum_{i=1}^{m} C_i \qquad (2)$$

Where $\sum_{i=1}^{m} C_i$ is the sum of the costs in selecting a new node of the experiment

The cost effectiveness to select computer node is denoted by β based on greedy algorithm

$$\beta = \frac{C(Q)}{Q-P} \qquad (3)$$

Where $C(Q)$ is the initial cost for selecting the nodes for each intrusion detection system and P is the set with minimum elements and Q is the minimum cost in selecting the new node.

4 APPROACHES AND METHODOLOGY

In a large number of Multi-sensor data fusion model, Bayesian and Dempster Shafer have been used for data analysis. Most of the existing work was in single threat detection (Wu, Siegel, Stiefelhagen, & Yang, 2002). Only couple of researchers tried to focus on multiple threat detection without using Set Cover theory. Set Cover has been identified as a new area which can be used to prioritize and schedule rule set on certain criteria in the fusion process. On this topic there are only a few papers available in the UNIX environment, therefore, it is difficult to compare literature on Multi-sensor threat detection in UNIX (Braun, 2000; Zamboni, 2000).

4.1 Multiple Simultaneous Threat Detection System

The main target of this research is to identify the exact threat(s) with a high degree of precision by using hybrid data fusion model comprised of Set cover, Bayesian theory of estimation, Dempster

and Extended Dempster Shafer theory. The origin and directions of the threats are exclusive of this research as that includes complicated, extensive and separate research.

In this distributed test environment which is conceptually the same as server client environment, a multiple simultaneous threat detection system has been set up on different nodes across the distributed subnets. Computer nodes are comprised of multiple operating systems and located at different networks, predominantly UNIX though include Wintel machines as well. Each computer node has different intrusion detection system that filters all the network data and collects threat related information and transfers them to the computer node hosting multiple simultaneous threat detection system for further accuracy and precision of the threat detection results. The computer nodes across different subnets receive different threats. As this is a controlled experiment, 4 types of threats mainly denial of service, man-in-the-middle, buffer overflow and Trojan will be initiated from one of the experimental computer node.

4. 2 Architecture of Multiple Simultaneous Threat Detection System

In this experimental test environment, 4 independent intrusion detection systems work as a separate Multi-sensor observers on different subnets. In order to monitor all data packets in the test environment, we used a switch on test network and configured a monitoring port to replicate all packets of the data traffic passing through the switch. Network data of layer 2 and 3 was also gathered. Data collecting software then decodes and analyse the data. We used following software for data collection: MARS, Sniffers, Snoop and Wireshark. Four types of threats: DoS, Denial of Service, Mom- man-in-the-middle attack or bucket-brigade attack or Janus attack, Buffer overflow or buffer overrun and Trojan Horses.

Each intrusion detection system collects network data and filters it using Cover set theory. Data may contain a single, two, three, four or any combinations of the above 4 x threats or false alarms and then move the data to next level of the data fusion within the multiple simultaneous threat detection system. The Multiple simultaneous threat detection system processes the data through different statistical and mathematical techniques and makes decision about the threats.

Then multiple simultaneous threat detection system's client nodes that exist on each computer uses the Set Cover Model as a middle tier data fusion tool which refines the data into small group of sets and schedules these groups of data for onward statistical and mathematical data fusion. Another benefit of the Set cover model is to choose computer nodes that cover all the anticipated threats at a minimum cost (Figure 1).

Figure 1. The architecture of the multiple simultaneous threat detection system

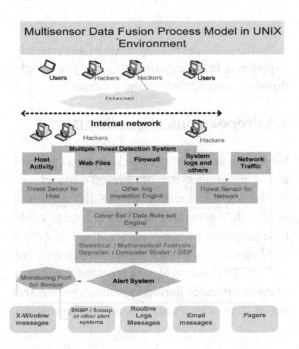

5. RESULTS OF THE TEST EXPERIMENT

Set Cover Fusion Model

The initial processing cost (in dollar) for selecting the nodes for each intrusion detection system is:

$C_{(A)}$ = 8 = cost of the 1st Node

$C_{(B)}$ = 5 = cost of the 2nd Node

$C_{(C)}$ = 12 = cost of the 3rd Node

$C_{(D)}$ = 8 = cost of the 4th Node

The sets with minimum number of elements denoted by P (number of threats) and set with minimum cost Q (in dollar) for each node were determined during the experiment. The total number of sets whose cost was lowest and set with minimum number of elements covered by node A, B, C and D of the experiment are given as:

$P_{(A)} = 0$, $P_{(B)} = 3$, $P_{(C)} = 3$, $P_{(D)} = 4$

$Q_{(A)} = 8$, $Q_{(B)} = 4$, $Q_{(C)} = 7$, $Q_{(D)} = 8$

Here we like to make it clear that the above values are the number of the sets not the elements of the sets, therefore, it should not cause any problem or mix up whilst reading Table 1. The optimal cost as per cost effectiveness β of the nodes using equation (3) would be A+D+C=8+8+12=28. The cost effectiveness of the node are A, D, C and B respectively (Sultan, 2009).

5.1 Set Cover's Set Generation

In order to collect 4 types of threats, 4 intrusion detection systems collected 2274 malicious substrings of 15 and above bytes from the experimental network. The threat data was a mixture of all 4 types of generated threats. Set Packing provided us the

Table 1. Set cover subsets reduced the sizes of the sets

Threat Data of Intrusion Detection Systems		
IDS	Before Set Cover	After Set Cover
Wireshark	128	122
Sniffers	439	82
Snoop	646	32
MARS	1061	59
Total	2274	295

ability to select the K = 4 number of subsets out of the union set N of 2274 such that each subset is a pair wise disjoint to other subsets. Thus each subset now has similar strings of the threat data whose union is N.

In order to find out pair wise disjoint subsets, we analysed N=2274 threat data using a small perlscript. The script separated pair wise disjoint strings of the threat data into 4 subsets of total 295 substrings. The number of elements or substring in each subset is given as seen in Table 1.

The client node sends all the above filtered data to next level of the data fusion system of the multiple simultaneous threat detection system. The multiple simultaneous threat detection system combines all the multi-sensor threat data that has already been filtered into different sets of minimum size using Set Cover model. In order to detect the real threats, improve the accuracy and precision in threat detection; the multiple simultaneous threat detection system fuses the multi-sensor data with Bayesian theory of estimation, Dempster, Extended Dempster Shafer and Generalized Evidential processing.

5.2 Dempster Shafer Theory to Fuse Data

In this experiment, frame of discernment θ will be a set of elemental propositions or combinations of the hypothesis statements. Threats denoted by T may be overlapping or different to each other.

In the set of n mutually exclusive and exhaustive set of hypotheses about threat(s) $T \dots T_n$.

$$\Theta = \{T_1, T_2 \dots T_n\} \quad (4)$$

If θ have set of n hypotheses, Boolean combination of the set will be θ^n hypotheses.

Dempster Shafer theory does not calculate the probability of a hypothesis but helps in finding out the probability of the evidential support for a hypothesis.

Unlike Bayesian and classical theory of inference, Dempster Shafer theory of inference helps in developing probability mass m (θ) by assigning evidence to each propositions or general propositions. Each intrusion detection system can assign evidence via probability mass to each of the 4 threats, e.g. M1 (T1), M2 (T2), M3 (T3) and M4 (T4). The total probability masses of all the propositions including general propositions will be equal to 1. The probability mass is represented as:

$$m (\theta) \leq 1 \quad (5)$$

$$\sum_{i=1}^{n} m (\theta) = 1 \quad (6)$$

m (θ) is the probability mass of any possible hypotheses. In this experiment that may be a single threat or combinations of the 4 threats.

5.3 Propositions / Hypothesis

We have 4 sensors (intrusion detection systems) and 4 different types of threats. Sensors can receive a single threat or any possible combinations of the 4 generated threats. The total possible base propositions using mathematical theory of combinatorics with and without repetitions are 340 and 15 respectively. As repeated threats are of no significance during hypothesis testing and will also unnecessary increase processing cost and time. Therefore, we will only concentrate on the propositions without repetitions.

Only 4425 (15 x 295) non repetitive propositions will be processed and tested by MTDS engine as compared to 773160 (340 x 2274) with repetitive propositions.

The general Combinations and Permutations formula is:

$$P(n,r) = \frac{n!}{r!(n-r)!} \tag{7}$$

Where n is the number of sensors (Intrusion Detection System), r is the number of threats to be selected ($0 \leq r \leq n$), where n =4 in this experiment, if r = n, P(n, r) = n!

Case 1: when single threat detected by each sensor, total # of hypothesis / propositions with and without repetitions would be 4 and 4

Case 2: when two threats detected by each sensor, total # of hypothesis / propositions with and without repetitions would be 6 and 16

Case 3: when three threats detected by each sensor, total # of hypothesis / propositions with and without repetitions would be 4 and 64

Case 4: when four threats detected by each sensor, total # of hypothesis / propositions with and without repetitions would be 1 and 256

Limitation

Due to high complexity of the probability mass and weights calculations, it is not possible for us to cover all the 15 non repetitive hypotheses during our research. Therefore, I'll test only four elementary hypotheses as mentioned in section 5.3.

5.4 Fusion without Using the Weights of the Intrusion Detection Systems

This experiment has 4 types of intrusion detection systems and each has its own way of threat detection. This means each intrusion detection system has different perception and reliability that it provides to multiple simultaneous threat detection system.

The Dempster Shafer model to combine the probability masses of the threats from more than two independent intrusion detection systems:

$$\sum_{i,j=0}^{n} M_i(T_{i,j}) = \sum_{i,j=0}^{n} \frac{p(\{T_{i,j}\})}{p(\{T_{i,j}\}) + p(\{\neg T_{i,j}\})} \tag{8}$$

Where $M_i(T_{i,j})$ is probability mass function, $T_{i,j}$ is the ith threat of the jth Intrusion Detection System and $p(\{T_{i,j}\})$ is the probability of an ith threat of the jth Intrusion Detection System for a particular type of the threat?

The calculation of the combined probability mass functions will be followed as:

$$P(\{T_{1,1}\}) = \frac{Detected\ Alerts}{Observed\ Alerts} = \frac{17}{51} = 0.3333 \tag{9}$$

$P(\{T_{1,1}\})$ is the probability assigned to the 1st threat by 1st Intrusion detection system.

$$P(\{T_{2,2}\}) = \frac{Detected\ Alerts}{Observed\ Alerts} = \frac{9}{33} = 0.272727273 \tag{10}$$

$P(\{T_{2,2}\})$ is the probability assigned to the 2nd threat by 2nd Intrusion detection system.

$$P(\{T_{3,3}\}) = \frac{Detected\ Alerts}{Observed\ Alerts} = \frac{5}{13} = 0.384615385$$

(11)

$P(\{T_{3,3}\})$ is the probability assigned to the 3rd threat by 3rd Intrusion detection system.

$$P(\{T_{4,4}\}) = \frac{Detected\ Alerts}{Observed\ Alerts} = \frac{9}{26} = 0.346153846$$

(12)

$P(\{T_{4,4}\})$ is the probability assigned to the 4th threat by 4th Intrusion detection system.

Putting the above values in the combined probability mass formula equation (12)

$$M_{1,2}(T_{1,2}) = 0.157894737$$

(13)

$M_{1,2}(T_{1,2})$ is the combined probability mass of threat 1 and 2 assigned by the intrusion detection system 1 and 2.

$$M_{1,2,3}(T_{1,2,3}) = 0.104895105$$

(14)

$M_{1,2,3}(T_{1,2,3})$ is the combined probability mass of the threat 1, 2 and 3 assigned by the intrusion detection system 1, 2 and 3.

Similarly the probability mass of the 4 intrusion detection system would be:

$$M_{1,2,3,4}(T_{1,2,3,4}) = 0.05841627$$

(15)

$M_{1,2,3,4}(T_{1,2,3,4})$ is the combined probability mass of the threat 1, 2, 3 and 4 assigned by the intrusion detection system 1, 2, 3 and 4.

In this experiment only 4 x threats and 4 x intrusion detection systems are participating in data gathering, therefore this combined probability mass formula for two, three and four threats was calculated.

5.5 Data Fusion Using Weights of the Intrusion Detection Systems

Unlike Bayesian decision theory, Dempster Shafer model can assign evidence to a single or group of propositions in an experiment and can combine probability masses of the propositions emerging from more than two sources but its self-evident definition of evidence (probability mass) is not very accurate. The Dempster Shafer theory of inference also has some issues in renormalization of the probability mass during probability masses combinations.

Thus it has become one of the most challenging tasks to find out the ways to perfect the evidential or probability mass combination techniques to increase the accuracy of the statistical decisions.

In our research, we used two different ways to improve decision making.

1. Weights of the observations
2. Generalized Evidential Processing

These methods minimized the effect of probability assignments to the propositions and renormalization of the rule of combinations of the probability masses of the preposition(s). For more detail please see a publication [26].

The Probability formula for calculating the probability mass and weights of an Intrusion Detection System for a particular threat is:

$$\sum_{i,j=0}^{n} M_i(T_{i,j})^{W_i^n} = \sum_{i,j=0}^{n} \frac{P(\{T_{i,j}\})^{W_i^n}}{P(\{T_{i,j}i\})^{W_i^n} + P(\{\neg T_{i,j}\})^{W_i^n}} \tag{16}$$

Where T is the threat and W is is the weight of the intrusion detection system and P is the probability of the ith threat of jth Intrusion Detection System.

and $P(\{T_{i,j}\})^{W_i^n} = 1 - P(\{\neg T_{i,j}\})^{W_i^n}$ (17)

$P(\{T_{i,j}\})^{W_i^n}$ is the probability assigned to the ith threat by jth Intrusion detection system with weight.

The Probability formula for calculating the weights of an Intrusion Detection System for a particular threat: $W_j^n = -\sum_{i,j=1}^{n} P_i \log P$ (18)

Where W is the weight of the Intrusion Detection Systems (sensors) and P is the probability of an ith threat of jth Intrusion Detection Systems.

Calculations of the Extended Dempster Shafer will be as followed:

$$P(\{T_{1,1}\})^{W_1^n} = \frac{Detected\ Alerts}{Observed\ Alerts} = \frac{18}{33} = 0.545454545 \tag{19}$$

$P(\{T_{1,1}\})^{W_1^n}$ is the weighted probability assigned to the 1st threat by 1st Intrusion detection system.

$$P(\{T_{2,2}\})^{W_2^n} = \frac{Detected\ Alerts}{Observed\ Alerts} = \frac{18}{28} = 0.642857143 \tag{20}$$

$P(\{T_{2,2}\})^{W_2^n}$ is the weighted probability assigned to the 2nd threat by 2nd Intrusion detection system.

$$P(\{T_{3,3}\})^{W_3^n} = \frac{Detected\ Alerts}{Observed\ Alerts} = \frac{8}{22} = 0.363636364 \tag{21}$$

$P(\{T_{3,3}\})^{W_3^n}$ is the weighted probability assigned to the 3rd threat by 3rd Intrusion detection system.

$$P(\{T_{4,4}\})^{W_4^n} = \frac{Detected\ Alerts}{Observed\ Alerts} = \frac{9}{17} = 0.529411765 \tag{22}$$

$P(\{T_{4,4}\})^{W_4^n}$ is the weighted probability assigned to the 4th threat by 4th Intrusion detection system.

The weights of the intrusion detection systems:

$$W_1^n = -\sum_{i=1}^{n} P1 \log P1 = 0.143586237 \tag{23}$$

W_1^n is the weight of the 1st intrusion detection system

$$W_2^n = -\sum_{i=1}^{n} P2 \log P2 = 0.123354981 \qquad (24)$$

W_2^n is the weight of the 2nd intrusion detection system

$$W_3^n = -\sum_{i=1}^{n} P3 \log P3 = 0.159757343 \qquad (25)$$

W_3^n is the weight of the 3rd intrusion detection system

$$W_4^n = -\sum_{i=1}^{n} P4 \log P4 = 0.146226924 \qquad (26)$$

W_4^n is the weight of the 4th intrusion detection system

$$M_{1,2}(T_{1,2})^{W_i^n} = \frac{P(\{T_1\})^{W_1^n} P(\{T_2\})^{W_2^n}}{P(\{T_1\})^{W_1^n} P(\{T_2\})^{W_2^n} + P(\{\neg T_1\})^{W_1^n} P(\{\neg T_2\})^{W_2^n}} \qquad (27)$$

$M_{1,2}(T_{1,2})^{W_i^n} = 0.753303965$, is the weighted combined probability mass of the probability assigned to 1st and 2nd threat by 1st and 2nd intrusion detection system using equation (23).

Similarly the other weighted combined probability masses of the other intrusion detection systems would be:

$$M_{1,2,3}(T_{1,2,3})^{W_i^n} = 0.373362445 \qquad (28)$$

$$M_{1,2,3,4}(T_{1,2,3,4})^{W_i^n} = 0.819596134 \qquad (29)$$

5.6 Data Fusion using Generalized Evidential Processing Theory

GEP is a generalization of Bayesian theorem. Similar to Bayesian theory, GEP can assigns evidence to hypothesis only whilst Dempster Shafer has an edge over an assigning the evidence to both conflicting propositions and hypothesis. As this research deals only with testing hypotheses, therefore, GEP and Dempster Shafer have exactly the same role in assigning evidences to the hypothesis. However, GEP assign and combine probability masses based priori conditional probability whilst Dempster Shafer updates priori probability of the hypothesis based on observation evidence. Therefore, in this research, priori probability of the hypothesis (threats) will be identified by any intrusion detection system of the test experiment.

Although, the main benefit of GEP is that it separates hypothesis from decision. GEP also describe the relationship of evidential assignments with fusion decision. This provides opportunity to test hypothesis at different quantization of the data.

The Generalized Evidential Processing model to combine the probability masses of the threats from more than two independent intrusion detection systems:

$$\sum_{i,j=0}^{n} M_i(T_{i,j}) = \sum_{i,j=0}^{n} \frac{P(\{T_{i,j}\})P(\{T_{i,j}/S_{i,j}\})}{P(\{T_{i,j}\})P(\{T_{i,j}/S_{i,j}\}) + P(\{\neg T_{i,j}\})P(\{\neg T_{i,j}/S_{i,j}\})} \qquad (30)$$

Where $\sum_{i,j=0}^{n} M_i(T_{i,j})$ is the combine probability mass of the independent intrusion detection systems.

$P(\{T_{i,j} / S_{i,j}\})$ is the probability of the test positive given ith threat of the jth intrusion detection system. That is the percentage of the detection accuracy by each Intrusion Detection Systems.

MARS, Sniffers, Snoop and Wireshark detection accuracy is 95%, 80%, 75% and 80% respectively.

$P(\Psi_{i,j})$ is the probability of the ith threat observed by the jth intrusion Detection systems.

As the numerical figures about accuracy of the Intrusion Detection Systems are not available in any literature, therefore, these values are purely on assumptions based on the detection accuracy in this experiment. However, it is strongly proposed if any reliable numerical figures become available, other workers must use those values to get better detection accuracy of their GEP identity fusion model. Putting the above values in the combined probability mass formula equation (12)

$$M_{1,2}(T_{1,2}) = 0.490870599 \qquad (31)$$

$M_{1,2}(T_{1,2})$ is the combined probability mass of the threat 1 and 2 assigned by intrusion detection system 1 and 2.

$$M_{1,2,3}(T_{1,2,3}) = 0.581137264 \qquad (32)$$

$M_{1,2,3}(T_{1,2,3})$ is the combined probability mass of the threat 1, 2 and 3 assigned by intrusion detection system 1, 2 and 3.

Similarly the probability mass of the 4 intrusion detection system would be:

$$M_{1,2,3,4}(T_{1,2,3,4}) = 0.62337544 \qquad (33)$$

$M_{1,2,3,4}(T_{1,2,3,4})$ is the combined probability mass of the threat 1, 2, 3 and 4 assigned by intrusion detection system 1, 2, 3 and 4.

5.7 Threat Results Based on Dempster Shafer Theory of Inference

After Set Cover data fusion we had a total of 295 threats (Table 1). This threat data is now further processed by the next part of the multiple simultaneous threat detection system that is Dempster Shafer as shown in Figure 1. In order to increase the precision of each threat was passed through multiple hypotheses testing as proposed in sec 5.3. The intrusion detection system classified the Dempster Shafer inferences into 4 types. Observed threats, Observed Alerts, Detected Alerts and Real Alerts that helped in determining the real threat detection and false positive rates. The final results of this part of the fusion have been given in Table 2.

False Positive rates are determined using the formula:

False Positive Rates =

$$1 - \frac{Real\ Alerts}{Observerd\ Alerts} * 100 \qquad (34)$$

Table 2. Threat results based on Dempster Shafer theory of inference

Threat Observations by the Threat Detection						
System Using Dempster Shafer						
IDS	OT	OA	DA	RA	FPR	Detect Rate
MARS	51	23	31	17	26	60.78431
Sniffers	33	19	21	9	53	63.63636
Snoop	13	7	7	5	29	53.84615
Wireshark	26	12	12	9	25	46.15385
Total	123	61	71	40		

And Threat Detection rate is calculated using the equation:

Threat Detection Rate =

$$\frac{Detected \ \ Alerts}{Observerd \ \ Threats} * 100 \qquad (35)$$

Where **OT** stands for Observed Threats, **OA** for observed Alerts, **DA** for Detected Alerts, **RA** for Real Alerts, **FPR** for False Positive Rate

5.8 Threat Results Based on Extended Dempster Shafer Theory of Inference

Just like the Dempster Shafer inference, 295 threats data analysed by the Extended Dempster Shafer inference and Intrusion Detection System then grouped as given in Table 3. It is obvious that real alerts have gone up from 40 to 53 that is a significant indication that False Positive Rates have reduced as compared to Dempster Shafer. Likewise there is an obvious improvement in threat detection rate as well.

5.9 Threat Results based on Generalized Evidential Processing

GEP has certainly improved the detection rats of almost all of the intrusion detection systems.

MARS detection and false positive rates showed the perfection of GEP model as a perfect fusion identity model at decision level. However, other 3 Intrusion Detection Systems (Sniffers, Snoop and Wireshark have also shown significant improvement in threat detection and there is a considerable drop in false positive rates as well (Table 4).

5.10 Performance of the Multiple Simultaneous Threat Detection System

The multiple simultaneous threat detection system is a multi-sensor data fusion system. Its major components statistical and mathematical techniques set covers, Dempster Shafer, extension Dempster Shafer and GEP are the main data processing cores and heart of the data processing unit for the system. The larger the number of sensors the greater should be the accuracy and precision in the results. Although Bayesian and Dempster Shafer provide best processing model in multi-sensor data fusion but involve too much complex iteration of the data fusion process in terms of its probability mass and weight calculations. Therefore, in real life, it would be a very hard task to use Bayesian and DS model for combining probability masses of an experiment having a more than four sensors, particularly in case of overlapping and conflicting propositions. The greater the number of sensors, larger would be precision in threat detection, that's

Table 3. Threat results based on extended Dempster Shafer theory of inference

Threat Observations by the Threat Detection						
System Using Extended Dempster Shafer						
IDS	OT	OA	DA	RA	FPR	Detect Rate
MARS	33	19	31	18	5.3	93.93939
Sniffers	28	21	26	18	14	92.85714
Snoop	22	9	14	8	11	63.63636
Wireshark	17	10	12	9	10	70.58824
Total	100	59	83	53		

Table 4. Threat results based on generalized evidential processing

Threat Observations by the Threat Detection						
System Using Generalized Evidential Processing						
IDS	OT	OA	DA	RA	FPR	Detect Rate
MARS	31	19	31	19	0	100
Sniffers	28	20	26	19	5	92.85714286
Snoop	15	10	14	9	10	93.33333333
Wireshark	18	10	17	9	10	94.44444444
Total	92	59	88	56		

why I'm looking into possibility of using more than 4 sensors in our next step.

In our experiment, we performed experiment in three steps using evidences of 2nd, 3rd and then 4th sensors (intrusion detection systems) to the 4 type of threats. The sensors were 4 intrusion detection systems. We compared their results and have proved the obvious fact that the combined results of the 4 sensors have improved threat detection significantly. Bayesian, Dempster Shafer and GEP theory of inferences provided us tools to combine evidences of these sensors and measure the uncertainty of a hypothesis or to gain better confidence in the combined probability measurements to the evidences or propositions.

The following are the graphs drawn in Microsoft Excel to display the results of multiple simultaneous threat detection system. Comparing efficiency of the Dempster Shafer and Extended Dempster Shafer data fusion techniques, Figures 2 and 3 show a significant increase in the combined probability masses in case of Extended Dempster Shafer Theory. That is a good indication of enhanced precision, accuracy and better performance of GEP data fusion in threat detection over the Dempster Shafer Data fusion techniques.

The average combined probability mass for threat detection by three methods; Dempster Shafer, Extended Dempster Shafer and GEP were 6%, 41% and 53% respectively. That clearly shows GEP as a most effective method which increased

Figure 2. Performance of the multiple simultaneous threat detection system

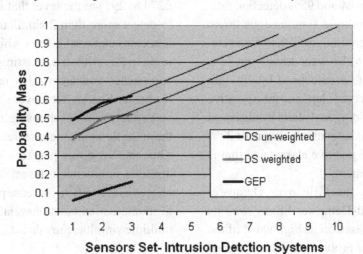

Figure 3. Effectiveness of the multiple simultaneous threat detection system

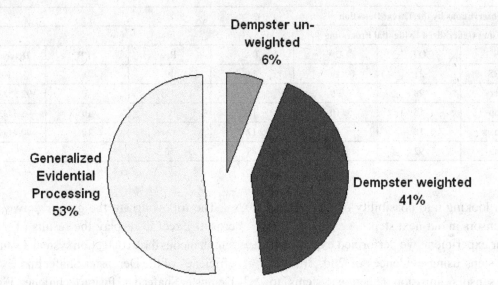

combined probability mass by 47%. General principle is that higher the probability mass greater would be the precision in threat detection.

6. CONCLUSION

The empirical experiment of multiple simultaneous threat detection system proved that the hybrid model had significant increase in precision in threat detection. Dempster Shafer inference produced 33% detection rate whilst extended Dempster Shafer and GEP had 80% and 95% detection rate. So on an average, multiple simultaneous threat detection System increased 39% detection rate. The false positive rate also went down from 33% to 6%. (Detection rate is calculated by dividing detected alerts by observed alerts and false positive rate is derived by dividing real alerts by observed alerts.) Thus there was a net improvement of 27% in getting rid of false positive alarms and that is a significant achievement.

Another edge of the GEP over Dempster Shafer and Extended Dempster Shafer was its better performance based on its high value of the combined evidential / probability mass assigned

by the 4 different Intrusion Detection systems. The combined probability mass of the GEP was 0.49 whilst Dempster Shafer and Extended Dempster Shafer had 0.06 and 0.40. GEP increased combined probability mass by 15% which in turn increased the overall efficiency of our simultaneous Multiple Threat Detection System.

Set Cover as a middle tier data fusion tool produced incredible results, particularly in data grouping that amazingly minimise the computational processing cpu and memory overhead cost and time. Set Cover reduce data population (from 2274 to 295) to the level that it became possible to detect more than 2 simultaneous threats with less computational efforts whist that was almost impossible with the existing threat detection approaches and others that used Bayesian and Dempster Shafer. Set Cover also determined the cost effectiveness of choosing a computer node for the multiple simultaneous threat detection system. Thus the Set cover played a vital role to assist multiple simultaneous threat detection system to improve its ability to increase precision and making numerical calculations relatively easier for the multiple simultaneous threat detection system.

Looking into the results, it is obvious that results of experiment has proven that the proposed threat detection system "multiple simultaneous threat detection system" remained successful to achieve our research goals.

In order to improve precision of threat detection, as a next step of our research, the main task we are planning is to implement weighted version of Generalized Evidential Processing (GEP) if possible. Plus also apply international standards for the test accuracy of the 4 sensors that we used in our experiment. GEP is an extension of the Bayesian and Dempster Shafer theory that presents a better evidential combination and separate propositions and the decisions. Therefore each proposition or set of propositions can be tested and analysed separately at different levels of the data. In addition to that we will focus to improve the quality of the test experiment and write the final thesis.

ACKNOWLEDGMENT

We would like to thank Dr. Paul Kwan (our principal supervisor) for his suggestion on the initial research direction and his valuable comments on how to structure this paper.

REFERENCES

Aickelin, U. (2002). An Indirect Genetic Algorithm for Set Covering Problems. *The Journal of the Operational Research Society, 53*(10), 1118–1126. doi:10.1057/palgrave.jors.2601317

Bass, T., & Gruber, D. (2005, August 18). A glimpse into the future of id. *Usenix*. Retrieved from http://www.usenix.org/publications/log-in/1999-9/features/future.html

Bendjebbour, A., & Delignon, Y. (2001, August). Multisensor Image Segmentation Using Dempster-Shafer Fusion in Markov Fields Context. *IEEE Transaction on GeoScience and Remote Sensing, 39*(8), 1–10. doi:10.1109/36.942557

Boston, J. R. (2000, February). A Signal Detection System Based on Dempster-Shafer Theory and Comparison to Fuzzy Detection. *IEEE Transactions on Systems, Man and Cybernetics. Part C, Applications and Reviews, 30*(1), 45–51. doi:10.1109/5326.827453

Braun, J. (2000). Dempster-Shafer theory and Bayesian reasoning in multisensor data fusion, Sensor Fusion: Architectures, Algorithms and Applications IV. *Proceedings of the Society for Photo-Instrumentation Engineers, 4051,* 255–266.

Brugger, S. T. (2004). *Data Mining for Network Intrusion Detection* (pp. 8-55). Retrieved from www.bruggerink.com/~zow/papers/dmnid_qual-pres.pdf

Burroughs, J., Wilson, L. F., & George, V. (2002). *Analysis of Distributed Intrusion Detection Systems Using Bayesian Methods*. Paper presented at IPCCC 2002 (pp. 142-147).

Chatzigiannakis, V., Lenis, A., Siaterlis, C., Grammatikou, M., Kalogeras, D., Papavassiliou, S., & Maglaris, V. (2002). *Distributed Network Monitoring and anomaly Detection as a Grid Application* (pp. 1-13).

Computer Society Institute. (2002, April). *Cyber crime bleeds U.S. corporations, survey shows*. Retrieved January 16, 2003, from http://www.gocsi.com/press/20020407.html

Dong, & Deborah. (2005). *Alert Confidence Fusion in Intrusion Detection Systems with Extended Dempster-Shafer Theory* (pp. 142-147). New York: ACM.

Gorodetski, V., Karsaev, O., Kotenko, I., & Khabalov, A. (2002). Software Development Kit for Multi-agent Systems Design and Implementation. In B. Dunin-Keplicz & E. Nawareski (Eds.), *From Theory to Practice in Multi- agent Systems* (LNAI 2296, pp. 121-130). New York: Springer Verlag.

Grocholsky, B., Makarenko, A., & Durrant-Whyte, H. F. (2003). *Information-theoretic coordinated control of multiple sensor platforms* (pp. 1521–1526). ICRA.

Habib, A., Hefeeda, M., & Bhargava, B. (2003). Detecting service violations and DoS attacks. In *Proceedings of the NDSS Conference* (pp. 439-446). Reston, VA: Internet Society.

Hall, D. (1992). *Mathematical Techniques in Multisensor Data Fusion* (pp. 99–105). Norwood, MA: Artech House.

Hugh, F. (2005). *Durrant-Whyte: Data fusion in sensor networks* (pp. 545–565). IPSN.

Klein, L. A. (1999). *Sensor and Data Fusion Concepts and Applications* (2nd ed., pp. 1-252). Melville, NY: SPIE Optical Engineering Press. ISBN 0-8194-3231-8

Koks, D., & Challa, S. (2005). *An Introduction to Bayesian and Dempster-Shefer Data Fusion* (pp. 1-52)

Kumar, K. S. (2000). *Intrusion Detection and Analysis*. Vancouver, Canada: University of British Columbia.

Ma, B. (2001). Parametric and Non Parametric Approaches for Multisensor Data Fusion (pp. 1-212). Unpublished PhD thesis, University Of Michigan, Michigan.

Ning, P., Xu, D., Healey, C., & Amant, R. (2004). Building Attack Scenarios through Integration of Complementary Alert Correlation Methods. In *Proceedings of the 11th Annual Network and Distributed System Security Symposium* (pp. 97-111).

Rehman, R. (2003). *Intrusion Detection System with SNORT* (pp. 1-288). Retrieved from http://www.snort.org/

Siaterlis, C., & Maglaris, B. (2004). Towards Multisensor Data Fusion for DoS detection. In *Proceedings of the 2004 ACM symposium on Applied Computing* (pp. 1-8).

Spafford, E. H. (1991). *The Internet worm incident* (Tech. Rep. No. CSD-TR-933). West Lafayette, IN: Purdue University, Department of Computer Science. LEM OS, R. (1991). *Counting the cost of slammer* (pp. 1-19).

Sultan, Z. (2009). Multiple Simultaneous Threat detection System in UNIX. *IJCSNS, 9*(1), 56–66.

Wu, H., Siegel, M., Stiefelhagen, R., & Yang, J. (2002). Sensor fusion using Dempster-Shafer theory. In *Proceedings of IEEE Instrumentation and Measurement Technology Conference*, Anchorage, AK (pp. 1-6).

Zamboni, D. (2000, October). *Doing intrusion detection using embedded sensors* (Tech. Rep. No. 2000-21, pp. 1-9). West Lafayette, IN: Purdue University, CERIAS.

This work was previously published in the International Journal of Web Portals 2(2), edited by Greg Adamson and Jana Polgar, pp. 51-67, copyright 2010 by Information Science Publishing (an imprint of IGI Global).

Chapter 10
Using Ajax to Track Student Attention

Jan Newmarch
Box Hill Institute and Monash University, Australia

ABSTRACT

Tracking the behaviour of users of online learning systems is an important issue, but current techniques have not been able to give deep views on what users do with Web-based learning systems. This paper shows how the use of Ajax can provide a richer model of how users interact with Web systems. In this paper, the authors will discuss a case study used to better track behaviours of online learning systems and how Ajax improves this understanding of user interactions.

INTRODUCTION

Any producer of web-based material is interested in what users do with the pages they visit: what do they visit, how long do they spend there, and what do they do while there? This can be of high commercial value, as information about users can be used to revise pages in order to draw customers into a commercial site, and hopefully to spend money. In the educational domain, knowledge of a user's activities can help to build a better educational experience. The intent is to build up

a model of the user and to customise the site to desirable users.

There have been three common techniques used to track user activity: web server logs (Schluting, n.d.), custom-built browsers (Edmonds, 2003; Velayathan & Yamada, 2006) or visual observation such as in a usability lab. They are all well-known to have significant drawbacks, as discussed in the next section. Recently a technique called Ajax (Holdener, 2008) (for Asynchronous JavaScript and XML) has come to the fore. Primarily this is used to give a more interactive experience with a web site, and has been used by companies such as Google (in Google maps).

DOI: 10.4018/978-1-4666-0336-3.ch010

HTML 4 compliant browsers support event tracking using languages like JavaScript, such as when a user enters and leaves a page. They also allow "focus" tracking, which can occur when a user switches to, say, an email program without leaving a web page. Combined with the asynchronous aspects of Ajax, we show in this paper how this can be used to give a clearer picture of what a user is doing. We demonstrate the use of this with a formal course for teaching Linux administration.

Consider the scenario. Johnny has been instructed to look at some courseware in his browser. He navigates to the page, but after 5 minutes he gets bored. He switches to another tab so he can read his Google mail for 20 minutes. Then he switches back to the courseware page. After another 5 minutes he decides to talk to a friend and starts up Skype. 10 minutes later he returns to the page and finally follows a link in that page to another page of the courseware.

Simple observation of server logs would suggest that Johnny spent 40 minutes on the first page, whereas a closer examination shows that he only spent 10 minutes. This paper shows how to perform some of this closer examination.

The structure of this paper is as follows: the next section discusses current techniques for tracking user behaviour. The section after that looks at Ajax and how we use this to generate information. Following this are a number of sections discussing issues arising from this use of Ajax and how to analyse the information gained. Finally an examination of actual server logs is given to show how to give a more accurate picture of a user's browsing habits, and future work is discussed.

The principal contribution of this paper is that it shows how deeper analyses of student use of web-based courseware can be performed, and illustrates this with a case study. Similar techniques could be used in other situations.

TRACKING USERS

HTTP logs are collected by HTTP servers such as Apache. Generally these logs use the Common Logfile Format (WWW Consortium, n.d.a). These record which pages are accessed, the date, which IP address made the request, and optional other information such as referring page. These logs form a relatively simple way of measuring what users are accessing. However, they only give partial information. They show the requests that actually made it to the server: many organisations now use proxy caches, and if there is a "hit" on a cache, then the request will be handled by the proxy and not make it back to the source server. This can be alleviated by setting the Expires time for each document to zero, but breaks the value of caching.

If the user makes use of the Back button in the browser, then the document will be retrieved from the browser's own cache. This cannot be avoided except by disabling the Back button.

The principal problem is that the server logs can only show that a page is requested from a server. What is done with that page is unknown. A user may examine it for a long time or simply discard it. Further, it is not clear whether it is a human using a browser or some automated agent such as a spider.

After any one request, if another is made to the same site then another entry is made in that server's log. This provides an upper bound to the time spent on the requested page. But the user may have been somewhere else, or may just never come back. A second technique is to use a special-purpose browser which logs each user activity. Such browsers can record a great deal of information. There is a minor problem of getting the information back to the server. The major problem is persuading people to use such a browser. Typically this can only be done with a relatively cooperative group of people, as a research experiment.

The third technique is to bring people into a special laboratory and to physically observe their behaviour. This is expensive and time consuming, and can only be done with small groups. However, it does offer the potential for discussion about what it being done, to give a "why" as well as a "what".

AJAX

Ajax is technically very simple: it consists of a JavaScript call that can be made asynchronously to a web server (Holdener, 2008). Typically such a request carries XML data, although this is not prescribed. The browser does not pause, or refresh while such a request is made. If a reply is received, the JavaScript engine may act on this. In the case of Google Maps it caches map data of the sides of the current map for use if the user wishes to view a nearby map. Other Ajax applications may use JavaScript to manipulate the browser's DOM model, to cause apparently interactive responses. The advantage of Ajax is that it can avoid the fetch-wait-refresh cycle usual in following hyperlinks or submitting forms.

Under the Web Consortium's Document Object Model (DOM), user actions in a browser can generate events (WWW Consortium, n.d.b). These events include loading pages, moving or clicking the mouse, and using the keyboard.

Ajax requests can be called from these Javascript events. We want to track user activity, where the interesting events are load, focus, blur and unload. There are many other events such as mouse motion etc, and it would be possible to track these as well. It is possible that HTML version 5 (WWW Consortium, n.d.c) will extend the set of events, but this is not yet standardised or consistently implemented.

The technique of this paper is to use Ajax to track load, unload, blur and focus events for each page and record them on the originating server. There they can be analysed by the web site's owner.

We include JavaScript in each page that has handlers for load, unload, blur and focus events. When a handler is called, it makes an Ajax asynchronous GET call back to the server. The browser does not use any returned information, so really all that is needed is to record on the server side the time, the page, the browser and the state change. One simple way is to use the Ajax call to just get a one-pixel image, tagged with the state change as in:

```
GET /dummyimage.png?state=loading
```

This will get recorded in, for example, the ordinary Apache server logs along with the referring page, which is where the state change occurred as:

```
192.168.1.11 --[21/Dec/2009:16:47:36
+1100] "GET /dummmyimage.
png?state=loading
HTTP/1.1" 200 266
"http://192.168.1.11/boxhill/ict213/
test.html" "Opera/9.80 (Windows
NT 6.1; U; en) Presto/2.2.15 Ver-
sion/10.10"
```

We also note two other systems which use Ajax to track user activity in different ways. The first is Robot Replay (Almaer & Galbraith, n.d.) which records mouse and keyboard events. This allows tracking of what a single user actually does on a page. Another is a service by Crazy Egg (Crazy Egg, n.d.) which builds up a record of many users and shows their interaction with heat maps - the hotter a point on the map, the more users interacted with elements there. These two approaches are complementary to the one here which measures how users navigate to and from web pages.

In both of the examples considered later, browser HTML pages are generated dynamically from server-side XML files. The generators were modified to include the required JavaScript. Any Content Management System can probably do the same, to quickly allow a site to be marked up to record user events.

EVENT GENERATION ISSUES

There are several different ways of attaching JavaScript code to DOM objects in order to generate events. One way is to attach JavaScript code code directly to an HTML tag as in <body onload = "sendGetRequest('http:/dummyimage. png?state=loading')"> This is an obtrusive method as it requires modification of the HTML of the document. However, it is reliable and produced the most consistent and useful results in event generation.

The second method is to include a Javascript file which attempts to locate the relevant DOM object and assign an event handler to it. There are many tutorials (e.g., Chapman, n.d.) which give example code such as window.onload =... This does not meet the HTML 4 specifications which state that the onload event should be attached to HTML body or frame tags. In practice, this produced inconsistent results, with some browsers failing to generate a focus event after loading, while others loaded and then unloaded, followed by focusing and blurring!

A third technique is to assign a name attribute to all body elements, search for these elements using the JavaScript getElementsByName() and then add an event handler to the element. This also turned out to be unreliable as the element needed to be loaded before it could be found and this invalidated the onload event.

The best method of adding event handlers for this project is to add the handler directly to the body or frame element. Where the HTML is generated from a content management system, this will need to be added to the generation mechanism. This was the mechanism used in the experiment described later.

BROWSER ISSUES

The HTML 4 event specifications are not very precise. For example, there is no state machine specification of what and when events should be generated during page loading. The forthcoming HTML 5 is more precise, but this is not yet standardised, or consistently implemented by browser vendors. In order to use this technique, the browser must support both JavaScript and the Ajax functions. This rules out many browsers such as Lynx and the W3C Amaya, but these have negligible market share. Even if we restrict attention to the major browsers of IE, Firefox, Safari, Opera and Chrome, there are still differences.

There are a large number of situations which could generate events. For example, focus events can be generated for a page after loading the document, by switching to it by using the Back or Forward buttons, by selecting a tab containing it, by selecting it from another application, or under most Linux GUIs, by switching from another desktop. Some events should be the result of the window system events such as switching focus between applications, while others belong to a browser such as switching focus between tabs.

Chrome is still at an early stage of development (at December, 2009) and fails many of the event generation possibilities. Even worse, I was unable to get Safari (under Windows) to generate any events. Firefox v3.0 failed to generate a focus event on tab switching, but this has been fixed in Firefox 3.5. Despite its generally poor reputation with regard to standards, all of Internet Explorer 6, 7, and 8 were consistent and nearly complete with respect to these events.

For the current major browsers, these are summarised in Tables One and Two. I initially carried out experiments with this technology in 2006, with Firefox 1.5. That version would generate a quite extended sequence of focus and blur events until it settled down to a stable state. This made it very difficult to analyse results.

In summary, browsers should not matter, but in practice still do.

BROWSER-GENERATED EVENTS

Many events are generated internally by user interaction with the browser. These include loading URLs, from the menu bar, by following a link or selecting a bookmark. But they also include opening or switching between tabs, closing tabs, or using the Back and Forward buttons. These are summarised in Table One.

IE has correct behaviour for almost all of these, even IE6. Firefox has a few minor errors. Chrome and Opera have a large number of errors. Safari is omitted as it does not generate any events.

There are some actions which lead to different event sequences between the browsers. For example, loading a URL generates load and focus events for IE and Firefox, but only load events for Opera and Chrome. If it is possible to load a URL without giving it the focus, then Opera and Chrome would have incorrect behaviour, otherwise it may be excusable.

OPERATING SYSTEM EVENTS

Browsers run within an environment supplied by the operating system or in the case of Linux also supplied by the X Window server and whatever window manager is used. There are many cases where these should signal to applications that a change of state is occurring. The major cases are focus changes between applications' windows, which includes iconification or de-iconification of an application's windows. But these events also include shutdown, hibernation, logging a user off or in the worst case, crashing. Of course, no-one could expect an operating system to generate events in a reliable manner if it is crashing! These are summarised in Table Two, with similar results as before: IE is good, Firefox is almost right and Opera and Chrome have many errors. Safari is omitted as before.

Virtual Machine Issues

Virtual machine technologies have been under development for many years. These allow a computer running one operating system to host a guest virtual machine running another operating system. For example, on my Linux laptop running Ubuntu I can run virtual machines under Virtual-Box (Sun MicroSystems, n.d.) hosting Windows XP, Windows 7 and Fedora Linux guests. While I am within one virtual machine, the task focusing and switching mechanism occurs according to that operating system. For example, when a Windows virtual machine has the focus, then Alt-Tab will switch focus between Windows applications on that virtual machine. However, for each virtual machine there is also an escape mechanism to switch focus from the guest virtual machine back to the host operating system. For example, in VirtualBox, it is the right control key by default.

Most GUIs for the major operating systems will not allow no window to have the focus. However, this will be required for accurate tracking of focus changes. Using VirtualBox, no blur events were generated for any guest operating system applications when the virtual machine lost focus, nor focus events when the virtual machine gained focus. That means that a browser window in a guest system will believe that it still has the focus even though it has been switched to another application in the host system.

Virtual machines are not common on the desktop yet, except for application developers, However, Windows 7 includes a virtual desktop for Windows XP so there may be an increase in virtual desktop utilisation. If that occurs then there will need to be agreement on focus management between virtual machines. At present this is probably ignorable, but needs work for future standardisation.

The effect of events not being generated by the operating system or by a virtual machine will result in some pages being recorded as obtaining focus but with no blur event being recorded even when focus is lost.

SERVER-SIDE ANALYSIS

Server-side programs can be used to analyse the log files. These programs can be in any language, and run in either batch or interactive modes.

I use the Apache HTTP server. The Common Logfile Format (WWW Consortium, n.d.a) includes date and time of access, referring URL (including host IP and page) and browser accessing the page. (It is possible for one browser such as Konqueror to pretend to be another such as IE, but this is usually to cope with badly designed browser-specific sites, and this practice should be decreasing.). Other Web servers may need to have their log formats adjusted to give appropriate data.

Analysis of logs must distinguish between valid users, i.e., those who are searching for or using the courseware, and between spiders trawling pages for search engines or other uses. This task may be simplified in general if the site is private or otherwise unknown to spiders. In our case, it is even simpler: spiders will not generate events, so by only looking at the event entries, we automatically exclude spiders!

The Ajax events measure what is generated in the browser. They are not filtered by intermediate proxies nor hidden by pressing the Back button in a browser. In addition, the events are generated in any browser which understands JavaScript events, which is the majority of browsers nowadays. This mechanism does not require custom-built browsers.

BROWSER INDENTIFICATION

In an ideal world, it should not matter which browser is used in creating the Ajax-augmented server logs. Unfortunately, Tables One and Two show that browsers still have differences in behav-

iour. In order to properly interpret the logs, it is still necessary to identify the browser generating the Ajax events.

Each browser (or more properly, each HTTP user agent) should send a string in each HTTP request giving the value of the USER-AGENT field (Fielding, Gettys, Mogul, Frystyk, & Berners-Lee, 2008). Identifying the browser from this is arcane, largely due to history: Netscape pretended to be Mozilla, Internet Explorer (IE) pretended to be Netscape, and then browsers pretended to be IE (Zakas, n.d.). A searchable list is maintained at (Staeding, n.d.).

PRIVACY

Capturing and manipulating user activities raises issues of privacy. Just using server legs or these Ajax extensions does not impinge directly on user privacy: no user identification is performed, and since any particular student may use a variety of IP addresses (home address, cafe hot-spot, DHCP-assigned address in the Institution network or logged in to a random computer), there is little opportunity for identifying any particular user through these logs.

It is becoming common, however, to only access to courseware through a Content Management Systems (CMS) such as Blackboard (Blackboard Inc., n.d.) or Moodle (Moodle Trust, n.d.). These generally require login to access the courseware, and maintain a session that tracks all activity. Generally this is restricted to navigation within the CMS, and as long as the courseware does not contain internal links invisible to the CMS, is able to track page visits and thus is able to give per user statistics on page visit activity.

There is a reasonable likelihood that this CMS page visit log data can be combined with the Ajax-extended server logs to link the focus activity to particular users. Further, if these techniques were adopted by a CMS, then it could make such activity part of the normal user activity log.

As long as the activity recorded is used for academic purposes only, then this should not be a serious issue. However, if it were to be used for other purposes such as showing whether or not an international student was serious in their study activity, then it may be more contentious.

COURSEWARE IN OTHER FORMATS

The techniques described in this paper use the Web formats of HTML, XHTML and XML. Many courseware designers make use of other formats such as PowerPoint or Flash. These formats are "web unfriendly" in that they do not directly follow any of the W3C content standards. In particular, they do not generate DOM events and thus use of these formats cannot be tracked directly using the techniques of this paper.

Flash files can make use of the Flex programming language (Adobe Systems, n.d.). Flex has an event handling model similar to the DOM model: "The Flex event model is based on the Document Object Model (DOM) Level 3 events model. Although Flex does not adhere specifically to the DOM standard, the implementations are very similar." In addition, a Flex application can communicate with JavaScript within its HTML "wrappper". Alternatively, it can use the HTTPService component to communicate directly back to an HTTP server. Thus it should be possible to adapt Flash pages to the concepts of the technology given here.

An alternative to Flash may be the forthcoming HTML 5, which will allow direct use of these techniques in multimedia pages using the W3C standards.

Powerpoint 2000 supports events as well and can call VBA scripts (Rindsberg, n.d.). Already, HTML 4, the DOM model and JavaScript are adequate to replace any use of PowerPoint, so although it may be possible to duplicate these techniques, it may not be necessary.

LIMITATIONS

In the introduction a scenario was posed whereby a user switched from web browsing to using Skype. Whereas the technology described here can detect loss of focus from the browser, it cannot detect that the application switched to was Skype. To do so would require far more invasive techniques than are currently available (or even desirable?).

Results

The subject ICT213 *Multi-user Operating Systems Administration* is a second year subject taught in the Bachelor of Computer Systems (Networking) at Box Hill Institute. In 2010 semester one it was a small class, of only seven students. Logs were kept over a three-week period, and no attempt was made to identify the students. The small size of this group means that results are indicative rather than statistically valid.

The structure of the courseware is that each "lecture" consists of one or two web pages. JavaScript is used so that the lecturer can display the pages in "slide mode" similar to PowerPoint, while the students usually view the pages as single documents. Other structures for courseware are of course possible, such as multiple linked small pages, and such a structure would produce different results.

The students over the logged period loaded courseware pages 40 times. The average load time was 1014 seconds, or about 16 minutes. By contrast, the students focused on pages 349 times. Many of these focus times were very short, less than 3 seconds, and may correspond to clicking on a page just to navigate away from it. Excluding these times, the students focused on the pages 179 times, so that each loaded page was gained and lost the focus on average 4.5 times. The average focus time was a mere 116 seconds, less than 2 minutes!

It is clear that the attention span of this group of students is very low. It should be noted that the logs were kept on the expository material only, and no significant assessment was carried out during this period. While one may expect higher use during assessment periods, these logs will actually provide a means of testing any such assertion.

CONCLUSION

This paper has demonstrated a technique based on Ajax for gaining more information about student interaction with courseware. While the current implementation deals only with documents in HTML, XHTML and XML formats, it should be possible to extend it to deal with non-W3C formats such as Flash and PowerPoint. More interesting would be extensions to deal with the expected multimedia components of HTML 5.

The technique presented was essentially standalone. However, it should be straightforward to use this within existing Content Management Systems such as Blackboard and Moodle to give them more sophisticated reporting capabilities on user activities.

The use of virtual machines is not yet very widespread among the user community, although it is likely to spread to some extent. There is not yet a defined model of event interaction between virtual machines and their guest operating systems, and this gap needs to be filled.

REFERENCES

Adobe Systems. (n.d.). *Adobe flex 3 developer guide*. Retrieved from http://www.faqs.org/rfcs/rfc2068.html

Almaer, D., & Galbraith, B. (n.d.). *Robot replay: Watch your users via ajax*. Retrieved from http://ajaxian.com/archives/ robot-replay-watch-your-users-via-ajax

Blackboard Inc. (n.d.). *Blackboard*. Retrieved from http://www.blackboard.com/

Chapman, S. (n.d.). *Using window.onload*. Retrieved from http://javascript.about.com/library/blonload.htm

Crazy Egg. (n.d.). *See where people click: Visualise the user experience on your website*. Retrieved from http://crazyegg.com/

Edmonds, A. (2003). A new tool for web usability testing. In *Proceedings of Behavior Research Methods, Instruments and Computers*. Uzilla.

Fielding, R., Gettys, J., Mogul, J., Frystyk, H., & Berners-Lee, T. (2008). *Rfc2068 -hypertext transfer protocol*. Retrieved from http://www.faqs.org/rfcs/rfc2068.html

Holdener, A. T. (2008). *Ajax: The Definitive Guide*. New York: O'Reilly.

Moodle Trust. (n.d.). *Moodle*. Retrieved from http://moodle.org/

Rindsberg, S. (n.d.). *Make your vba code in powerpoint respond to events*. Retrieved from http://www.pptfaq.com/FAQ00004.htm

Schluting, C. (n.d.). *Analyzing web server logs*. Retrieved from http://www.serverwatch.com/tutorials/article.php/3518061/Analyzing-Web-Server-Logs.htm.

Staeding, A. (n.d.). *List of user-agents (spiders, robots, crawler, browser)*. Retrieved from http://user-agents.org

Sun MicroSystems. (n.d.). *Virtualbox*. Retrieved from http://www.virtualbox.org/

Velayathan, G., & Yamada, S. (2006). Behavior-based web page evaluation. In *Proceedings of the Web Intelligence and Intelligent Agent Technology Workshops*.

WWW Consortium. (n.d.a). *Common* logfile format. Retrieved from http://www.w3.org/Daemon/User/Config/Logging.html#common-logfile-format

WWW Consortium. (n.d.b). *Document object model (dom) level 2 events* specification. Retrieved from http://www.w3.org/TR/2000/ REC-DOM-Level-2-Events-20001113/

WWW Consortium. (n.d.c). *A vocabulary and associated apis for html and xhtml*. Retrieved from http://dev.w3.org/html5/spec/Overview.html

Zakas, N. C. (n.d.). History of the user-agent string. Retrieved from http://www.nczonline.net/blog/2010/01/12/history-of-the-user-agent-string/

APPENDIX

Table 1. Browser behaviour for browser events

User action	Firefox 3.0	IE6/IE7/IE8	Opera 10	Chrome beta
New page loaded (from link, url, bookmark)	load focus	load focus	load	load
Focus away to another tab pane	none (error) (Firefox 3.5: blur)	blur (IE6: N/A)	blur	blur
Focus from another tab pane	focus	focus	focus	focus
Open link in same pane	unload	unload	unload	none (error)
Open link in new window	none (error)	unload	blur	blur
Open link in new tab pane	none, but no focus change	blur but no focus change (error)	blur	none, but no focus change
Browser is closed	unload	unload	none (error)	unload
Tab pane is closed	unload	unload	none (error)	unload
Back Button to another page	none	unload	none (error)	none (error)
Back Button to this page	load focus	load focus	none (errr)	none (error)
Forward button to another page	unload	unload	none (error)	none (error)
Forward button to this page	load focus	load focus	none (error)	none (error)

Table 2. Browser behaviour for system events

User action	Firefox 3.0	IE6/IE7/IE8	Opera 10	Chrome beta
Focus away to another application	blur	blur	blur	blur
Focus away to another browser window	blur	blur	blur	none (error)
Focus away to another desktop (Linux)	blur	N/A	none (error)	none (error)
Focus from another application	focus	focus	focus	focus (Linux) none (error) (Windows 7)
Focus from another browser window	focus	focus	focus	focus
Focus from another desktop (Linux)	focus	N/A	focus	none (error)
Window is closed	blur unload	unload	none (error)	unload
Iconify	blur	blur	blur	blur
De-iconify	focus	focus	focus	focus
Computer hibernates	blur focus blur	blur	none (error)	?
Restore from hibernation	focus blur focus	?	?	?

Chapter 11
How Thick Is Your Client?

Ed Young
Victoria University, Australia

Michael Jessopp
Object Consulting, Australia

ABSTRACT

Average Revenue Per User (ARPU) is a measure of the revenue generated by users of a particular business service. It is a term most commonly used by consumer communications and networking businesses. For mobile devices, they generate ARPU through network and content services (value-added services) that they make accessible to the user. The more accessible these services are the greater the ARPU generated. The harder something is to find, the less likely someone is to use it. This paper explores the potential continuum between ARPU and service discoverability for mobile services by comparing and contrasting various technologies with respect to development, user experience, security, and commercialisation.

INTRODUCTION

Average Revenue Per User (ARPU) is a measure of the revenue generated by Users of a particular business service. It is a term most commonly used by consumer communications and networking businesses. For mobile devices, they try to generate ARPU through network and content services (value-added services) that they make accessible to the User. It seems that the more accessible these services are, the greater the ARPU

generated - the harder something is to find, the less likely someone is to use it.

Therefore, a Continuum appears to exist between ARPU and accessibility.

This is by no means the only factor that affects ARPU, for instance usability for instance plays a large major role in retaining Users and sustaining ARPU.

The problem appears to be that the more accessible services are the more closely integrated with the mobile device they have to be. The tighter this integration is, the more complicated and costly it becomes to implement.

DOI: 10.4018/978-1-4666-0336-3.ch011

A common method for integration is a 'client' where a locally device-hosted piece of software delivers a service from over a network to the User. Clients vary in 'thickness'. Client thickness is often measured in terms of the size of their resource footprint on the host - the greater the footprint, the thicker the client. Commonly, the thicker a client is, the better able it is to integrate with local functions, the more capable it is of local processing and interaction, and ultimately, the better it is at exposing services to a User through a mobile device.

Moreover then, there appears to be a Continuum between ARPU and client thickness.

This begs the question, how thick is your client? The answer to this question is more often than not, a business one. The thicker a client is, the more expensive it tends to be to develop and maintain. While not directly a factor in ARPU, this expense would have to be offset against ARPU to justify a Business Case.

Significant technologies that constitute this Continuum include:

- Mobile Browser;
- Browser Plug-In;
- Web Portal;
- On Device Portal (ODP);
- Thick Client;
- Widget and App Store.;
- The Idle Screen.

This paper compares and contrasts these technologies for service discovery by considering each with respect to:

- Development;
- User Experience;
- Security;
- Commercialisation.

MOBILE BROWSER

Browsers are the thinnest of clients. The Mobile Browser (Figure 1) is much like its larger brethren, albeit a cut down version specifically engineered to operate within the constraints of its environment - limited memory, Central Processor Unit (CPU), network connectivity, and storage. They are native to the device as standard and require no Operator or service provider intervention with the Original Equipment Manufacturer (OEM).

As device capabilities have increased over time, mobile browsers have kept pace and have increased their capabilities by taking advantage of the increased memory, CPU and storage offered by the handset. This has allowed modern Mobile Browsers to support newer rendering technologies (Extensible Hypertext Markup Language (XHTML), Cascading Style Sheets (CSS), JavaScript), and provide a better experience. Native browsers, such as Safari and the Palm WebOS browser, also offer deeper integration with the device and expose some of the device capabilities, such as accelermoter to mobile web applications.

Despite sharing a common 'client', mobile web applications are notoriously difficult to develop. The mobile web developer has to keep front of mind the numerous restrictions that the mobile device presents - limited screen real estate, input and navigation controls (Young, 2009a). Integration with technology such as Wireless Universal Resource File (WURFL), can exploit the unique

Figure 1. Mobile Browser

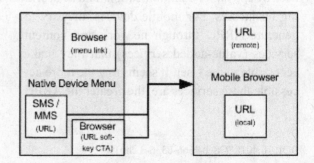

capabilities of each device. Some platforms such as WebOS and the iPhone OS provide a Mobile Browser that offers deeper integration into the device, such as the recent addition of Geo-location to Safari 3.0. There are advantages for development of purely browser based applications; centralised content - change once and is available everywhere.

Whilst providing increasing universal access via the use of standard web technologies, Mobile Browser based applications do suffer from poor discoverability. Users must first know the location (Universal Resource Locator (URL)) of the application in question, and then attempt to enter the URL into the browser to navigate to the application. Entering URL's on mobile devices is notoriously difficult; the vast majority of handsets do not have a physical keyboard, and even for those that do, the use of the ':' and

'/' characters make input laborious and device dependant. There have been various attempts to make this experience easier for handset Users; through the ability to bookmark URL's via the browser; sending an Short Message Service (SMS) with an embedded URL, or reducing the length of the application URL, through Top-Level Domain (TLD) such as.mobi. Applications provided by carriers can be pre-provisioned as out-of-the-box bookmarks in the browser, links on carriers' mobile portals, or links via on device portals. Telcos try to direct consumers towards their services by providing links from device menus and soft-keys to firm-coded URL's (server proxy).

Mobile browser based application have typically suffered from poor User experience. Previous incarnations of rendering technologies (Wireless Markup Language (WML), i-mode) delivered a poor visual experience, whilst the form factor of handsets made text input and scrolling arduous. Applications tended to be simple in functionality, to cope with the statelessness of the protocols used, poor battery life, and the vagaries of wireless connectivity. Indeed, network connectivity is a difficult issue to resolve - without a network connection, it's not even possible to provide the

application consumer with evergreen content. Representation of state of the service is accurate at the time of the response to original request. Only and stale if the User does not refresh. No evergreen contingency or network outage tolerant. And not all Operator networks are created equal, so it is not possible to assume connectivity on a per handset basis. Though very similar to the old days of web browsers but with far more implementation diversity, mobile devices do not suit the fixed model.

Jorstad and Dustdar (Ivar Jorstad & Dustdar, n.d.) discuss the issues and technologies used to profile devices over a network.

While there is no real device integration beyond loading Multipurpose Internet Mail Extensions (MIME) types handled by the browser, this does ensure a sandbox secured that restricts applications from potentially un-authorised access to resources and information. Further content processing - installing ring-tones, games - is at the mercy of the device handlers.

While most people view mobile web applications as free, they do often come with a hidden price tag - they consume data. Unless agreement has been reached with a carrier, the data associated with the application is charged to the customer. While undeniably a simple model, it is not without its challenges. Most consumers do not understand the quantity, or price point of a KiloByte (KB). Indeed, the price point of a KB actually depends on the charging model for the data - be it 'pay as you go', bundled, data pack, or unlimited. Sam (2008) provides and interesting insight into the SMS pricing model with some extraordinary conclusions.

The introduction of 3G networks, coupled with increased consumer demand for smarter handsets, is rapidly changing the mobile application landscape.

Some other considerations for browser based applications included:

- Information always has to be request - never pushed to the device except via SMS/MMS;
- Lowest amount of client-side processing for resource constrained devices - just render;
- Limited persistence and customisation - the only real way to store information about the Users is through cookies. Their capacity to store information is limited and not always permitted.

Web Browser sits on the far left of our Continuum. They are the thinnest and also the least discoverable of mobile network service access technologies.

MOBILE BROWSER PLUG-IN

Browser Plug-in clients (Figure 2) extend Mobile Browser clients with the judicious use of technologies such as JavaScript and Adobe Flash Lite. These technologies extend the capabilities of the browser and permit greater interaction with the native device functions. They act as extensions to the browser capabilities. With these extensions come increased security problems because plug-ins has access to more local resources as they are installed directly on the device.

Each plug-in requires explicit installation before its functions can be addressed by a browser 'extended' application. This is usually free to

the User. While the installation is only required once, it means that there is an initial delay when accessing services. There is an increase in Client-side processing since there are more functions hosted on the device but this generally means that User interaction is more responsive and richer. There are some examples of plug-in technologies used to control the complete device; Flash for instance.

There is little support for this style of development, due to fragmented support for these technologies across the spectrum of devices, which complicates significantly the development, deployment and support of such clients.

While offering a much richer User experience than 'vanilla' Mobile Browser clients, the client still suffers from the discoverability issues inherent in Mobile Browser based solutions. So, while further to the right of Mobile Browsers on our continuum because of the increased native function integration and full device interface usage, plug-ins do not necessarily offer a great deal in the way of discoverability over them.

WEB PORTAL

Web Portals are a unified and uniform view of services. Portals are composed of portlets that represent a services' state.

Web Portals do not address the issues of mobile device service discoverability directly. Entirely browser-based, they are afflicted by the

Figure 2. Mobile browser plug-in

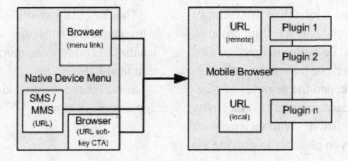

Figure 3. Web portal

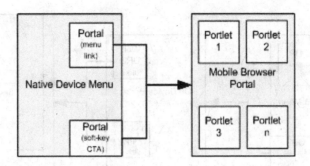

same limitations as any browser-based mobile application (see Web Browser) and benefit from the advantages.

Once the User has accessed the Portal entry point (perhaps via a native menu link or soft-key) (Figure 3), they are able to choose the services they wish to engage with. This is a similar approach to an application store without the need to download complex client-side applications.

Benefiting from much larger screen sizes, richer plug-in technologies and Web 2.0 innovations, Web Portals perform well for static browsers allowing Users to customise, choose and arrange the information they want (or are permitted to have). The principle of permitting Users to amalgamate small pertinent service representations to suit their requirements is what is appealing in the context of this discussion. Mobile Portal presentation is nowhere near as mature as static but with the rapid development of mobile browser plug-ins and better browser to device integration, mobile portals have a bright future. Potentially, the native phone menu could be implemented as a Web Portal with services available both locally and remotely, and collaborated as the User requires. The point of discovery starts at the web browser.

Web Portals move the POO (Point Of Orchestration) to the client. Usually, services are orchestrated and amalgamated at the server and then delivered to the client just for rendering. Web Portals allow the orchestration decision to take place to an extent 'at the glass'.

See Young (2009) for a further discussion and Haenel (2004) for a discussion on Multi-Device Portals.

Web Portals do not present any advantage over other browser based applications in terms of discoverability for mobile devices. They do not offer a richer User experience or greater integration with native functions offered by Web Browser Plug-Ins. However, the flexibility they offer the User to control the services and information they want facilitates a level of customisation and choice prevalent in thicker client technologies discussed later. Therefore then, the Web Portals principle takes its place after Web Browser Plug-Ins on the Continuum.

Mobile Portals are a potential solution to bringing the enterprise to mobile Users (Young, 2009a).

ON DEVICE PORTAL (ODP)

Positioned somewhere between thick client and web on the Continuum, an On Device Portals (ODP) is a mechanism for surfacing network functions to Users and directing them towards specific services. A service surfacing layer, if you will, on the mobile device.

ODP implementations (Figure 4) usually take one of the following forms:

1. Replacement for the native device menu;
2. Accessed as a secondary menu from the native device's main menu;

Figure 4. On-Device Portal

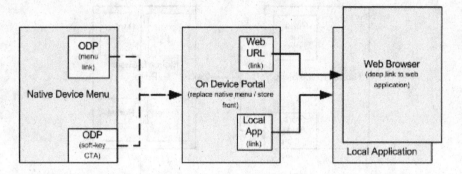

3. Via a pre-configured soft-key Call to Action (CTA);
4. As a 'store front' application;
5. Downloaded by the User from a service vendor and accessed as any other application.

Implemented client-side with little or no direct device integration, ODP's are usually stand-alone applications that launch with the device and are accessed as a secondary menu from the device's native main menu usually by a pre-configured soft-key Call To Action (CTA) or downloaded by the User from a specific service vendor as a launching point to their services.

ODP's often resemble the native device menu (or replace it) and launch web applications and 'deep-links' through the native browser and sometimes, local native or proprietary applications in some cases. The User is not required to recall or enter long and error-prone URL's to access information and services. This allows the ODP provider to prescribe the URL's to direct Users to their monetary services, in this case, referred to as a 'Store Front'.

ODP's bring the discovery of services to the fore requiring very few User actions (or 'clicks' or CTA's) before a service is accessed. The User is not usually permitted any choice regarding which services are promoted, though ODP's often vary between User segment targeted mobile devices. If an ODP is downloaded from a provider, discovery is not as easy since downloaded applications can be difficult to find in many layers of native menus. However, there is additional complexity if the ODP is to be pre-installed and further commitment from Original Equipment Manufacturers (OEM)'s is required. The User experiences a rich initial client-side experience with a stateful, responsive interface. Links from the ODP to web applications can often be disappointing as the transfer of control to the native web browser can be disjointed and the final web application does not provide as rich an experience as the ODP menus. Sometimes this transition is not clear and can cause confusion over the cost of the service; the ODP is free and then the web experience is potentially not. To counter this, warning notifications are sometimes used about potential costs that tend to further decrease the quality of the User experience. Transition from the web browser back to the ODP is often not clear and can often confuse the User giving the impression of a navigational 'dead-end'.

Since they don't require close integration with the native device's functions, ODP deployment can be easier than a truly integrated client. Over The Air (OTA) updates of the ODP are often possible so that the menu can be re-branded or changed to publicise a new service or campaign (and fix faults). This requires that the client have permissions to access the network exposing the device to a limited security threat as the client does not have extensive access to potentially sensitive User data.

All clients have the potential to become 'orphaned' should a defect occur that prevents the client from gaining access to the network and receiving software updates. Correction of this type of defect can be highly disruptive and potentially commercially damaging to the device supplier and network operator. Mobile device Original Equipment Manufacturers (OEM's) are often reluctant to incorporate third-party applications into their device firmware releases as they introduce a complexity and consequent, increased potential for malfunction while not offering them any benefit; ARPU is only usually a concern for network operators.

The motivation behind ODP is to provide the discoverability and richness of experience of a device integrated client with the centralised development and maintenance benefits of web. Accordingly, the approach suffers the short comings of both but to a lesser degree than either one alone; client integration and maintenance is costly and difficult, while mobile web application experiences are cumbersome. This approach requires that a software vendor be proficient at both client and web development across multiple devices.

ODP is not a distinct technology but an approach through the amalgamation of two others. The term ODP coined by ARCchart Research in 2001, is a little pretentious in this context and seems potentially contrived so that the mobile community could congratulate themselves with

another best 'x of y' award but the concept is still deserving of its place on the Continuum.

THICK CLIENT

Thick Clients (Figure 5) follow the basic model of Personal Computer (PC) based applications; applications are typically developed for a single platform, using platform specific Software Development Kit (SDK)'s and Application Programming Interface (API)'s, and offer a User experience on par with the underlying platform. Such applications also benefit from having superior access to the underlying device capabilities, as provided by the platform.

Thick Clients for mobile device have been around for many years, on mobile platforms such as Palm OS, Microsoft Windows Mobile and Symbian. Thick Clients suffer from many problems that have plagued the PC based application markets. Developers must be aware of different hardware, firmware (device driver), and Operating Systems versions (and combinations thereof). Use of platform SDK's, API's and technology stacks makes supporting multiple platforms significantly more challenging.

It should be noted that Java based applications attempt to solve many of the problems associated with proprietary technology stacks. Conventional wisdom is that Java based clients are a 'write once,

Figure 5. Thick client

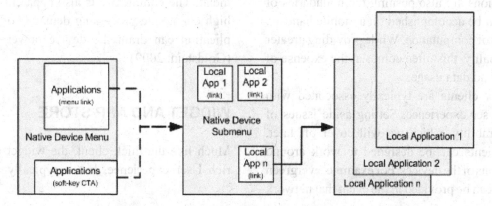

run everywhere' model - which is simultaneously correct and incorrect, hence the phrase, 'write once, test everywhere'. Further complicating use of Java base clients, is the differing support for various Java Specification Request (JSR)'s, and runtime versions.

The deployment model for mobile devices is significantly different from the PC based model. Typically, clients deployed on the various mobile platforms must be digitally signed, either by the handset manufacturer (e.g. Nokia), Platform provider (Symbian) or carrier. This process adds significant overhead to the deployment of Thick Clients, and can even act as a barrier for smaller developers. While true that these client don't have to be signed, the User experience for unsigned clients is extremely poor – during the installation process Users can experience various prompts seeking confirmation at all stages.

Thick clients also increase the potential attack surface, in particular because of their tighter integration with the device. Modern platforms typically run clients in a sandbox to mitigate this risk. Other platforms rely on extensive testing before signing clients, although there have been occurrences where malicious clients have passed the rigorous testing and been deployed.

Thick clients, much like PC applications, become to push the boundaries of complexity, and introduce configuration options that can confuse Users. General Users can't configure Access Point Node (APN)'s or POP3 as these are considered too technical. As well as increasing complexity, applications are also pushing the boundaries of what can be accomplished on a mobile handset, in terms of computation. While providing greater functionality, this often comes at the expense of battery and data usage.

Thick clients are typically associated with better User experience. Setting aside issues of discoverability, which we will cover off later, thick clients can be designed to work around limitations of the devices. For example, evergreen content can be provided in the event that network

connectivity is not available. Clients can cache content so that they can continue to work offline. And they can take advantage of device orientation to render content appropriately (Capra, Emmerich, & Mascolo, n.d.).

Despite the many advantages that thick clients offer, Telcos are finding it hard to manage the myriad of device vendors and application vendors. It seems that governance in this area is in its infancy; compounded by the desire of the Telcos to provide additional applications out of the box. OEM's often fear that Telco applications will adversely affect their devices by giving the impression that a pre-installed application was developed and supported by them. Commercially, there is very little for the OEM's except potentially increased deployment complexity particularly if the Clients are pre-installed. Client vendors are often very immature organisations parasitic to the larger Telcos for survival. This makes the whole production life-cycle precarious.

Another issues, related to governance, is managing the ongoing updates to clients. Typically, each application manages the update process itself, while platforms such as the iPhone OS providing this facility natively. In any case, governance over updates, including testing, is becoming onerous. Updates can be 'pushed' and 'pulled'.

Because of the very close integration with the device, Thick Clients are often highly surfaced and easy to discover, and consequently, on the far right of our Continuum. They often represent a complete interface layer or high level native menu. The complexity is also apparent and the high client-side processing demands of the application can drain the device power quickly (Goldstein, 2009).

WIDGET AND APP STORE

Much like the thick client, the widget offers a rich User experience, but is typically focused on a specific task, game, or complement a web based experience.

The Widget and App Store model (Figure 6) attempts to resolve the issue of discoverability experienced with Thick Clients. Clients are included in a catalogue, and are purchased and installed by the User on demand. This is extremely empowering to the User in much the same way as Web Portals. The User is able to decide what they want to use on the device without it being dictated to. Often there are default widgets or apps that encourage the User to use certain services provided by the OEM or Operator.

Despite the meteoritic rise of the App Store model on specific high end platforms, it should be noted that the model is still in its infancy, and there are many issues with the model that require attention. Discoverability is becoming harder in a significantly crowded marketplace – indeed the marketplace itself is experiencing growing pains, with shop-fronts struggling with how to validate and authorise, catalogue, promote, and manage the vast array of clients available. It can be argued that an App Store is simply a containing Thick Client and hence, suffers from the same short-comings discussed in regard to them. The container permits control and security regulation of the applications delivered through it.

Developers, typically those new to mobile development, are becoming to appreciate the complexities of developing clients for mobile devices.

Figure 6. Widget and app store

The Apple iPhone, for example, in such a short time span, already has three unique hardware profiles (2G, 3G, and 3GS, and not including the iPod touch which shares the same base OS). And clients developed on the iPhone are not platform independent, and therefore must undergo significant redevelopment to target additional mobile platforms such as Windows Mobile, Palm WebOS and Android.

There is currently much consideration for Enterprise Applications available via App Store. Lune, (2009) explores the viability of these applications to enable the mobile enterprise (Young, 2009a).

The ultimate current level of surfacing and consequently, discoverability is achieved though the utilisation of the Idle Screen device real estate (Figure 7). Thick Client applications, application stores and widgets are made accessible through the default entry screen of the device. This approach requires very close integration with the device, introduces the complexity of the Thick Client, Widget and App Store technologies with an even less flexible and immature integration surface location. Updates and information available through these applications is available without the User interacting with the device at all - zero-click away. This high level surfacing combined with the client-technologies occupies the furthest right-hand side of our Continuum.

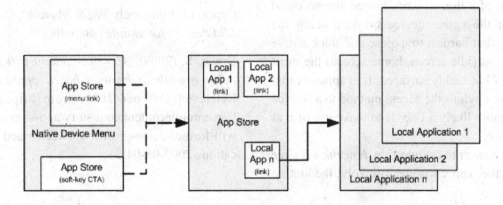

Figure 7. Idle screen

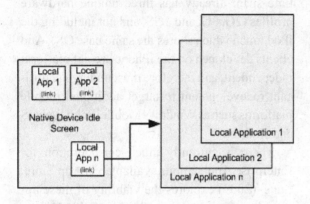

CONCLUSION

Exposing a network service to the greatest number of Users increases the potential for ARPU generation. That is not to say that all services should be blanketly disseminated and not targeted towards appropriate Users but that a User should have the best chance of being able to consume a service with the equipment they have. The vast, fluid range of different devices varying in Operating Systems (OS), versions and capabilities, makes catering for them all extremely challenging. A 'lowest common denominator' approach is relatively simple but sells short Users of more capable equipment while close device integration provides superior User experience but alienates the vast majority of the market and is high maintenance and complex.

From this discussion, it seems clear that increasing discoverability of services often involves more complex device integration efforts with the creation of a thin network hosted site accessed through the native device browser being the simplest but hardest to expose and thick native integration (idle screen, home screen) the most complex but highly surfaced. It is apparent that the more obvious the access method to a service is, the more likely a User is to make use of it at least once.

The answer to the question, *how thick is your client?,* then appears to ideally involve facilitating the best User access possible to network services on a device-by-device basis. Not only that but offer the User the choice of all possible access mechanisms (web, plug-in, portal, client) supported by their device; 'horses for courses' as it were. The consideration then is what the Business can financially justify to support this approach.

FURTHER RESEARCH

The technology for mobile devices is evolving rapidly. It is following a well-worn path described primarily by static Internet technologies. However, it lacks the (potentially oxymoronic) standardised freedom of the Internet. Device manufacturers typically control access to the device's functions through a closed OS (though this is changing) and vet client applications through their prescribed delivery channels. Perhaps the victor here is not going to be a technology but a manufacturer. It is common for Users to define their preferences for mobile devices by manufacturer way above all else. Would a stalwart device manufacturer devotee User deviate from their preference if the OS was changed? Perhaps it is a big enough market to go round.

Two areas of some discussion are Enterprise Applications for mobile devices (Drake, 2009) and Mobile Virtualization (VMWare, 2009).

REFERENCES

Capra, L., Emmerich, W., & Mascolo, C. (n.d.). *Middleware for mobile computing.*

Drake, S. (2009). *App store mania will further delay growth of browser-based applications.* Retrieved October 2009, from http://www. fiercemobilecontent.com/story/app-store-mania-will-further-delay-growth-browser-based-applications/2009-08-04

Goldstein, P. (2009). *Handset requirements outpacing battery life.* Retrieved October 2009, from http://www.fiercewireless.com/story/report-handset-requirements-outpacing-battery-life/2009-09-29

Haenel, W. (2004). Multi Device Portals (Multi Device Portals). *it - Information Technology, 46*(5), 245-254.

Ivar Jorstad, D. V. T., & Dustdar, S. (n.d.). *Personalisation of next generation mobile services.*

Luna, L. (2009). *Finally, a mobile enterprise app store.* Retrieved October 2009, from http://www.fiercemobileit.com/story/finally-mobile-enterprise-app-store/2009-09-16

Sam. (2008). *COST OF SMS v Cost of ISP analysis.* Retrieved October 2009, from http://gthing.net/the-true-price-of-sms-messages/

VMWare. (2009). *VMWare Mobile Virtualization Platform (MVP).* Retrieved November 2009, from http://www.vmware.com/technology/mobile/

Young, A. E. (2009). Service Oriented Architecture Conceptual Landscape PART II. *International Journal of Web Portals* 3.

Young, A. E. (2009a). Mobilising the Enterprise. *International Journal of Web Portals, , 6.*

This work was previously published in the International Journal of Web Portals 2(2), edited by Greg Adamson and Jana Polgar, pp. 1-11, copyright 2010 by Information Science Publishing (an imprint of IGI Global).

Chapter 12
An Integration Ontology for Components Composition

Sofien Khemakhem
CNRS and University of Toulouse, France, & University of Sfax, Tunisia

Khalil Drira
CNRS and University of Toulouse, France

Mohamed Jmaiel
University of Sfax, Tunisia

ABSTRACT

Software components composition can improve the efficiency of knowledge management by composing individual components together for complex distributed application. There are two main areas of research in knowledge representation for component composition: the syntactic based approach and the semantic-based approach. In this paper, the authors propose an integrated ontology-supported software component composition. The authors' approach provides dual modes to perform component composition. Ontologies are employed to enrich semantics at both components description and composition. The authors demonstrate that their search engine SEC++ fulfills automated component composition, in particular, and knowledge management in general.

1. INTRODUCTION

The development of distributed software based on components composition is becoming increasing important because of its potential to reduce product development cost and time-to-market. The successfulness of the composition is important and depends essentially on two key factors: (1) Knowledge management: components are

knowledge which necessitates a solution for organization, representation and sharing to approve the search and the composition process. This work contributes to the body of knowledge management research by suggesting an ontology-supported and component-oriented approach to organizational knowledge management. We introduce an integrated system for component composition by leveraging the syntactic-based and the semantic-based approaches. The system can support semantic and automated component

DOI: 10.4018/978-1-4666-0336-3.ch012

composition effectively. (2) QoS-based optimization of component composition: component composition creates new functionalities by aggregating different components. When two or more functional-qualified components are available, they can form different combinations. These combinations deliver the same functionality, but they differ from each other in QoS performance. Obviously, component requesters should be able to select the optimal component set without trying all possible combinations.

Current component-based approaches concentrate mainly on functional properties, and ignore component non-functional ones, which are crucial in many application domains. Few examples of quality parameters are: dependability, reliability, availability. In a component-based approach, it is relatively easy to glue components together to provide the desired system.

This paper is organized as follows: section 2, section 3 and section 4 present respectively the related work, the discovery and the integration ontology and the ontology-supported component composition. We will devote section 5 to describe the shared ontology. Section 6 presents the implementation. In conclusion, we will suggest some openings and prospects related to this study.

2. RELATED WORK

Component composition is to construct higher-level components based on existing multiple individual ones in order to fulfill more sophisticated business requirements. An example of components composition is generating a comprehensive conference travel plan, including conference registration, flight ticket booking, hotel reservation, car rental, map request, and so forth, from existing components. Depending on whether a composition decision is made at design time or at run-time, it falls into either static or dynamic composition, respectively (Cardoso, Busslerand, Shethand, & Fensel, 2002). From a process standpoint, com-

ponent composition can be done horizontally, vertically, or both. The aforementioned example belongs to vertical composition, because hotel booking cannot be carried out until the flight ticket is issued. However, car rental and map request can be performed simultaneously in a horizontal way. Component composition poses challenges from the following multiple aspects along the composition course (Cardoso et al., 2002): (1) description or representation of components; (2) components discovery; (3) integration of individual components; (4) QoS-based optimization of component composition as well as other issues.

The syntactic-based component composition approach already has been used widely in the industry (Agarwal, Chafle, Mittal, & Srivastava, 2008). Although more vocabularies are added for component description, messaging, those constructs are still concerned mainly with document structure or syntax. The component discovery, matching, and integration utilize keyword searching, which has been usually proved ineffective by information retrieval researchers.

The semantic-based component composition addresses the semantics-absent problem of the syntactic-based approach. In the component composition context, the RDF+OWL technology can help component description, advertisement, discovery, integration, interoperation, invocation, execution, and monitoring, which all converge at component composition (Cardoso et al., 2002). In the context of component composition, ontologies can be employed to distill all concerned concepts in a certain domain as a centralized repository, which shows superiority for on-the-fly component choreography by specifying semantic relationships between component terms.

There are four lines of research that are related to this study. The first one centers on architectures for components description and composition. Some researchers have started incorporating ontologies into conceptual modeling and component architecture (Kim, Sengupta, Fox, & Dalkilic, 2007; Loucopoulos & Zicari, 1992). The second line of research aims to map syntactical component description to semantic specifications (Li, Madnick, Zhu, & Fan, 2009; Shen, Yang, & Lalwani, 2004). The third line of related work is concerned with ontology development for software components (Ma, Ma, Liu, & Jin, 2009; Mika, Oberle, Gangemi, & Sabou, 2004). The fourth stream is called compositional modeling (Deokar Amit & El-Gayar Omar, 2008). Their knowledge description framework includes both models' conditions and domain theories, which are analogous to the semantic description scheme and business rules in our proposed framework, respectively.

3. THE DISCOVERY AND THE INTEGRATION ONTOLOGY

We describe the semantics of components to express knowledge about functional and non-functional aspects of a component. This knowledge comprises:

- The structural aspects that specify the component's internal structure. The developer uses these aspects to determine if interaction exists between component operations and other components used to build the current project.
- The functional aspects that identify the functionalities of the component is expected to provide through many features. These features include methods that are used to adapt the behavior of the component to his context. The adaptation is made by specializing and customizing. The other kinds of features are used by the application specific part of component-based software. Generally this type of information is specified by the component's methods.
- The non functional aspect specifies the component constraints related to communication or computation. The non functional aspect includes features such as

performance, availability, reliability, security, adaptability and dependability. We distinguish static and dynamic categories of non functional features. Static features, such as security-related constraints, do not change during component execution. Dynamic features, such as performance-related properties, depend on the deployment environment.

All these features represent different and complementary views of a component. The feature set used to describe a component, depends on the developer action: discovery and integration. The discovery of a component is made by sending a query to the repository manager. Once a set of components has been selected, additional features are specified to select a component before integration. For the discovery action, the query includes functional and/or non functional features. For integration action, the structural features have to be specified.

The underlying approach is based on the following ontologies (see Figure 1):

- The discovery ontology that specifies functional and non functional features.
- The integration ontology that describes the problem solving method (PSMs) used to specify the component's structural features.

As illustrated in Figure 1, the main information contained in constraints, interface and model are respectively the non-functional properties, the functional information (operation names, input, output, precondition and postcondition) and the internal structure of the component. We use RDF language to describe the discovery ontology. One step further, the elements in the discovery ontology link to the corresponding properties in the integration ontology for example, the *interface* concept in the discovery ontology corresponds to *Tasks* concept in the integration ontology.

Figure 1. Discovery and integration ontologies

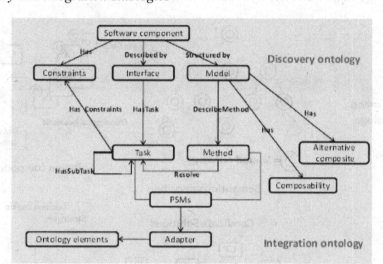

As for the integration ontology, we employ problem solving method (l, 1998) to develop a local ontology for component. In the integration ontology we try to divide the component process into tasks. Tasks are either solved directly (by means of primitive methods), or are decomposed into subtasks (by means of decomposition methods). We use the Unified Problem-Solving Method Language (UPML) (Fensel et al., 2003) to describe the components of PSMs (*task, method and adapter*). Similarly, the component model subclass is especially beneficial for composition. The proposed approach utilizes the component model class in two ways. For base components, a component model keeps information about composability, which specifies when the component can be used in a composite component. For composite components, a component model maintains alternative composite solutions incrementally for reuse. This semantic enrichment provides a self-learning capability of component composition.

4. ONTOLOGY-SUPPORTED COMPONENT COMPOSITION

Our approach foe components composition exploits the advantages of semantic composition approaches, powered by ontologies at both component discovery and integration levels. Building on top of that, we introduce an ontology-based semantic approach. First, the semantic component specification provides a mechanism to enrich atomic components with more semantics than the syntactical method. Second, mapping atomic components and other relevant concepts into a centralized shared ontology offers a knowledge repository for software components. The objective of semantic enhancement is to support ontological heuristics in order to enable automated and dynamic component composition (see Figure 2). When our enhanced search engine SEC++ receives a query from a consumer, it first searches the discovery ontology. Our approach enhances the discovery ontology with a shared ontology. This centralized ontology represents relevant components and concepts in a specific domain, constructed by mapping and integrating individual integration ontologies for software components. Here, the ontological heuristics serves as guidelines to respond to a developer request. After using ontological heuristics on the shared ontology, SEC++ generates a number of alternative solutions to component composition. These alternatives are then evaluated by a deci-

Figure 2. An ontology-supported system for component composition

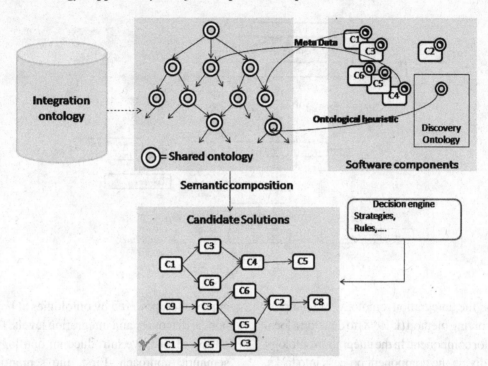

sion engine using a set of criteria specified by the developer. Such criteria may include QoS-based optimization of component composition, business rules and strategies. A selected optimal composition scheme is then executed.

5. SHARED ONTOLOGY

Local integration ontologies are consolidated in a server by ontology mapping and integration. As a result, all relevant concepts and components in a domain are in the shared ontology, local integration ontology for a component is mapped into the shared ontology, appearing as a node in the ontology tree. How to organize all components into the repository depends on domains and application requirements. For example, for calculating Matrix we can maintain semantic relationships (e.g., hierarchical and sibling relationships) between Matrix operations. The shared ontology also represents other application-specific concepts for mapping

and integrating components. The mapping and integration not only unite component descriptions and concepts but also add more semantics.

Moreover, the shared ontology enables ontological heuristics, thus facilitating dynamic component composition. For example, we can study composability of components based on some generic concepts.

As a simple example, when composing component $C2$ calculates the determinant of a real matrix by receiving the output parameters of a component $C1$ that calculates the sum of two matrix which have a natural type. At first glance, these two components cannot be composed. However, the relationship between real and natural is revealed in the type ontology: natural is included in real. The RDF+OWL document shows how OWL uses unionOf vocabulary to represent this relationship. Similarly when composing two components which conducted at different periodical levels: annual and quarterly. These two components cannot be composed if time period is a parameter. However, the

Figure 3. An ontology-supported system for component composition

```
<rdfs:comment>Time Concepts.</rdfs:comment>
</owl:Ontology>
- <rdfs:Class rdf:ID="Year">
    <rdfs:subClassOf rdf:resource="http://www.daml.org/Process#TimePeriod" />
    <rdfs:subClassOf rdf:resource="http://www.daml.org/Process#Sequence" />
  - <owl:subClassOf>
    - <owl:Restriction>
        <owl:onProperty rdf:resource='http://www.daml.org/Process#components' />
      - <owl:toClass>
        - <owl:subClassOf>
          - <owl:unionOf rdf:parseType="owl:collection">
              <rdfs:Class rdfs:about="#FirstQuarter" />
              <rdfs:Class rdfs:about="#SecondQuarter" />
              <rdfs:Class rdfs:about="#ThirdQuarter" />
              <rdfs:Class rdfs:about="#FourthQuarter' />
            </owl:unionOf>
```

relation between annual and quarterly is revealed in the time ontology (see Figure 3).

In an industrial context, a specific team would be responsible for the description of local integration and shared ontologies. This team mainly considers functional features should focus more on the analysis part (e.g., determine the domain and scope of ontologies, and enumerate important terms in ontologies), while the technical part takes charge of the design and implementation (e.g., define classes and class hierarchy, define properties of classes, define facets of the slots, and create instances). The developed ontologies should be reviewed periodically. Our proposed ontology represents an enhanced approach to organizational knowledge management. The shared ontol-

ogy incorporates systematically relevant knowledge into a centralized repository.

6. IMPLEMENTATION

As mentioned before the composability property of the component model class can have values denoting possible ways for component composition. Taking, for illustration, the *binary operation Matrix* component, the inputs to this component include two matrix *M1* and *M2*. The outputs are sum, product and determinant. The inputs and outputs of their composability contains a list of possible parameter flows (from inputs to outputs): *M1* to *determinant*, (*M1* and *M2*) to *product*, *M2*

Figure 4. The search engine SEC and its different version

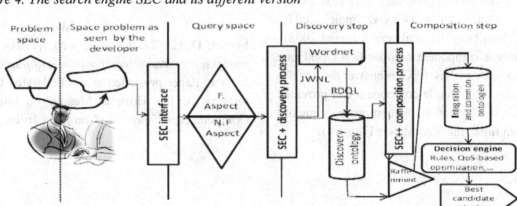

to *determinant* and so forth, each of which can be a part of an alternative path in a composite component. Another way to exploit composability is first to attach composability to other properties with concrete meanings, then associate composability with composition rules. For example, assuming composability is a property Another way to use composability is first to attach composability to other properties with concrete meanings, then associate composability with rules of composition; for example, assuming composability is a property of time. If a component *C1* is time period based, while *C2* is time point based, these two components should not be composed together. As a result, the value of the composability property for the time of *C1* can be ¬timepoint.

All designed local integration ontologies are mapped together following Matrix operation organization, appearing as nodes or subclasses in the shared ontology, as each component described in discovery ontology. After organizing components into a shared knowledge repository, we can add other concepts relevant to Matrix operations, either domain-specific or generic, such as Type and operation. The semantics obtained so far are limited to hierarchical and sibling relationships. Ontological mapping and linkage supplement a richer set of semantics, which can be performed through the value type constrained.

SEC++ is a novel version of SEC (Search Engine for Component based software development) (Khemakhem, Drira, & Jmaiel, 2006) which guaranties the composition step. It is an extension of SEC+ (Khemakhem, Drira, & Jmaiel, 2007; Khemakhem, Drira, Khemakhem, & Jmaiel, 2008) by adding a component composition based on ontological heuristics. SEC++ answer the developer query if no single component can provide all required information, but composing some of them can fulfill the request (see Figure 4).

7. CONCLUSION

In this article, we have proposed an integrated ontology-supported composition system by leveraging both syntactic-based component and semantics-oriented technologies. Our new version search engine has implications for organizational knowledge management. We believe that this integrated ontology- supported software component is an effective approach toward dynamic component composition. The proposed search engine offers an innovative approach to knowledge extraction, representation, organization, conversion, and creation. The employ of ontological heuristics through the shared ontology tree may consume computational resources, in particular when the tree grows very large. More efficient ontology structures and searching algorithms need to be developed. Third, some other approaches to component composition, such as AI planning techniques and workflow technology (Yen, 2008); (Thiagarajan & Stumptner, 2006), might provide other solutions, although they are beyond the scope of the current study.

REFERENCES

Agarwal, V., Chafle, G., Mittal, S., & Srivastava, B. (2008). Understanding approaches for web service composition and execution. In *Compute '08: Proceedings of the 1st Bangalore Annual Compute Conference* (pp. 1–8). New York: ACM.

Cardoso, J., Busslerand, C., Shethand, A., & Fensel, D. (2002). *Semantic web services and processes: Semantic composition and quality of service*. Paper presented at the Federated Conferences on the Move to Meaningful Internet Computing and Ubiquitous Computer, Irvine, CA.

Deokar Amit, V., & El-Gayar Omar, F. (2008). A semantic web services-based architecture for model management systems. In *HICSS '08: Proceedings of the 41st Annual Hawaii International Conference on System Sciences*, Washington, DC: IEEE Computer Society.

Fensel, D. (2003). The unified problem-solving method development language UPML. *Knowledge and Information Systems, 5*(1), 83–131. doi:10.1007/s10115-002-0074-5

Khemakhem, S., Drira, K., & Jmaiel, M. (2006). SEC: A search engine for component based software development. In *SAC '06: Proceedings of the 2006 ACM Symposium on Applied Computing* (pp. 1745–1750). New York: ACM.

Khemakhem, S., Drira, K., & Jmaiel, M. (2007). SEC+: an enhanced search engine for component-based software development. *SIGSOFT Softw. Eng. Notes, 32*(4).

Khemakhem, S., Drira, K., Khemakhem, E., & Jmaiel, M. (2008). An experimental evaluation of SEC+, an enhanced search engine for component-based software development. *SIGSOFT Softw. Eng. Notes, 33*(4), 1–3. doi:10.1145/1384139.1384143

Khemakhem, S., Jmaiel, M., Hamadou, B. A., & Drira, K. (2002, May). *Un environnement de recherche et d'intégration de composant logiciel.* Paper presented at the Seventh Conference on Computer Sciences, Annaba, Algeria.

Kim, H. M., Sengupta, A., Fox, M. S., Dalkilic, M. M. (2007). A measurement ontology generalizable for emerging domain applications on the semantic web. *Database Manag., 18*(1).

Li, X., Madnick, S., Zhu, H., & Fan, Y. (2009). An approach to composing web services with context heterogeneity. In *ICWS '09: Proceedings of the 2009 IEEE International Conference on Web Services* (pp. 695–702). Washington, DC: IEEE Computer Society.

Loucopoulos, P., & Zicari, R. (1992). *Conceptual Modeling, Databases, and Case: An Integrated View of Information Systems Development.* New York: John Wiley & Sons.

Ma, Y., Ma, X., Liu, S., & Jin, B. (2009). A proposal for stable semantic metrics based on evolving ontologies. In *Proceedings of the International Joint Conference on Artificial Intelligence* (pp. 136–139).

Mika, P., Oberle, D., Gangemi, A., & Sabou, M. (2004). Foundations for service ontologies: aligning OWL-S to dolce. In *WWW '04: Proceedings of the 13th International Conference on World Wide Web* (pp. 563–572). New York: ACM.

Shen, J., Yang, Y., & Lalwani, B. (2004). Mapping web services specifications to process ontology: Opportunities and limitations. In *FTDCS '04: Proceedings of the 10th IEEE International Workshop on Future Trends of Distributed Computing Systems* (pp. 229–235). Washington, DC: IEEE Computer Society.

Thiagarajan, R., & Stumptner, M. (2006). A native ontology approach for semantic service descriptions. In *AOW '06: Proceedings of the Second Australasian Workshop on Advances in Ontologies* (pp. 85–90) Darlinghurst, Australia: Australian Computer Society, Inc.

Yen, V. (2008). Business Process and Workflow Modeling in Web Services. In *Electronic Commerce: Concepts, Methodologies, Tools, and Applications* (pp. 202–208). Hershey: Idea Group.

This work was previously published in the International Journal of Web Portals 2(3), edited by Greg Adamson and Jana Polgar, pp. 35-42, copyright 2010 by Information Science Publishing (an imprint of IGI Global).

Chapter 13
The Philosophy of Software Architecture

Amit Goel
RMIT University, Australia

ABSTRACT

Computer Software Intensive systems have become ingrained in our daily life. Apart from obvious scientific and business applications, various embedded devices are empowered with computer software. Such a diverse application of Computer Software has led to inherent complexity in building such systems. As civilizations moved forward, the concept of architectural thinking and practice was introduced to grapple with the complexity and other challenges of creating buildings, skyscrapers, townships, and cities. The Practice of Software Architecture is an attempt to understand and handle similar challenges in Software Intensive Systems. This paper introduces software architecture and the underlying philosophy thereof. This paper provokes a discussion around the present and future of Software Architecture. The authors discuss skills and roles of Software Architect.

INTRODUCTION

The invention of automated machines dates back to seventeenth century. These automated machines were run by mechanical and electrical control mechanisms and performed simple tasks. The advent of electronics based computing machines increased the potential of these machines making them complex. The concept of software has manifested in all forms of computing machines whether mechanical, electrical or electronic, being the lifeline thereof.

As the computer systems became more powerful and smaller in size, their usage diversified from scientific computations to business systems. It wasn't long before they were used to automate various devices such as Phones, Airplanes and Cruise Control Systems in cars. Today most of

DOI: 10.4018/978-1-4666-0336-3.ch013

our devices are embedded with a computer of one kind or another. The diverse usage, heterogeneous systems and structure of computers systems lead to further complexity for software, which has now become the essential part of any computer system, large or small.

In order to manage complexity, a journey of abstractions was observed which passed through machine language (language of 0 and 1), assembly language (language of instructions and mnemonics such as add, load), high level languages the (C, C++, Java) and fourth generation (4GL) or domain specific languages (DSL). From another viewpoint this complexity was being addressed by using concepts such as top-down and bottom-up software development approach. The theory of software design and design patterns was formed during these developments. As the complexity increased, the need was felt to make decisions at much higher levels of abstraction, and to make strategic decisions before making tactical (as in design) or operational decisions (as in code). The theory of Software Architecture started taking shape in order to manage the complexity at higher levels of abstraction and to embed strategic decision making in the building of software systems.

In this paper we explore few fundamental thoughts on software architecture to provoke discussion around some basic questions. We start by discussing the meaning and definition of the term 'Software Architecture' in section 2. We ask "Why do we need to do Software Architecture?" in section 3 and hence outline the rationality for doing the software architecture. Section 4 discusses what skills and qualities are required by a software engineer engaged in the practice of software architecture. Section 5 discusses the software architecture metaphor and how is it similar to or different from art, engineering and science. This section leads us to think whether software architecture is an art, science or engineering or a mix of these. We conclude by providing a summary and future direction.

This paper covers few key issues about philosophy of software architecture in breadth. Hence the discussion is brief. However, we point the reader to various references to dive deeper into details of various concepts presented in this paper.

The Pursuit of Software Architecture

Software architecture is a generally overused term. However, if we ask someone about software architecture generally the conversation is like the one below:

"What is software architecture?"

"The set of decisions an architect makes."

"What are these decisions?"

"The architecturally significant ones"

"Ok. What is architecturally significant?"

"The architect decides".

Kent Beck articulated such situation humorously that "Software architecture is what software architects do and therefore by implication what software architects do is, well, they architect software" (Booch, 2006).

Let us first understand the meaning of word architecture in context of computer software. Software engineering community has a common understanding that architecture enables transformation of requirements to code or working application. Yet another view is that architecture is the glue between Business and IT and closes the Business-IT alignment gap. Hence software architecture is positioned in the middle of requirements/code (Figure 1) or business/IT (Figure 2). We do not deny the importance of architecture in both these roles, but mainly software architecture sits in the middle of strategy and implementation (Figure 3). Strategy is the owner's vision and

Figure 1. Architecture as a transformation between requirements and code

Figure 2. Architecture closing the business IT gap

Figure 3. Architecture lies between strategy and execution

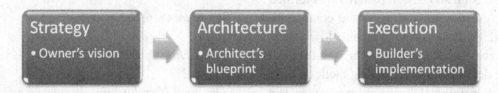

implementation is the execution of strategy. Architecture, positioned in the middle, is architect's blueprint which allows owners to implement or execute their strategy. Positioning architecture in the middle of strategy and execution allows it to scale conceptually from software architecture to enterprise architecture, and relates architecture to important aspects discussed in section one, i.e., strategic decision making and higher levels of abstraction.

We find many definitions of Software Architecture in the literature. Let us have a look at some of them:

- "Software architecture is a set of architectural (or design) elements that have a particular form." (Perry & Wolf, 1992)
- "Software architecture is a collection of computational components—or simply components—together with a description of the interactions between these components—the connectors." (Garlan & Shaw, 1993)
- "Software is an abstract system specification consisting primarily of functional components described in terms of their behaviors and interfaces and component-component interconnections. The interconnections provide means by which components interact. Architectures are usually associated with a rationale that documents and justifies constraints on component and interconnections or explains assumptions about the technologies which will be available for implementing applications consistent with the architecture." (Hayes-Roth, 1994)
- "Software architecture is the structure or structures of the system, which comprise software elements, the externally visible

properties of those elements, and the relationships among them." (Bass et al., 1997; Bass et al., 2003)

Seminal paper written by Perry and Wolf in 1992 is quite important as it laid the foundations for research in software architecture and attempted to put forward a definition of software architecture (Perry & Wolf, 1992). Perry and Wolf defined software architecture as a particular form of design or architectural elements, and this form is defined in terms of properties and relationships among elements. Just one year later, Shaw and Garlan gave the component and connector based definition of software architecture (Garlan & Shaw, 1993). The definition by Bass et al. (1997) adds "externally visible properties" to the existing definitions (Bass et al., 1997; Bass et al., 2003). The externally visible properties reflect the assumptions about services and qualities provided by components in architecture such as performance, security, fault tolerance etc.

A common pattern in these definitions is that software architecture is a description of the system (or software) at a very high level of abstraction which defines the core of the system. The high level abstraction describes the components and their static and dynamic view. Static view describes the interconnection of components to form the structure, and dynamic view describes the interaction of components to form the behavior. The relationship of components or system to the environment is also part of abstraction at architectural level. Many more classical and contributed definitions can be found at the website of Software Engineering Institute of Carnegie Mellon University, located at URL: http://www.sei.cmu.edu/architecture/start/definitions.cfm.

Today we find a commonly adopted definition of software architecture which was earlier released in IEEE standard 1471-2000, titled *"Recommended Practice for Architecture Description of Software-Intensive Systems"*. This standard was also adopted by ISO/IEC and named as ISO/IEC 42010. According to ISO/IEC 42010, "the software architecture is the fundamental organization of a system, embodied in its components, their relationships to each other and the environment, and the principles governing its design and evolution". (ISO/IEC/(IEEE), 2007)

Based on our industry experience, we find that software architecture is the process of thinking about the systems at a strategic level. This strategic level thinking leads a business to benefit either by reducing costs or by increasing profits (or by both). For example by implementing business process system software, the business is able to reduce costs by optimizing its processes, and by using web based shopfront software the business is able to increase sales and profits. Strategic level decision making in software also enables a business to benefit from innovation. For example by introducing iPhone application for Australian Post, the cost may not have reduced, or profits may not have increased directly, but the value of customer experience is increased by such innovation. We summarize above discussion on software architecture in the following definition.

Definition 1: *Software architecture* is a strategic thought process for planning and making decisions about structure and behavior of software in such a way that enables a business to increase profits, reduce costs or innovate.

We find different kinds or genre of "Architecture" in practice in the field of Information Systems and Software Engineering. Figure 4 gives a map of some of such terms. This map shows where software architecture is positioned. We give below definition of some of the other architecture terms so as to differentiate them from software architecture.

Definition 2: *Technology Architecture* describes the technology components of a system from the infrastructure perspective. These components are of two types, hardware compo-

Figure 4. "Architecture" terminology landscape in information systems

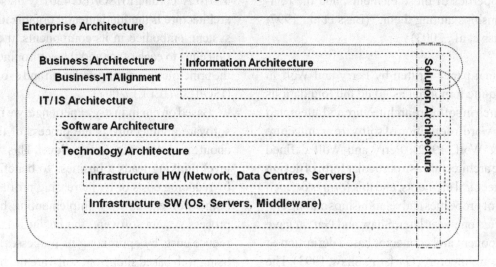

nents such as computers, network, switches, data centers, server machines etc., and software components such as operating systems, server software and middleware software etc. The middleware described as part of technology architecture could consist of software as well as hardware components.

Definition 3: *Information Systems Architecture* addresses the overall information system components in a business, which could be application software components or technology components. This is also referred to as Information Technology Architecture.

Definition 4: *Information Architecture addresses* creation, storage, archival, search and retrieval of information in business and includes metadata, taxonomies, ontologies, transaction-data, master data and information flows etc. Information Architecture has overlapping knowledge areas with IT Architecture and Business Architecture.

Definition 5: *Business Architecture* addresses business strategies, processes, services, structure, policies and governance etc. Business architecture and Information System Architecture have the perennial problem of Business-IT alignment gap.

Definition 6: *Solution Architecture* refers to architectural description of a single solution which cuts across domains of all the above mentioned architecture genres and hence involves components from some or all of them, but addresses a particular solution within the business.

Definition 7: *Enterprise Architecture* (EA) is the expression of key strategies around architectural decisions, variations, generic families, patterns and building blocks for architecting complex enterprises and systems that are subject to dynamic change. Enterprise Architecture centers on modeling, predicting and managing key properties such as profits, costs, risks, changes and innovation from an architectural perspective and in a holistic way (Goel et al., 2010).

These definitions and the map in Figure 4 clarify to certain extent the positioning of software architecture. A detailed discussion is beyond the scope of this paper. Now let us understand in next section the need to do software architecture and the difference from software design.

Rationale Behind Software Architecture

Winchester House is a beautiful residence located in San Jose, California, USA (Winchester House, 2010). The house looks so beautiful that we can hardly think that it might have any flaws. This house is a gigantic structure with 160 rooms, 40 bedrooms, 6 kitchens, 2 basements, 950 doors, 467 doorways, 1257 window frames, and 10,000 window panes. It is said to be a result of efforts of total 147 builders.

However such a huge structure has various flaws and has been converted into a museum for that reasons. The structure did not have a cohesive blueprint or architect working on it when it was being built. The result was tremendously uncoordinated structure. It has 65 doors which lead to blank walls. There are 13 staircases which were abandoned because some other structure appeared at the other end, and various staircases just appear out of nowhere. There are 24 skylights in floors. The fragility and weakness of structure was exposed when 3 stories were destroyed in a minor earthquake in 1906.

Does that mean we need an architect for every structure we build? Building a pet house would be different from building a human house. For building a pet house you may only need some nails, wood, hammer, saw and something to stick the pieces together. It will be ready in a few hours to a few days of work. However building a house requires sophisticated methods and tools. The time spent in building a house is between few weeks to few months. Generally an architect makes a blueprint which is then used by builder to build the house. Electrical, structural and other engineers just follow the blueprint which gives a cohesive plan. How about building a skyscraper? As we might have observed from practice, usually a team of architects or sometimes even a team of architecture firms works on building the blueprints for skyscrapers.

The software engineering equivalents of these examples would be:

- Building a small script/macro for your own computer (pet house)
- Writing a small application for a purpose (human house)
- Developing a product line (such as Operating systems, word processors) or enterprise application software to be used by huge enterprises such as (SAP ERP, Air Traffic Systems) (skyscrapers)

We learn from this discussion that there are certain differentiators which separate one kind of building activity from another. Some of these differentiators are:

- *Team size*: The team size for writing a script or macro is usually one. Simple application software is generally written by a team of few professional and engineers, and a large team consisting of sub teams usually works on huge product lines and enterprise software.
- *Scale of work*: The scale of work in writing a script is quite lower than that of application software. In case of a macro or a script, number of lines of codes is less, size of executable is small and resource requirements in terms of memory and CPU are quite less.
- *Cost*: Cost of writing script is only few many hours; cost of writing simple application is still less than the cost of writing product lines and huge software. Most importantly, the cost of mistakes or having an erroneous script is much less then having a buggy SAP ERP system.
- *Processes*: The process of writing macro or script by person is very simple. The level of process complexity increases as the team and scale of the application and enterprise software gets bigger.

- *Technology*: The technology used in writing a small program is much less complex whereas for large systems the technology complexity is compounded by heterogeneity.
- *Tools*: The tools required for writing a small program are simple. Whereas writing large programs is not possible without sophisticated tools for software engineering such as project management, release management, testing, configuration and versioning etc.
- *Models*: The simple program, script or macro could be written without any models, or the simplest model would be a flowchart. For writing an application or enterprise software would require much more complicated tools such as state charts, message sequence charts, UML diagrams etc.

There have been examples similar to Winchester Mystery House in software engineering. The software architecture is required to create a blueprint of the system when the complexity of a system increases in terms of the above mentioned differentiators. Software architecture ensures cohesiveness and integrity among the system components which cannot be achieved if we decide to build in a bottom up approach. The result would be something like Winchester Mystery House. In bottom up approach we would be optimizing the parts only while compromising the whole at the same time. Using software architecture for modeling and decision making ensures we optimize the whole as well.

Furthermore, software architecture gives a system-wide perspective to address several cross cutting concerns across different aspects and to make the necessary tradeoffs. For example, information security is a cross cutting concern, which needs to be woven cohesively throughout the whole system. At the same time, using too much information security may require too much processing speed, and may make the interaction between human and machine too complicated. Software architecture allows us to do a tradeoff analysis in such situations at the whole system level.

Software architecture allows us to reduce waste, rework and redundancy and leads to increased reuse of several components or system. This results in increased consistency and integration among the different parts of the system. Thus complexity of systems becomes tractable and enabled by different software architecture views.

The Identity of Software Architect

The identity of architect is defined by the actions performed in this role and the skills required. In this section we look at the skills required by a software architect. Defining the skills required for a profession which is undergoing a continuous evolution is quite a challenge in itself. We reviewed and collected advertisements in web portals for careers and job opportunities over a period of three years. However we found it difficult to find a common theme among the skills wanted in a software architect. Some of the advertisement required narrow skills very specific to the task and domain, and on the other end of extreme the other advertisements required varied and broad skills ranging from leadership and project management to technical depth and breadth.

The TOGAF standard (The Open Group Architecture Framework) (Spencer, 2004), which has roots in Information System architecture and is considered a generic Enterprise Architecture framework requires an architect to possess skills in following categories:

- **Generic Skills**: This category of skills includes leadership, team working and interpersonal skills etc.
- **Business Skills and Methods**: This category of skills includes developing business

cases, engineering business processes and strategic planning, etc.

- **Enterprise Architecture Skills**: This category of skills includes modeling, building block design, applications and role design and systems integration etc.
- **Program and Project Management Skills**: This category of skills includes managing business change, applying project management methods and tools, etc.
- **IT General Knowledge Skills**: This category of skills includes brokering applications, asset management, migration planning and managing SLAs etc.
- **Technical IT Skills**: This category of skills includes capabilities related to software engineering, security, data interchange and data management etc.
- **Legal Environment**: This category of skills includes knowledge of different related laws such as data protection laws, contract law, procurement law and fraud etc.

However, this skills set is quite broad and involves different skill domains. One of the simplest and concise frameworks for skills and knowledge required by a software architect is given by Dana Bredemeyer and Ruth Malan in their paper "Role of Software Architect" (Bredemeyer & Malan, 2002). This framework divides the skills and knowledge in five domains of competency: Leadership, Consulting, Organizational Politics, Business Strategy and Technology. Each domain is then further described using three aspects of "what you know", "what you do", and "what you are", reflecting the knowledge, actions and traits required for each competency. Table 1 shows a summary for of the knowledge, actions and traits required for each of the 5 competency domains.

Increasing focus on leadership, consulting and politics domains as compared to strategy and technology domains is required as the architect grows in seniority. Further, another observations

made by Bredemeyer and Malan is that the higher domains of competency such as leadership and consulting require lesser focus on knowledge and more focus on personal traits from the architects. This competency framework seems less complex and easier to follow and at the same captures all the essential elements of skills required by a software architect.

Many times identity of Software Architect is confused with Project Manager or Team Lead. This identity overlap is due to the fact that team leads and managers perform the role of software architect themselves in practice instead of delegating this role to a specialist. However, we distinguish between roles of software architect and project manager. Some of the major differences are listed in Table 2.

We find that roles of both Manager/Lead and Architect are central to any software project. James O. Coplien articulated that "A common pattern you find within the hyper-productive organizations is the binary star of the systems architect and the project manager orbiting one another, and the rest of the team surrounding them" (Coplien, 2006).

The Metaphor of Software Architecture

The philosophical discussion of Software Architecture brings us to another question: What metaphor best describes Software Architecture: Science, Engineering or Art? The purpose of this section is not to give definitive answers to this question, but to provoke a discussion around it.

Science has been defined as a body of useful and practical knowledge and a method of obtaining it (Campbell, 2009). Although software architecture has manifested itself in computer systems since their inception, but still an explicit body of knowledge about this field is not very mature and rich. We do not find many scientific and analytical methods to formulate software architecture or to reason about software architecture. Even the few existing methods are difficult to apply and thus

Table 1. Domains of competency for a software architect by Dana Bredemeyer and Ruth Malan (Brede-meyer & Malan, 2002)

Competency Domain	What you Know (Knowledge)	What you Do (Actions)	What you Are (Traits)
Leadership	• Yourself	• Set team context (vision) • Make decision and stick to them • Build teams • Motivate people	• Others see you as a leader • Charismatic and credible • Believer that it can be and should be done, and that you can lead the effort • See the entire effort in a broader business and personal context
Consulting	• Elicitation techniques • Consulting frameworks	• Build trusted advisor relationships • Understand what the developers want and need from the architecture • Help developers see the value of the architecture and understand how to use it successfully • Mentor junior architects	• Committed to other's success • Empathic, approachable • Effective change agent, process savvy • Good mentor, teacher
Politics	• Who the key players are in the organization • What they want, both business and personal	• Communicate, Listen, network, influence • Sell the vision, keep the vision alive • Take and retake the pulse of all critical influencers of the architecture project	• Able to see from and sell to multiple viewpoints • Confident and articulate • Ambitious and driven • Patient and not • Resilient • Sensitive to where power is and how it flows
Strategy	• Organization's business strategy and rationale • Competition (products, strategies, processes) • Organization's business practices	• Influence business strategy • Translate business strategy into technical vision and strategy • Understand customer and market trends • Capture customer, organizational and business requirements on architecture	• Visionary • Entrepreneurial
Technology	• domain and pertinent technologies • Understand what technical issues are key to success • Development methods and modeling techniques	• Modeling • Tradeoff analysis • Prototype / experiment / simulate • Prepare architectural documents and presentations • Technology trend analysis / roadmaps • Take a system viewpoint	• Creative • Investigative • Practical / Pragmatic • Insightful • Tolerant of ambiguity, willing to backtrack, seek multiple solutions • Good at working at an abstract level

Table 2. Major differences in roles of project manager / team lead and software architect

	Manager / Lead	Architect
Process	Manages schedule, resources, budget, risks	Manages quality and dependencies, Gives input to manager
Requirements	Negotiates requirements, Approves estimates	Reviews requirements, Estimates timelines, Performs impact analysis
Technology	Follows architect's recommendations	Recommends technology, tools and trainings
Quality	Ensures quality of product Quality reporting	Implements tools to measure defects and productivity
People	Hires, fires, retains, motivates, appraises	Mentors and collaborates with people

used rarely in industry practice, except a few niche areas. There is nothing called perfect architectural design. The practice of software architecture involves managing situations and information which are extremely ambiguous and sometimes even contradictory. This becomes evident when we study the literature on software engineering from industry as well as academia.

The definition of art is difficult and has been controversial (Adajian, 2007; Tolstoy & Tolstoy, 2009). A common aspect of art is "originality" of expression by the artist. In practice however, even the best architects assemble the new software from the borrowed proven working solutions, such as design patterns and frameworks. They may improve or reconfigure the reused part before assembling in.

Engineering is defined as the profession of applying scientific knowledge to create economical (cost-effective) solutions for the benefit of humanity. The focus in engineering is on building and optimizing the parts which could be integrated after their production. Thus the engineering has various streams associated with it such as electrical, structural, mechanical etc. Architecture on the other hand has a broad focus on the whole and on the integration of products. The focus of architect is in optimizing and striking a balance between quality, usability, composition and appearance in the end product. Thus the scope of application architect (software architect) is in architecting an end product which utilizes the work of J2EE engineer, database engineer, and others.

CONCLUSION AND FUTURE OUTLOOK

Our thoughts on philosophy of software architecture could be summarized by saying that software architecture is inherently strategic in nature and it enables the achievement of business strategy. The software architecture lies between strategy and execution. The strategy is owner's vision of business which is captured using requirements engineering and execution is builder's implementation of architectural blueprint which is realized in IT systems and software code.

There are various terms related with software architecture, a definition for each of these was given in section 2 with a visual map in Figure 4. The rationale behind doing software architecture is to gain benefit from holistic system wide perspective leading to system wide optimizations. We discussed the identity of software architect as defined by skills required, although this topic in itself requires detailed empirical investigation and has been continuously under research. We proposed from our experience that a concise architect competency model given by Bredemeyer and Malan is easy to use as compared to other complicated models such as the one arising from a review of job advertisements of architects or the one from TOGAF. The metaphor of software architecture is contrasted with science, art and engineering and reader is left with a provocation to further explore this area.

Software Architecture has been studied and researched for over 18 years now since its first definition appeared in print by Perry and Wolf (1992). In future, we see the focus broadly on following areas:

- **Software Architecture Representation**: The main focus in this area has been on defining Architecture Modeling Languages such as UML (Booch et al., 2005; Medvidovic et al., 2002), SysML, Abstract Architecture Definition/Description Languages (Clements, 1996; Medvidovic & Taylor, 1997; Medvidovic & Taylor, 2000; Mishra & Dutt, 2006) such as AADL (Feiler et al., 2006), ACME (Garlan et al., 1997), Architecture Documentation and Tools to support them. There are also attempts to formalize the software architecture representation so as to use them for automated validation, verification, analysis and execution.

- **Software Architecture Execution and Automation:** Model Driven Architecture (MDA) by OMG (Kleppe et al., 2003) has been a key focus area in this space. MDA proposes to build infrastructure of meta-modeling languages in multi-level structure such that the system would be automatically executed from software architecture definition. The intermediate step in this direction could be generation of software first, before executing in a container or platform. Finally when the MDA platforms are mature enough, then the architectural description of a system would be executable through various internal transformations.

- **Software Architecture Evolution:** The software systems continuously undergo change due to various internal and external factors, creating a need for software architecture to evolve. Thus we need to find representations, formal methods, models and frameworks for evolution of software architecture (Garlan et al., 2009; Garlan & Schmerl, 2009) from one state to another. Research in this area has been growing rapidly (Aoyama, 2002; Barais et al., 2008; Falcarin & Alonso, 2004). Major challenges in software architecture evolution are description and representation of software architecture evolution, analysis models to predict and check consistency due to change in software architecture and standard frameworks for software architecture evolution.

We see from our experience that although a significant research has gone into the software architecture field, there is still plenty of potential for solving the unsolved problems. The philosophy of software architecture is getting richer and mature with such research efforts.

REFERENCES

Adajian, T. (2007). *The Definition of Art*. Stanford Encyclopedia of Philosophy.

Aoyama, M. (2002). Metrics and analysis of software architecture evolution with discontinuity. In Proceedings of the International Workshop on Principles of Software Evolution (p. 107). New York: ACM.

Barais, O., Meur, A., Duchien, L., & Lawall, J. (2008). Software architecture evolution. *Software Evolution, 233-262.*

Bass, L., Clements, P., & Kazman, R. (1997). *Software architecture in practice* (1st ed.). Reading, MA: Addison-Wesley Professional.

Bass, L., Clements, P., & Kazman, R. (2003). *Software architecture in practice*. Reading, MA: Addison-Wesley Professional.

Booch, G., Rumbaugh, J., & Jacobson, I. (2005). *Unified Modeling Language User Guide*. Reading, MA: Addison-Wesley Professional.

Booch, G. (2006). *Software architecture*. IBM Rational Software Group Presentation.

Bredemeyer, D., & Malan, R. (2002). *The Role of the Architect*. Resources for Software Architects.

Campbell, N. (2009). *What is science? Biblio-Bazaar*. LLC.

Clements, P. (1996). A survey of architecture description languages. In P*roceedings of the 8th International Workshop on Software Specification and Design* (p. 16). Washington, DC: IEEE Computer Society.

Coplien, J. (2006). Organizational Patterns. *Enterprise Information Systems, 6,* 43–52.

Falcarin, P., & Alonso, G. (2004). Software architecture evolution through dynamic aop. *Software Architecture, 57-73.*

Feiler, P., Gluch, D., Hudak, J., & INST, C.-M. U. P. P. S. E. (2006). *The architecture analysis & design language (AADL): An introduction.*

Garlan, D., Monroe, R., & Wile, D. (1997). Acme: An architecture description interchange language. In *Proceedings of the 1997 conference of the Centre for Advanced Studies on Collaborative research* (p. 7). IBM Press.

Garlan, D., Barnes, J., Schmerl, B., & Celiku, O. (2009). Evolution Styles: Foundations and Tool Support for Software Architecture Evolution. In *Proceedings of the Joint Working IEEE/ IFIP Conference on Software Architecture 2009, European Conference on Software Architecture.*

Garlan, D., & Schmerl, B. (2009). Ævol: A tool for defining and planning architecture evolution. In *Proceedings of the 2009 IEEE 31st International Conference on Software Engineering* (pp. 591-594). Washington, DC: IEEE Computer Society.

Garlan, D., & Shaw, M. (1993). An introduction to software architecture. In *Proceedings of the Advances in software engineering and knowledge engineering* (Vol. 1, pp. 1-40).

Goel, A., Schmidt, H., & Gilbert, D. (2010). Formal Models of Virtual Enterprise Architecture: Motivations and Approaches. In *Proceedings of 14th Pacific Asia Conference on Information Systems (PACIS)*. Association for Information Systems.

Hayes-Roth, F. (1994). *Architecture-based acquisition and development of software: Guidelines and recommendations from the ARPA domain-specific software architecture (DSSA) program. Teknowledge Federal Systems (Version 1). ISO/ IEC/(IEEE) 2007ISO/IEC/(IEEE). (2007). ISO/ IEC 42010 (IEEE Std) 1471-2000: Systems and Software engineering - Recommended practice for architectural description of software-intensive systems*. Washington, DC: IEEE.

Kleppe, A., Warmer, J., & Bast, W. (2003). *MDA explained: the model driven architecture: practice and promise*. Reading, MA: Addison-Wesley.

Medvidovic, N., Rosenblum, D., Redmiles, D., & Robbins, J. (2002). Modeling software architectures in the Unified Modeling Language. *ACM Transactions on Software Engineering and Methodology, 11*(1), 57.

Medvidovic, N., & Taylor, R. (1997). A framework for classifying and comparing architecture description languages. In *Proceedings of the ACM SIGSOFT Software Engineering Notes* (Vol. 22, No. 6, p. 76).

Medvidovic, N., & Taylor, R. (2000). A classification and comparison framework for software architecture description languages. *IEEE Transactions on Software Engineering, 26*(1), 70–93.

Mishra, P., & Dutt, N. (2006). Architecture Description Languages. In Ienne, P., & Leupers, R. (Eds.), *Customizable and Configurable Embedded Processors*. San Francisco: Morgan Kaufmann Publishers.

Perry, D., & Wolf, A. (1992). Foundations for the study of software architecture. *ACM SIGSOFT Software Engineering Notes, 17*(4), 40–52.

Spencer, J. (2004). *Togaf* (enterprise ed., version 8.1).

Tolstoy, C., & Tolstoy, L. (2009). *What is art? BiblioBazaar*. LLC.

Winchester House. (2010). *Winchester Mystery House Homepage*. Retrieved from http://www. winchestermysteryhouse.com/

This work was previously published in the International Journal of Web Portals 2(4), edited by Greg Adamson and Jana Polgar, pp. 28-39, copyright 2010 by Information Science Publishing (an imprint of IGI Global).

Section 3
Practical Experiences of Business Today

Chapter 14
Impact of Web Portal Announcements on Market Valuations:
An Event Study

Manish Gupta
State University of New York, Buffalo, USA

Raj Sharman
State University of New York, Buffalo, USA

ABSTRACT

Organizations providing enhanced electronic services to their customers have exponentially increased in past years. The benefits of web-portals to companies and to customers are well evident and are considered an IT artifact manifested in entry points to Internet-based information presentation and exchange by communities of common interest. Despite much research done on the benefits of web portals to companies, no research exists that focuses on impact of adoption of web-portals on a company's market valuation. In this paper, the authors look into impact of web-portal announcements on company's stock prices (market value). Using event-study methodology, they provide empirical evidence on the effect of announcements of web portals on the market valuation of the company for a sample of 25 publicly traded companies in 2008. The study examines stock data to access investors and shareholders' reactions to web portal announcements. Results indicate that web portal announcements significantly and positively influence investors' perceptions toward financial worth and future prospects of the company. The authors discuss these findings in detail and present implications for both research and practice. Findings offer insight that can be used by managers and executives in understanding the role and effect of a companies' market value.

DOI: 10.4018/978-1-4666-0336-3.ch014

INTRODUCTION

It has been almost two decades since the first web portals were launched. Given their utility and functions, they have been considered a "killer application" ever since they were introduced. Web portals have hailed top have endowed businesses a platform for integrating their collective services in an attempt significantly enhance user experience and convenience (Shuler, 2002). Over years, an increasing number of companies have established Web portals to "*complement, substitute for, or extend their existing services to users*" (Van Real et al., 2002). A web portal is an Internet-based site providing a wide array of online information-related services and functions to its users including search, collaboration, syndication, information, offerings, productivity tools, channel of communication, etc (Eisenmann & Pothen, 2000; Yang et al., 2004). Web portals have come a long way and have evolved in ways that was not even conceivable a decade ago. Portals also commonly used for providing access to multiple applications and databases targeted to a community of common interests such as customers of a specific company or enterprise focused to provide access to organizational information (Mahdavi et al., 2004). Today, they are complete hubs of electronic commerce, electronic communications, online collaboration and sharing, and customized and personalized content and services and they have become the most visited sites on the web (Sieber & Volor-Sabatier, 2005). Some definitions of web portal:

"*A portal is an integrated and personalized Web-based application that provides the end user with a single point of access to a wide variety of aggregated content (data, knowledge, and services) anytime and from anywhere using any Web-enabled client device.*" *(Polgar et al., 2004, p. 97)*

"*Enterprise information portals are applications that enable companies to unlock internally and externally stored information, and provide users a single gateway to personalized information needed to make informed business decisions.*" *(Shilakes & Tylman, 1998)*

"*A Web portal or public portal refers to a Web site or service that offers a broad array of resources and services, such as e-mail, forums, search engines, and online shopping malls. The first Web portals were online services, such as AOL, that provided access to the Web, but by now most of the traditional search engines have transformed themselves into Web portals to attract and keep a larger audience.*"*(Webopedia, 2010)*

Companies can provide improved customer service quality, enhanced operational efficiencies, increased collaboration and information dissemination, improved potential for revenue generation and increased savings (Gehrke & Turban, 2000; Hamel & Sampler, 1998; Kalakota & Whinston, 1996). It has been proved that introduction of new services through web portals or introduction of new web portals will attract new customer segments while improving experiences of existing customers. There are common functions of a web-portal that a company may elect to provide to its users, customers, partners or employees, which includes (Collins, 2001): Search Capabilities, Content Management, Process and Action, Help Features, Data Points and Integration, Taxonomy, Presentation, Administration, Collaboration and Communication, Personalization, and Security. Companies have realized enormous benefits through such web portals. Such initiatives should be perceived as companies' proactive efforts to improve customer service quality, introduce newer services and reduce costs, in an attempt to improve firm performance and profits. So, such web portal announcements in media should have positive effect on the stock price performance of the company due to investor's positive reflection on the company and their anticipation of potential reviews and benefits (Chang et al., 2003; Geyskens et al., 2002; Subramani & Walden, 2001). Therefore, investors and shareholders of the company will be more inclined to react positively to announcements of such initiatives yielding a positive abnormal return on the stock value of the company, around the date of an e-service announcement (Lin et al., 2007). Therefore, we hypothesize that:

H1: Announcement of web portal related initiatives will have positive abnormal return for the stock of the company around the date of the announcement.

Since value appraisal of web portal type of e-service initiatives is a difficult undertaking (Geyskens et al., 2002), we conduct an event study to study this phenomenon. There are many studies in extant literature that use survey and/or case study methodology, but there are none that look specifically into web portal arrangements from a market valuation of the firm perspective to measure the impact of such announcements (positive or negative). Hence, we believe that there is a gap in literature to understand the impact of announcement of web portal initiatives on the market valuation of the firm as would be reflected in abnormal return on the stock around the date of announcement. This will be immensely helpful for both practitioners and researchers alike to get unique perspective into the phenomenon. This will also help companies understand under what circumstances would the announcements their stock value, if at all. So we frame our research question as follows, which we study through announcements of web portal initiatives:

What is impact of web portal announcements on market valuation of the firm?

The extent of impact on stock prices due to web portal announcements is likely to be different for different companies. There are capabilities and resources that specific to the firms, including their market position, that will moderate the extent of impact (Bowman & Gatignon, 1995). The market reaction aside, the effectiveness of the introduction of the new service on web portal also is likely to affect the impact. For our study, we have not evaluated merits and effectiveness of the service offering on the web portal, but have considered an aggregate effect of such announcements on the firm's stock price. Another factor that has also been found to be moderate impact is size of the firm, which reflects on expansion plans and growth strategies (Mishina et al., 2004; Cross et al., 2001; Koh & Venkatraman, 1991). Also the intent of the web portal initiative has also been studied along two dimensions: service expansion (new services to existing customer items) and market expansion (new services for new customers).

The contributions of the paper are two-fold. One, it provides a state of research in the area of effect of web portals on valuation of the firms performance. Secondly the paper investigates if the media announcements of web portal initiatives affect the market valuation of the firm. The paper is organized by presenting the background and a survey of extant literature on web portal initiatives from organizational perspective and on case studies' use to evaluate impact of similar events on stock prices. Next a methodology employed in this study including data collection, analysis and results are presented. Finally the paper concludes with discussions and future directions of research.

BACKGROUND AND LITERATURE REVIEW

We carried out a systematic review of extant literature by evaluating and interpreting available research that is particular to our research question (Kitchenham, 2004). We selected works that are pertinent to web portals' role in affecting performance and quality of service and to similar event studies that investigate impact on market valuations of firms due to similar announcements.

Web Portals

Portals exemplify the concept of augmented services via Internet (Gounaris & Dimitriadis, 2003; Payne & Holt, 2001). The augmentation of existing services comes from the fact that they provide services such as communication, collaboration, information and personalization under single umbrella. This conforms to Afuah and Tucci's (2001) integration of four Internet-based business models of "*content, context, communication and commerce*" into one unified model (see also Bauer & Hammerschmidt, 2002). Today they, more often than not, provide both information and support for transactions together (Huizingh, 2002). Numerous other studies have referred to them as "one-stop shopping" that provide single point of access to a rich and targeted portfolio of services (see Gounaris & Dimitriadis, 2003; van Riel et al., 2002). Some literature have suggested that concept of portal is highly specific to the functions and support that they provide based on "*certain standards*" and "*certain specific features*" they host (Polgar & Polgar, 2007; Tatnall, 2005). The web portals can be classified as "hortals", for horizontal portal, that provide a wide range of services under single access to a large number of users or as "vortals", for vertical portal, that provide very targeted and specific functions to users. Both types can be providing customized interface and services based on their purposes (Liu & Dub, 2009).

There are several studies in research literature in the area of web portals. Some investigate service quality of transaction-oriented portal sites (Cho & Park, 2001; Donthu, 2001; Loiacono et al., 2002; Wang et al., 2001; Wolfinbarger & Gilly, 2002; Yang et al., 2001; Yoo & Donthu, 2001; Zeithaml et al., 2001; Zeithaml et al., 2002) and some on the design quality of the portals (Bell & Tang, 1998; Liu & Arnett, 2000; Zhang & von Dran, 2001; Zhang & von Dran, 2002). Some researchers have looked into specific functionality provided by the web portals such as content quality and reliability and richness of search feature (Aladwania & Palvia, 2002; Koller, 2001; Parasuraman & Zeithaml, 1988; Paulin & Perrien, 1996). Service quality is one of the most researched areas within portals, where adequacy and reliability of information has been found to have most impact in quality perception about the web portal (Yang et al., 2005; Liu & Dub, 2009). Webb and Webb (2004) developed a model "SiteQual" to measure web site quality using 21 service quality items (Parasuraman et al., 1994) and deriving seven quality factors.

Event Study

Researchers have used the event study methodology in information systems literature to understand the impact of a specific event on stock performance of that company. The event study methodology is basically borrowed from financial economics domain, where it has been used to study stock price trends for several decades (see Ball & Brown, 1968; Brown & Warner, 1985). Its use in information systems research is relatively new, starting in early 1990s. Effect of IT investments have been studied in IS literature from different perspectives including resource-based view and process-theoretic view. It investments are important for any organization to meet its objectives (Bharadwaj, 2000). It is therefore very important to understand impact of those investments and impact of announcements about them on firm's and its stock's performance (Dehning et al., 2005; Hayes et al., 2001; Im et al., 2001; Barua et al., 2000).

There are many methodologies in IS literature that have been used to investigate impact on firm's performance, event study being one of the most used ones in recent literature with great effectiveness (Richardson & Zmud, 2002). At its core, the relevant extant literature in this area tries to investigate if there is any effect of specific IT event on stock price and also what can companies do to maximize the return on their "*events*" (Richardson & Zmud, 2002; Dehning et al., 2003; Oh et al., 2006). Since mid 1990s, there have been a relatively large number of studies to understand this phenomenon of impact of IT-related announcements on stock price (Dehning et al., 2004; Im et al., 2001). In those studies, the areas within IS include IT investment in general (Dos Santos, 1993), outsourcing (Peak et al., 2002; Agrawal et al., 2005), e-commerce, security and knowledge management (Chatterjee et al., 2002), specific system such as ERP or CRM system (Hayes et al., 2001), etc. Some studies have shown some events positive impact on the stock price (Im et al., 2001; Richardson & Zmud, 2002; Dos Santos, 1993; Hayes et al., 2000; Meng & Lee, 2007), while some don't (Hayes et al., 2001; Oh et al., 2006; Chatterjee et al., 2002; Dardan et al., 2006; Dewan & Ren, 2007; Lee et al., 2002; Ranganathan & Brown, 2006; Subramani & Walden, 2001). Dehning (2004) have also found out that time period in which the event type is being investigated can also affect the results. Appendix 1 summarizes results of some of the studies and their domains.

METHODOLOGY

Researchers have used the event study methodology in information systems literature to understand the impact of a specific event on stock performance of that company. The event study methodology is basically borrowed from financial economics domain, where it has been used to study stock price trends for several decades (see for example, Ball and Brown, 1968; Brown and Warner, 1985). Its use in information systems research is relatively new, starting in early 1990s. We use event study to investigate if web portal announcements have impact on stock price on the companies making the announcements. The details of the methodology are presented next.

Sample Selection Procedure

Media announcements and information on web portal arrangements were collected using a text search of news sources (PR Newswire and Business Wire) from the Lexis-Nexis search engine for one year of 2009. A data set of more than 1600 companies available from Lexis-Nexis returned around 320 news articles. The keywords we used for the search include ("web portal" OR "web-portal" OR web portal), AND (NYSE OR NASDAQ OR AMEX OR OTC). To determine inclusion of the announcement in our study we used the following set of checks:

1. The company making the announcement should be listed in one of the US stock exchanges (NYSE, NASDAQ). This significantly reduced the sample by about 70%.
2. The announcements were clearly regarding web portal initiatives or arrangements.
3. The announcement pertains directly to the company making the announcement.
4. The company's stock price information was available for a continuous estimation period of 200 days and also for the event window if 5 days.
5. The companies that also had other announcements such as earnings, mergers or other initiatives near the date of web portal announcement were eliminated to reduce any confounding effect on the analysis.
6. In case of multiple announcements of the same event, only the first announcement was used and others were discarded.

Using, these selection criteria we were able to retrieve around 25 media announcements from publicly traded companies in the database for the year 2009 from an initial set of around 325. A sample of the announcements is provided in Table x and the list of companies and event date is shown in the Table y. The daily returns of the individual stock prices for the companies in study were retrieved from the Center for Research on Security Prices (CRSP) database using Eventus® software. We examined the daily abnormal returns over a 200-day estimation period and an event window of 2 days.

Data Analysis

The event-study methodology is a widely used method, in the fields of finance, accounting and information systems, to study effect of events on market valuations of firms. The premise of event studies is that any new information about a company is efficiently incorporated in the stock price of the company due to changes in perception about expected future performance. Like other event studies, we also use the market model to estimate abnormal returns on the stock prices of the companies. The market model assumes a linear relationship between the daily stock returns of a firm and the returns on the market portfolio of its stocks. The market model, for any specific stock, can be represented as:

$$R_{it} = \alpha_i + \beta_i R_{mt} + \varepsilon_{it} \tag{1}$$

R_{it} denotes the return of the i stock on day t; R_{mt} is the return on the market portfolio of stocks; α_i is the intercept term and β_i is the slope parameter representing systemic risk of the stock i and ε_{it} is the disturbance or error term for stock i on day t. According to the efficient-market hypothesis any news announcements made by a company is immediately used by the investors through their reaction to yield an abnormal return, which can be positive (higher stock price) or negative (lower stock price). The abnormal return on stock price of a firm i on day t of the event window can be estimated as:

$$AR_{it} = R_{it} - (\hat{\alpha}_i + \hat{\beta}_i R_{mt}), \tag{2}$$

$\hat{\alpha}$ and $\hat{\beta}$ are the ordinary least-square (OLS) parameter estimates of α and β, the intercept and slope terms, respectively. We estimate these parameters using the market model over a 200 day period ending 45 days before the event day. These parameter estimates were obtained from the regression of R_{it} on R_{mt} over an estimation period (T) preceding the event, 255 days prior to the event. AR_{it} is the rate of return on the stock derived after subtracting the expected return on the stock from its actual return. The return on the market portfolio of stocks is defined as the change of the stock market value as a whole (Keown et al., 2004). We used 255 estimation days of the stock price to find the parameters in the market model; we started from t = -300 to t = -45 of the event date to ensure that the event returns would not influence the market parameters (Armitage, 1995), which is in accordance with other previous studies (Chatterjee et al., 2002; Ranganathan & Brown, 2006; Sabherwal & Sabherwal, 2005). The cumulative abnormal return, sum of the daily abnormal returns, is computed over the event window (T1, T2) as:

$$CAR_{i(T1,T2)} = \sum_{t=T1}^{T2} AR_{it} \tag{3}$$

The mean cumulative abnormal return, for a sample of n stocks, is the average CAR over the event window, represented as:

$$CAR_{i(T1,T2)} = \frac{1}{n} \sum_{i=1}^{n} CAR_{i(T1,T2)} \tag{4}$$

In this study, we looked at event windows of (-1, 1), (-2, 2), (-1, 0), (0, 2) and (0, 1) which is line with other prior event studies. Event window is duration in days during which the impact of any announcement is measured (Ranganathan & Brown, 2006). Event window is considered one of the important choices in event study research design (McWilliams & Siegel, 1997). Our major focus for this study was 2-day window, which is consistent with other event studies of similar type (see Hayes et al., 2000; Koh & Venkatraman, 1992; Oh e t al., 2006; Peak et al., 2002). Event windows should be long enough to capture any announcement's effect on market valuation, but short enough to avoid confounding of results due to other events (Armitage, 1995). Brown and Warner (1985) have also demonstrated that the longer windows tend to reduce the power of the empirical tests causing incorrect conclusions and misleading results of significance tests. Usually, the day of the announcement has been found to capture the primary market reaction to the announcement, beyond which the effects of other events seep into the results. Table 1 shows event study research design parameters used in our study.

Results

The results from this study of web portal announcements support our hypothesis that the announcements market generally reacts positively to such investments. These announcements were associated with an average cumulative excess return of 2.05 percent on the day of announcements. The finding is significant in terms in noticing that on day -1 (the day before the announcements), the mean CAR was -0.70 percent (Table 2). The results are statistically significant at 0.10

level for Patell Z test, Portfolio Time series t test and Rank Test (Table 2). While Jackknife Z test gave us better result that is significant even at 0.05 levels. This excess return is comparable to excess returns reported in previous event studies discussed earlier, which clearly demonstrates that the announcements have yielded a positive return in excess of what was predicted based on historical price returns (calculated for the estimation window of 200 days).

The observation of a positive return on the stocks due to announcements is not theoretically strong evidence, because the magnitude of the returns should also be statistically significant to be academic proof for an empirical support for the hypothesis. On statistical tests also, we see that for the window of study (0, 1), we have a mean CAR of 2.27% with both Rank Test and Jackknife Z tests statistically significant at 0.10 levels with 2.068 and 2.702 scores, respectively (Table 3). We also see that the strength of the tests decrease as we move away from the day of announcement or when we increase the size of the event window. We used CARs as a dependent variable, which yielded statistically significant results on both the regression models (Table 3). Figure 1 and Figure 2 shows the mean cumulative abnormal returns and statistical test results, re-

Table 1. Event study design parameters

Event Study Parameter	Parameter Selection
Market Index	CRSP Value Weighted
Benchmark Options	market model + Market-Adjusted Returns (MAR)
Estimation Period:	
End Before Event Date (EST)	45 days
Minimum Estimation Length (MINESTN)	3 days
Maximum Estimation Length (ESTLEN)	255 days
Autodate	Back
Estimate Method	EGARCH
Event Period:	PRE = -2, POST = -2
Statistical tests	PATELL, CDA, JACKKNIFE, RANKTEST

Table 2. Day-wise CARs and test results

Days	Mean Cumulative Abnormal Return	Positive/Negative Signs of CAR	Patell Z	Portfolio Time series (CDA) t	Rank Test Z	Jackknife Z
-8	0.58%	16:9)	1.191	0.55	1.515$	1.927*
-7	-0.37%	9:16	-0.514	-0.352	-0.383	0.107
-6	-1.01%	11:14	-1.244	-0.956	-1.423$	-1.395$
-5	0.06%	12:13	-0.324	0.058	-0.421	-0.376
-4	0.42%	10:15	0.836	0.398	-0.658	-0.137
-3	0.63%	13:12	0.79	0.595	0.866	1.215
-2	0.04%	14:11	0.506	0.035	0.633	0.095
-1	-0.70%	11:14	-0.013	-0.661	0.095	-0.786
0	**2.05%**	**19:6>>**	**2.252***	**1.936***	**2.314***	**2.915****
1	0.17%	12:13	-0.199	0.162	0.103	0.324
2	-0.70%	14:11	-0.393	-0.662	-0.373	-0.826
3	0.02%	12:13	-0.034	0.016	0.019	-0.696
4	-1.23%	11:14	-0.266	-1.158	-0.037	-0.218
5	-0.14%	8:17<	-1.158	-0.132	-1.429$	-1.639$
6	-0.71%	12:13	-0.603	-0.671	-0.356	-0.759
7	-0.28%	11:14	-0.454	-0.268	0.072	0.389
8	-0.01%	11:14	-0.421	-0.013	-0.61	-0.224
9	0.39%	11:14	0.04	0.365	-0.362	-0.57
10	0.15%	13:12	-0.173	0.145	0.002	-0.126
11	0.33%	13:11	0.623	0.316	0.392	0.581

The symbols $,*,**, and *** denote statistical significance at the 0.10, 0.05, 0.01 and 0.001 levels, respectively, using a generic one-tail test. The symbols (,< or),> etc. correspond to $,* and show the direction and generic one-tail significance of the generalized sign test.

spectively, for the study. The figures also show the spike in trend on the day of the announcements.

This results and analysis based on the data, for web portal announcements during year 2008, show that the hypothesis made in this paper is supported. The study showed that for the sample of announcements studied, the investors did see them in positive light by positively reacting on the stock prices. For other event windows (1,1), (-1, 0), (0,2) and (-1, 2), the mean CARs are positive even though they are statistically significant. Thus, the event's economic impact can be measured using asset prices observed over a relatively short time period around the occurrence of the event.

CONCLUSION AND DISCUSSION

We sought to investigate the impact of web portal announcements in media on the market valuation of the firm as is reflected in its stock prices. In analyzing a sample of 25 relevant web-portal related announcements, during year of 2008, the results of our event study indicated that web portal announcements were associated with positive increases in the market value of the firms, giving us evidence that investors perceive such initiatives in positive light about the company and favorably treat the stock prices.

Portals exemplify the concept of augmented services via Internet (Gounaris & Dimitriadis, 2003; Payne & Holt, 2001). The augmentation

Table 3. CARs and Significance results

Days	Mean Cumulative Abnormal Return	Positive / Negative Signs of CAR	Patell Z	Rank Test Z	Jackknife Z
(-1,+1)	1.31%	13:12	1.017	1.584$	0.686
(-1,0)	1.08%	13:12	1.305$	1.629$	0.398
(0,+1)	**2.27%**	**18:7>>**	**1.534$**	**2.068***	**2.702****
(0,+2)	1.66%	13:12	1.026	1.443$	1.315$
(-1,+2)	0.71%	16:9>	0.685	1.159	0.068

The symbols $, *, **, and *** denote statistical significance at the 0.10, 0.05, 0.01 and 0.001 levels, respectively, using a generic one-tail test. The symbols (,< or),> etc. correspond to $,* and show the direction and generic one-tail significance of the generalized sign test.

Figure 1. Statistical test results (Patell, Rank test and Jackknife)

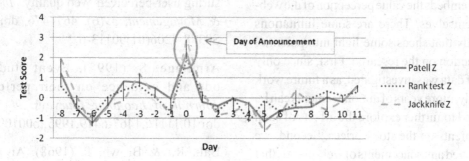

Figure 2. Mean cumulative abnormal return trend

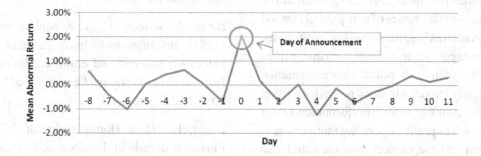

of existing services comes from the fact that they provide services such as communication, collaboration, information and personalization under single umbrella. Web portals have come a long way and have evolved in ways that was not even conceivable a decade ago. Portals also commonly used for providing access to multiple applications and databases targeted to a community of common interests such as customers of a specific company or enterprise focused to provide access

to organizational information (Mahdavi et al., 2004). Today, they are complete hubs of electronic commerce, electronic communications, online collaboration and sharing, and customized and personalized content and services and they have become the most visited sites on the web (Sieber & Volor-Sabatier, 2005). With great advances in Internet-based technologies, web-portals are increasingly becoming ever-available and promising option for firms. Given such benefits, our results assert that announcement of such initiatives can increase firm's market value and perception. Since web-portals play a significantly beneficial role in a company's performance and bottom-line, the announcement is perceived as proactive move by the company, which is rewarded. Our study can help firms get insights into when to invest in and implement web-portals. The current results of this study are helpful for both web-portal and electronic services researchers and practitioners. This study brings forth a viable and effective approach for assessment of web-portal announcement values, which also embeds the value perception of the web-portals themselves. There are some limitations of this study that sheds some light into potential future direction on the research. First, since only one year of data was investigated, as a future work on this study, more years of announcements can be investigated to further explore the effects of such announcements on the stock prices. Second, we only examined announcements of web-portals that affected publicly traded companies only, which might not be a true reflection on general market served by web-portals. So, further research can be look into how performance of non-publicly traded companies such as hospitals, medical institutions, government agencies and educational institutions affected by such web portal announcements. Third, we only looked into stock prices for market valuation or firm's economic performance. Other variables such as profits, operating numbers, revenue, customer base, market share etc could also be investigated to completely understand impact of such announcements on different aspects of the company. Finally, nature of web-portals can also be looked into to see if they affect the degree or direction of impact of announcements. For example, web-portal announcements can be for any type of service offerings such as e-tailing, customer service, financial, etc. It will be interesting to see examine impact of announcements for different types of web portal.

REFERENCES

Afuah, A., & Tucci, C. (2001). *Internet Business Models and Strategies*. Boston: Harvard.

Agrawal, M., Kishore, R., & Rao, H. R. (2006). Market reactions to e-business outsourcing announcements: An event study. *Information & Management*, *43*(7), 861–873. doi:10.1016/j.im.2006.08.002

Aladwania, A. M., & Palvia, P. C. (2002). Developing and validating an instrument for measuring user-perceived Web quality. *Information & Management*, *39*(6), 467–476. doi:10.1016/S0378-7206(01)00113-6

Armitage, S. (1995). Event study methods and evidence on their performance. *Journal of Economic Surveys*, *9*(1), 25–52. doi:10.1111/j.1467-6419.1995.tb00109.x

Ball, R., & Brown, P. (1968). An empirical evaluation of accounting income numbers. *Journal of Accounting Research*, *6*(2), 159–178. doi:10.2307/2490232

Barua, A., Kriebel, C. H., & Mukhopadhyay, T. (1995). Information technologies and business value: An analytic and empirical investigation. *Information Systems Research*, *6*(1), 3–23. doi:10.1287/isre.6.1.3

Bauer, H. H., & Hammerschmidt, M. (2002). Financial portals in the internet. In *Proceedings of the WSEAS Conference on E-Commerce*, Athens, Greece.

Bell, H., & Tang, N. K. H. (1998). The effectiveness of commercial internet Web sites: a user's perspective. *Internet Research: Electronic Networking Applications and Policy, 8*(3).

Bharadwaj, A. S. (2000). A resource-based perspective on information technology capability and firm performance: An empirical investigation. *Management Information Systems Quarterly*, *24*(1), 169–197. doi:10.2307/3250983

Bowman, D., & Gatignon, H. (1995). Determinants of competitor response time to a new product introduction. *JMR, Journal of Marketing Research, 32*(1), 42–53. doi:10.2307/3152109

Brown, S. J., & Warner, J. B. (1985). Using daily stock returns: The case of event studies. *Journal of Financial Economics, 14*(1), 3–31. doi:10.1016/0304-405X(85)90042-X

Chaney, P. K., Devinney, T. M., & Winer, R. S. (1991). The impact of new product introductions on the market value of firms. *The Journal of Business, 64*(4), 573–610. doi:10.1086/296552

Chang, K. C., Jackson, J., & Grover, V. (2003). E-commerce and corporate strategy: an executive perspective. *Information & Management, 40*(7), 663–675. doi:10.1016/S0378-7206(02)00095-2

Chatterjee, D., Pacini, C., & Sambamurthy, V. (2002). The shareholder-wealth and trading-volume effects of information-technology infrastructure investments. *Journal of Management Information Systems, 19*(2), 7–42.

Cho, N., & Park, S. (2001). Development of electronic commerce user consumer satisfaction index (ECUSI) for internet shopping. *Industrial Management & Data Systems, 101*(8), 400–405. doi:10.1108/EUM0000000006170

Collins, H. (2001). *Corporate portal definition and features*. AMACOM.

Cross, J., Hartley, S. W., Rudelius, W., & Vassey, M. J. (2001). Sales force activities and marketing strategies in industrial firms: relationships and implications. *Journal of Personal Selling & Sales Management, 21*(3), 199–206.

Dardan, S., Stylianou, A., & Kumar, R. (2006). The impact of custmer-related IT investment on custmer satisfaction and shareholder returns. *Journal of Computer Information Systems, 47*(2), 100–111.

Dehning, B., Richardson, V. J., & Stratopoulos, T. (2005). Information technology investment and firm value. *Information & Management, 42*(7), 989–1008. doi:10.1016/j.im.2004.11.003

Dehning, B., Richardson, V. J., Urbaczewski, A., & Wells, J. D. (2004). Reexamining the value relevance of E-commerce initiatives. *Journal of Management Information Systems, 21*(1), 55–82.

Dehning, B., Richardson, V. J., & Zmud, R. W. (2003). The value relevance of announcements of transformational information technology investments. *Management Information Systems Quarterly, 27*(4), 637–656.

Dewan, S., & Ren, F. (2007). Risk and return of information technology initiatives: Evidence from electronic commerce announcements. *Information Systems Research, 18*(4), 370–394. doi:10.1287/isre.1070.0120

Donthu, N. (2001). Does your Web site measure up? *Marketing Management, 10*(4), 29.

Dos Santos, B. L., Peffers, K., & Mauer, D. C. (1993). The impact of information technology investment announcements on the market value of the firm. *Information Systems Research, 4*(1), 1–23. doi:10.1287/isre.4.1.1

Eisenmann, T., & Pothen, S. T. (2000). *Online portals* (Case No. 9-801-305) (pp. 1-29). Boston: Harvard Business School.

Ferguson, C., Finn, F., & Hall, J. (2005). Electronic commerce investments, the resource-based view of the firm, and firm market value. *International Journal of Accounting Information Systems, 6*, 5–29. doi:10.1016/j.accinf.2004.08.001

Gehrke, D., & Turban, E. (2000). Determinants of successful web-site design: relative importance and recommendations for effectiveness. In *Proceedings of the 32nd Hawaii International Conference on System Sciences*, HI.

Geyskens, I., Gielens, K., & Dekimpe, M. G. (2002). The market valuation of internet channel additions. *Journal of Marketing, 66*(2), 102–119. doi:10.1509/jmkg.66.2.102.18478

Gounaris, S., & Dimitriadis, S. (2003). Assessing service quality on the web: evidence from business-to-consumer portals. *Journal of Services Marketing, 17*(5), 529–548. doi:10.1108/08876040310486302

Hamel, G., & Sampler, J. (1998). The e-corporation (cover story). *Fortune, 138*(11), 80–87.

Hayes, D. C., Hunton, J. E., & Reck, J. L. (2000). Information systems outsourcing announcement: Investigating the impact on the market value of contract-granting firm. *Journal of Information Systems, 17*(2), 109–125. doi:10.2308/jis.2000.14.2.109

Hayes, D. C., Hunton, J. E., & Reck, J. L. (2001). Market reaction to ERP implementation announcements. *Journal of Information Systems, 15*(1), 3–18. doi:10.2308/jis.2001.15.1.3

Huizingh, E. K. R. E. (2002). The antecedents of web site performance. *European Journal of Marketing, 36*, 1225–1248. doi:10.1108/03090560210445155

Im, K. S., Dow, K. E., & Grover, V. (2001). A reexamination of IT investment and the market value of the firm: an event study methodology. *Information Systems Research, 12*(1), 103–117. doi:10.1287/isre.12.1.103.9718

Kalakota, R., & Whinston, A. (1996). *Frontiers of Electronic Commerce*. Reading, MA: Addison Wesley.

Keown, A., Martin, J., Petty, J., & Scott, D. (2004). *Financial Management: Principles and Applications*. Upper Saddle River, NJ: Prentice Hall.

Khallaf, A., & Skantz, T. R. (2007). The effects of information technology expertise on the market value of a firm. *Journal of Information Systems, 21*(1), 83–105. doi:10.2308/jis.2007.21.1.83

Kitchenham, B. (2004). *Procedures for Performing Systematic Reviews* (Tech. Rep. No. SE0401). Newcastle-under-Lyme, UK: Keele University.

Koh, J., & Venkatraman, N. (1991). Joint venture formations and stock market reactions: an assessment in the information technology sector. *Academy of Management Journal, 34*(4), 869–892. doi:10.2307/256393

Koller, M. (2001). Tool offers personalization on the fly. *Internet Week, 857*(16), 15.

Lee, H. G., Cho, D. H., & Lee, S. C. (2002). Impact of e-business initiatives on firm value. *Electronic Commerce Research and Applications, 1*(1), 41–56. doi:10.1016/S1567-4223(02)00005-4

Lin, J. C., Jang, W., & Chen, K. (2007). Assessing the market valuation of e-service initiatives. *International Journal of Service Industry Management, 18*(3), 224–245. doi:10.1108/09564230710751460

Liu, C., & Arnett, K. P. (2000). Exploring the factors associated with Web site success in the context of electronic commerce. *Information & Management, 38*, 23–34. doi:10.1016/S0378-7206(00)00049-5

Liu, C., Dub, T. C., & Tsai, H. (2009). A study of the service quality of general portals. *Information & Management, 46*, 52–56. doi:10.1016/j.im.2008.11.003

Loiacono, E. T., Watson, R. T., & Goodhue, D. L. (2002). WebQual: a measure of Website quality. In *Proceedings of the Marketing Educators' Conference: Marketing Theory and Applications* (Vol. 13, pp. 432-437).

Mahdavi, M., Shepherd, J., & Benatallah, B. (2004). A collaborative approach for caching dynamic data in portal applications. In *Proceedings of the fifteenth conference on Australian database* (Vol. 27, pp. 181-188).

McWilliams, A., & Siegel, D. (1997). Event studies in management research: Theoretical and empirical issues. *Academy of Management Journal, 40*(3), 626–657. doi:10.2307/257056

Meng, Z. L., & Lee, S. Y. (2007). The value of IT to firms in a developing country in the catch-up process: An empirical comparison of China and the United States. *Decision Support Systems, 43*(3), 737–745. doi:10.1016/j.dss.2006.12.007

Mishina, Y., Pollock, T. G., & Porac, J. F. (2004). Are more resources always better for growth? Resource stickiness in market and product expansion. *Strategic Management Journal, 25*(12), 1179–1197. doi:10.1002/smj.424

Oh, W., Gallivan, M. J., & Kim, J. W. (2006). The market's perception of the transactional risks of information technology outsourcing announcements. *Journal of Management Information Systems, 22*(4), 271–303. doi:10.2753/MIS0742-1222220410

Parasuraman, A., Zeithaml, V. A., & Berry, L. L. (1988). SERVQUAL: a multiple-item scale for measuring consumer perceptions of service quality. *Journal of Retailing, 64*(1), 12–40.

Parasuraman, A., Zeithaml, V. A., & Berry, L. L. (1994). Alternative scale for measuring service quality: A comparative assessment based on psychometric and diagnostic criteria. *Journal of Retailing, 70*(3), 201–230. doi:10.1016/0022-4359(94)90033-7

Paulin, M., & Perrien, J. (1996). Measurement of service quality: the effect of contextuality. In Kunst, P., & Lemmink, J. (Eds.), *Managing Service Quality* (3rd ed., pp. 257–273). London: Chapman.

Payne, A., & Holt, S. (2001). Diagnosing customer value. *British Journal of Management, 12*, 159–182. doi:10.1111/1467-8551.00192

Peak, D., Windsor, J., & Conover, J. (2002). Risks and effects of IS/IT outsourcing: a securities market assessment. *Journal of Information Technology Cases and Applications, 4*(1), 6–33.

Polgar, J., & Polgar, T. (2007). WSRP Relationship to UDDI. In Tatnall, A. (Ed.), *Encyclopaedia of Portal Technology and Applications* (*Vol. 1*, pp. 1210–1216). Hershey, PA: IGI Global.

Polgar, P., Bram, R., & Polgar, T. (2004). Building and Managing Enterprise Wide Web. In *Proceedings of the 2004 Informing Science and IT Education Joint Conference, Portals – Tutorial*, Monash University, Melbourne, Australia.

Ranganathan, C., & Brown, C. V. (2006). ERP investment and the market value of firms: Toward an understanding of influential ERP project variables. *Information Systems Research, 17*(2), 145–161. doi:10.1287/isre.1060.0084

Richardson, V. J., & Zmud, R. W. (2002). The Value Relevance of Information Technology Investments Announcements: Incorporating Industry Strategic IT Role. In *Proceedings of the 35th Hawaii International Conference on System Science*, HI.

Sabherwal, R., & Sabherwal, S. (2005). Knowledge Management Using Information Technology: Determinants of Short-Term Impact on Firm Value. *Decision Sciences, 36*(4), 531–568. doi:10.1111/j.1540-5414.2005.00102.x

Shilakes, C. C., & Tylman, J. (1998). *Enterprise information portals*. New York: Merril Lynch. Retrieved from http://www.sagemaker.com/home.asp?id=500&file=Company/WhitePapers/lynch.htm

Shuler, J. (2002). Of Web Portals, E-Gov, and the Public's Prints. *Information Policy the Journal of Academic Librarianship*, *28*(6), 410–413.

Sieber, S., & Volor-Sabatier, J. (2005). Competitive dynamics of general portals. In Tatnall, A. (Ed.), *Web portals: The new gateways to Internet information and services* (pp. 64–79). Hershey, PA: IGI Global.

Subramani, M., & Walden, E. (2001). The impact of e-commerce announcements on the market value of firms. *Information Systems Research*, *12*(2), 135–154. doi:10.1287/isre.12.2.135.9698

Tatnall, A. (2005). *Web Portals: from the General to the Specific*. In *Proceedings of the 6th International Working for E-Business (We-B) Conference*, Victoria University, Melbourne, Australia.

Van Riel, A. C. R., Liljander, V., Lemmink, J., & Streukens, S. (2002). *Boost customer loyalty with online support: the case of mobile telecomms providers*. Retrieved from http://www.fdewb.uni-maas.nl/blokken/9010/documents/onlinesup.pdf

Wang, Y.-S., Tang, T.-I., & Tang, J.-T. E. (2001). An instrument for measuring customer satisfaction toward Web sites that market digital products and services. *Journal of Electronic Commerce Research*, *2*(3), 1–14.

Webb, H. W., & Webb, L. A. (2004). SiteQual: An integrated measure of Web site quality. *The Journal of enterprise information management*, *18*(4).

Webopedia. (2010). Retrieved from http://webopedia.com/TERM/P/portal.html

Wolfinbarger, M. F., & Gilly, M. C. (2002). *comQ: dimensionalizing, measuring and predicting quality of the e-tailing experience* (Tech. Rep. No. 02-100). MSI.

Yang, Z., Cai, S., Zhou, Z., & Zhou, N. (2005). Development and validation of an instrument to measure user perceived service quality of information presenting Web portals. *Information & Management*, *42*(4), 575–589. doi:10.1016/S0378-7206(04)00073-4

Yang, Z., Peterson, R. T., & Huang, L. (2001). Taking the pulse of internet pharmacies: online consumers speak out on pharmacy services. *Marketing Health Services*, *21*, 4–10.

Yoo, B., & Donthu, N. (2001). Developing a scale to measure the perceived quality of internet shopping sites (SITEQUAL). *Quarterly Journal of Electronic Commerce*, *2*(1), 31–47.

Zeithaml, V. A., Parasuraman, A., & Malhotra, A. (2001). *A conceptual framework for understanding e-service quality: implications for future research and managerial practice* (Tech. Rep. No. 00-115, pp. 1-49). Cambridge, MA: MSI.

Zeithaml, V. A., Parasuraman, A., & Malhotra, A. (2002). Service quality delivery through Web sites: a critical review of extant knowledge. *Journal of the Academy of Marketing Science*, *30*(4), 362–375. doi:10.1177/009207002236911

Zhang, P., & Von Dran, G. (2001). Expectations and rankings of Website quality features: Results of two studies. In *Proceedings of the 34th Hawaii International Conference on System Sciences*.

Zhang, P., & Von Dran, G. (2002). User expectations and rankings of quality factors in different Web site domains. *International Journal of Electronic Commerce*, *6*(2), 9–33.

APPENDIX 1

Table A1. Sample of event studies on impact of IT announcements

Domain	Study	Years	Sample	Main Results
IT outsourcing	Hayes D C, 2000	1990 to 1997	76	No impact
	Peak D A, 2002	1988 to 1993	64	No Impact
	Oh W, 2004	1998 to 2001	97	Positive impact
	Agrawal M, 2006	1999 to 2002	96	Positive impact for 2 of 3 types of announcements.
	Oh, W, 2006	1995 to 2003	192	Positive impact
IT Investment	Dos Santos B L, 1993, P.1-23	1981 to 1988	97	No Impact
	Im K S, 2001, P.103-117	1981 to 1996	238	No Impact
	Chatterjee D, 2002, P.7-42	1992 to 1995	112	Positive impact
	Dardan S, 2006, P.100-111	1996 to 2001	57	Positive impact
	Oh W, 2006, P.19-44	1985 to 1999	430	Positive impact.
	Meng Z L, 2007, P.737-745	1999 to 2002	128	Positive impact - Chinese IT No impact for US.
E-Commerce	Subramani M, 2001, P.135-154	4th Qtr 1998	251	Positive impact
	Ferguson C, 2005, P.5-29	1988 to 2001	232	Positive impact
	Dewan S, 2007, P.370-394	1996 to 2002	640	No Impact
	Lin J C, 2007, P.224-245	1999 to 2002	179	Positive impact
Specific System / Process	Ranganathan C, 2006, P.145-161	1997 to 2001	116	Positive impact (ERp)
	Sabherwal R, 2007, P.409-422	1995 to 2002	103	Positive impact
CIO hiring	Chatterjee D, 2001, P.43-70	1987 to 1998	113	Positive impact
	Khallaf A, 2007, P.83-105	1987 to 2002	461	No Impact
New Product	Chaney et al. 1991	1975 to 1984	1101	Positive impact

APPENDIX 2

Table A2. List of companies

COMPANY NAME	EVENT DATE
CANON INC	Monday, September 28, 2009
COMCAST CORP NEW A	Thursday, September 10, 2009
DIGITAL REALTY TRUST INC	Tuesday, December 15, 2009
EASTMAN KODAK CO	Tuesday, April 14, 2009
EXTREME NETWORKS INC	Thursday, April 16, 2009
FIBERNET TELECOM GROUP INC	Monday, March 2, 2009
IBM Company	Monday, May 25, 2009

continued on following page

Table A2. Continued

COMPANY NAME	EVENT DATE
KEYNOTE SYSTEMS INC	Friday, August 28, 2009
LIFE TECHNOLOGIES CORP	Tuesday, July 7, 2009
LOCKHEED MARTIN CORP	Thursday, October 22, 2009
M G T CAPITAL INVESTMENTS INC	Monday, June 29, 2009
MERGE HEALTHCARE INC	Monday, November 16, 2009
MICROSOFT CORP	Friday, November 6, 2009
N D S GROUP PLC	Tuesday, January 13, 2009
NAVISITE INC	Wednesday, February 4, 2009
NETFLIX INC	Monday, August 3, 2009
RED HAT INC	Tuesday, September 1, 2009
REDIFF COM INDIA LTD	Friday, May 22, 2009
SOHU COM INC	Monday, February 9, 2009
VEOLIA ENVIRONNEMENT	Monday, September 21, 2009
VERIZON COMMUNICATIONS INC	Friday, April 17, 2009
WIPRO LTD	Friday, February 13, 2009
XATA CORP	Wednesday, August 19, 2009
YAHOO INC	Wednesday, February 18, 2009
YAHOO INC	Tuesday, August 25, 2009

APPENDIX 3

Table A3. Sample of web portal announcements

Date	Title
August 24, 2009	Yahoo Buys Arabic Web Portal Maktoob.com [T1]
Yahoo has agreed to buy Maktoob.com, an Arabian portal combining news, business and sports information with mail and chat services. The deal will allow Yahoo to **expand into a new region** *and to serve a linguistic market that it does not currently reach: Maktoob will give Yahoo the* **capability to develop** *Arabic versions of the Yahoo Mail and Yahoo Messenger communication services, it said Tuesday. Maktoob began life in 2000 as a Web-based e-mail service, and in May* **claimed around 16.6 million unique monthly visitors**. *The company is based in Jordan, with offices in Egypt, Kuwait, Saudi Arabia and the United Arab Emirates.*	
April 14, 2009	Kodak Offers eService Web Portal [T2]
ROCHESTER, N.Y. -- Kodak's eService, a new KODAK Service and Support web portal, makes it **easier for customers** *of KODAK Service and Support to submit, check and manage orders through a centralized location. The service is available for Kodak's Document Imaging Channel & Manufacturing Service Partners and Kodak's Retail Print Services customers.* *"Kodak's eService application* **provides users with the immediate ability** *to view their customers' equipment base, make changes on the fly to that base, place service calls, and monitor call status. The centralized, on-demand web portal serves as a* **differentiator and a value-add capability** *for the users of Kodak's service."With eService, ..., offering users* **an easier, faster method** *for submitting, viewing and managing their service requests.* *"With the launch of eService we have matched our* **best of breed onsite support** *with a trackable method of recording and monitoring service performance. The eService platform takes our partners' support to a new level of detail and availability: the proof of their value can be customized to* **meet their most demanding end customer requirements**.	

continued on following page

Table A3. Continued

Date	Title
January 13, 2009	Partner Communications Selects NDS PC Show™ to Power New VOD Content [T3]
*LONDON, UK – NDS, the leading provider of technology solutions for digital pay-TV, today announced that leading Israeli mobile operator Partner Communications, part of Hutchison Telecom International, has chosen NDS PC Show™ to deliver Video On Demand (VOD) securely over the Internet for its **newly launched content portal**. By implementing NDS PC Show, together with NDS Unified Headend™, Partner Communications is able to provide Israeli consumers who register on the website with a **wealth of video content** that can be viewed on their PCs. Partner Communications has almost **three million mobile customers** in Israel. NDS PC Show **provides the ideal solution** for enabling the delivery of VOD services and linear channels to PCs over the open Internet. Incorporating the highly robust content protection of NDS' VideoGuard PC™, it allows subscribers to watch content via an operator's branded web portal.*	
19 August 2009	XATA to Launch New Web-Based, Online Training Tool [T4]
*MINNEAPOLIS, Aug. 19 /PRNewswire-FirstCall/ -- XATA Corporation (Nasdaq: XATA), the expert in fleet optimization, today announced the September **launch of a new Web portal** that will allow XATA customers to **more effectively train** on the company's XATA-NET technology.* *"The key benefit of this online training is how it will streamline the adoption of XATANET with our customers," said Kevin Haus, director of training and installation for XATA Corporation. "Over time, it will empower fleet management to increase technology use and get full adoption from drivers and dispatchers."* *The new online training **offers several key benefits** over other training formats, including 24/7 access to self-directed coursework. Interactive features in the XATANET online-training modules make the website a more involved learning experience for users, and company fleet managers can customize the level of passing scores for all online testing.*	
Feb 18, 2009	Yahoo launches Yahoo! Mobile personalized Web portal [T5]
*Today, Yahoo! launched its multi-platform Yahoo! Mobile Web service that provides users with a **personalized Web portal** and Web starting point. Using the service, consumers can assemble content into a single location with choices from editor-selected top news, websites, RSS feeds, weather, stocks, and more. They can also **access a variety** of email, instant messaging, and social networking accounts. The service is accessible by mobile Web and an application is available for Apple's iPhone, Nokia, RIM, Samsung, Sony Ericsson.*	
October 22, 2009	LM launches geo-intel Web portal [T6]
*HERNDON, Va., Oct. 22 (UPI) -- U.S. company Lockheed Martin announced the **launch of its new Web portal** to provide users access to a geospatial images library to support mission planning.* *Lockheed Martin says the new Intelligence on Demand Web portal, launched with support from partner Pictometry International Corp., includes more than **100 million geospatial images** for register users. The Intelligence on Demand site was developed using Lockheed Martin's analytical tools and images from Pictometry as part of an effort to address the growing demand for geospatial intelligence for operational planning.* *"More and more U.S. federal government agencies are relying on geospatial intelligence to plan and conduct their operations," Roger Mann, Lockheed Martin Information Systems and Global Services-Intelligence director of advanced programs, said in a statement.*	

[T1] http://www.businessweek.com/technology/content/aug2009/tc20090825_293120.htm

[T2] http://members.whattheythink.com/news/index.cfm?id=39897

[T3] www.webwire.com/ViewPressRel.asp?Id=D84332

[T4] www.redorbit.com/news/business/1739872/xata_to_launch_new_webbased_online_training_tool

[T5] http://www.mobileburn.com/news.jsp?Id=6404

[T6] http://www.upi.com/Business_News/Security-Industry/2009/10/22/LM-launches-geo-intel-Web-portal/UPI-75251256242212/

This work was previously published in the International Journal of Web Portals 2(4), edited by Greg Adamson and Jana Polgar, pp. 1-17, copyright 2010 by Information Science Publishing (an imprint of IGI Global).

Chapter 15
Part of the Tool Kit:
SOA and Good Business Practices

Kee Wong
e-CentricInnovations, Australia

Greg Adamson
University of Melbourne, Australia

ABSTRACT

Portals, and Service Oriented Architecture in general, simplify the process of delivering services to users. But this doesn't represent a fundamental change to the user experience. Changing the user experience depends on business intent, and while Web 2.0 functionality is available for users today, corporate and government department practices are often not ready to embrace it. In fact the most effective uptake of new technologies may not be the company intranet at all, but an external company community hosted on MySpace or Facebook. This case study examines the experiences of delivering both strategy and implementations to Fortune 500-type companies and Australian government departments. It compares the experience of delivering web and pre-web services, and notes the impact of the global financial crisis on innovation, concluding with the observation that in this changing climate SOA remains part of the industry practitioner's toolkit.

INTRODUCTION

While Portals and Service Oriented Architecture have held a high profile in planning user facing technologies in recent years, in practice their implementation runs up against user uncertainty about what they provide. In part is due to the

DOI: 10.4018/978-1-4666-0336-3.ch015

traditional approach of many company and government senior managers, and in part it reflects the fact that while Portals can simplify customer solution delivery, they don't provide a uniquely different end-user experience. To gain a practitioners' perspective on this, the following case study was undertaken with Kee Wong, CEO of e-CentricInnovations (http://www.e-centricinnovations.com.au), who is interviewed by Dr. Greg

Adamson, co-Editor-in-Chief of the *International Journal of Web Portals*.

Question: Can you describe the sector that your company works in and its activities in relation to portal and Service Oriented Architecture [SOA] implementations?

We are a consulting company and we also do systems integration. So for us the boundary between portals and SOA, and integration in general, is not hard defined. We could develop strategy involving a lot of thinking around a portal. Alternatively we could implement a portal technology solution in a particular business unit within a multinational company, or within government. Every time we do a portal implementation we have to think about the architecture: how to integrate the application that the user sees as a portal interface to back-end systems that may reside within an organisation or sometimes external to the organisation. So integration becomes important as well. We find that SOA becomes an acceptable way for people to build the integration layer, because it helps shield the application and the user from the changes that might occur in the back-end. By default SOA is a key part of designing a good portal solution, architecting it and then implementing it.

We do business in government, retail, manufacturing, supply chain, banking and finance. They are all the same in that a portal solution is about providing the right application to the audience you are giving information to, and then abstracting that information from systems. Some of those systems are transactional, others are non-transactional. The information could be a policy document that sits in a document management system, for example. It could be information that has been extracted from publicly available websites. It could be HR [human resources] information that is merged out of a policy document and a transaction system that relates to payroll information. It could combine superannuation system information

from a superannuation provider and business-to-business connectivity with the company you are dealing with. It could go in any direction. There can be portals for HR, portals for supply chain, portals for executive dashboards, portals for sales information, portals for occupational health and safety, portals for supplier performance, portals for customer satisfaction, and so on.

Typically our customers are larger sized companies. We tend to work with customers who are in the Top 200 category, whether they are multinationals with a presence in Australia, or Australian multinationals, and also government, federal and state. We tend not to work with smaller companies than this, because of our origins. Before I started eCentricInnovation I used to run a division in IBM for enterprise integration, integrating front-end and back-end systems, so we were used to dealing with Fortune 500-type companies.

Q. How are your customers using the technologies that you advise on and implement?

In the business world nothing much has changed in terms of managing human resources and managing enterprise resources. A few years ago they coined the term ERP [Enterprise Resource Planning]. It provided information that an information worker could work with. Taking that forward, how do you get more citizens and people interacting through new technology? E-mail is a wonderful tool that traditionally didn't exist. Now we just take it for granted because it is being used more extensively in the last 10 or 12 years. Now we have Twitter (http://twitter.com) and Facebook (http://www.facebook.com) and others, and Google (http://www.google.com) as a portal. People are able to connect because of the availability of tools for the consumer across many devices, not just a laptop or a desktop with a web browser but on a mobile phone, on a PDA [personal digital assistant] and so on. But the premise is still the same. You have an interface that a user can interact with, and then information that can come from a source somewhere. With the proliferation of the Internet it means that the source can be not necessarily from a particular domain of your company, a domain of the country you live in, or your own government. We can get access to information that is government-related from any country in the world, if we are given the access to it.

For SOA and portals, what proportion of it is being done in a traditional way, basically just accepting information from a legacy system, and what proportion is being applied in a more innovative way that allows people new use of it? I think that it's happening on both fronts. A large proportion of the work that we and a lot of organisations are doing in the corporate world, in government, is the traditional business model. A small portion is now starting to become more innovative. You find that organisations are still run by CEOs [chief executive officers] who are our age, and if you did a survey of the number of CEOs who have their own Facebook page you will find a surprisingly low proportion. They still don't get it, but they don't care, because in five or ten years they are going to retire. Somebody else can come behind them and take the organisation into a new direction. Having said that, there are middle managers who are getting into applying some of these technologies to the workforce and maybe beyond, to other stakeholders that use them. So you find that the best ways to apply Web 2.0, Web 3.0 technologies are still being discovered.

Q. So your customers are grappling with how to use these technologies?

To come back to portals, lots of portal software is being sold, but very little has been applied well. A lot of people are looking at the portal as an interface that is a bit puzzling, asking "what do we put there?" A lot of people think of content. So behind that is a web content management system that allows people to author, approve, publish and retire content. But you could do that without a portal. So what do you do after content? Well, we'll add a calendar. Fine: And then maybe we access our e-mail on that. And then some productivity tools. Then we put something sticky [changing content that encourages viewers to return to a site], some sort of banner-type things, whether it is the temperature of a particular city or a stock price or whatever the case may be. But beyond that what do people think they ought to put on a portal?

We do a lot of work with organisations that want a portal to be about business process integration, about application integration efficiency. So now, in the corporate world, implementing a portal is about having the right application for a particular user of that portal. The innovative way in the corporate world is making the portal personalised for a worker who is looking at a particular piece of information. For example, you may be in the Sales department and I may be in the HR department. The company is not going to build one portal for me and one portal for you. They will have one portal. What they do is apply the innovation in, for example, security systems. These say that when you sign on they known your profile, your job function, and the mandatory things that you need to see on your portal. Then they allow you the latitude of choosing other things that are not mandatory but you like to add on, individually selected information. And I can do the same thing. But when I sign in I am HR, and see the HR portal first. You sign in and you see the Sales portal first. The information has some common parts, a company bulletin and so on, but there are others that mostly fit each job role. The way they do that is that the security system and software identifies you as a person with a certain profile, and then automatically splits the right information into your portal and gives you access to certain systems that you get and I don't. Then the ability to have personalised profiling on your preferences means you can add a function to it.

But there are limitations. Here is one example, the intranet. Intranet is a portal isn't it? Can you tell me, if we had them in this room, how many organisations would put their hand up and say we have a very successful intranet project? The sorts of comments I get are universal. "We can't find things on the intranet." "We've got a lot of outdated stuff on the intranet." "The thing we are looking for isn't there." "It's very hard to find the stuff we need." A lot of this has nothing to do with technology. It is about managing the content in a way that meets people's expectations. The only intranets that work well are those with mandatory applications people have no other access to: payroll, leave applications, expense management. There are HR-related things that people have a personal interest in and so they have to go to: job applications and so on. Other than that you find people very rarely want to go and look at a new company policy, or what the CEO has to say. In a company that incents people on how well the stock price is performing, you can bet everybody will be looking at the stock price every day. Those are the sticky things that make people want to go to the intranet. But other than that they won't, funnily enough.

There is a de facto intranet in any organisation. It is called MySpace and Facebook. It connects people who are employees of a company, but outside the company. You will find that a major telecommunications or airlines Facebook community or the Victorian government Department of so-and-so Facebook community has more activity than on a corporate created intranet. Why? It is not the technology. It is "what's in it for me, and why do I want to come?" That I think is the most important need to understand when you try to create a portal environment, whether an intranet, an extranet or whatever. What makes people want to come to these? Maybe it is because they don't like people to monitor what they do. Maybe they don't have the freedom to say what they want to say. Maybe there isn't the glue that gels a particular clique together. Maybe they don't want to talk about the next event they want to have because they have a union issue at work, who knows. And some organisations put a stop to

any external information they don't want you to have. There are organisations that say you can't go to Facebook during work hours, and just stop people from doing that. So I think in the corporate world where I spend a lot of time, and in government, depending on the objective of the particular solution, there's not a lot of innovation in terms of being out there, allowing people to interact in a social sense. But people do that from home anyway. You will find that the de facto intranet happens outside the organisation. Now isn't that interesting? But is that portal? Of course it is.

Q. What are the challenges for your customers?

Most of the companies we deal with already had awareness in portal technology. More than half had them installed and kept them for two or three years but struggled to find how to apply them. Others come to us because our business is consulting. As trusted advisers to business we provide people who sit with the C[chief]-level executives, whether they are marketing, finance or sales, or the CEO or CIO [chief information officer]. We can say, here is something that other organisations are doing in the space of CRM [customer relationship management] or procurement, or managing performance for their distributors or suppliers or customer. Here is what other organisations are doing building a community of interest. One of our clients is a major motorcycle and power equipment company. There is a strong community of motorcycle riders who like to tell other people what they are doing: extending the performance of their machine, or doing a trip, or running a certain event, and so on. Some people like to discuss technically related stuff. Without the Internet how do you do it? You go to a club, you put on biscuits, you put on coffee, people talk. You use a telephone and you meet physically. With the Internet maybe you don't have to meet. People still like to socialise physically, but a lot of those things can be done electronically. People can do research, they can find out more about how they can improve the performance of things. Maybe they can have a dialogue with an expert, either within the company or outside the company. They can interact with people in other parts of the world.

Some of the portal concepts are brought to our customers through things that we know, industries that we understand and work that has been done elsewhere, that we are aware of. In other cases the customer prompts us. They come to us and say, "My people in marketing tell me we should be doing this. What do you think?" I say, it is a good thing to have an idea put on the table, let's explore that a little bit more. We could start with prototyping: why we are doing this, what outcome do we want, where is the starting point? Are they fully aware of all the issues and challenges, all the requirements that need to be in place? Then, how fast do they want to do it? How sophisticated do they want on Day 1. If the idea is there, then paint the vision, because it takes just as much energy to be bold as to be timid. But then scale back and say, realistically, what expectation do we need to set so that we don't disappoint people when we take the first step? How many resources do you have practically to make that happen, because if you set an expectation and deliver short you will disappoint people and maybe lose the opportunity for them to ever come back again? Those softer issues are more important in a successful portal implementation than the technical issues. The technical issues are pretty well established in a lot of cases. Our value-add to people that we deal with is managing expectations, knowing the change requirement, the change management aspect, and the need to take people along. Everybody is focussed more on one dimension of making technology work, but what is required to manage success? My entire experience is that technology is the easy bit. Making people want to adopt it is hard.

Q. What is new about SOA and portals?

The concept behind Service Oriented Architecture, believe it or not, is not new. Its principle has been part of good design for many years.

The difference with SOA is that the technology available now to manage that architecture is more sophisticated. When people talk about Service Oriented Architecture it means that you have "services". People tend to put the word "web" in front of "services", but they don't have to be web services. These services are specific in their purpose. They might be providing information about an employee, providing information about sales figures, or just doing a calculation routine to work out the compensation for a particular line of insurance. The idea is "invent it once and use it many times". It embeds business rule so that people don't need to know those rules. All they know is that they can trust that when they put something in they will get something out that is always going to be consistent.

The same application that you now build using portal as a platform, you could have built 10 years ago. The difference with portal technology is that it shields the difficulty. You don't have to hand-code user registration, profiling, identity management, access management, integration, portal-to-portal communication. So a lot of the stuff that you do with portal today you could do without portal technology, but it needed hand coding. If you did the right thing componentising everything yourself, architecting it so that the framework is scaleable, layered correctly and so on, by default you could have built a portal engine. Most organisations that did that were not software companies, so they didn't take the assets and package them into something they could sell to someone else. Nevertheless there is nothing today in a portal platform that you couldn't do without it. A user doesn't see anything differently when something is implemented as a portal. To some extent a portal is actually less flexible, because you have to fit in with the framework and template that is provided. To go beyond that template is pretty hard. There are key limits and supports in place that you can't remove. They are like pillars in a building: if you remove them the building will collapse. Today Service Oriented

Architecture provides a framework for managing the discovery of services that have been built, the ongoing maintenance of that framework, business rules for organisation changes so that people can still find and use the framework and have a cycle of management for maintaining the system so there is no duplication or slight variation of the same rules for example. That didn't exist in the past. People built their own services and managed them. Having an inventory of services and lifecycle management plan has always been a challenge.

In the past you could walk into any organisation that called themselves [quality standard] ISO9000 compliant and ask, "Can I audit the documentation of your system?" I can bet you everyone would fail. They were never up to date, and they never could be. Think about SOA as a variation of that and say, "Can you tell me all the web services that are being used in your organisation? Are you 100 per cent accurate in your inventory? Can you absolutely ensure that your governance rules are satisfied?" The answer will be No as well. When you become serious, SOA software vendors are providing frameworks and tools to help manage that better. But the situation today is no different to 20 years ago. I build a software routine that is sitting there centrally. I allow people to apply a business rule or whatever it executes. I call it a "service", and it provides the right answer back to the person who called that function. These days it tends to be written as a web-based application, and therefore you call it a web service.

Q. How sophisticated are your customers in relation to SOA governance?

At its simplest form, take the "governance" word out and replace it with "govern". How do you govern a good environment so that it doesn't break or doesn't get misused? First of all that means there is a level of understanding of statements and quality. You wouldn't make a web service available unless it has been tested and the description of its function is clearly specified.

Then you would define who is allowed to play the web service, who is allowed to manage it, who is allowed to take out the system. There needs to be some level of ownership, which is part of the governance. Then you define how it is made accessible to people, who is going to maintain it on an on-going basis, who is allowed to request it and who is allowed to use it. The rules of the game have to be clearly specified. Different roles require different ownership. Who supervises to make sure that all of the rules are kept relevant, and change with time as changes are required? That, for me, is governance.

I don't think there is a really well established SOA environment anywhere in the world. I think it is a new game. There are different degrees of sophistication. People have rules that they make up as they go along. I don't know of anyone in the corporate world or any government department with a governing body that says absolutely, "We are the body that governs this SOA environment and this is how we interact with external people; this is how we interact with internal people". A lot of companies have external suppliers that come in and build systems for them and integrate with existing systems. Such a governing body would say: "The first thing you need to do before you come in is to understand we have an SOA environment and you need to understand the rules of the game here. Here are the people with authority that you need to speak to and here is the induction." I don't think there is one. Yet this is how you should run an SOA environment. So I would say that there are different levels of sophistication and understanding about SOA.

Q. In your experience over the past one to two years, how has the global financial crisis affected customers in terms of their interest in innovation?

I think the global financial crisis has severely impacted most organisations that I know, including government. I chair the AIIA (Australian Information Industry Association, http://www.aiia.com.

au) report into federal government procurement, and every state now is looking towards the federal government and saying "that's what we want to do too". I think the global financial crisis has cut tremendously into people's capital expenditure, and typically innovation comes under capital expenditure rather than operational expense. Operational expenses are being cut as well. At the moment most organisations do not have the latitude to do R&D or innovation that adds value to the business in a more intangible way. Most companies are just keeping the lights on at the moment, having less on.

Even technology-based cost reduction is very hard to justify. If you ask to spend $1 million with a view that you might get $2 million back in three years, they say no. If you spend $1 million that reduces headcount to the value of $1.5 million within a short timeframe, in the next three to six months, then they will spend it. It has to be a direct return that is putting money in the bank. Otherwise it is very hard to convince people to spend money these days.

Q: In many organisations we are seeing a widespread adoption of the Microsoft SharePoint portal product (http://sharepoint.microsoft.com). Is this an important trend?

SharePoint is catching up to its competitors. The person who is revolutionising what Share-Point is doing is Ray Ozzie. Ray invented Lotus Notes. He joined Microsoft in 2005 and it was a real coup for Bill Gates. Bill has always admired Ray Ozzie. When Ray left Lotus and IBM he created a technology called Groove. Groove is built on Microsoft technology, and Microsoft bought Groove and got Ray into the organisation. Groove was meant to be the non-Lotus version of Lotus: a collaborative platform that allowed people to share things, that empowered a user to be flexible. SharePoint is that, and now SharePoint is catching up with Lotus Notes. It has Forms, you can do Workflow with it, it is a reasonable Document

Management System, it allows collaboration. Lotus has always been a portal. I would go further. Remember PKI [Public Key Infrastructure]? Lotus has had PKI from Day 1, with public and private keys for authentication. Any organisation that uses Lotus Domino (http://www-01.ibm.com/software/lotus/products/domino/) internally has by default engaged PKI, including electronic signatures, identifying someone through their certificate, so that you can't circumvent the security model. So MOSS, Microsoft Office SharePoint Server (http://office.microsoft.com/sharepointserver) continues an existing trend. People who don't want to go to the Lotus Domino environment have an alternative Microsoft space.

I think it is easier to adopt a Microsoft environment than it is to adopt a Domino environment. You have to get used to the UI [user interface] for Domino. The thick client performance is still not as good. It is acceptable. But if you have never been in a Lotus environment and you came in you would be on a learning curve. It is not intuitive. Once you get used to it you accept it. If an organisation hasn't got Domino and hasn't got SharePoint, I don't think they are going to pick Domino. They will go with SharePoint. And some people who have already got Lotus Notes may migrate to Microsoft Exchange and Outlook. Once you go down that direction you are not going to use Lotus Domino. So I think over time Microsoft will just overtake Lotus. It is like VHS and Beta [video cassette recorder standards]. It doesn't matter whether your technology is good or not, it is just where the crowd is going. The crowd went with VHS and that was the end of Beta.

Q. IBM has played a important part in establishing the SOA roadmap. Where do you see that in IBM's strategy today?

IBM is still the biggest patent submitter in the world, and they have been for many years. So there is a lot of innovation from IBM. I think a lot of the R&D goes towards features to do with green planning, green technologies and smart grid. Its focus is on making machines more green and efficient, about power consumption and requirements, and also about making software more clever in terms of managing demand at the point of use: power generation to suit demand, a pull model rather than a push model. The power industry is probably the last remnant of "it doesn't matter what the demand is, we will keep making it and pushing it out. If it is not used it is fine, if there is a peak period and we don't produce enough then that is bad luck, we'll install something in between." So I think the smart grid approach is to say "No, we'll produce just what is required, and if we have excess we will store it so we can draw it down at some point in time." That means we have got less at the point of generation in terms of unnecessary greenhouse gasses. In this and in other areas of technology development, SOA will be part of the toolkit.

Chapter 16
Interview:
Portal Experiences of Not-for-Profit Organisations

Greg Adamson
University of Melbourne, Australia

Rick Noble
N2 Services, Australia

ABSTRACT

Not-for-profit organisations are significant users of IT services, including Portals, for the use of public outreach and service delivery. While lacking the resources of the commercial sector, many not-for-profit organisations' needs may be similarly complex if they are relying on a portal for service delivery to a vulnerable client sector, or for the protection of medical records. In this paper, the authors examine the experience of service delivery to two medium-sized not-for-profits in Melbourne, Australia.

INTRODUCTION

Not-for-profit organisations make extensive use of portal technology for public outreach and service delivery. This case study looks at the challenges of a resource-poor sector and how it meets often sophisticated requirements. The study is based on the experience of industry practitioner Rick Noble, who has worked with not-for-profits in a technology development, support and man-agement capacity for more than 10 years. He is interviewed by Greg Adamson, co-Editor-in-Chief of the *International Journal of Web Portals*.

Can You Provide An Introduction to the Use of Portals by Not-For-Profit Organisations?

Various not-for-profit organisations will think of portals in different ways. It depends on the maturity of the organisation and which area or sector they are in as to what their interpretation and sense of

DOI: 10.4018/978-1-4666-0336-3.ch016

meaning of the word portal is. It is a generic term for many, perhaps not well understood by some. In one sense portal for some organisations just refers to a web site. It is an entry point for their service users. It could mean a collection of sites that have a common thread.

There are a number of organisations I have worked with that have been developing web sites for service users as an entry point to a range of service models. There are three types of web sites that not-for-profits engage with.

First is the primary web site. The main web site is their public facing marketing and information site. It is their reference point of contact for potential funding partners, service users and general public.

The second type of site that not-for-profits engage in is specifically service driven, so it needs to deliver a product via the web. A couple of good examples are amphetamine type sites www.meth.org.au and www.bluebelly.org.au. These sites are about meth and amphetamine use and harm minimisation. They are two pertinent examples around a service based web site, provided by medium sized not-for-profits.

The third is an ancillary web site, developed as an additional entry point or complementary service to a core project. This is typically a 'landing page' style or a small set of pages with a limited amount of information.

Each one of these three traditionally has a different funding source. That is key for not-for-profits. The main site is rarely funded: not-for-profits when they go for tenders rarely get infrastructure funding, as opposed to universities and others, who do get the money to do a job, and money to support the workers in providing that service. The third one, the ancillary site, is very rarely funded so that needs to come from other sources, whether it is an internal funding stream or development funds.

So Funding is a Major Issue?

The funding model for service-based sites is a really interesting one. It is an external environment which sets up a competition between organisations that would otherwise be collaborative. So there is a tension between collaboration and competition when portals are set up in a tendering environment. The problem is with the cost in time of responding to tenders. The Collaborative Internet Innovation Fund (CIIF) tendering model is a little different. They will seek expressions of interest, and then the shortlisted candidates receive money to develop their proposal. Rather than have to find the time and money internally, it is a funded process. That is a key change. CIIF is in their second round of funding. If you look at most of the major Australian government departments, they seek response to tenders in a competitive manner.

Each of the three types of sites tends to be underfunded compared to commercial areas, so the level of funding provided to produce a particular web site or portal of a particular quality is normally sub-standard, and to some degree the lack of funding has to be compensated for by additional effort and input from the staff involved.

I've worked on all three types of portals, primarily with two different organisations, one of which is Moreland Hall. Both are around the 100 EFT [equivalent full time] mark, about $10 million in terms of expenditure and therefore funding, on which they aim to break even. The client base is either drug users; drug affected groups such as families, or wider society, maybe a particular community; and policy makers within government. Both the organisations I have worked with operate on a harm minimisation model.

I think it is worth looking at two meth/amphetamine sites, which have a lot in common. Certainly the two organisations have similarities and those sites, meth.org.au and bluebelly.org.au have a close relationship and a similar commonwealth funding stream.

Funding certainly has an impact in terms of the technology that is used and the type of resourcing that is supplied. If we look at the funded service models, a site that is built with funding, they can be and normally are outsourced to a web developer. They tend to have a slightly higher level in terms of quality, needing to meet expectations of professionalism, even though it's a not-for-profit rather than a commercial site. They tend to use open source technologies.

This sits within a wider technologic requirement of not-for-profits. Technology is absolutely important, and increasingly so over the last five years. One not-for-profit I worked closely with has a high emphasis on research as a core business line. On-line surveying as a technology has become increasingly important and relevant to both delivering service and to success for getting funding. The degree of dependence or reliance on IT is increasing. Whether that is acknowledged at a business level within an organisation is up for further consideration.

Given This Shortage of Funds, are the Needs of the Not-for-Profit Sector Therefore Simpler?

Not at all. The expectations of a product delivered by a not-for-profit compared to a commercial one are the same in many ways. There is an expectation of quality, of presentation, of function. A not-for-profit is expected to have a good site, but it can't be too good, because it looks to funders as if they have spent too much money on it.

The functionality requirements are fairly high. For service provision we need to have integrated content: video content, RSS feeds, branching out to newsrooms, distributions, linking YouTube and other social media platforms into these sites. Given that the sector in general uses open source platforms, the demands on these are quite high. For example, Wordpress doesn't quite cut it, either for the main sites or service based sites. We

need a platform that has a reasonably high level of integration and sophistication.

Then there are the requirements for privacy. This is a challenge, although not necessarily a problem or issue. Anonymity is a key positive in the clients' eyes. If you look at meth/amphetamine users they seem to be typically bordering on paranoia, or having dual health issues such as having a combination of drug and mental health issues. The maturity of a site or portal is measured by the ability of a client to interact with a degree of anonymity.

Looking at meth.org.au, the client can register to receive harm reduction tips around amphetamine use via SMS and by e-mail. Anonymity is a key requirement there. So there are strong statements around privacy for the client. They can register just a mobile phone number without any other details. They can browse and read some of the content without any registration process. Meth.org.au was developed about three years ago. The bluebelly.org.au site is more recent and far more interactive. It provides service from the organisation as well from peers. So meth/amphetamine users can bounce ideas off other meth/amphetamine users in a totally anonymous way. Anonymity is absolutely key. Guaranteeing anonymity can be a real challenge and requires strong content systems that are monitored, attention to the setup of infrastructure, and good presentation. When creating these sites, some of the scoping feedback from the ground pointed to a need to not reference the organization building the site, or to mention government involvement even at a funding level. There is an important issue of trust for these people.

If we were to draw a map of meth/amphetamine users and web sites, there are sites like bluelight, pill reports (both by Enlighten - http://www.en-lighten.org.au/wordpress/about/) and, the heroin diaries (theaustralianheroindiaries.blogspot.com), which essentially are just out there in the cloud. They have been started by individuals or small groups and grown organically. There are a whole lot of services sites that have been funded and provided at no charge. The web of use is quite a complex one. There is some involvement from police, journalists and other agencies in these sites. A pseudonym may be used by a researcher who wants to get a thread for the next batch of research that might be relevant. They may present themselves as a user and get a lead on the inside. When journalists and police do this it undermines the sites, and raises some ethical questions.

Privacy is particularly important when an organisation deals directly with clients. There are regulations that not-for-profits need to comply with. In Australia in terms of portals, if a not-for-profit is getting funding for a service-based site or even their main site, by 2012 they will need to comply with the web accessibility guidelines AA standard. I am not aware of any that are pursuing that actively. They are certainly aware that it needs to be done, but in an environment like this I expect it is not going to happen in advance of the requirement coming into force.

Given the Environment You Describe, What are the Decision Processes and Key Requirements of a Portal Product?

Issues include cost and support. There is certainly advice taken from vendors and vendors have preferred content management systems. In contrast to medium sized commercial organisations, the not-for-profit area tends to be more collaborative. The experience of other organisations feeds into the decision process for an organisation. That collaborative environment is a huge positive among the mid-sized not-for-profits. We can see this particularly in the case of human resource management. Human resources in not-for-profits improved its form about a year ago. HR folk in around 400 not-for-profit organisations in the Victorian region have organically grown into a group. They have regular e-mail, some newsletters, they bounce ideas off peers. I think this group has

the potential to use a portal based system across all the participating organisations. To a lesser degree there is also interaction between IT folk in the sector.

Despite the shortage of money, a web portal is a very cost effective method of providing a web based service. Not-for-profits tend to use open source platforms. The choice of platforms is often not well informed in the not-for-profit sectors and once staff is used to a platform there is tendency to not explore other platforms that may be better solutions. There is also a degree of reliance on the preferences of outsourced providers.

Among the various open source solutions, the difference comes down whether they have adopted a user centric design. There are a couple of open source platforms that have been built by technologists for technologists. They function very well, but they are difficult to use for the lay person. These include Joomla, Drupal and WordPress, which are very common both in not-for-profit and other spaces. They are strong platforms, but the usability is not as high as others.

The change from 'tech for tech' to 'tech for users' is a core move. It is attractive to not-for-profits and sits better with a human service provision approach. Systems that are built with a person in mind are far closer to the core values of the not-for-profit sector.

Concrete5 (released under the MIT software license) is the one that I have been using and seen being used more frequently. It is built by technologists for non-technical users. In my own experience I have seen that someone with clinical experience doesn't need a degree of technical experience to effectively host and manage a content and functionally rich site. The next one that is going to be a real contender in about six months is Typo3 version 5 (released under the GNU General Public License). It has recently moved from a technology focus, built by techies for techies, to a user-centric focus, built by techies for users. I've used Typo3 (older versions) for a couple of moderate sized sites. It is more of a framework than a system, and has huge flexibility.

The move towards design for users is driven by usage. The Concrete5 folk and the people developing the next version of Typo3, clearly identify the usage aspect. They have realised that even with the greatest technology setting and the greatest platform, if people managing and using a site can't use it, then its efficacy is reduced.

In the Concrete5 model, a couple of guys who had worked in the commercial space made enough money to do the things that they really wanted to do, to help people. They were able to pursue more philanthropic ambitions. From that technology starting point Concrete 5 was rewritten viewing the user as the central point. The MVP (http://www.concrete5.org/documentation/introduction/model-view-controller), model is applied with the user centric focus. It is a methodology that takes a number of things into account. So Concrete 5 has MVP and the user centric focus. Typo3 which is a fantastic product is taking that step now. They are going back and rewriting their core products with MVP and a user centric approach as two principles.

Do the Commercial Portal Systems Have Much Presence in the Not-For-Profit Sector?

No, there is a double cost barrier: cost of function, and usability for non-technical staff. The outlay costs are more. IBM WebSphere has functionality but lacks usability from a not-for-profit perspective. As for Microsoft SharePoint, most not-for-profits get not-for-profit licensing, or leverage educational licensing if they have a strong education arm of their organisation. For this reason the cost of SharePoint licensing is about one-tenth of the commercial cost. However, implementation costs are no cheaper for not-for-profits. SharePoint 'out of the box' is quite a good product. Some organisations I know do use SharePoint for their internal knowledge management and document management, but they are not using it effectively. Licensing is lower, but implementation is still as expensive, so not-for-profits often can't afford to implement it effectively.

On the other hand, you can implement an open source product more cost effectively than a commercial one. The key is support. The level of user community based support and advice, around implementation issues and problem solving, is higher and more current than it is with commercial products. The commercial product implementation is done by a third party, a specialist in the area, at a cost. All it takes for a not-for-profit to implement an open source system is to be aware of the right system for their needs and to be aware of the support structures that exist in terms of implementation, maintenance and ongoing support. Most of the open source platforms have fairly strong support communities. It is peer support, but paying for support where it is available is also a possibility.

How Do Not-for-Profits You Have Worked With Address the Issue of Support?

One of the challenges for not-for-profits is to attract and develop staff with relevant technical skills. Staffs that have had content knowledge in the alcohol and drug sector, for example, and have content knowledge in the IT space, are not that common. It is certainly different for the not-for-profits to recruit to those positions. This staffs is also typically expected to provide input to ICT projects in addition to providing core services.

It's siloed. You tend to get staff who have the context expertise in, for example, clinical areas. Then at a certain size the not-for-profit starts to have its own internal lines where ICT staff are developed. There is a correlation between the two groups I have worked with regarding the combined skill sets across a couple of areas. Moreland Hall is a good example. There are two staff out of 100 who have both clinical and IT knowledge.

Because of this they are effectively the leaders of the organisation in terms of its on-line aspirations.

Where a not-for-profit looks to an external commercial organisation to deliver services, the external organisation won't begin with specialist clinical or other knowledge. They will generally follow the same flow or business process that they would apply to any client to undertake a needs analysis, develop a specification, develop a draft, and so on. It is a fairly typical flow, with staff at the not-for-profit providing the context.

There are advantages and disadvantages to depending on external service providers. At one not-for-profit I set up all the hosting internally: we housed it in a data centre, but the infrastructure was owned by the organisation. Moreland Hall has gone down a slightly different path. All the infrastructure is outsourced, so they are using a purely hosted model. That ties back into a lack of infrastructure funding for core tenders for not-for-profits. The skill set at Moreland Hall is that they know where to go to find that support, not to deliver the support themselves.

At the other not-for-profit, there was a degree of knowledge and experience held internally in by IT and content staff around particular products that are being used. I think the advantage of an in-sourced model is you get greater synergy. A good example would be the search capability across sites. There may be a number of different funded service based sites, a couple of main sites for business itself and then an overarching search function across all of those sites. You can't really do that unless you have a degree of ownership around the infrastructure and the models that are being used. The Moreland Hall model is outsourced, different hosting platforms, different developers, different providers. Trying to get an oversight of all of those sites and the content particularly from a search perspective and from the site management perspective is not quite there yet.

I think the in-sourced model is a better one for that, but the costs were moderate to implement that and maintain it. It is hard to exactly compare the costs. With the in-sourced model it is possible to calculate the cost of wages, of infrastructure and get a fairly accurate estimate. The outsourced model is more difficult to add up. Some of that is around the support costs. It may or may not be paid support.

How Aware are Not-For-Profits of Technology Governance?

I would describe them as not quite mature. On a Gartner scale they are mid-way, 'ad hoc' or just coming into the 'managed' classification. ICT tends to be driven by the skill sets of internal staff. If staff has reasonable skill sets then the level of maturity of the organisation in terms of its provision of ICT services from governance through to management and operations tends to be reasonable. It is certainly not high.

Then we have standards compliance. Not-for-profits are just starting to get their heads around practices such as ITIL, looking at the Australian Standards for guiding their internal support services. The Australian ICT Standards (i.e. AS AS8015 and ISO38500) are quite good in terms of their scalability to be applied at the medium level. However, organisations are only just starting to come to the point of realising the value of IT in their organisation. I think that is a comment back to the maturity level of the organisations. The larger not-for-profits are essentially run as businesses. The mid-sized not-for-profits are still getting their heads around some fundamental business practices. In a smaller not-for-profit, it is the staff who have an interest in IT who tend to help build or deliver the services or support them. A good comparison is finance. Most organisations look after their finances well, but most small to medium not-for-profits still aren't looking after their IT as well as they should. The better financial management is partly due to regulation. The finance area is a regulated one. There are mandatory standards that need compliance.

Looking at the two organisations I have worked with, Moreland Hall was a little more ad hoc. I think one of the hurdles you need to go through to adopt the in-sourced model is demonstrating value, and I think that would have resulted in a higher maturity level around issues such as governance. But the outsourced model can have a greater degree of flexibility and responsiveness. An organisation has greater choice about when they need to go to get something done.

Does the Lack of Money Lead to Experimentation?

As they say, necessity is the mother of invention. On-line surveying is an example. Looking back five years ago the commercial on-line surveying market was fairly immature. When the initial requirement to undertake on-line surveying in the research environment emerged, nothing was out in the market. At one not-for-profit I worked closely with, we built an on-line surveying system, contributed to the code developers, made some of that code available to other developers. A system called PHP Surveyor led to another fork named Lime Survey - a fantastic open source system published under the GNU GPL.

Some of the more progressive not-for-profits, such as Moreland Hall, are very supportive of innovative risk taking. As an example exploring the use and benefit of Web 2.0 technologies and social media for their staff and clients is encouraged.

There isn't enough research into use of these technologies to provide evidence yet. There is some anecdotal evidence around the ability of workers in the Health sector to access Web 2.0 technologies: Can they access Twitter in their workplace? Is it supported in their workplace? The anecdotal evidence is that about one third of the alcohol and drug workforce can access social media at their workplace.

For some innovative uses there is a privacy implication. If an organisation is looking to hold clinical data on Google Docs, EyeOS or any of the others, then that is a bit of a trap because that data may be physically held outside of Australia, which breaches Australian privacy legislation. There are a couple of regulatory areas to clarify, but in terms of convenience and benefit for clients there is a lot of potential. A client from a low socio-economic sector or one who is about to re-engage with mainstream society would likely have a need to access computing resources. Cloud-based storage and desktop systems make a lot of sense for that individual.

This work was previously published in the International Journal of Web Portals 2(4), edited by Greg Adamson and Jana Polgar, pp. 45-51, copyright 2010 by Information Science Publishing (an imprint of IGI Global).

Chapter 17
Portals, Technology and E-Learning

Greg Adamson
University of Melbourne, Australia

ABSTRACT

E-learning promises to improve the learning process through the application of technology, including portal technology. Portals can provide the personalisation and interactivity functionality that e-learning requires. However, the long-held promise that technology will improve learning has often failed to deliver. This paper examines the promise of this technology and compares the specific demands of e-learning to the actual capability of portals and the underpinning Internet and World Wide Web. It then identifies four "costs" of using technology for e-learning, and points to existing project management tools that may minimise the effect of these "costs".

1. INTRODUCTION: THE CHALLENGE

The 1999 science fiction cinema classic *The Matrix* provides one future view of e-learning (Wachowski & Wachowski, 1999). Trinity and Neo steal a helicopter to rescue Morpheus. After telling Neo that she doesn't know how to fly a helicopter, in seconds Trinity is able to download a helicopter pilot program into her brain. This se-

ductive promise works on two levels. First, in the future it will be possible to learn instantly. Second, and more importantly, it feeds the mystique that technology by one means or another can meet any need of pedagogy, the study of teaching. That future promise has existed for decades. Former US Federal Communications Commission chairman Reed Hundt (2000) describes a 1993 meeting he attended with US Vice-President Al Gore and others regarding the Information Superhighway, an Internet precursor:

DOI: 10.4018/978-1-4666-0336-3.ch017

'Telephone lines are surely in every school's principal's office,' I said. 'But if we want to make a difference in the way teachers teach and the way kids use technology, we have to build networks that connect to kids in their classrooms.'

The immediate goal is modest, while the promise is large: improve the quality of technology available for teacher and student use; this will improve the overall effectiveness of education.

From an enterprise perspective, many information technology projects appear to follow the same logic: install a program or portal for electronic learning or knowledge management and it will 'make a difference'. Evidence for this is ambiguous. McKinsey Global Institute (2001) reviews technology and fails to find evidence that spending on information technology per se leads to an increase in productivity, but rather is part of a complex and not fully understood process. Specifically, information technology investment may fail to raise productivity, or as in the case of retail banking may lead to less improvement than expected. In an application such as industrial process control or a financial spreadsheet, where tasks are clearly defined and IT systems complete them more quickly and accurately than people, then it is likely that the technical outcome will be approximately what was expected. Even here the change management implications (change to work practices, the organisation's structure, training and hiring practices, and the organisation's informal culture) may be extensive and unexpected. When we come to less clear goals such as learning or knowledge management the relationship is far less clear.

This paper examines a range of expectations or hopes that technology is currently promising to e-learning. It then examines underlying Internet, World Wide Web, and portal technology characteristics to point to gaps between the expectation and the inherent technology capability. The effect of these gaps is shown to be an ongoing challenge in the application of technology to requirements.

It then suggests that tools of project management can reduce the dissonance between technology promises and e-learning needs. This work builds on research into the unexpected results of Internet investment (Adamson, 2004). This work is multi-disciplinary, but takes a primarily technological view of the challenges of e-learning.

2. WHAT TECHNOLOGY OFFERS EDUCATORS

The promise list for e-learning infrastructure is long. The following is a typical set, drawn from a recent e-learning conference call for papers by the Interactive Computer Aided Learning (ICL, 2010), with a description of each topic added.

1. Web based learning (WBL): Learning based on the ubiquity of web access, familiarity of the interface and the hyperlink and search functionality.
2. Lifelong learning: Education as an ongoing process requiring a range of tools available to a people of a diverse range of ages.
3. Adaptive and intuitive environments: Teaching environments that modify what is presented to a student based on identification of needs for a particular student, using the Internet or other means.
4. Responsive environments: Environments that use sensor technologies to modify and augment the learner experience.
5. Mobile learning environments and applications: Access not bound to a desk (or desktop computer) but available on a range of devices anywhere and at any time.
6. Platforms and authoring tools: Technology that facilitates preparation of material for the non-technical educator.
7. Educational MashUps: The ability to gather multiple information streams and present these in a single view useful to a student.

8. Knowledge management and learning: Intra-organisation processes for information storage and self-service. This is separate from data management and content management, which are distinct technology tools, and information management which is a broader function supported by technology.

9. Collaborative learning: Virtual teams replicate the experience of a class team in producing collaborative work for assessment.

10. Pedagogical and psychological issues: Understanding the difference between direct and technology mediated learning from a teaching perspective.

11. Immersive learning models thanks to technological advancements: Applying virtual reality methods to learning providing learners with simulated environments.

12. Personal Learning Environments: Learning environments where the student can modify their goals and the content that they receive in order to suit their needs.

13. Information retrieval techniques for e-learning: Linking traditional learner information gathering activities to on-line information stores such as academic databases.

14. e-Learning readiness: Barriers to using technology for training purposes including institutional, educator and individual learner, and specially whether a conventional classroom will prepare a student for e-learning.

3. CORE INTERNET AND PORTAL STRENGTHS

While these goals are broadly based, the technology of the Internet and its extensions is specific and reflects its actual development path over the past half century. The earliest development of the Internet occurred in a military context in the 1960s, and it remained a US military network until 1983. Between then and 1995, when the US National Science Foundation withdrew from funding Internet backbone services, the Internet was primarily an education and research network (Hafner and Lyon 1998).

Between the end of 1982 and 1990 the number of Internet hosts (connected computers) grew approximately one thousand-fold, to 313,000, and by a further order of magnitude to 3.8 million by 1994, with the World Wide Web (Zakon, 2010). Proportionally this was the Internet's greatest period of growth, the period during which it unexpectedly transformed itself from a legacy network to the first open global data network, surpassing the US proposed Information Superhighway, the European focused International Standards Organisation approach, and other contenders in the process. This educational core of the Internet's original usage success is often overlooked in the post-1994 commercial Internet era. It is one of the reasons that the Internet is potentially so helpful for e-learning.

There are several areas in which the Internet in general help e-learning, including the following:

- Common representation: the basis for diverse 'content' is the common representation of text, photos, graphics, sound, video, music, speech and more as binary digits. The mathematical basis of this was published by Nyquist (1928). Its practical application was undertaken in the telecommunications field to improve voice traffic over networks from the 1960s and in media for new distribution methods from the 1980s. In contrast to previous systems it allows the distribution of perfect (non-degraded) copies of information over large areas. While this is common to all digital computing and communication, the Internet provides new value from this.

- Ubiquitous any-to-any data communications network: the global spread of the Internet was based on the linking of academic communities, primarily for e-mail and then for exchange of files. In this sense, what is known as Web 2.0 is interactivity built in to the early Internet. It is different to the three other main global information networks: The postal network (the world's largest information network) doesn't support concurrent interactivity. The voice telephone network natively supports neither data distribution nor one-to-many communication. The global satellite television network lacks interactivity, and has a high cost of entry for information distribution.

- Low cost of publication: The Internet can be contrasted to pay-TV. While there are many potential digital television channels, the cost per channel is very high. In Australia the Foxtel network in 2002 reduced the price for content providers per channel per year from $2.3 million to $0.75 million (Kohler, 2002). By contrast the Internet provides almost no financial barrier to entry.

For comparison, it should be noted that the Internet lacks several characteristics of other commercial communication networks: It is best effort, has no inherent security, does not identify users, and has no facility for micro-payments. Tim Berners-Lee's original proposal to develop the World Wide Web's prototype shows that like the Internet, while commercial distribution of the World Wide Web may have become important, the requirements of commerce were absent at the beginning. Under the specification heading of 'Non Requirements' he listed 'copyright enforcement and data security' (Berners-Lee & Fischetti, 2000). This is in contrast to the functional requirements of commercial data communication alternatives of the time.

The World Wide Web created the Internet as it is currently recognised in the early 1990s. This introduced three key characteristics of relevance to e-learning:

- Hyperlinking: This is the ability to link from any web location to any other. A concept originally proposed by Vannevar Bush (1996), this establishes a key characteristic of cyberspace, that every location on the web 'sits beside' every other location.
- Search: Previous attempts to develop a large, scalable network of information sources foundered on the question of how to catalogue the information (Gillies & Cailliau, 2000). The conceptual leap achieved by the World Wide Web was that an information system does not have to 'know' where it stores information, whether the information is fact or fiction, or whether it has any value to anyone. Searching through a large and unorganised mass of information produces a sufficiently meaningful result to be worth the effort.
- Simple interface, with respect for text (a known basis for experiencing unknown learning content): the World Wide Web in particular has become a technology that tens or hundreds of millions of people are familiar with. Its use of text can be contrasted to the experience of television.

A portal may be described as a web site that can offer specific content based on an individual customer or their segment. The first generation of portals were developed by Yahoo and Altavista. They were meant to provide a single site that would become the user's home page for the entire web. Today the term 'portal' describes at least eight different on-line approaches: web searching; e-commerce; self-service; business intelligence; collaboration; enterprise information; e-learning; and communication (Boye, 2006). In contrast to web site content management systems, portals are entry points to services and information rather than information containers.

From around 2005 portal technology functionality and performance achieved the long-term promise of portals as effective business tools. It then became feasible or even easy to create an individual customer experience for large numbers of customers based on varied data services, with reasonable performance. Beyond the Internet and web, portals are able to provide some additional characteristics:

- Single location for variously sourced material: In addition to the simple representation of many items electronically, a portal provides information from multiple sources in various ways. A classroom may have a teacher, a white board, text books, wall charts and the opportunity to ask questions. A portal is able to provide an interface to multiple applications approximating these functions.

- Personalisation of content: By recognising an individual, the opportunity is created for individually tutored classes. This may be as simple as keeping track of where an individual user has reached in self-paced learning, or something more complex such as providing additional material in areas of learning difficulty.

These eight relatively simple features provide the basis for a wide variety of services relevant to e-learning. These include:

- Flexible: Delivering a wide variety of services; achieving the promise of digitisation; from fully interactive to multi-cast or broadcast; same time or across time zones
- Responsive: Innovative; easily and quickly updated
- Inclusive: Alternative formats for people with disabilities
- Convenient: Familiar; any time; any place; ubiquitous; user configurable
- Low cost: As a publishing channel; through self-service
- Reliable: No single point of failure.

4. THE TECHNOLOGY 'PRICE'

A comparison of the anticipated needs of e-learning and the technological characteristics of the Internet, web and portals suggests a strong benefit. At the same time a sense of caution needs to be added. The use of any technology to deliver a service comes at á cost to usability. For media theorist McLuhan (1994) writing in a television dominated period a medium's technology provides a message of its own, independent of any programming content. This approach is relevant to subsequent electronic media, including the Internet.

Is this the experience of the web? Qualitative research by Adamson and Wong (2010) suggest "yes". The decision to implement Web 2.0 technologies in large enterprises is based more on the generation of the responsible Chief Executive Officer, rather than identified benefits or costs involved. In this case the CEO gives the message they want heard through their selection of technology channel.

As described above, in regard to education infrastructure there is a widely held view that more technology is better. Internet usage veteran Dyson (1998) gives a warning to this:

The downside of our obsession with the miracle of multimedia is that we lose the power of mere words, which are relatively cheap to create (requiring only a single author's time) and cheap to distribute. The challenge is that they require more work and attention—from the recipient, and from the creator, too. It requires work to create a coherent argument (I know; I'm trying to do it right now), and it requires work to follow the argument. However, that work produces something of value that multimedia, for all its cost, often doesn't: knowledge and understanding.

Adamson (2004) identified multiple success factors for Internet investment. First, the application should be matched to the actual ways that users already use Internet, web and portal technology, rather than attempting to impose different use patterns as a precondition for success of the application. Second, the application must be designed with an understanding of the specific technical limitations of Internet, web and portal technology, not expecting the user to adopt additional add-ons or processes before they can use the application. Third, for commercial investments, the application must be able to achieve sustainable competitive advantage, not simply provide an idea which others can immediately replicate.

There are several 'costs' associated with the use of technology. Here are four that have both general and specific e-learning applicability.

First is the financial cost. A large proportion of all capital investment is devoted to information technology. Technology spend may close off and can be at the expense of other approaches, from more face-to-face teaching staff to hot meals for children who are otherwise hungry and lack the ability to concentrate in class.

Second, technologists in general are not reflective. Technology investment is generally accompanied by unbounded optimism. While many IT projects fail completely, and the majority fail to provide their expected benefits (Johnson, 2010), in general little time is spent determining why. Technologists, particularly ones working for a technology vendor, will rarely recommend a low-technology or non-technology solution.

Third is the effect of introducing technology and technologists to a role which was previously not technology based. This is particularly evident in the selection and implementation stages of technology providing educational functions. For Winner (1978) technologists are socialised to see the world as 'a set of "problems" awaiting technically refined "solutions".' This view is relevant to the question of why technically driven solutions are most successful when dealing with narrowly defined challenges, such as 'automate this process' and least successful with broadly defined challenges such as 'improve staff learning'.

Fourth is the cost of creating material that can then be copied: once a site is available for use, it is available to be copied. Where an e-learning site is primarily one or more sets of information provided using a standard set of tools, it may be easy to copy. In these circumstances, regardless of how many users the approach attracts, if these users are viewing copies of the material on other sites there is no benefit or competitive advantage for the original developer. (On the other hand, if the site's purpose is dissemination of information, such as a public awareness campaign, this ease of duplication becomes a benefit rather than a cost.)

Technology's strength has been its ability to do simple things quickly. Calculating thousands of mathematical equations in order to draw a picture on a screen, or examining a measuring device output every second, year after year, are beyond human capacity. Eventually these trillions and quadrillions of computations will add up to something more, but for the moment each passing decade shows little qualitative change in the capacities of artificial intelligence applications. Unlike a three-year-old child, computers 'cannot tell the difference between a dog and a cat' (Negroponte, 1995). Nicholas Negroponte of MIT Media Labs attributed this to a lack of attention by an industry more interested in marketable applications, but 15 years and much effort later 'AI' still makes little fundamental difference.

At the other end of the e-learning combination is learning, a complex and partially understood process. Take something as basic as learning to read and write. Throughout the 20th-century national adult literacy programs were attempted in many countries but only achieved lasting effect in one (MacDonald, 1986).

Combine these together and we have the challenge of getting non-bright machines to succeed where very bright people often fail.

5. MATCHING CAPACITY TO REQUIREMENTS IN DELIVERY

The previous section identified challenges of applying technology possibility to e-learning. The following identifies tools from project management that can assist in uptake, and user centred design.

A typical technology selection process may have the following steps:

1. Purpose: identify and analyse the strategic purpose and objective alignment for which the technology may be applied, eg management of internal information resources.
2. Approach: review the available technology approaches for this purpose, eg a document management approach, a centrally managed intranet, or a distributed authoring approach. Select the approach that best meets the needs identified.
3. Selection: review offerings that use the approach selected. Select the most suitable offering that supports the chosen approach (based on price, stability, supported within a country or region, proven, appropriate size, difficulty of learning), and test it.
4. Implementation: if the tests are successful, use a staged implement and train staff in its use. Then hand over to operational support and ongoing review.

A poorly selected technology application will commence with product selection, often at the urging of a vendor or industry peer pressure, and then attempt but fail to fit the requirement around it.

Technology-driven technology selection is widespread, and often unsuccessful because it ignores user requirements. A requirements approach that starts with the user will prioritise non-technical questions first. For example, a technologist may expect significant cost savings from the introduction of e-learning tools and assume this will benefit

business. However, a business perspective may ask different questions. These could be:

*   What is the purpose of training our workforce?
*   Are we in the business of training?
*   Could our efforts be better used in some other way, such as only recruiting fully trained staff?

In the human dimension the key stakeholder could be the human resources manager, with questions such as:

*   How would this training approach affect workflow practices?
*   What is the business impact if this approach fails?
*   How do we measure success?
*   What change management do we need in place to achieve success?

In the technical dimension many assume the next step is to go out and build or buy a technology 'solution'. For a prospective user of e-learning systems, there is a wealth of experience in business information technology selection. Buying and customising a single solution, assembling a 'best of breed' suite of applications, or developing an application to meet the particular requirements are some of the options. At this point, however, additional technical-business and technical-human dimensions emerge.

Once investigation of requirements is complete, and a technology-based approach is considered, a new set of business issues emerges. Where a technologist often looks for evidence of improved efficiency from a particular solution, the relevant business goal in a commercial environment is return on investment. This can be thought of as the crystalisation of efficiency improvements through reduced cost of production or increased sales, not just making people's jobs easier.

The human aspect also re-emerges, with the question: 'From whose perspective is the solution being designed or selected?'

We can learn something from the User Centred Design approach to technology implementation. This approach places the user's needs at the centre early in the product development cycle. This is widely used in electronic environments such as web sites. Early writers including Nielsen (2000) identify several ways in which this can be overlooked, including ignorance of the audience needs, where site structures reflect the organisational structure, rather than the tasks of users, and how these uses need to access information.

Singh (2000) describes the barriers to maintaining interest in user representation through a technical development process, as technical priorities such as schedules focus a production team on (possibly irrelevant) deliverables.

These business and human investigation issues and techno-business and techno-human implementation issues regularly make themselves felt, either explicitly as considerations or implicitly as problems. Once they are dealt with the technology itself can be approached, including not just hardware, operating systems, networks and software, but application and project management methodologies that include such aspects as testing, risk management, security, and business continuity management.

6. CONCLUSION

Education and training represent a significant challenge for technology implementers due to the inherent complexity of the learning process and the limitations of what technology can achieve. E-learning must bridge this gap if it is to be successful. To do this requires two things:

Firstly, this can be partially achieved by understanding what Internet, web and portal technologies do well. This includes a common digital representation of all stored or communicated information, a network that spans the globe based on a wide range of access speeds and devices, a familiar, text friendly interface, self-service, and low cost of entry for information providers. These factors lend themselves to many of the requirements of e-learning, partly reflecting the origins of the Internet's usage growth as an education and research network, once it ceased to be a military network. As a technology the Internet will continue to impose the limitations of its technology on e-learning. Its greatest technical limit is the difficulty of using it to achieve many traditional commercial purposes.

Secondly, the inherent weaknesses in a technological approach to technology selection need to be understood. These include the challenge of getting non-bright machines to succeed where very bright people often fail.

The point at which the problems most clearly show themselves is during the technology selection process. Here e-learning can benefit from other business experience with technology selection, in particular identifying user requirements and maintaining focus on these during a selection and implementation process that repeatedly favors the technological. The tools of project management that have been developed to address the experience of repeated project failure are valuable here.

REFERENCES

Adamson, G. (2004). *The mixed experience of achieving business benefit from the Internet: A multi-disciplinary study.* Retrieved April 18, 2010, from http://adt.lib.rmit.edu.au/adt/public/adt-VIT20041105.112155/index.html.

Adamson, G., & Wong, K. (2010). Case study: SOA, part of the tool-kit. *International Journal of Web Portals, 2*(1).

Berners-Lee, T., & Fischetti, M. (2000). *Weaving the Web*. New York: HarperBusiness.

Boye, J. (2006). *The enterprise portals report.* Olney, MD: CMS Watch.

Bush, V. (1996). As we may think. In Stefik, M. (Ed.), *Internet dreams: archetypes, myths, and metaphors* (pp. 15–22). Cambridge, MA: MIT Press.

Dyson, E. (1998). *Release 2.1: a design for living in the digital age.* London: Penguin.

Gillies, J., & Cailliau, R. (2000). *How the web was born.* Oxford, UK: Oxford University Press.

Hafner, K., & Lyon, M. (1998). *Where wizards stay up late: the origins of the Internet.* New York: Touchstone.

Hundt, R. E. (2000). *You say you want a revolution: a story of information age politics.* New Haven, CT: Yale University Press.

ICL. (2010). *Academic and corporate e-learning in a global context.* Retrieved April 18, 2010, from http://www.icl-conference.org/icl2010/index.htm

Johnson, J. (2010). *CHAOS Chronicles III.* Retrieved April 16, 2010, from http://www.standish-group.com/chaos/

Kohler, A. (2002). Access to Foxtel network may be a dog of a deal. *Australian Financial Review, 72.*

MacDonald, T. (1986). *Making a new people.* Vancouver, BC, Canada: New Star Books.

McKinsey Global Institute. (2001). *US productivity growth 1995-2000: understanding the contribution of information technology relative to other factors.* Washington, DC: McKinsey & Company.

McLuhan, M. (1994). *Understanding media: The extensions of man.* Boston: MIT Press.

Negroponte, N. (1995). *Being digital.* London: Coronet.

Nielsen, J. (2000). *Designing web usability: The practice of simplicity.* Indianapolis, IN: New Riders Publishing.

Nyquist, H. (1928). Certain topics in telegraph transmission theory. *Trans. AIEE, 47*(2).

Singh, S. (2000). *User-centred design of smart Internet technologies.* Melbourne, Australia: Smart Internet Technology CRC.

Wachowski, L., & Wachowski, A. (1999). *The Matrix.* Retrieved April 18, 2010, from http://www.screenplay.com/downloads/scripts/The%20Matrix.pdf.

Winner, L. (1978). *Autonomous technology: technics-out-of-control as a theme in political thought.* Cambridge, MA: MIT Press.

Zakon, R. H. (2010). *Hobbes' Internet timeline, version 10.* Retrieved April 20, 2010, from http://www.zakon.org/robert/internet/timeline/

This work was previously published in the International Journal of Web Portals 2(3), edited by Greg Adamson and Jana Polgar, pp. 56-64, copyright 2010 by Information Science Publishing (an imprint of IGI Global).

Section 4
Learning for Future Portal and SOA Implementations

Chapter 18
Improving Our Approach to Internet and SOA Projects

Neil Richardson
SkyBlue Consulting Ltd, UK

BOOM

In the late 1990s, the internet boom required new techniques and practices from project management that were more overtly agile and (perceived as being) outside of the realm of traditional methodologies. At the time, and to this day to a large extent, traditional methodologies had been the single recognised toolset available to a project manager: and then only really addressing the 'harder' disciplines required of project managers. During the internet boom project management methodologies (such as PRINCE2, APMP) were apparently, and in some cases deliberately, ditched

in favour of the JFDI (Just Do It) approach to delivering websites and, perhaps more importantly, business objectives (because for the first time, new technology permitted instant delivery).

In reality the swing from one extreme to the other merely served to demonstrate a truism known to project managers but never clearly articulated: that the 'hard' methods alone were insufficient to assure project success and that the perceived, structured, rules for applying methodological tools and techniques were being flaunted on a need-to-deliver-now (or else).

Yet still the problem of some projects delivering and some succeeding remained - though it had not escaped the attention of many project

DOI: 10.4018/978-1-4666-0336-3.ch018

managers that projects could be delivered without (apparently) following the "rules" of disciplined methodologies: a thought so heretical, it better not be spoken out loud.

BUST

Within a few short years the internet boom was so rapidly followed by bust, and it was in the interests of methodology pedlars to insist that the reasons for bust had clearly been the lack of discipline in project management. Subsequently PRINCE2 and APM exam courses around the world have made, and continue to make, rich these pedlars of project management half-truths.

More than a decade later I (and other experienced programme and project managers) find ourselves asking the question of what we lessons we should have learned from that time. There were many new and genuinely transformational insights that emerged yet curiously, no one else appears to have either recognised or grasped these lessons either, based on the evidence available (and it remains in the interests of project management examination bodies to ignore anything that may threaten their income stream from would-be candidates).

LESSONS LEARNED?

It is clear to me that best practice project management consists of a combination of 'hard' PM methods, soft skills (because people, not processes deliver projects) and a 'project-intelligent (?)-ability to recognise the specifics of the situation to provide the correct combination of skills necessary to assure project success and deliver a business objective.

Like the internet, a decade later Service Oriented Architecture is challenging many aspects of project management methodology. Having

emerged from many years of speculation there is, perhaps, a mixed blessing with SOAs: while solving one type of problem, it merely serves to create an alternative set. But for the business objective focused professional who manages the risk-reward balance for an organisation success is found in determining which set of problems is more manageable - on the assumptions that (i) we recognise the varying problem sets (ii) we can define them correctly and rigorously and (iii) we can deliver on that promise! And it is in the failure to validate these relatively simplistic but necessary assumptions (at the very start of any projects work) that I focus because we are still not getting the message!

The promises of SOA such as a standardised approach and reusability are accompanied by new challenges such as governance and the integration of legacy environments. In this sense it is like the promise of outsourcing: problems and inefficiencies are taken off our hands, but we simultaneously find new problems and lack the immediate levers of control that we could have used to resolve an in-house development. Yet in the UK (just like the early days of outsourcing) people are heading down that same route of 'act first, think later!' And it is exacerbated by the need (or organisations) to see activity (sic not the same as progress) that projects commence with a focus on the JFDI method referenced earlier... even when everyone believes they are following a well-defined structured method.

DELIVERING PROJECT CERTAINTY...THE PLAN

Whether the purpose is SOA (as it was this week when I was reviewing a project health check report for a client) or internet based opportunities, project management methodologies and project planning tools have to assist the practitioner in achieving their goal: to deliver a successful project in a period when many projects fail. And projects involving innovative technologies struggle to succeed because, by definition of innovation, they are more difficult therefore the requirements of a project manager to be competent are increased.

Although you, the reader, is already recognising the obvious truth of what you are reading, we still have to reflect on the empirical nature of the evidence that supports our assertion. For today I shall content myself to take the simplest and perhaps most trivial example to demonstrate the shortcomings of how we begin to achieve a business objective: the plan.

When planning a project (whether SOA, outsourcing, business transformation, so-called IT project or whatever) project managers are still focused on the correct and necessary rigour to plan. However (and I guess we have all done this ourselves), the first thing we do is open a software application (such as Microsoft Project) and begin to "deliver" our plan...but are we really delivering?

Over the past 20 years I have observed project managers using planning application software and the effect it has on the user and their community. I have distilled, from my observations, the ten top shortcomings that I find with currently available tools as evidence for the complete absence of thought application (leadership) that project managers should be demonstrating...but are not!

1. Visibility

It's a fundamental challenge for project planning software to provide sufficient visibility of the schedule. No screen (not even iMac size screens) can provide enough so that it can be viewed easily. How many people have free and easy access (even at work) to A1 plotters; as well as the physical space and time required to stick the various plots together? And even if you have all of the above, who is skilled enough to plot them correctly (I certainly find it really tricky) and how much does it cost?

2. Working calendars

Resource and working calendar functionality is available and reflects their many and varied complexities. However these views are rarely presented at the top level: this presents the problem of maintenance (both target and actuals) - not insurmountable but incredibly arduous, time-consuming and often, sadly, retrospectively.

In particular, hammock tasks (tasks that exist throughout the project but typically have no specific dependencies with other tasks but is usually dependent on external dates for both its start and finish - an obvious example is the very activity of project management itself) are difficult to plan in a precise and timely manner; let alone retrospectively capture the actuals.

3. Simplicity

Gantt chart creation is all too easy in much planning software - so how can that be bad news? The temptation to start by creating a Gantt chart simply because it is possible is great. So great, in fact, that they can be generated by almost anybody (alone) without reference to the essential gathering of the project team to create the work breakdown structure; and the veracity and integrity of the Gantt chart is entirely dependent on the quality of the input data (and delivering against it, based on the singularity of purpose as a cohesive team).

Equally the (truly or partially) uninitiated can tend to believe that planning is a simple exercise capable of being completed quickly and with little knowledge or understanding. Terms such as duration, effort, slack, float, EV milestone type can look harmless enough but, for the uninitiated, can leave an accident waiting to happen in the middle of their plan.

4. Over-complexity

Using planning software correctly is complex. A new breed of resource, Project Planners (usually "Software Jockeys") has emerged that requires intensive software application training that is necessary to make use of the functionality required to best reflect the reality of a project in its plan. The resulting problems then stem from planners not fully understanding what the project manager understands and from the project manager not being able to use the software themselves.

5. Functionality versus cost

No planning software that I have yet discovered has sufficient planning aids to truly reflect the planning process. Even the generation of work breakdown structures or dependency networks are tedious and time-consuming. Risk management (the reality that turns a 'happy-day plan' into a real one) does not yet appear to have made its presence felt within planning applications. Though risk and opportunity databases exist within other applications, the link to such requisite functionality for such as Monte Carlo simulations when used in planning, has not yet arrived.

6. Cost versus functionality

Simplistic planning software tends to be relatively easy to start to use; and its cost reasonable. However it is constrained by its inability to truly reflect the real complexity of planning a project. In order to better reflect missing functionality, other software applications are required to make up the shortfall (requiring further cost and skill-sets).

By contrast heavyweight project planning software tends to be very difficult to use, can reflect a much greater level of project reality though its costs are commensurately high both initially and on an ongoing basis.

7. Cost versus cost

Reconciliation of duplicated systems has never been an easy task. And for all project planning software applications there is usually an auto- mated batch or manual batch link to the finance systems of parent organisations making real-time accounting almost impossible (and that is always assuming effort-data collected is complete, timely and correct).

8. The mythical man-month

All planning software I have encountered does not (and probably cannot ever) take into account the concept of the mythical man-month. A one-person, 20 day effort task when split between four people (according to the software) takes five days. Even if Weinberg's rules were applied, the reality depends on the specific availability and skills of the individual resources available.

9. Project data quality

The overcomplexity of functionality can easily put-off the trained user, let alone the untrained one. Consequently where individual project team members are required to enter data directly, the chances of that data actually reflecting reality is inversely proportional to the complexity of the software.

Even when skilled user(s) perform regular and frequent updates, the level of effort required to capture and enter precise and timely data that truly reflect a top-quality granular plan is (currently) very significant. The question of whether it is worth retrospectively capturing such quantities of information remains a matter for conjecture.

Furthermore when progress is captured there can be a tendency to make use of the calculations within the software to generate information of highly dubious quality such as 'Task A is 43.5% complete.'

10. Planning horizons

The reality of planning is that we can only plan a relatively short distance into the future with any degree of certainty. Thereafter we are increasingly at the mercy of risk, opportunity and uncertainty. Consequently the best plans make use of planning horizons (rolling wave planning) where our view of the project end-date becomes increasingly precise over time. Sadly planning software takes no account of the necessary lack of precision; referring instead to its innate algorithms to provide a (relatively) meaningless, but nevertheless specific, end-date. And isn't that what we were trying to achieve at the outset?

A BAD WORKMAN...

The tools are driving incorrect and wholly inappropriate behaviours: the usual excuse is to blame the inadequacy of the tool but as the old adage goes "a bad workman always blames his tools..."

Chapter 19
Challenges in Researching Portals and the Internet

Greg Adamson
University of Melbourne, Australia

ABSTRACT

The portal is a point of convergence for many uses and users. Along with the Internet itself, the portal crosses or combines many traditionally separate areas of research, each with its own perspective or perspectives. Such a combination creates a challenge for researchers on how to combine these various perspectives in examining portal and Internet use. This paper examines the methodological challenge by combining five perspectives: historical, technical, media, regulatory and business theory. The paper provides examples of the misunderstanding found regarding concepts that are fundamental and widely understood within a single field, but unknown or misunderstood outside of that field. This misunderstanding between business, technologists, media theorists and regulators contributed to the gulf between Internet investment expectation and the 2000 to 2001 results, the US$4 trillion 'tech wreck'. Avoiding them will be important to the effective implementation of portal-based business solutions.

INTRODUCTION

The influence of the Internet is such that there is probably no research area, from biology to law or theology to material sciences, that could be excluded from the field of Internet research. Analysing the Internet from the traditional

DOI: 10.4018/978-1-4666-0336-3.ch019

perspective of the technology workshop, the boardroom, the user community or the government policy committee provides only part of the story. Combining these perspectives provides a richer, multi-dimensional analysis. This paper describes a set of multi-disciplinary challenges found through an examination of literature in five areas of research: historical examinations of the Internet; sociological and media studies of communication usage; technology development; the regulatory context; and business studies of strategy and the 'Internet economy'.

The Internet is primarily viewed as a communication medium. That doesn't reduce the multi-disciplinary challenge. McPhail (1989) considers communication an inherently multi-disciplinary field of study. This research adopts a multi-disciplinary approach. Multi-disciplinary research may begin from a 'meta-discipline'. For example, in geospatial studies the single common element of physical location can be used as a means of grouping botanical, geological, historical, geographic, demographic and many other types of information. Such research may comprise multi-disciplinary teams of researchers representing the separate disciplines. Alternatively, multi-disciplinary research may result from research that follows a question beyond the traditional boundaries of a single discipline. Such research may remain oriented to the initial audience, but be written in a way that extends its knowledge into the separate field. DiMaggio et al. (2001) point to the example of Lessig, who manages to identify the technical aspects important to non-technical approaches to the Internet. This may result over time in the modification of a discipline's area of focus. This research is aligned to the first of these, the 'meta-discipline' approach. There are many examples of such an approach, of sociologists, historians, technologists and business theorists working outside of their traditional perspective, particularly in the context of technology history, user-centred design, technology philosophy and business strategy. Brown (1997) describes the multi-disciplinary perspective as 'seeing differently'.

Understanding of the Internet and Web applications such as the portal requires a multi-disciplinary approach. However, as soon as specialists in one field move into other fields, we are vulnerable to beginners' mistakes. To give a simple example, to learn lessons about the Internet from researching the history of technology, it isn't sufficient to look at what happened in the past. It is necessary to apply the tools of the historian to the available evidence. While historians debate which tools and how to use them, approaching the past with no tools and no realisation of this is likely to limit the value of any result. The insights in this paper were gained during preparation of a thesis on e-business and commercial benefit (Adamson, 2004). Some of these insights were presented to a conference of the Association of Internet Researchers, September 2006.

HISTORY

Assembling the information necessary to understand the development of the Internet requires an historical approach using the tools of historiography, the study of history. The Internet is young in historical terms. The impetus for its development, the 1957 launch of the Soviet satellite Sputnik, is still within living memory of many people. With some notable exceptions many of the key participants during its technology development since the early 1960s remain alive and professionally active. The main historical methodological challenge is examining issues so soon after the event when historical significance is measured in decades rather than years:

The important effects of the printing press era were not seen clearly for more than 100 years. While things happen more quickly these days, it could be decades before the winners and losers of the information age are apparent. Even today, significant (and permanent) cultural change does not happen quickly (Dewar, 2000).

This is separate from a related debate in the study of history described by Fischer (1970, p. 141), 'that a history of ongoing events ought not to be attempted, because objectivity is impossible, evidence is incomplete, and perspective is difficult to attain'. Fischer himself suggests that these same problems relate to all study of history.

Problems in the study of Internet history include:

- The Internet is political: As the Internet moves towards a global regulatory environment analogous to the world telephone or world postal systems, it is facing significant problems, including control of a multilingual Domain Name System, and top level domain control. This makes precedent and interpretation of recent events a politically significant issue.
- Secrecy: Coming out of the US Department of Defense, the history of the Internet at least partly remains the subject of government secrecy.
- History as told by leading participants: Much writing to date is provided by or based on the recollections of key technology development figures from the early years of the Internet. Evans (1997, p. 214) raises the difficulty that, 'Much if not most military history written by generals, for example, is hopelessly narrow and ignorant of the wider social, political and diplomatic aspects of the subject'. Where histories focus on the individuals involved in developing the Internet there is also a tendency to the 'heroic theory of invention' identified by Maclaurin (1971, 1947) in his study of radio.
- The success of the Internet presented as inevitable: Outside of the Internet context Fischer (1970, p. 135) criticises this approach as 'to prune away the dead branches of the past, and to preserve the green buds and twigs which have grown into the dark forest of our contemporary world'. The assumed inevitability of later events becomes a substitute for examining the detail of the events. Geyl (1958, p. 257) writes in relation to the period before the United States

Civil War, 'we cannot do justice to the pre-war years if we will see them only in the light of the war *we* know was coming.'

These examples could be true of any new media technology. They are exacerbated in relation to the Internet by its importance to human communication. In contrast, for example, each of satellite broadcast and mobile telephony have had a large impact as communication technologies. But they simply fitted into the existing media landscape, while the Internet, including Web 2.0, has significantly disrupted it.

MEDIA AND COMMUNICATION STUDIES

Within media studies it is generally recognised that the Internet is a communication medium, and that communication media follow common phases of development. It was widely assumed that the Internet would follow a similar path to other 20th century media. In contrast, the Internet was the first 19th or 20th century communication medium where widespread usage preceded commercial investment, which began in earnest in 1995 (Adamson, 2004). Sources of cross-field confusion for communication media include:

- Usage surveys: Following the experience of television media research, much late 1990s Internet usage research has been based on understanding which viewers are seeing which Internet web sites. In the television context this information provides the basis for evaluating the reach of advertising, and for establishing advertising rates. The predominance of advertising as a funding mechanism for information-based web sites lends itself to a similar approach, and commercial surveys such as Clickz, <http://www.clickz.com/>, provide this. This approach had two immediate shortcomings. First, the definition of advertisement viewer was unclear. Commercial models for Internet advertising were continually revised during the dotcom era. Second, the Internet still continues to poorly meet the expectations of a broadcast medium, where there is no direct equivalent to Google, for example.

- Web 2.0 and broadcast: In the first half-decade of commercial Internet development from 1995, the television watching experience was considered the 'gold standard' (Herman & McChesney, 1997). The rise of Web 2.0 signaled media recognition of the changed relationship between production and consumption of media. While this had been the case with telephone through the 20th century, as each telephone user was a 'content producer' (they spoke the words that the telephone network carried), the Web enabled a qualitative extension of this. This is typified by the popularisation of the term Web 2.0 by publisher Tim O'Reilly (2005).
- Audience meaning: Silverstone, Hirsch and Morley (1991) focus on media and information technology actual practices. This changes the focus from the intentions of technology and media content producers to the experiences of consumers in their homes. While this research predates the widespread dissemination of the Internet, it was motivated by the environment from which the Internet emerged: an awareness that what was becoming available in terms of new technologies, new services and new systems was likely, suddenly, to expand quite dramatically. The diversity of Internet content types and the absence of a single stable media delivery equivalent to broadcast television places audience research at a much earlier stage than that of television. The Internet changes the de-

bate about 'active' and 'passive' audiences (Singh, 2001).

- Rate of communication technology uptake: Descriptions of the Internet and its uses often focus on the speed of growth, compared to previous media or technologies. Such comparisons are unreliable for two reasons. First, rates of growth for pre-20th century technologies are often difficult to determine, including the telephone (Marvin, 1988). Second, a basis of comparison may be difficult to establish. Comparisons between media can be based on when a device is invented, which could refer to its prototype, a patent, a working device, or a commercial release. It could consider the launch of a medium such as the Internet or of a service provided on it such as the World Wide Web, which occurred decades later. It could consider absolute numbers, the relative rate of growth, or the proportion of the population using a service. Proportions could refer to a city, country, or the world. The figures might be provided by an industry or by an independent observer. One or many geographical markets could be considered. Potential ambiguity is typified by Barua and Whinston (2001, p. 7), who conclude that the Internet economy is 'bigger' than the Industrial Revolution: 'Starting around 1994, the Internet Economy has grown [at a] much faster pace than the Industrial Revolution that began in the 18th century.'
- Clarifying meaning: The first generation of portals were developed by Yahoo and Altavista. They were meant to provide a single site that would become the user's home page for the entire web. Merrill Lynch coined the term 'enterprise information portal' in 1998. Today the term 'portal' describes at least eight different on-line approaches, including: web searching; e-commerce; self-service; business

intelligence; collaboration; enterprise information; e-learning; and communication (Boye, 2006).

- The basis of success: Livingstone (1999) argues that media success as defined by its influence on everyday life is more a product of the way a medium is positioned for consumers than its specific technology. This suggests that the success of the Internet should be understood in a social context rather than from its technology or individual use.
- Invention and use: Examination of the relationship between technology invention and use has a long history, and comprises the key consideration within the philosophy of technology. Mary Wollstonecraft Shelley's 1818 classic *Frankenstein: The Modern Prometheus* is described by Winner (1978, p. 307) as 'still the closest thing we have to a definitive modern parable about mankind's ambiguous relationship to technological creation and power'.

The medium of the Internet itself provides a poor basis for persistent reference. The basic address element of a World Wide Web page is its Uniform Resource Locator (URL), such as <www.isoc.org>. Research published by the Association for Computing Machinery shows that: 'Approximately 28% of the URLs referenced in *Computer* and [*Communications of the ACM*] articles between 1995 and 1999 were no longer accessible in 2000; the figure increased to 41% in 2002' (Spinellis, 2003, p. 77).

Within the communication media industry it is widely known that new media don't replace old. Newspapers, magazines, radio, cinema and television are now joined by the Internet. Technologists on the other hand are used to new technologies replacing old, the hydroelectric turbine supersedes the water-wheel. Because the Internet came from a technical environment, and technologists 'understood it', there was a technology-led

expectation that the Internet would usurp many other commercial media.

TECHNOLOGY

There are many themes in technological writing regarding the Internet. Most relate to the relative benefits of various technologies. A major gap in this literature concerns the capacity of the Internet to support commercial applications, particularly as a transactional medium. Areas of potential confusion in technological literature regarding the Internet include:

- Understanding the Internet's technology: While several historians of the Internet provide an introduction to its technology, these are often insufficient for understanding. A technology is designed to do something. Technological writers are writing about technology in its own context, which may be more easily understood than a descriptive historical approach. Huston (1999) is an example of a technological writer, providing his description in a business context. Even Comer (2000), a technical writer who provides a very detailed examination of TCP/IP, may be more useful to the non-technical reader attempting to understand a concept such as the Domain Name System than a non-technical writer.
- Confusing the service provided and the underpinning technology: A portal is distinguished from a simpler Web offering by its ability to present audience-specific information. This may be done using commercial or open source portal products or toolkits, or it may be done without them (Boye, 2006). The equation of 'portal' with 'portal technology' is not valid.
- Defining the Internet: The US Federal Networking Council (1995) definition of the Internet is clearly technological, us-

ing 'Internet Protocol', 'globally unique address space', 'layered' services, and other technical terms in its definition. This emphasises the technological basis for Internet-based services, but also serves to obscure the Internet in non-technical discussion. For example, among networks that are not part of the Internet have been those based on Japan's iMode, Wireless Application Protocol (WAP) networks, mobile telephone 'texting' and private global TCP/IP networks. The usage and business implications of this distinction are important, but the distinction can only be described technologically.

- The cultural separation between voice and data communication: A significant difference of perspective exists between technologists in the traditional voice telephony field and the data communication technologists who developed the Internet. In North America technologists from these two perspectives were named 'bellheads' and 'netheads' respectively. 'Bellhead' refers to technologists who were trained in the culture of the US Bell telephone system (Denton, Menard, & Isenberg, 2000). These differences are reflected in discussions on the relative merits of 'packet switching' and 'circuit switching', for example. The early years of Internet usage were dominated by a haphazard and accidental evolution of technology guided by a sense of technology cooperation. This stands in contrast to the telecommunications culture of the time, including the mission of a telephone in every house and 'five nines' availability for business, service available 99.999 per cent of the time.

- The separation of technologists from users: Technologists are trained to adopt a problem-solving perspective. When considering the various possible uses of the Internet from a technological perspective,

Stefik (1996) identifies four archetypes: the keeper of knowledge or conservator, the communicator, the trader, and the adventurer. He presents these four views as collectively exhaustive, missing the technologist, and thereby providing no reflective examination of the Internet itself. The technologist sits above or outside of the world of problems to be solved. If technology is 'out of control' (in either a negative or positive sense), who better than a technologist to intercede on a business's behalf? This recalls Babbage's 19th century view of the factory with the engineer as an agent of God's order (Agre, 1999). Fischer (1970) suggests that the use of archetypes blocks the development of historical understanding. Giving priority to unchanging elements, the archetypes, prevents an understanding of the things that change, the subject of historical study.

- The separation of technologists from business: Joseph Schumpeter (1934, pp. 14-15) describes a relationship that can be seen at the beginning of the 21st century:

Economic reality does not necessarily carry out the methods to their logical conclusion and with technological completeness, but subordinates the execution to economic points of view... Economic logic prevails over the technological. And in consequence we see all around us in real life faulty ropes instead of steel hawsers, defective draught animals instead of show breeds, the most primitive hand labor instead of perfect machines, a clumsy money economy instead of a cheque circulation, and so forth.

- Business assumption: From a technical perspective, it is understood that the TCP/IP protocol suite is non-deterministic and that the Internet is a 'best effort' network. For business investors used to the telephone network or pre-1990 commercial data networks, this concept was difficult to grasp, or to include in investment calculations.

Technologists know that the Internet is a technology that reflects the design activities of a wide range of technologists. It was widely assumed that the limitations of the Internet as a commercial transactional medium would be resolved by appropriate technical design effort. As mentioned above, the Internet experienced mass uptake prior to commercialisation, making it different to most other successful technologies. The Internet has proven strongly resistant to commercial technical modifications, and from a commercial service view essentially retains its pre-1995 character.

REGULATORY POLICY

The Internet originated in the United States, and for this reason a key regulatory role sat with the US Federal Communications Commission (FCC). Two issues of importance had received little attention. First, how regulation of the early Internet compares to early regulation of previous emerging media. In the absence of specific regulation directed at the early Internet, little research examines indirect regulation. Winston (1998) approaches the question, but primarily focuses on non-Internet media. Second, whether late 1990s regulation of the Internet represents the continuation or a break with early 1990s regulatory activity. The 'information superhighway' term dominated discussions of network services up to 1995, but was then replaced by references to the Internet and the World Wide Web. A late pre-Internet vision of the Information Superhighway is provided in a marketing video from Pacific Bell (1994). There has been little examination of whether the Internet represents the implementation of the 'information superhighway', or a break from the commercial expectation of that approach. Other areas of potential confusion include:

- Regulatory experimentation during the period of the Internet's development: This has a primarily United States focus prior to the 1980s, followed by an international discussion of issues such as deregulation. While international deregulation in telecommunications developed strongly in the late 1980s and early 1990s, the basis of this had developed over decades. Schiller (1999) writes that a business agenda for corporate use of telecommunications independent of AT&T control developed between the mid-1950s and 1970s based on banks, insurance companies, retail chains, automobile manufacturers, oil companies and aerospace firms. The United States government has yet to establish a single approach, in place of a regulated national monopoly along the AT&T model. Winston (1998) describes an experiment in privatised regulation through the 1960s Comsat group responsible for commercial satellite communication. He attributes to this deregulated approach a significant lost opportunity for United States commercial interests. A second experiment was division of the United States into 500 separately licensed areas for first generation mobile telephony, producing what Hundt (2000, p. 14) describes as 'the worst quality, most out-of-date cellular systems of any developed country in the world.' This experience is the background for discussion of the 1990s approach to Internet regulation.

- How regulation and technical architecture intersect: Lessig (1999) argues, through an examination of law, the market, norms and architecture, that technology may be used to establish regulatory restrictions. Lessig places major emphasis on the 'end-to-end effect' described by Saltzer, Reed, and Clarke (1984). In a traditional telephone network, new services (such as call-forwarding) are provided from within the network. The Internet in contrast sits outside of the network. For example, the World Wide Web was added to the Internet without any 'approval'. In turn Web 2.0 applications such as Wikipedia were then added to the Web without an approval requirement. This has a regulatory aspect. Networks using digital technologies can either provide an unrestricted platform for new applications or they can control new applications. This is also described in the term 'net neutrality' (http://en.wikipedia.org/wiki/Net_neutrality).

- What regulation encourages electronic commerce: As a global network the Internet provides a basis for international electronic commerce. This creates potential friction between different legal traditions. These include privacy of information, specifically the difference between European and United States legislation. There are also strongly opposed perspectives in relation to intellectual property rights and the Internet. One is provided most clearly by the Recording Industry Association of America, <http://www.riaa.org>. The other is represented by the 'digital commons' approach led by Lawrence Lessig, <http://creativecommons.org>.

- What regulatory environment encourages innovation: While including an international dimension, the relationship between innovation and monopoly is vigorously debated in the United States, specifically whether the resources of large corporations or the ambitions of small companies are more conducive to innovation. Writing at the end of World War II, Maclaurin (1971, 1947) argues that in conditions of monopoly, small competitors are unlikely to be able to afford research, including both the cost of development and cost of protecting resulting discoveries. He cites the example of a conflict between two radio patents filed in 1913 and 1914, the outcome of which was not resolved by the Supreme Court until 1934. Similar views were voiced at the time by Schumpeter (1939). Porter (1990), writing some decades later, finds historical evidence for Schumpeter's view lacking, and attributes innovation to smaller firms and 'outsiders'. During the period of development of the Internet, the US Federal Communications Commission described its role as being: 'to create a level playing field where telephone companies using their economic might could not unfairly enter the enhanced service provider market and destroy its competitive and innovative nature' (Cannon, 2000, p. 7). TCP/IP co-inventor Kahn (1994, p. 11) suggests that active government support was required to maintain innovation in the Internet: 'What guarantees that the same degree of vitality will be part of its future evolution if market forces alone determine what new capabilities are added to the Internet?'. In 2009 the US Federal Communications Commission chair stated that this principle should be extended beyond wired to wireless Internet connections (Genachowski, 2009).

The United States regulatory community knows that throughout the 20th century each US communication technology system has been the subject of extensive regulation, including telephony, radio and television. It was widely assumed that the new interactive medium would depend on regulation for its success. The regulatory environment and specifically the US Federal Communications Commission played a key (if unintentional) role in the success of the Internet, by preventing telecommunication companies in the United States from monopolising the emerging data communication field. Yet there is a widely expressed view among both technologists and business theorists that the Internet's success was due to an absence of regulation. The Internet did depend on regulatory intervention for its success, but in an accidental way.

BUSINESS

Business theorists generally view the Internet along with other technology as a potential (not inevitable) source of what leading business theorist Michael Porter calls competitive advantage (Porter, 1985). In order for that potential to be realised, a company or industry needs particular circumstances to ensure that profits are not 'competed away'. Technologists and media theorists generally assume to the contrary that widespread uptake will result in profitable communications medium investment.

Business literature generally considers the Internet as part of broader information technology investment rather than as a communication medium. The additional features of the Internet as a communication medium are described using theories of the Internet's peculiarity as a technology, such as Tapscott (2000, p. 4), for whom: 'the Internet precipitates one of those rare occasions in economic history when we must think even more broadly in order to understand how the entire infrastructure for wealth creation is changing'. Notable relevant debates regarding technology investment are: the productivity paradox, whether information technology investment 'matters', how to measure a 'business benefit' and competitive advantage:

- The productivity paradox: Roach (1987) showed that although white-collar service sector computer use rose dramatically in the 1970s and 1980s, productivity of the sector had not risen. Fifteen years later, 'No one has yet made the connection between IT investment and non-IT-producing sector MFP [multi-function productivity] growth clear and incontrovertible' (Hayward, 2002). Krugman (1997, p. 127)

suggests that much business restructuring of the 1980s and 1990s did not improve productivity because it did not eliminate jobs: 'it merely outsources them from large corporations that pay high wages to smaller suppliers that often pay less'. Several reports on information technology and productivity from McKinsey Global Institute are combined in a widely cited report, 'Whatever happened to the New Economy?' (McKinsey Global Institute, 2002). This found supporting evidence for the productivity paradox: 'At the economy-wide level, MGI found no correlation between jumps in productivity, and jumps in IT intensity. Moreover, our sector studies revealed specific instances where IT failed to raise productivity'. While this relates to IT rather than just the Internet, it challenges many of the assumptions used to identify Internet business benefit: It isn't sufficient to show that the Internet is the latest form of IT, and therefore assume that a productivity benefit inevitably follows.

- Technology confidence: The perspective of technologists regarding the value of previous technologies has no necessary relationship to a business perception. What for a technologist may be a 'legacy technology' of little value requiring replacement may from a commercial perspective be a reliable and satisfactory solution to a requirement. One example is the competing business and technical opinions of three supply chain approaches, Electronic Data Interchange (EDI), Business-to-Business exchanges, and portals (Adamson, 2009).

- Business benefit: There is a difference between the concept of a business benefit and the technological concept of a solution to a problem, as this may or may not provide some type of financial value to a company employing it. Economists know that there is no necessary relationship between productivity and a financially defined business benefit. 'In economic theory, corporate profits growth has no clear or unambiguous relation to productivity growth, and so it is no surprise that historical data show no such relation' Shiller (2001).

- Competitive advantage: Michael Porter developed the theory of competitive advantage in a series of works published between 1980 and 1990. He later applied this analysis to the Internet (2001), where he identified the difficulty of companies benefiting from the 'network effect' (the increasing value of a network, such as the telephone network, as more users join it). His work is widely known within business studies, but not well known outside of that field, although his technical term 'value chain' has become part of technological marketing jargon. In contrast to Porter, Castells (2000) argues that, under pressure from the Internet, old-style hierarchical corporations are in crisis, and that network enterprises, made up of multiple smaller parts, would replace them. In this view the network rather than the company has become the basic operating unit. While to a non-business audience this view appears to be based on economic analysis, and received some attention in business journals, the lack of supporting evidence and collapse of Enron has left the 'networked company' approach out of favor among business audiences. In a later work Castells moves from an economic to a cultural approach (2001).

- The value of information technology investment: The 'productivity paradox' debate received fresh impetus from Carr (2003). For Carr the lack of research into the role of technology in influencing competition has led to incorrect assumptions. He suggests that the generalised availability of standard technology, especially the Internet, was reducing the capacity for information technology spending to provide competitive advantage.

- Failure of Internet infrastructure commodity trading: An attempt to position the Internet within traditional commercial frameworks led to an expectation that the underpinning bandwidth carrying Internet traffic would itself become a tradeable commodity. Enron capitalised on the belief, pretending that it had a 'broadband operating system' which allowed applications developers to dynamically allocate bandwidth on demand. In 2009 co-CEO of Enron Broadband Services was sentenced to 16 months in prison for his part in the fraud (Department of Justice, 2009).

From mid-1995, widespread commercial attention to the Internet was based on an understanding that it fulfilled the expectations of a new interactive medium. It was generally assumed that widespread use of the Internet would also meet the commercial expectations of a medium such as the 'information superhighway'. The sudden transfer of commercial expectations from the promised 'information superhighway' to the Internet from 1995 was not accompanied by commercial analysis of the Internet's actual technical or usage characteristics.

CONCLUSION

This research points to a common pattern, that issues understood within a single area may be unknown, ignored or misunderstood beyond that area.

As shown in this paper, while each of the five examined fields has a different range of issues, there is a similarity across the fields:

- The issues are well known within each field, not hidden.

- Their basic concepts are not hard to understand for people outside the field.
- When practitioners in other fields are aware of the concepts they often believe that they understand them when they don't, this is typified by the incorrect technology marketing statement, 'technology provides competitive advantage', which is inconsistent with the business meaning of competitive advantage, or as Porter puts it, 'anything that a company can access over distance is almost never going to be a competitive edge: if you can buy machines from Germany, so can anyone else' (Trinca, 2002, p. 39).

What makes this a more important issue for portal and Internet research than for other technologies such as mobile telephony uptake, is the Internet's unique development path, its mass uptake prior to commercial investment. The reason that the different path was not more easily understood in part relates to the cross-field confusion described here.

REFERENCES

Adamson, G. (2004). *The mixed experience of achieving business benefit from the Internet: a multi-disciplinary study* (Tech. Rep.). Melbourne, Australia: RMIT University, Melbourne. Retrieved October 15, 2009, from http://adt.lib.rmit.edu.au/adt/public/adt-VIT20041105.112155

Adamson, G. (2009). Portals and the challenge of simplifying Internet business use. *International Journal of Web Portals, 1*(1).

Agre, P. E. (1999, September). *The fall of Babbage's theology*. Paper presented to People and Computers seminar, University of Newcastle upon Tyne, Newcastle upon Tyne, UK.

Barua, A., & Whinston, A. (2001). *Measuring the Internet economy*. Paper presented at the Cisco Systems/Center for Research in Electronic Commerce, University of Texas, Austin, Texas.

Boye, J. (2006). *The enterprise portals report*. Olney, MD: CMS Watch.

Brown, J. S. (1997). *Seeing differently: insights on innovation*. Boston: Harvard Business School Press.

Cannon, R. (2000, September 23-25). *Where Internet service providers and telephone companies compete: a guide to the Computer Inquiries, enhanced services providers and information service providers*. Paper presented to TPRC Research Conference on Communication, Information and Internet Policy, Alexandria, VA.

Carr, N. G. (2003). IT doesn't matter. *Harvard Business Review, 81*(5), 41–49.

Castells, M. (2000). *The rise of the network society* (2nd ed., *Vol. 1*). Oxford, UK: Blackwell.

Castells, M. (2001). *The Internet galaxy: reflections on the Internet, business, and society*. Oxford, UK: Oxford University Press.

Comer, D. E. (2000). *Internetworking with TCP/IP: principles, protocols, and architectures* (4th ed., *Vol. 1*). Upper Saddle River, NJ: Prentice Hall.

Denton, T. M., Menard, F., & Isenberg, D. (2000). *Netheads versus Bellheads*. Ottawa, Canada: Federal Department of Industry.

Department of Justice. (2009). *Former Enron Broadband Co-Chief Executive Officer Sentenced for Wire Fraud*. Retrieved October 15, 2009, from http://houston.fbi.gov/dojpressrel/pressrel09/ho092809.htm

Dewar, J. A. (2000). *The information age and the printing press: looking backward to see ahead.* New York: ACM. Retrieved October 15, 2009 from http://portal.acm.org/citation.cfm?id=347 634.348784&coll=GUIDE&dl=GUIDE&CFID =56515123&CFTOKEN=92433459

DiMaggio, P., Hargittai, E., Neuman, W. R., & Robinson, J. P. (2001). Social implications of the Internet. *Annual Review of Sociology, 27,* 307–336. doi:10.1146/annurev.soc.27.1.307

Evans, R. J. (1997). *In defence of history.* London: Granta Books.

Federal Networking Council. (1995). *Definition of 'Internet'.* Retrieved October 15, 2009, from http://www.itrd.gov/fnc/Internet_res.html

Fischer, D. H. (1970). *Historians' fallacies: toward a logic of historical thought.* New York: HarperPerennial.

Genachowski, J. (2009). *Improving broadband and mobile communications.* Washington, DC: Brookings Institution. Retrieved October 15, 2009 from http://www.brookings.edu/~/media/ Files/events/2009/0921_broadband_communica- tions/20090921_broadband.pdf

Geyl, P. (1958). *Debates with historians.* Glasgow, UK: Fontana/Collins.

Hayward, B. (2002). *The impact of IT invest- ment on the Australian economy.* Stamford, CT: Gartner Group.

Herman, E. S., & McChesney, R. W. (1997). *The global media: the new missionaries of corporate capitalism.* London: Cassell.

Hundt, R. E. (2000). *You say you want a revolution: a story of information age politics.* New Haven, CT: Yale University Press.

Huston, G. (1999). *ISP survival guide: strategies for running a competitive ISP.* New York: Wiley Computer Publishing.

Kahn, R. E. (1994). *The role of government in the evolution of the Internet.* Paper presented to Revolution in the U.S. Information Infrastructure, Washington DC.

Krugman, P. (1997). How fast can the U.S. economy grow? Not as fast as "new economy" pundits would like to think. *Harvard Business Review, 75*(4), 123–129.

Lessig, L. (1999). *Code and other laws of cyber- space.* New York: Basic Books.

Livingstone, S. (1999). New media, new au- diences? *New Media & Society, 1,* 59–66. doi:10.1177/1461444899001001010

Maclaurin, W. R. (1971). *1947). Invention and innovation in the radio industry.* New York: Arno Press.

Marvin, C. (1988). *When old technologies were new: thinking about electric communication in the late nineteenth century.* New York: Oxford University Press.

McKinsey Global Institute. (2002). *Whatever happened to the new economy?* San Francisco, CA: McKinsey & Company.

McPhail, T. L. (1989). Inquiry in international communication. In Asante, M. K., Gudykunst, W. B., & Newmark, E. (Eds.), *Handbook of in- ternational and intercultural communication* (pp. 47–66). Newbury Park, CA: Sage Publications.

O'Reilly, T. (2005). *What is Web 2.0?* Retrieved October 15, 2009, from http://oreilly.com/web2/ archive/what-is-web-20.html

Pacific Bell. (1994). *The Information Superhigh- way.* Retrieved October 15, 2009, from http:// www.youtube.com/watch?v=QQS6gTdbOsk

Porter, M. E. (1985). *Competitive advantage.* New York: Free Press.

Porter, M. E. (1990). *The competitive advantage of nations.* New York: Free Press.

Porter, M. E. (2001). Strategy and the Internet. *Harvard Business Review*, *79*(3), 62–78.

Roach, S. (1987). America's technology dilemma: a profile of the information economy. *Special Economic Study*.

Saltzer, J. H., Reed, D. P., & Clarke, D. (1984). End-to-end arguments in system design. *ACM Transactions on Computer Systems*, *2*(4), 277–288. doi:10.1145/357401.357402

Schiller, D. (1999). *Digital capitalism: networking the global market system*. Cambridge, MA: MIT Press.

Schumpeter, J. A. (1934). *The theory of economic development: an inquiry into profits, capital, credit, interest, and the business cycle*. Cambridge, MA: Harvard University Press.

Schumpeter, J. A. (1939). *Business cycles: a theoretical, historical and statistical analysis of the capitalist process* (*Vol. 1*). New York: McGraw-Hill.

Shiller, R. J. (2001). *Irrational exuberance*. Princeton, NJ: Princeton University Press.

Silverstone, R., Hirsch, E., & Morley, D. (1991). Listening to a long conversation: an ethnographic approach to the study of information and communication technologies in the home. *Cultural Studies*, *5*(2), 204–227. doi:10.1080/09502389100490171

Singh, S. (2001). Studying the user: a matter of perspective. *Media International Australia*, (98), 113-128.

Spinellis, D. (2003). The decay and failures of web references. *Communications of the ACM*, *46*(1), 71–77. doi:10.1145/602421.602422

Stefik, M. (1996). *Internet dreams: archetypes, myths, and metaphors*. Cambridge, MA: MIT Press.

Tapscott, D. (2000). Rethinking strategy in a networked world: or why Michael Porter is wrong about the Internet. *Strategy+Business*, *24*. Retrieved October 15, 2009 from http://www.theecademy.com/downloads/Strategy+Business.pdf

Trinca, H. (2002, September). Absolute Porter. *Australian Financial Review: Boss magazine*, pp. 34-39.

Winner, L. (1978). *Autonomous technology: technics-out-of-control as a theme in political thought*. Cambridge, MA: MIT Press.

Winston, B. (1998). *Media technology and society: a history from the telegraph to the Internet*. London: Routledge.

This work was previously published in the International Journal of Web Portals 2(2), edited by Greg Adamson and Jana Polgar, pp. 26-37, copyright 2010 by Information Science Publishing (an imprint of IGI Global).

Chapter 20
Containers and Connectors as Elements in a Portal Design Framework

Joe Lamantia
MediaCatalyst B.V., The Netherlands

ABSTRACT

This article defines the standardized elements used in the building blocks portal design framework in detail, as the second in a series of articles on a Portal Design Framework. This article explains the (simple) rules and relationships for combining Containers and Connectors into portal structures. This article shares best practices, examples, and guidelines for effectively using the building blocks framework during portal design efforts.

OVERVIEW OF THE CONTAINER BLOCKS

The building block system includes seven types of Containers, beginning with the Tile at the lowest level of the stacking hierarchy, and increasing (conceptual) size and complexity to include a collection of interconnected Dashboards or Portals, called a Dashboard or Portal Suite. From smallest to largest, the Container blocks are:

- Tile
- Tile Group
- View
- Page
- Section
- Dashboard or Portal
- Dashboard or Portal Suite

Like musicians in a band, the different kinds of Container blocks in the system play different roles in the overall effort to construct dashboards or portals. The smaller (lower in the stacking hierarchy)

DOI: 10.4018/978-1-4666-0336-3.ch020

blocks - Tiles, Tile Groups, and Views—enable the display of content, and support users' interactions with content. Sections, Dashboards or Portals, and Dashboard or Portal Suites—the larger blocks, that are higher in the stacking hierarchy—enable the navigation, organization, and management of collections of content. Pages straddle the middle of the size continuum; they are the largest block whose role is primarily to provide a framework for display of and interaction with dashboard or portal content, and the smallest Container which plays an important navigational / organization role in the system.

The Connectors (described later in this article) 'hold things together'; thereby creating navigation paths amongst destinations, establishing a tangible architecture or structure, providing referential cues for orientation with the environment, and allowing movement into and out of the environment. The different kinds of Containers work in concert with Connectors to enable the creation of scalable, navigable, and easily maintainable information architectures that support high-quality user experiences.

Each Container definition includes:

- Mandatory components
- Optional components
- Stacking size
- Detailed description
- Example rendering (for illustrative purposes only)
- Rendering description

TILE

Mandatory Components: Tile Header, Tile Body
Optional Components: Tile Footer
Stacking Size: 1

Description

Tiles are the fundamental building block of the dashboard or portal framework. Tiles locate con-tent and functionality within the coherent information and navigation structure of the dashboard or portal environment. Tiles clearly identify the sources and broader contexts of the information or tools they contain (very important in situations where terminology is ambiguous, conflicting or overlapping, or when differing data sources provide differing values for the same metrics), and offer consistent access to onvenience functionality such as printing and emailing the Tile contents for use outside the dashboard.

Tiles consist of two required components—a Tile Header and Tile Body—and one optional component—the Tile Footer. Tiles may include multiple Control Bars (note: adding multiple Control Bars can quickly increase development complexity and lower usability levels). The Tile Header contains a mandatory Title, optional Subtitle, mandatory source indicator identifying the origins of the content, and may include buttons or links for Convenience Functionality (described in detail in a subsequent part of this series).

The mandatory Tile Body can contain nearly any form of content. Tiles commonly contain text, charts, tables, interactive maps, scrolling news feeds, RSS consoles, video, slideshows, syndicated XML structured documents, links to documents and resources, and complex transactional functionality. Of course, this is only a small subset of the tremendous diversity of Tile-delivered content available in the rapidly growing libraries of widgets published for Apple's OSX desktop, Yahoo's widget platform, Google Gadgets, web desktops such as NetVibes, and the many social networking platforms including FaceBook and MySpace. In the end, the range of content that can appear within a Tile is limited only by imagination and ingenuity.

The optional Tile Footer is a structurally consistent location for contextual links, pointers to related destinations and content. The Tile Footer commonly offers links to additional resources or source data in another format (tab delimited,. pdf, etc.), links to other Tiles, Pages or areas of the Dashboard that provide related content or functionality, links to other applications and environments offering comprehensive functionality or information out of scope for the Tile, etc.

The sizes and internal layouts of individual Tiles will vary depending upon several factors including, but not limited to their content, priority vs. neighboring Tiles or other building blocks, and expectations for reuse. It is good practice to define a grid for screen layouts that prescribes standard sizes for Tiles and all screen elements, and match the sizes and internal layouts of Tiles to this reference grid.

Here are a few guidelines on information design and interaction design standards within Tiles:

- Each chart, table, or text block within a Tile needs an accurate title or label
- Charts may have a footer area that offers additional data values, a key or legend for the items shown in the chart, links to additional resources, or source data in another format
- Tiles that contain long lists, large tables, or other large objects may scroll, depending on the interaction and design standards and capabilities of the dashboard or portal platform
- Tables in Tiles often allow users to change sorting order or open and hide columns
- Charts summarizing large amounts data can offer interactions or drill-down behaviors allowing users to navigate deep data sets

Many of these interaction behaviors and design best practices are now offered as standard functionality - making them 'free' or 'low-cost' in design and development terms - by leading business intelligence and portal platform vendors. Additionally, these capabilities are also becoming standard in many general purpose presentation frameworks, including RUBY and AJAX libraries, and the various for-purchase (Adobe AIR, Flex, Laszlo Webtop, etc.) and open-source development toolkits.

Stacking Note: Tiles stacked inside larger building blocks retain their individual Tile Header, Tile Body, and any optional components. (See Figure 1)

Figure 1. Tile components and structure

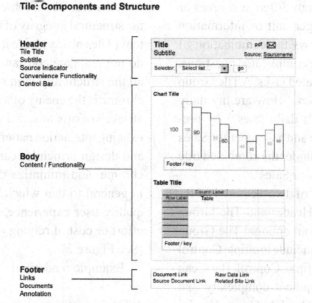

Example rendering:

{tile_structure_2.ai}

Rendering Description

This wire frame style illustration shows the structure of a Tile with an attached Control Bar. The Tile Header offers several types of convenience functionality (print, email, and pdf export of the Tile). The Control Bar offers a single selector. The Tile Body contains a chart and table, each with a title and footer or key. The Tile Footer contains four links, to a mixed set of destinations either within or outside the portal.

TILE GROUP

Mandatory Components: Tile Group Header, Tile Group Body
Optional Components: Tile Group Footer
Stacking Size: 2

Description

A Tile Group typically combines two or more Tiles together—likely from different sources or perspectives—into a larger unit of information or functionality that allows the combination of resources to answer more complicated questions, or achieve more complicated tasks. A Tile Group might answer the question, "How are my daily sales vs. my competitor's daily sales?" by presenting a Daily Sales Tile and a Competitor Sales Tile next to one another, under the combined title 'Daily Sales vs. Competitor Sales'.

Tile Groups consist of two required components—a Tile Group Header and Tile Group Body—and may include an optional Tile Group Footer. Tile Groups may include multiple Control Bars (note: adding multiple Control Bars can quickly increase development complexity and lower usability levels). The Tile Group Header contains a mandatory Title, optional Subtitle, mandatory content source indicator, and may include buttons or links for Convenience functionality.

In the scenario above, the two stacked Tiles likely present information that comes from different data sources (perhaps one internal, and one licensed from a third party market metrics service), and it's likely that the Tiles were created by different organizations that used the Building Blocks system to coordinate user experience design and development efforts that rely on a common enterprise portal or platform foundation. The consumers of the individual Tiles are likely affiliated with separate business units or operating groups, and may not need or be aware of the other Tiles, or the Tile Group. The consumers of the Tile Group could easily be part of a third element of the organization – or perhaps they are affiliated with the originating groups for the separate tiles, but share a common management perspective or performance incentive that requires a comparative presentation of the source information.

Stacking Note: Tile Groups stacked inside larger building blocks retain their individual Tile Group Header, Tile Group Body, Tile Group Footer, and any optional components.

Design Note: While Container defintions require the presence of some components to maintain the structural integrity of the Buildng Blocks system (Tiles always have a Tile Header, etc.), they do not mandate constant *visibility* or *display* of all the structurally required components. Excess chrome is the enemy of a good user experience at all levels of structure, and should be avoided. Many existing interaction patterns, control mechanisms and design principles can help eliminate excess chrome, and minimize the presence of chrome in general to that which is necessary for a high quality user experience, without increasing the effort or cost of relying on the Building Blocks. (See Figure 2)

Example rendering:

{tilegroup_structure_2.ai}

Figure 2. Tile group components and structure

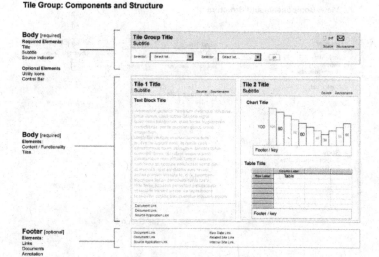

Rendering Description

This wire frame illustration shows the structure of a Tile Group with an attached Control Bar. The Tile Group Header offers several types of convenience functionality (print, email, and pdf export of the Tile as rendered). The single Control Bar offers two selectors. The Tile Group Body contains two stacked Tiles; one Tile offers text, the other contains the combination of a chart and table seen previously. Note that both stacked Tiles retain their individual Tile Headers and Tile Footers. In this rendering, neither stacked Tile offers convenience functionality, though it is possible for stacked Tiles to offer convenience functionality.

VIEW

Mandatory Components: View Header, View Body
Optional Components: View Footer
Stacking Size: 3

Description

Views consist of two required components—a View Header and View Body—and may include an optional View Footer. Views may include multiple Control Bars (note: adding multiple Control Bars can quickly increase development complexity and lower usability levels). The View Header contains a mandatory Title, optional Subtitle, mandatory source indicator, and may include icons for accessing standard convenience functionality.

A View typically combines Tiles and Tile Groups together to present a comprehensive set of information resources that address a single perspective within an area of interest. In common use, Views allow Dashboard or Portal users to see the most logical subsets of all available Tiles related to one aspect of an area of interest. For example, many Tiles might provide information about a single product—too many to appear on one Page—but the Customer View of a product presents only those Tiles that show information about a single Product in relation to major Customers. Another defined View could offer marketing information for that same product, and a third

Figure 3. View components and structure

View: Components and Structure

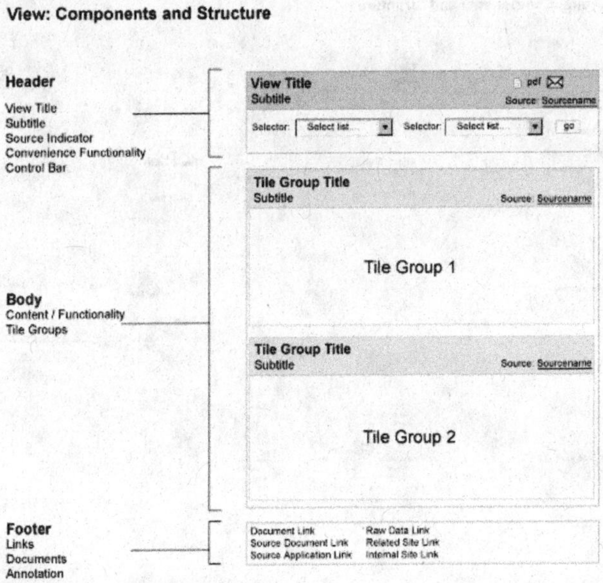

might allow executives to check inventory levels for the product at various storage facilities.

Views stacked inside larger building blocks retain their individual View Header, View Body, View Footer, and any optional components. (See Figure 3)

Example rendering:

{views_structure_2.ai}

Rendering Description

This wire frame shows the structure of a View with an attached Control Bar. The View Header offers several types of convenience functionality (print, email, and pdf export of the View as a single unit). The Control Bar offers two selectors. The View Body contains two stacked Tile Groups, one Tile offering text, the other offering the combination of a chart and table seen previously. The stacked Tile Groups retain their individual Tile Group Headers, but do not include Tile Group Footers. In this rendering, neither stacked Tile Group offers convenience functionality, though it is possible for stacked Tiles to offer convenience functional-

ity. The View Footer contains links to a variety of documents, applications, and destination sites.

PAGE

Mandatory Components: None
Optional Components: Page Header, Page Footer
Stacking Size: 4

Description

It's best to talk about Pages in two senses; specifically as Containers from the Building Block system, and generally as destinations for users navigating dashboard or portal environments. In the first sense, as part of the hierarchy of building blocks in the dashboard or portal system, Pages are simply a larger kind of Container without mandatory components. They are governed by the same principles of portability, openness, independence, etc. as the other blocks, which means individual Pages may not be visible to some types of users, depending on security restrictions, and could consist of a mix of smaller building blocks and elements of free-form content. One possible alternate name considered for Pages was 'nodes,' to emphasize the distinction between their building block system role and their browser navigational role, but that felt too abstract.

In the second sense, Pages take on their traditional role as presentation canvases for content and functionality, linked together by navigation mechanisms: they serve as the single-screen units of display and interaction familiar from the Web paradigm. In this role, Pages become the delivery vehicle for combinations of Containers and Connectors that allow users to work with content, and move through the dashboard or portal environment. Pages typically combine collections of Tiles, Tile Groups, and Views with a set of accompanying Connectors (Section Connectors, Page Connectors, Crosswalk Connectors, Geography Selectors, and Utility Navigation) to create a navigable user experience. Pages – following the principle of Openness – may include free-form content or navigation mechanisms. Common examples of free-form content include search functionality,

global navigation, links to intranets and extranets, feedback forms for requesting new features, and branding elements.

A Page can consist of a single Tile, or only free-form content, may or may not have a Page Header or Page Footer managed as building blocks assets, and might not be connected to or accessible from other areas of the Dashboard or Portal. For example, a Page dedicated to account administration functions might only be visible to members of the user group Administrators, who themselves cannot see other areas of the Dashboard or Portal, and thus would not require navigation connections to other Pages in the Dashboard or Portal. (See Figure 4)

Example rendering:

{page_structure_2.ai}

Rendering Description

This wire frame shows the structure of a Page that mixes free-form content with building block content. The free-form elements appear in the form

Figure 4. Page components and structure

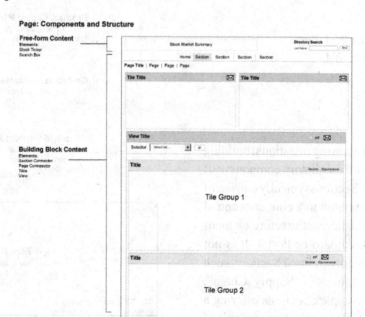

of a stock ticker, market summary, and a staff directory search box. Branding elements such as logos identifying the individual dashboard often appear as free-form content. These free-form content elements could also appear as a formally defined Page Header building block, managed as an asset in a library of reusable Tiles.

The building block content includes a navigation cluster made of a Section Connector and a Page Connector, two stacked Tiles, and a View that contains two stacked Tile Groups (Tiles not shown). On this Page, the two independent Tiles and the View are stacked at the same level within the containing Page. The layout of this Page places the Tiles above the View to ensure they remain visible without scrolling, but this layout is not necessary by the rules of the building block system. The individual Tiles on this Page do not include either Control Bars or Footers. The View includes a Control Bar with two selectors. None of the blocks offers Convenience Functionality, though of course this is possible across all levels of the stacking hierarchy, and is commonly available for the Page itself.

SECTION

Mandatory Components: 1 Page
Optional Components: NA
Stacking Size: 5

Description

The Section is primarily an organizational building block, but it does have a mandatory component of at least a single Page. Sections typically consist of collections of Pages related to a core conceptual element of the information architecture or mental model for the Dashboard or Portal. It is not uncommon to see broadly defined Sections such as "Products", "Customers", "Supply Chain", or "Sales". Deep or complex Sections offering a considerable number of Pages or a large amount of

content commonly include summary style Pages that condense or introduce the full contents of the Section in an overview. Shallow sections offering few Pages often do not require a summary style Page. (See Figure 5)

Example rendering:

{section_products.eps}

Rendering Description

This site map style rendering shows a Section, titled Products, which contains five Pages that of-

Figure 5. Example section

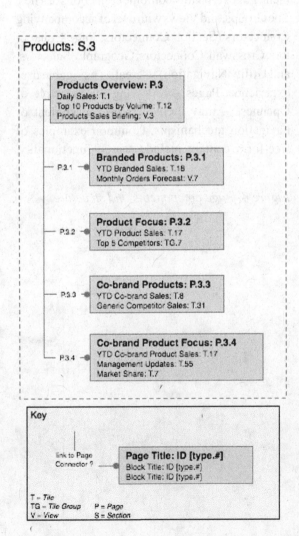

fer a variety of content related to the two types of Products produced and sold by a fictional company. The Section begins with a summary Page titled Products Overview. The four additional Pages are titled Branded Products, Product Focus, Co-Branded Products, and Co-brand Product Focus. The five pages contain a mixture of stacked Tiles, Tile Groups, and Views. The summary Page, titled Products Overview (P.3), offers the following: two stacked Tiles, Daily Sales (T.1) and Top 10 Products by Volume (T.12); and a stacked View, titled Products Sales Briefing (V.3).

By personal preference, only the blocks stacked at the level of the Page – level 3 – are individually identified on this map-style rendering; the Views and Tile Groups would obviously include further Tiles stacked within. I use this rendering convention to cut down on visual clutter in maps of large dashboards or portals. For your own renderings, feel free to itemize every stacked block at every level on the Page, or even list the dashboard or portal contents in simple outline fashion without pictures. Each stacked block in the rendering is identified by its Title, and a unique ID code or label, to allow synchronization with a master list of building blocks available across all dashboards. The numbered lines indicate that each Page includes a standard Page Connector, offering navigation between all the numbered Pages in the Section.

DASHBOARD OR PORTAL

Mandatory Components: 1 Section
Optional Components: N/A
Stacking Size: 6

Description

The Dashboard or Portal is the largest single unit of meaning possible to assemble from stacked building blocks. A Dashboard or Portal must consist of at least one Section (itself made of at least a single Page). Dashboards or Portals typically consist of several connected Sections, assembled from connected Pages that contain a variety of stacked building blocks, combined with a smaller number of stand-alone Pages dedicated to utility functionality or administration. Most Dashboards or Portals rely on a variety of Connectors to link assembled building blocks into a cohesive and navigable whole. A Dashboard or Portal's information architecture often aligns with a single mental model, or a small set of closely overlapping mental models, though this obviously depends on the needs and goals of the expected users.

To most users of internal tools situated withing an enterprise, a Dashboard or Portal is the total set of Sections, Pages and other stacked building blocks their security and access privileges permit them to see and use when they visit a URL or some other user experience destination (note: for web-delivered Dashboards or Portals, it is common practice to create a URL and expose this address via an intranet or other internal gateway). Since each user has an individually determined and potentially different set of security and access rights to each possible Section, Tile, View, and Page, each user will likely see a different combination of Dashboard or Portal content that is tailored to his or her own needs.

In this way, individual Dashboards or Portals often draw from a pool of defined Tiles and blocks which:

- Serve a group of executives running a large organizational unit within an enterprise, such as Marketing, Manufacturing, or Information Technology
- Provide a class of information resources giving insight across an enterprise, such as inventory monitoring, sales forecasting, financial reporting, quality control assessment
- Offer functionality in support of specific roles that entail responsibilities across the en-

terprise, such as regional directors, account managers, or human resources directors

I recommend labeling or branding these kinds of internally focused Dashboards or Portals clearly, to help communicate their contents and purpose to users and administrators who will likely have to work with many different tools and environments, and may easily suffer disorientation as a result. A simple title such as "Corporate Finance and Accounting Dashboard" can help distinguish one Dashboard or Portal in a Suite from another for busy users. I also recommend creating a log-in or destination page that orients users and confirms they are accessing the correct Dashboard or Portal to meet their needs.

In more public and social settings, the patterns of architecture, usage, and design at this level of size and complexity naturally differ.

Design Note: Depending on the depth and complexity of the assets offered within any one Dashboard or Portal, it may make sense to create a separate Home Page that introduces the structure and contents of the Dashboard, and offers unique content. Home Pages in this style commonly provide trend charts with roll-ups of more granular metrics, score-card style visualizations that communicate status for major areas of interest, alerts that require business attention, and

high-level summarizations of the more extensive information available deeper inside. (See Figure 6)

Example rendering:

{dashboard.eps}

Rendering Description

This sitemap style rendering shows a medium-sized Dashboard or Portal designed to meet the information and business functionality needs of a large enterprise with multiple operating units and business lines. In this context, the Dashboard provides cross-unit summaries of many important metrics for senior managers, and could even provide them business functionality to alter business processes, change supply chain structures, or revise finance and resource allocations.

This Dashboard or Portal consists of a dedicated Home Page, and five major sections: Marketing, Finance, Products, Supply Chain, and Administration. The first four sections – S.1 through S.4 – are linked via a Section Connector, offering direct navigation between these Sections. Each of these Sections includes a summary style Page. The Administration Section is not linked and navigable via the Section Connector: access to this Section would come via another path, generally direct URL entry or at the Dashboard or Portal log-in prompt

Figure 6. Example dashboard or portal

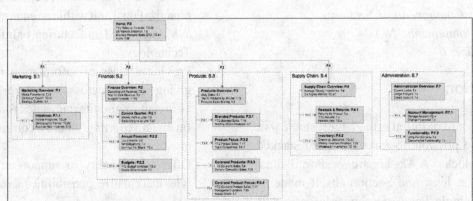

(not shown). Within the major sections, all Pages are linked and navigable via Page Connectors.

DASHBOARD OR PORTAL SUITE

Mandatory Components: Dashboards
Optional Components: N/A
Stacking Size: 7

Description

A Dashboard or Portal Suite consists of a group of stacked (though at this high level of structure, the construct is more akin to a collection of interlinks rather than hierarchically arranged) Dashboards or Portals sharing integrated content and common infrastructure. Stacking Dashboards or Portals as a Suite allows design and support teams to organize and manage distinct but related Dashboards or Portals as a single unit, and can help users by giving them quick and direct access to the collection of interconnected Dashboards or Portals. These Suites generally serve a diverse population of users who draw on a variety of business intelligence resources or other functionality to execute job functions at a variety of levels

within the enterprise. The goals or purposes of the Dashboards or Portals in a Suite may vary dramatically; hence their individual content offerings will also vary dramatically. Users whose business needs or functions require them to work with single Dashboards or Portals in a Suite may not realize the commonalities underlying the various individual Dashboards or Portals they use. Users whose needs span multiple Dashboards or Portals in a Suite typically rely on a Dashboard or Portal Connector to move from one Dashboard or Portal to another within the Suite.

From an enterprise level architectural or IT administrative viewpoint, the Dashboard or Portal Suite can become the connection point to other enterprise level systems, such as metadata registries and repositories, ERP and SCM applications, enterprise data stores, security and authentication platforms, intranets, extranets, etc. The Dashboard or Portal Suite is also a useful unit for enterprise level perspectives including IT portfolio management, business process management, strategic information management, and knowledge management. (See Figure 7)

Example rendering:

{dashboard_suite.eps}

Figure 7. Example dashboard suite

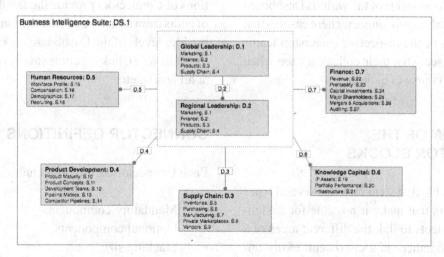

Rendering Description

This sitemap style rendering shows an enterprise level Dashboard Suite made up of seven individual Dashboards that share assets. Five of the seven provide depth of content in major domains of a global enterprise: Supply Chain, Human Resources, Product Development, Knowledge Capital, and Finance. Each of these domain Dashboards has a distinct internal structure, with the individual Sections identified on this map.

The remaining two Dashboards—Global Leadership and Regional Leadership—aggregate assets for presentation to the different levels of executive leadership within the enterprise. Within this scheme, the information architecture of the two leadership Dashboards is closely parallel, but the scope of the assets shown in each would differ; users of the Regional Leadership Dashboard would have a view of Finance assets for their individual regions, and not globally, as in the Global Leadership Dashboard.

In this Suite, The five domain Dashboards are linked to the two Leadership Dashboard via a Dashboard Connector, meaning that each of these is navigable from the Leadership Dashboards. The Regional Leadership Dashboard is also linked to the Global Leadership Dashboard via another Dashboard Connector. Whether these Connectors allow two-way access is dependent on the individual access rights of the various Dashboard users. The Dashboard Connector here ensures that the members of the respective leadership teams can literally see what their colleagues see when discussing a course of action.

OVERVIEW OF THE CONNECTOR BLOCKS

The building block system includes several types of Connectors that make it possible for designers and architects to link the different areas of a Dashboard together via a consistent, easily un-

derstandable navigation model. The system also ensures the resulting information architecture can grow in response to changing needs and content. There's no special stacking hierarchy for the Connectors. However, they do have an official stacking size (most are size 3) in order to keep Dashboards constructed with the building blocks internally consistent.

The defined Connectors are:

- Control Bar
- Section Connector
- Page Connector
- Dashboard Connector
- Crosswalk Connector
- Contextual Crosswalk Connector
- Utility Navigation
- Geography Selector

Control Bars allow access to deeper collections of similar blocks, such as Tile Groups and Tiles offering narrowly focused content. Section, Page, and Dashboard Connectors offer hierarchically driven navigation paths between larger Containers. Crosswalk Connectors and Contextual Crosswalks extend the capabilities of the default Building Blocks navigation model to include links that express context-driven associative relationships between Containers, regardless of their location within the Dashboard or Portal structure. Combinations of Connectors provide the familiar patterns of paths from a user's current location to higher or broader levels of the Dashboard, links to items at the same level, links to contextually related items at all levels, etc.

CONNECTOR DEFINITIONS

Each Connector definition includes:

- Mandatory components
- Optional components
- Stacking size

- Detailed description
- Example rendering (for illustrative purposes only)
  - Rendering description

CONTROL BAR DEFINITION

Mandatory components: Controls for manipulating Container content
Optional components: None
Stacking size: special – can be attached to Tiles, Tile Groups, or Views

Control Bar Description

A Control Bar increases the amount of content offered by a Tile, Tile Group, or View by giving users the ability to change the content displayed within the block. Designers attach a Control Bar to a block to increase the effective depth (or scope) of the block's content. Control Bars allow dashboard designers to increase the depth of a new or existing Container block without increasing the on-screen size of the block or creating a large number of very similar blocks.

One common way of using Control Bars is to allow users to perform repeated tasks on one object that is a member of a group of similar objects. For example, a Tile that allows users to approve or reject purchase orders for one operating unit could be augmented with the addition of a Control Bar. The Control Bar will expand the scope of purchase order approval functionality by allowing the user to choose one or more operating units from a list of all available operating units. The approval functionality itself should appear and remain within the Tile, though the scope may expand with successive revisions of the Tile.

Another common use for Control Bars is to provide tools for choosing different combinations of data parameters for display within a block, such as selecting a single item for focus (or rendering of available data) from a list of many other items of the same type, shifting the start or end dates for a time period, changing a measurement unit or referencing an axis for comparison.

The controls—buttons, sliders, actuators, etc.—in a Control Bar are often rendered as standard form elements such as radio buttons or select lists, or hyperlinks. They could just as easily appear as custom scripted elements, applets, or AJAX / RIA delivered sliders. The types and styles of controls presented should be driven by the guidelines of good user experience design. And perhaps your budget!

A primary benefit of Control Bars is to reduce the total number of blocks necessary for a dashboard—though they do increase the complexity of individual blocks—thereby lowering overall development costs and saving valuable screen real estate. For example, consider a single product that is part of a family of fifteen related products: placing a Control Bar on a Tile that shows the inventory for one of those products allows users to change between displaying the same kind of inventory data for any product in the family, instead of simultaneously displaying fifteen separate Tiles with the same inventory data for all the different products in the family. Control Bars also work well when users need to compare metrics, items, or groups of metrics or items, in a side-by side fashion.

Control Bars attached to stacked blocks retain their functionality. Stacking Containers with attached Control Bars can lead to complex possible permutations of scope and depth for block content. Explore the potential combinations and permutations carefully, especially in regards to security and access rights. Control Bars should not replace functionality already located within a block, or serve as a means of combining wildly different sorts of content together into a single block that is incoherent or inconsistent. I recommend limiting the use of Control Bars to one per Container. (See Figure 8)

Figure 8. Example control bar

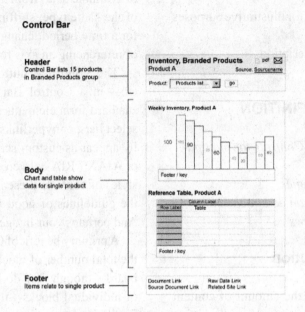

Example rendering

{Control_bar.ai}

Rendering Description

This rendering shows a Tile with attached Control Bar that allows users to shift the focus of the Tile to any of a list of fifteen individual products, chosen via the select list shown. When the user chooses a product, the contents of the Tile refresh to show weekly inventory data for the new product, as well as a reference table and associated documents and links for the same new product.

PAGE CONNECTOR DEFINITION

Mandatory components: links to all Pages in the parent Section
Optional components: None
Stacking size: 3

Page Connector Description

The Page Connector links all the Pages stacked within a single Section of the Dashboard. The Page Connector typically appears on every Page within a Dashboard, though this is not required. As users navigate from Section to Section, the links in the Page Connector change to reflect the different Pages stacked in each Section. Of course, placing a Page Connector on any Page does not preclude creating other groups of links to other Pages located throughout the Dashboard. The Building Blocks are an open system—architects and designers should introduce additional (Free Form, within the view of the blocks) navigation models and mechanisms into the experience as needed. (See Figure 9)

Example rendering:

{page_connector.eps}

Rendering Description

This rendering shows the navigation links to Pages appearing in a Page Connector for a Section titled

Figure 9. Example page connector

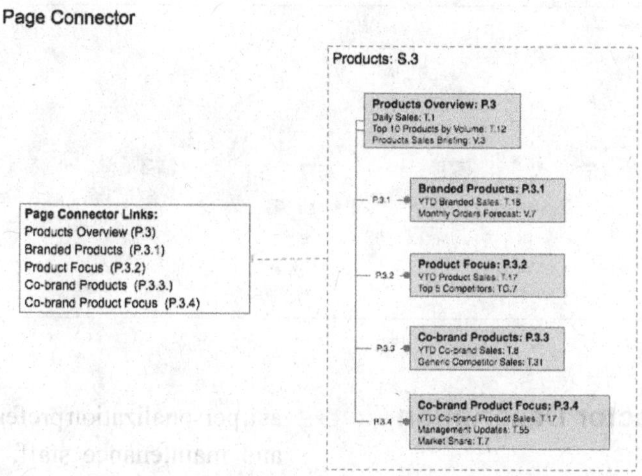

Products, which contains a Section summary page and four other Pages.

SECTION CONNECTOR DEFINITION

Mandatory components: links to all Sections in the Dashboard
Optional components: link to Dashboard Home Page
Stacking size: 3

Section Connector Description

The Section Connector is a high level Connector that provides a link to each Section making up the Dashboard. The Section Connector typically appears on every Page within the Dashboard, though this is not required. The Section Selector is akin to the ubiquitous global navigation element familiar from many web sites, though its actual content when displayed to a user will vary based on security settings or access rights. The links in the Section Connector should take users either to the Section Summary Page for that Section or to the chosen default Page within the Section. Include a link to any Dashboard Home Page in the Section Connector, especially if it offers unique

content not available elsewhere in the dashboard. (See Figure 10)
Example rendering:

{section_connector.eps}

Rendering Description

This rendering shows the navigation links to Section summary Pages appearing in a Section Connector for a Dashboard that includes a Home Page and five Sections. Four of the Sections are navigable via the Section Connector, the remaining fifth Section—S.5 Administration—is dedicated to administrative uses, and is not navigable or linked via the Section Connector.

DASHBOARD CONNECTOR DEFINITION

Mandatory components: links to each Dashboard in a Dashboard Suite
Optional components: NA
Stacking size: 3

Figure 10. Example section connector

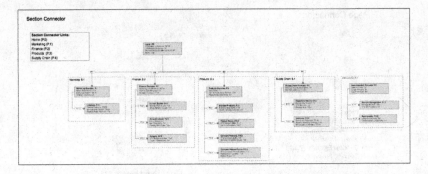

Dashboard Connector Description

The Dashboard Connector allows users with access to two or more Dashboards within a Dashboard Suite to move quickly and directly amongst all the Dashboards they may access, without passing through multiple log-in or authentication interfaces. Dashboard Connectors typically appear on every Page of a Dashboard, though this is not required. The individual links in a Dashboard Connector often point to the Homepage for each listed Dashboard. A less-common linking behavior for Dashboard Connectors is to connect to the last visited Page in each linked Dashboard or to a default Page of the users choosing that is stored

as a personalization preference. For administrators and maintenance staff, Dashboard Connectors can offer the same quick and direct access to the separate administrative areas of each Dashboard in a Suite. (See Figure 11)

Example rendering:

{dashboard_connector.eps}

Rendering Description

This rendering shows the Dashboard links appearing in the Dashboard Connector for the Business Intelligence Suite described above.

Figure 11. Example dashboard connector

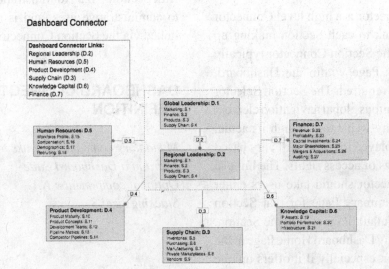

CROSSWALK CONNECTOR DEFINITION

Mandatory components: recurring item (link origin), destination building block
Optional components: None
Stacking size: None

Crosswalk Connector Description

A Crosswalk Connector is a direct navigation path between individual building blocks, regardless of origin and destination locations in the Dashboard structure. Crosswalk Connectors provide a hub and spoke style path from many locations to a single destination, rather than a uniquely occurring link between two blocks. Crosswalks often take the form of a recurring name, term, or object that consistently links to another single building block offering content related to the linked item.

Common examples of Crosswalk Connectors include:

- product names linked to a summary Page or View of the identified product
- topic terms linked to a news aggregator or RSS aggregator block that shows recent items related to that topic
- competitor names linked to a profile snapshot or market intelligence block

- market or product family names linked to sales performance blocks
- colleague names linked to profile information blocks showing their role, responsibilities, and direct reports (See Figure 12)

Example rendering:

{crosswalk_connector.eps}

Rendering Description

This rendering shows all the appearances of a Crosswalk Connector that links the instances of a product name to a destination Page in the Products Section (S.3) titled "Product Focus" (S.3.2), in this case a Page offering detailed information and tools related to a single product.

CONTEXTUAL CROSSWALK DEFINITION

Mandatory components: linked term (recurring item), origin contexts associative relationship, destination building blocks
Optional components: None
Stacking size: None

Figure 12. Example crosswalk connector

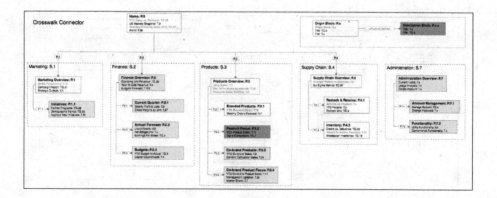

Contextual Crosswalk Description

Contextual Crosswalks allow dashboard architects to create a direct link between blocks that is sensitive to context, instead of simply point to point. Contextual Crosswalks typically link a recurring item, such as a product name, to a destination block that varies based on the location of the originating link within the Dashboard's information architecture. With a Contextual Crosswalk, the destination block of each occurrence of the product name is determined by the location or context of the link within the Dashboard structure; that is, by relying on the users' current location to offer insight into the things they are most interested in seeing.

For example, each occurrence of a product name throughout a Dashboard could link either to a block offering inventory information for that product, or to a block offering sales information for competing products. When the product name is located in the Supply Chain section of the Dashboard, it would connect to the inventory block: when the product name is located in the Sales section, the link would connect to the competitor sales block.

Contextual Crosswalks are useful when Dashboards offer a substantial amount of content that addresses several different facets or aspects of an important and recurring topic, term or item. Contextual Crosswalks often appear in the form of a Page showing Views for an item, both of which are chosen via Control Bar to give users ready access to the other available collections of blocks matching the other origin contexts.

Keeping the broader principles of the Building Blocks in mind, it's perfectly logical for Contextual Crosswalks to link from one of several Dashboards or Portals within a Dashboard Suite to another destination Dashboard.

While Contextual Crosswalks can express any kind of associative relationship, in practice, it's best to define a limited set of types of Contextual Crosswalk in advance and apply them consistently across the Dashboard or Portal Suite. We know well that complex navigation models increase the work required for designers, developers, users and administrators. Prescribing the available set of Crosswalk Connectors (Contextual and standard) in advance will make it much easier to maintain consistent and easily understood navigation models. (See Figure 13)

Example rendering:

{contextual_crosswalk.eps}

Figure 13. Example contextual crosswalk

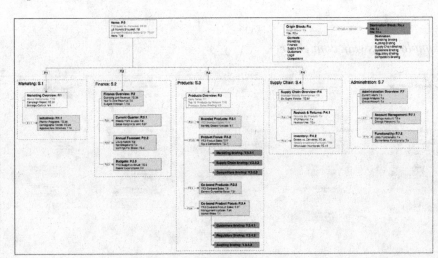

Rendering Description

This rendering shows the navigation paths for a Contextual Crosswalk that links from a number of different origin contexts (or locations) to one of a number of similar destinations within the Products Section of a medium-size Dashboard. The legend on the map identifies the origin contexts and destinations for the Contextual Crosswalk, as well as the linked term: a Product Name. In this case, the Contextual Crosswalk directly links product names in six possible origin contexts (Marketing, Finance, Supply Chain, etc.) with six matching briefings that provide detailed information on the status of a that same product. Those briefings appear as Views available from the Branded Product Focus Page (which contains the Marketing, Supply Chain, and Competitors briefings) or the Co-brand Product Focus Page (which contains the Customers, Regulatory, and Auditing briefings). After clicking the linked product name in the Supply Chain Section, a user navigates to the Branded Product Focus Page (P.3.2), which presents them with the Supply Chain Briefing (V.3.2.2).

UTILITY NAVIGATION DEFINITION

Mandatory components: links to Dashboard Utility Functionality
Optional components: None
Stacking size: 3

Utility Navigation Description

This Connector gives users consistent access to the most important utility functions and features for a Dashboard or Portal, gathering ubiquitous links to these necessary tools into a single building block. Utility Navigation should include links to any Utility Function that must be accessible from most or all Dashboard Sections or Pages.

Utility Navigation is typically considered to have a stacking size of 3, meaning it is placed at the Page level of the stacking hierarchy and not within individual Tiles, Tile Groups or Views. This approach is common practice in design settings and enterprise environments where standardized functionality is often supplied by or closely connected to externally defined services supplied via SOA – situations where some sort of dependency links the Dashboard or Portal to another system or environment. (See Figure 14)

Example rendering:

{utility_navigation.jpg}
{ltd_utilitybar.tif}

Rendering Description

This Utility Navigation component uses icons to provide links to eight distinct Utility Functions, an enterprise directory, a news feed aggregator, managed documents (Resources), a calendar, enterprise search, KPI driven alerts, prioritized

Figure 14. Example utility navigation

staff updates and personalization settings. As you review the illustrations and examples of Utility Navigation and the other Connectors, keep in mind that no rule from the Building Blocks system requires Utility Navigation to appear onscreen collected together in a single location (though good conceptual and practical reasons for doing so often apply). Likewise, the design decision about how to provide access and use – via icons, text, or other features – should be driven by the particulars of your project and user needs. (See Figure 15)

GEOGRAPHY SELECTOR DEFINITION

Mandatory components: controls or links for shifting the geographic context of a Container
Optional components: None
Stacking size: special – can be attached to Tiles, Tile Groups, Views, or Pages,

Geography Selector Description

The Geography Selector allows designers and architects to decouple the information architecture of a Dashboard from the shifting organizational structures based on geography that many enterprises rely on to understand the fundamentals of their

Figure 15.

Recalling the example business intelligence dashboard
designed with the Building Blocks system from Part 1, this
illustration shows a Dashboard Page which includes several
of the Connectors.
{us_products_example_callouts.jpg}

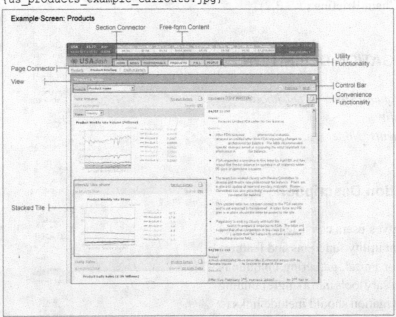

This Page includes a Section Connector, a Page Connector, a
View and a Tile with attached Control Bars, Utility
Navigation (labeled 'Utility Functionality' here) and
Convenience Functionality (described in more detail Part 5)

activities. The Geography Selector presents users with controls or links allowing them to change the geographic reference point of a Container, while maintaining the structure of that Container. In the same way that Control Bars increase the depth of a Tile, Tile Group, or View, a Geography Selector increases the scope or depth of a Container while reducing the number of additional Containers to manage. For example, a Geography Selector might allow users the ability to change the focus of a sales activity chart located in a Tile from one US state to another.

Large enterprises often operate in or with reference to multiple states (or provinces, departments, etc.), regions, countries or even continents. These geographic concepts or schemes frequently differ from unit to unit within an enterprise. They often change dramatically from year to year to suit external environmental changes or internal reorganizations. Just as aligning a site map to an organization chart creates a brittle structure subject to disruption during reorganization, tying a Dashboard's information architecture to an enterprise's current geographic scheme is a recipe for frustration.

Some Geography Selectors allows users to choose from a single set of geographic units, such as states or counties, with respect to the parameters determining the data shown for a defined set of KPI's (fixed Containers, variable scope for their content). Other Geography Selectors allow users to traverse a hierarchy of geographic units, with respect to the parameters determining the data shown for a defined set of KPI's (fixed Containers, variable scope for their content). It's possible to attach Geography Selectors to Containers with Control Bars. In these cases, the Geography Selector typically drives the Container contents before the Control Bar. (See Figure 16)

Example rendering:

{geography_selector.ai}

Rendering Description

This rendering shows a Tile Group with attached Geography Selector and Control Bar. The geographic scheme represented is hierarchical, spanning three tiers, beginning with State, moving to district and concluding with territory. Of course, many businesses use non-hierarchical geographic schemes, irregular schemes, or a combination of these options; in these cases the structure and quality of the underlying data, functionality and

Figure 16. Example geography selector

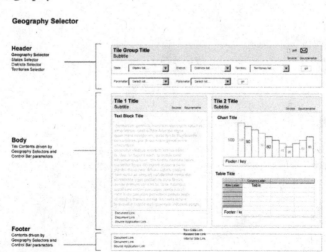

business logic may require creative solutions to the problems spawned by unusual intersections of the various choices.

CONCLUSION

This set of Connectors provides the minimum tools necessary for the assembly of coherent Dashboards across a wide variety of circumstances. I encourage you to refine this starting set, or create additional types of Connectors to meet new challenges.

When combined in a fashion that meets the specific needs and context of a tile-based design effort, the Containers and Connectors can strike a good balance between cost, flexibility, and cus-

tomization in terms of the user experience, systems and technology efforts and business perspective.

With proper assembly, using the stacking hierarchy and the small set of required elements, portal designers can create a consistent and scalable structure that supports a high quality user experience, lowers development costs and establishes a basis for sharing of resources across the enterprise.

The next paper of this series will describe a common set of utility and convenience functionality often used to extend the reach and relevance of portal content to other contexts of use, making practical suggestions for following the principles of Openness, Independence and Portability underlying the Building Block system.

This work was previously published in the International Journal of Web Portals 2(1), edited by Greg Adamson and Jana Polgar, pp. 58-81, copyright 2010 by Information Science Publishing (an imprint of IGI Global).

Chapter 21
Enhancing the Portal Experience

Joe Lamantia
MediaCatalyst BV, The Netherlands

ABSTRACT

This article presents strategies for enhancing the long-term business and user value of portals as the third in a series of articles describing a Portal Design Framework. This article identifies essential Enterprise 2.0 functionality for collaboration and dialog—capabilities that support emerging Social Business practices—included in the Building Blocks Design Framework. The author discusses portal management and governance best practices and describes strategies for maintaining and enhancing the user experience of portals designed using the Building Blocks Framework.

A PORTAL DESIGN VISION: TWO-WAY EXPERIENCES

Portals gather and present content from a wide variety of sources, making the assembled items and streams more valuable for users by reducing the costs of content discovery and acquisition. By placing diverse content into close proximity, specialized forms of portals such as the dashboard support knowledge workers in creative and interpretive activities including synthesis, strategy formulation, decision making, collaboration, knowledge production, and multi-dimensional analysis.

At heart, however, aggregation is a one-way flow. In the aggregation model common to many portals, content is collected, organized, and perhaps distributed for use elsewhere, but nothing returns via the same channels. Savvy users quickly see that the greatest value of aggregative experiences and tools lies in their potential contributions to two-way flows. They understand that experiences capable of engaging direct and indirect audiences transform portal and dashboard content into a broadly useful resource for communities of much greater scope and impact. Further, business staff and IT users comfortable in the new world of Enterprise 2.0, DIY / mash-ups and shadow IT now often create their own information tech-

DOI: 10.4018/978-1-4666-0336-3.ch021

nology solutions, assembling services and tools from many sources in new ways that meet their individual needs.

Accordingly, portal designers should create experiences that support increased discussion, conversation, dialog and interaction, and allow for the potential value of remixing content in innovative ways. We might summarize a broad design vision for two-way portals that synthesizes these audiences, environmental factors and imperatives as follows:

- Provide rich contextual information about the origin and nature of dashboard or portal content to users (context is crucial, especially in a fragmented and rapidly moving enterprise environment).
- Improve the quality and consistency of the user experience of aggregated content.
- Improve the portability of content, making it useful outside the boundaries of the dashboard.
- Allow dashboard users to take advantage of other tools available from outside the immediate boundaries of the portal.

Operatively, this means providing two-way channels that make it easy to share content with others or even 'take it with you' in some fashion. The building block framework is ideal as a robust foundation for the many kinds of tools and functionality – participatory, social, and collaborative – that support the design vision of two-way flows within and outside portal boundaries.

RECOMMENDATIONS

Based on this vision, and experience with the long-term evolution and usage of many portals, I recommend five ways to enhanced two-way capabilities, and the overall quality of user experiences designed with the building blocks framework:

1. Define standardized convenience functionality that could apply to all blocks: This will provide a baseline set of common capabilities for individual blocks such as export of Container content, printing, etc.
2. Define utility functionality offered at the Dashboard or Dashboard Suite level: This captures common productivity capabilities for knowledge workers, linking the dashboard to other enterprise resources such as calendars and document repositories.
3. Define common metadata attributes for all Container blocks, to support administration and management needs.
4. Define presentation standards that balance flexibility with appropriate consistency within Container blocks, and across the user experience.
5. Define user roles and types of blocks or content to allow quick management of items and functionality in groups.

As with the rest of the building blocks design framework, these recommendations are deliberately neutral in terms of business components and processes, technology platforms and development frameworks (RUBY, AIR, Silverlight, etc.), and design methods. They describe capabilities and / or functionality that design, business and technology decision makers can rely on as a common language when deciding together what a given portal or dashboard must accomplish, and how it should do so. (Besides allowing extension and reuse of designs, neutrality is consistent with the principles of Openness, Independence, Layering and Portability that run throughout the building blocks system.)

CONVENIENCE FUNCTIONALITY

Convenience functions make it easier for users to work with the content of individual Container blocks. Good examples of convenience functionality include printing the contents of Containers for use outside the Dashboard, or subscribing to an RSS feed that syndicates a snapshot of the contents of a block. Convenience functionality is associated with a single Container, but is not part of the content of the Container.

This collection is a suggested set of convenience functionality meant to help establish a baseline that you can adapt to the particular needs of your users. Assign convenience functions to individual blocks as appropriate for circumstances and as endorsed by users, business sponsors, and technologists. Some of these features make sense at all levels of the block hierarchy, and some do not (how would one print an entire Dashboard in a way that is useful or readable?).

The collection is broken into five groups:

- Understanding Content Sources and Context
- Making Dashboard Content Portable

- Controlling the User Experience
- Staying Aware of Changes / Subscriptions
- Social and Collaborative Tools

The illustration below shows Convenience functionality associated with a Tile (Figure 1).

GROUP 1: UNDERSTANDING CONTENT SOURCES AND CONTEXT

Preserving accurate source indication for the contents of each block is critical for the effective use of heterogeneous offerings. Dashboards that syndicate Tiles from a library of shared assets may contain conflicting information from different sources, so users must have an indication of the origin and context of each block. (Wine connoisseurs use the term 'terroir').

Figure 1. Tile convenience functionality (by group)

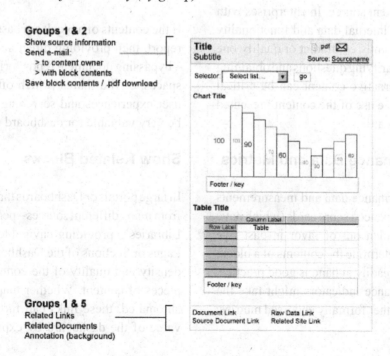

Show Detailed Source Information for a Block

For business intelligence and data content, the source information commonly includes the origin of the displayed data in terms of operating unit and internal or external system (from partners or licensed feeds), its status (draft, partial, production, audited, etc.), the time and date stamp of the data displayed, the update or refresh cycle, and the time and date of the next expected refresh.

For widgets, web-based applications, and content that takes the form of transactional functionality such as productivity or self-service applications delivered via an intranet or web-service, source information commonly includes the originating system or application, its operating status (up, down, relevant error messages…), and identifying information about the group, operator, or vendor providing the functionality.

Send Email to Source System Owner / Data Owner

This allows portal users to directly contact the 'owners' of a content source. In enterprises with large numbers of internal data and functionality sources that frequently contradict or qualify one another, asking clarifying questions and obtaining additional or alternative content can be critical to making effective use of the content presented within the Dashboard.

Show Performance Data and Metrics

If standard performance data and measurements such as KPIs or balanced score cards (which have risen and then fallen out of favor in past five years) affect or determine the contents of a block, presenting them readily at hand is good practice.

Such performance indicators might take the form of KPIs or other formally endorsed metrics, and require:

- Showing displayed KPIs
- Showing supporting KPIs (rolled up or included in the summary KPI on display)
- Showing related KPIs (parallels by process, geography, industry, customer, etc.)
- Showing dependent KPIs (to illuminate any 'downstream' impact)

For performance indicators defined by number and name – perhaps they are recognized and used across the enterprise or operating unit as a comparative baseline, or for several different measurement and assessment goals – provide this important contextual information as well.

Show Related Documents or Assets

Whether automated via sophisticated information management solutions or collected by hand, related documents and assets increase the range and applicability of dashboard content. Bear in mind that less is often more in a world drowning in electronic assets and information.

Show Source Reports or Assets

If the contents of a block are based on an existing report, then providing direct access to that item – bypassing document repositories, collaboration spaces, or file shares, which often have terrible user experiences and searching functions – can be very valuable for dashboard users.

Show Related Blocks

In large portals or Dashboards that aggregate Tiles from many different sources – perhaps several Tile Libraries – providing navigable links to related Pages or Sections of the Dashboard increases the density and quality of the connections between pieces of content. Whether mapped by hand or automated, these links can further enhance the value of the dashboard by exposing new types of relationships between informational and functional content not commonly placed in proximity in source environments.

Search for Related Items and Assets

If individual Container blocks carry attached metadata, or metadata is available from the contents of the block, search integration could take the form of pre-generated queries using terms from local or enterprise vocabularies, directed against specifically identified data stores.

GROUP 2: MAKING DASHBOARD CONTENT PORTABLE

These capabilities enhance the portability of content, supporting the two-way communication and social flows that make content so useful outside the boundaries of the dashboard. The items below include several of the most useful and commonly requested portability measures.

- Print contents of block
- Email contents of block (HTML / text)
- Email a link to block
- Create a .pdf of block contents
- Create a screenshot / image of block contents
- Download contents of block (choose format)
- Save data used in block (choose format)
- Download source report (choose format)

GROUP 3: CONTROLLING THE USER EXPERIENCE

Individual blocks may offer users the ability to change their on-screen layout, placement, or stacking order, collapse them to smaller sizes, or possibly activate or deactivate them entirely. If designers have defined standard display states

for Containers (see *Presentation Standards and Recommendations* below), blocks may also allow users to choose the display state

Functionality:
- Change layout or position of block on screen block
- Collapse / minimize or expand block to full size
- Change display state of block
- Deactivate / shut off or activate / turn-on block for display

GROUP 4: STAYING AWARE OF CHANGES / SUBSCRIPTIONS

Aggregation models lower information discovery and acquisition costs, but do not obviate the costs of re-finding items, and do little to help users manage flows and streams of content that change frequently. Many portals and dashboards aim to enhance users' awareness and make monitoring the status of complex organizations and processes simpler and easier. This group includes functionality allowing users to subscribe to content through delivery channels such as RSS, or to receive notice when dashboard content changes.

Functionality:
- Send email on block change (it is optional to include contents)
- Subscribe to RSS feed of block changes (it is optional to include contents)
- Subscribe to SMS message on block change
- Send portal Page on block change

GROUP 5: SOCIAL AND COLLABORATIVE TOOLS

This group includes social features and functions that engage colleagues and others using social mechanisms. Introducing explicitly social mechanisms and capabilities into one-way dashboard and portal experiences can dramatically enhance the value and impact of dashboard content.

When designed properly and supported by adoption and usage incentives, social mechanisms can encourage rapid but nuanced and sophisticated interpretation of complex events in large distributed organizations. Social functions help preserve the insight and perspective of a diverse community of users, an intangible appreciated by many global enterprises.

Annotate Block

Annotation allows contributors to add interpretation or a story to the contents of a block. Annotation is typically preserved when blocks are syndicated or shared because annotations come from the same source as the block content.

Comment on Block

Commentators can provide locally useful interpretation for a block originating from 'elsewhere'. Comments are not always portable, or packaged with a block, as they do not necessarily originate from the same context, and their relevance will vary.

Tag Blocks

Tagging with either open or predetermined tags can be very useful for discovering unrecognized audiences or purposes for block content, and quickly identifying patterns in usage that span organizational boundaries, functional roles, or social hierarchies.

Share / Recommend Blocks to Person

Combined with presence features, sharing can speed decision making and the growth of consensus.

Publish Analysis / Interpretation of Block Content

Analysis is a more thorough version of annotation and commenting, which could include footnoting, citations, and other scholarly mechanisms.

Publish Contents of Block

Publishing the contents of a block to a team or enterprise wiki, blog, collaboration site, or common destination can serve as an communication vehicle, and lower the opportunity costs of contributing to social or collaborative tools.

Rate Block

Rating blocks and the ability to designate favorites is a good way to obtain quick feedback on the design / content of blocks across diverse sets of users. In environments where users can design and contribute blocks directly to a Tile Library, rating allows collective assessment of these contributions.

Send Contents of Block to Person (With Comment)

Sending the contents of a block – with or without accompanying commentary – to colleagues can increase the speed with which groups or teams reach common points of view and serve as a useful shortcut to formal processes for sharing and understanding content when time is important, or individual action is sufficient.

Send Link to Block to Person (With Comment)

Sending a link to a block – with or without accompanying commentary – to colleagues can increase the speed with which groups or teams reach common points of view and serve as a useful shortcut to formal processes for sharing and understanding content when time is important, or individual action is sufficient.

Commenting and annotation, coupled with sharing the content that inspired the dialog as a complete package, were the most requested social capabilities among users of many of the large enterprise dashboards I have worked on.

Figure 2. Combinations of functionality

STACKING BLOCKS

Some combinations of Convenience functionality will make more sense than others, depending on the contents of blocks, their purpose within the larger user experience, and on the size of the blocks in the stacking hierarchy (outlined in part 2). Figure 2 illustrates a Page composed of several sizes of Containers, each offering a distinct combination of Convenience Functionality.

Convenience or Connector Component?

Several of the Connector components (described in part 4 of this series) – especially the Control Bar and the Geography Selector – began life as examples of Convenience functionality. Over the

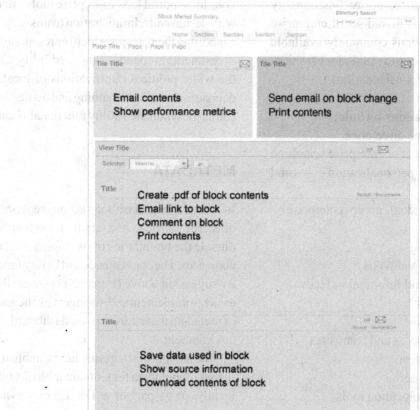

course of many design projects, these pieces were used so frequently that their forms standardized, and they merited independent recognition as defined building blocks (The change is a bit like receiving a promotion).

With sustained use of the blocks framework, it's likely that designers will identify similar forms of Convenience functionality that deserve identification as formal building blocks, which can then be put into the library of reusable design assets. This is wholly consistent with the extensible nature of the blocks system, and I encourage you to share these extensions!

UTILITY FUNCTIONALITY

Utility functionality enhances the value of content by offering enterprise capabilities such as calendars, intranet or enterprise searching, and colleague directories, within the portal or dashboard setting. In practice, utility functionality offers direct access to a mixed set of enterprise resources and applications commonly available outside portal boundaries in a stand-alone fashion, (e.g., in MS Outlook for calendaring).

Common Utility functions include:
- Team or colleague directories
- Dashboard, intranet or enterprise searching
- Dashboard personalization and customization
- Calendars (individual, group, enterprise)
- Alerting
- Instant messaging
- Corporate blogs and wikis
- Licensed news and information feeds
- RSS aggregators
- Attention streams
- Collaboration spaces and team sites
- Profile management
- Document repositories
- Mapping and geolocation tools

- Business intelligence tools
- SCM, ERP, and CRM solutions

MY EXPERIENCE OR YOURS?

One important question designers must answer is where and how portal users will experience and work with Utility functionality, whether within the portal experience itself, or within the user experience of the originating tool? Or as a hybrid of these approaches?

Enterprise productivity tools and large software packages such as CRM and ERP solutions often provide consumable services via SOA or APIs, as well as their own user experiences (though they may be terrible). The needs and goals of users for your portal may clearly indicate the best presentation of Utility functionality syndicated from elsewhere is to decompose the original experiences and then integrate these capabilities into your local portal UX. Enterprise tools often come with design and administration teams dedicated to supporting them, teams which represent significant investments in spending and credibility. Consider the wider political ramifications of local design decisions that affect branding and ownership indicators for syndicated utility functionality carefully.

METADATA

In portals and dashboards, aggregation often obscures origins, and content may appear far outside the boundaries of its original context and audiences. The convenience and Utility functionality suggested above (Figure 3) is generally much easier to implement and manage with the assistance of metadata that addresses the dashboard or portal environment.

The attributes suggested here establish a starting set of metadata for Container blocks managed locally, or as part of a Tile Library syndicated

Figure 3. Local vs. source experiences

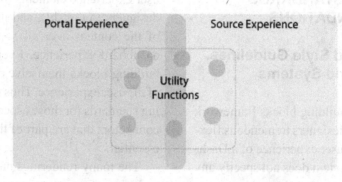

across an enterprise. The goal of this initial collection is to meet common administrative and descriptive needs, and establish a baseline for future integration metadata needs. These attributes could be populated with carefully chosen values from a series of managed vocabularies or other metadata structures, or socially applied metadata provided by users as tags, keywords, facets, etc.

Administrative Attributes:
- Security / access level needed for content
- System / context of origin for content
- System / context of origin contact
- Data lifecycle / refresh cycle for content
- Most recent refresh time-date
- Effective date of data
- Block version #
- Block release date

Structural Attributes:
- Container blocks stacked in this block
- Crosswalk Connectors present within block
- Contextual Crosswalk Connectors present within block

Descriptive Attributes:
- Title
- Subtitle
- Subject
- Audience

- Format
- Displayed KPIs (defined by number / name)
- Supporting KPIs (defined by number / name)
- Related KPIs (defined by number / name)
- Related Documents / Assets
- Source Report / Assets
- Related Blocks
- Location

Metadata Standards

The unique needs and organizational context that drive the design of many portals often necessitates the creation of custom metadata for each Tile Library or pool of assets. However, publicly available metadata standards could serve as the basis for dashboard metadata. Dublin Core, with a firm grounding in the management of published assets, offers one useful starting point. Depending on the industry and domain for the users of the dashboard, system-level integration with enterprise vocabularies or public dictionaries may be appropriate. Enterprise taxonomies and ontologies, as well as metadata repositories or registries, could supply many of the metadata attributes and values applied to building blocks.

PRESENTATION STANDARDS AND RECOMMENDATIONS

Visual Design and Style Guidelines, Page Layouts, Grid Systems

The neutrality of the building blocks framework allows architects and designers tremendous flexibility in defining the user experience of a Dashboard or portal. The system does not specify any rules for laying out Pages, defining grid systems, or applying design styles or guidelines. Responsibility for these design questions should devolve to the local level and context; the architects and designers working on a given user experience must make these critical decisions.

Standards for Containers and Connectors

One of the paramount goals for the building blocks system is to minimize the presence of un-needed user experience elements (no excess chrome for designers to polish!), and maintain the primacy of the content over all secondary parts of the dashboard experience. Even so, aspects of the building blocks themselves will be a direct part of the user experience. Thus setting and maintaining standards for those aspects of Containers and connectors that are part of the user experience is essential.

The many renderings and examples of Tiles and other components seen throughout this series of articles show a common set of standards that covers:

- Location and relationship of Tile components (Tile Body, Tile Header, Tile Footer)
- Placement of Convenience functionality
- Placement of Utility functionality
- Treatment of connector components
- Boundary indicators for Tiles and Containers

Figure 4. Presentation standards for containers and connectors

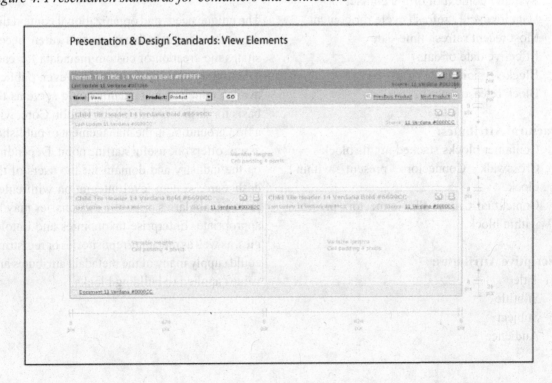

- Boundary indicators for mixed content (block and free-form)

Figure 4 shows one set of standards created for the Container and Connector components of an enterprise dashboard.

This is a starting set of elements that often require design standards. Architects and designers working with the building blocks will need to decide which block elements will be part of the user experience, and create appropriate standards. (If using lightweight and modular user experience development approaches relying on standards and structured components, it's possible to effect quick and easy design iteration and updates.)

Standards for Content Within Containers

Setting standards and defining best practices for layout, grid systems, and visual and information design for the contents of Container blocks will increase the perceived value of the dashboard or portal. In the long term, offering users a consistent and easy to understand visual language throughout the user experience helps brand and identify Tile-

based assets that might be syndicated or shared widely. a strong and recognized brand reflects well on its originators. Figure 5 shows example standards for chart content in Container blocks.

Standards for Mixed Building Block and Freeform Content

Setting standards for layouts, grid systems, and information design for the freeform content that appears mixed with or between Containers makes sense when the context is known. When the eventual context of use is unknown, decisions on presentation standards should devolve to those designers responsible for managing the local user experiences.

Container States

The core principles of openness and portability that run throughout the building blocks framework mean the exact context of use and display setting for any given block is difficult for designers to predict. Defining a few (three or four at the most) different but standardized presentation / display states for Containers in a Tile Library can help

Figure 5. Presentation standards for chart content in container blocks

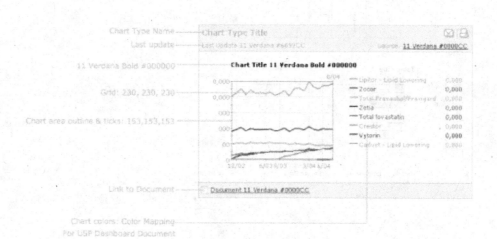

address the expected range of situations and user experiences from the beginning, rather than on an ad-hoc basis. This approach is much cheaper over the long-term, when considered for the entire pool of managed Tiles or assets.

Since the on-screen size of any element of the user experience is often a direct proxy for its anticipated value and the amount of attention designers expect it to receive, each standard display state should offer a different combination of more or less content tuned to an expected context. Using a combination of business rules, presentation logic, and user preferences, these different display states may be invoked manually (as with Convenience functionality) or automatically (based on the display agent or surrounding Containers), allowing adjustment to a wide range of user experience needs and settings. In practice, states are most commonly offered for Tiles and Tile Groups, but could apply to the 'larger' Containers with greater stacking sizes, such as Views, Pages and Sections.

One of the most commonly used approaches is to assume that a Container will appear most often in a baseline or normal state in any user experience, and that all other states cover a sliding scale of display choices ranging from including the greatest possible amount of content, to the least. The four states described below represent gradations along this continuum.

Normal state is the customary presentation / display for a Container, the one users encounter most often.

Comprehensive state is the most inclusive state of a Container, offering a complete set of the contents, as well as all available reference and related information or Containers, and any socially generated content such as comments, annotations, collective analyses, etc. Figure 6 shows a Tile in comprehensive display state.

Figure 6. Tile: comprehensive display

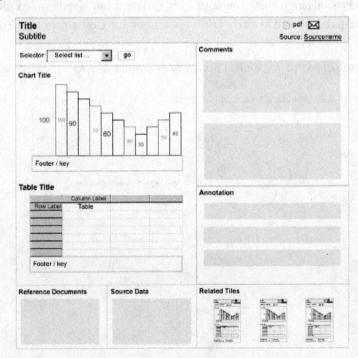

Figure 7. Tile: summary display

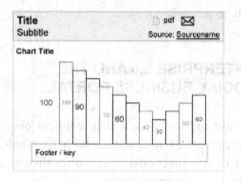

Summary state condenses the block's contents to the most essential items, for example showing a single chart or measurement. The summary state hides any reference and related information, and places any socially generated content such as annotation or comments in the background of the information landscape. Figure 7 shows a Tile in summary display state.

Snapshot state is the most compact form of a Container block, offering a thumbnail that might include only the block's title and a single highly compressed metric or sparkline. Snapshot states often represent the Container in discovery and administrative settings, such as in search experiences, in catalogs of assets in a Tile Library, or in dashboard management interfaces. Figure 8 shows a Tile in snapshot display state.

Convenience and Utility Functionality

New platforms such as AIR and Silverlight, and the freedom afforded by AJAX and RIA based experiences in general offer too many possible display and interaction behaviors to discuss in detail here.

Accordingly, I suggest designers keep the following principles in mind when defining the interactions and presentation of convenience and Utility functionality:

- Convenience functionality is meant to improve the value and experience of working with individual blocks.
- Utility functionality addresses the value and experience of the portal as a whole.
- Convenience functionality is less important than the content it enhances.
- Convenience functionality is always available, but may be in the background.
- Utility functionality is always available, and is generally in the background.
- Convenience functionality does not replace Utility functionality, though some capabilities may overlap.
- Usability and user experience best practices strongly recommend placing convenience functionality in association with individual blocks.
- Usability and user experience best practices strongly recommend presenting Utility functionality in a way that does not associate it with individual Container blocks.

MANAGE FUNCTIONALITY BY CREATING GROUPS

Most users will not need the full set of convenience and Utility functionality at all times and across all Tiles and types of Container blocks. Usage contexts, security factors, or content formats often mean smaller subsets of functionality offer the greatest benefits to users. To keep the user experience free from the visual and cognitive clutter of un-needed functionality, and to make management easier, I recommend designers define groups of

Figure 8. Tile: snapshot display

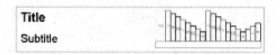

functionality, users, and content. Create groups during the design process, so these constructs are available for administrative use as soon as the portal is active and available to users.

Other recommendations include:

- Define bundles of convenience and Utility functionality appropriate for different operating units, business roles and titles, or access levels of users.
- Allow individual users to select from bundles of convenience and Utility functionality. Customization commonly appears in a profile management area.
- Create roles or personas for dashboard users based on patterns in content usage, and match roles with relevant and appropriate functionality bundles.
- Define types of user accounts based on personas, or usage patterns and manage functionality at the level of account type.
- Define types of Tiles or Containers based on content (informational, functional, transactional, collaborative, etc.). Apply bundles of convenience functionality to all the Tiles or Containers of a given type.
- Define standard levels of access for social features and functionality based on sliding scales of participation or contribution: read, rate, comment, annotate, write, edit, etc. Manage access to all social functions using these pre-defined standard levels.

Larger portals may warrant the creation of a dedicated administrative interface. The building blocks make it easy to define an administrative console accessible via a Page or Section apparent only to administrators.

ENTERPRISE 2.0 AND THE SOCIAL BUSINESS PORTAL

Portals and dashboards that augment one-way aggregation of information with Convenience and Utility functionality can offer diverse and valuable content to savvy users – customers who expect Enterprise 2.0, Web 2.0, and Social Business software capabilities from all their experiences and tools. As these recommendations demonstrate, the building blocks can serve as an effective design framework for portals that serve as two-way destinations.

Many of these recommended Convenience and Utility capabilities come 'out of the box' in portal or dashboard platforms and the interactions that make them available to users follow standard behaviors in the resulting user experiences. When first identified as valuable for users (going on five years ago), these capabilities almost universally required teams to invest considerable amounts of time and money into custom design, development and integration efforts. Thankfully, that is no longer the case.

Part Four of this series will present a case study on how the building blocks framework solved recurring problems of growth and change for a series of business intelligence and enterprise application portals by reviewing the evolution of a suite of enterprise portals constructed for users in different countries, operating units, and managerial levels of a major global corporation.

This work was previously published in the International Journal of Web Portals 2(2), edited by Greg Adamson and Jana Polgar, pp. 12-25, copyright 2010 by Information Science Publishing (an imprint of IGI Global).

Chapter 22
Using the Building Blocks:
Evolution of a Portal Suite

Joe Lamantia
MediaCatalyst BV, The Netherlands

ABSTRACT

This article is a case study that explores the use of the Building Blocks portal design framework over a series of enterprise portal projects spanning several years. This article describes the business contexts that shaped each portal as it was designed, showing the use and reuse of design and development elements based on the Building Blocks. This article discusses the changes and adaptations that shaped the elements of the Building Blocks design framework over time.

A BRIEF WORKING HISTORY OF THE BUILDING BLOCKS

The Building Blocks began life as an internal tool used by technical and user experience architects at my services firm to lower development costs and speed design work. Over a span of ~36 months, its use expanded rapidly, and the blocks become a shared framework for the design and integration of almost a dozen different enterprise portals created for a long-term client.

In retrospect, the portal suite went through four stages of evolution and growth.

The first portal to be built was a business intelligence application meant to test the value of a dashboard style experience for small groups of executives. Even at this early stage, the vision was to create a collection of interlinked portals that aggregated functionality and content from within the enterprise, with the first dashboard acting as prototype.

Based on the success of the first dashboard, the client commissioned many new types of portals -- including role-based, enterprise productivity, and geographically focused -- for different busi-

DOI: 10.4018/978-1-4666-0336-3.ch022

ness and operating units. This stage corresponds roughly, or metaphorically to the rapid speciation [http://en.wikipedia.org/wiki/Speciation] that occurs when an ecological niche is opens, or is unoccupied.

Following rapid expansion, efforts shifted to consolidating and integrating technical architectures and user experiences across the different portals in the suite in order to keep pace with waves of organizational changes reshaping the client's business.

In the fourth stage, the emphasis was on stability and efficiency, making the portal suite cost-effective for the client to govern without our direct involvement.

We built numerous portal-based enterprise applications, running the gamut from finance and collaboration to geographic information visualization during this time. Rather than survey these by type (another case study), it is easier to understand the different roles the building blocks played throughout all four stages of the suite's evolution by following the history of one of the larger portals, which I will call the U.S. Portal.

THE USA DASHBOARD: PATIENT ZERO

Like many inventions, the Building Blocks were born as the most expedient solution to a pressing problem, when I joined a struggling design effort for an overdue new portal. The design of what I'll refer to as the USA Dashboard (for confidentiality) was supposed to be a quick and easy 'tweaking' of its predecessor, the prototype Global Executive Dashboard. Since the audiences for the two portals were very different, however, nearly every aspect of the existing Executive Dashboard from content, structure and information design, to security model and data update schedule required revisiting.

Our team needed a way to quickly accommodate many new assets into an existing portal structure, define and iterate multiple content placement options, abstract repeated elements for code reuse, coordinate the interaction design of a rapidly growing library of functionality, and resolve a collection of information design challenges. We also had to create a system that could allow for unforeseeable future changes and expansions without disrupting the user experience.

To meet these ambitious goals, we needed a new design language for the portal environment. This new language needed to be internally consistent, flexible, and simple enough for clients to understand.

Relying on lessons learned from the design of the prototype dashboard, the Building Blocks simplified and standardized the components and relationships that could be used to build a portal. The first version of the Building Blocks included only three Containers, the Tile, Tile Group, and Page; three Connectors; the Control Bar, the Crosswalk Connector, and the Section Connector; and an initial set of Convenience Functionality. At the time, we did not identify the Blocks as a framework, or even label the different kinds of blocks as Containers or Connectors.

The most immediate benefit of introducing the Building Blocks into the design effort was to help the clients move beyond an all-or-nothing style of decision making that relied on large numbers expensive, hard to create, full-color mockups of interfaces populated by live data.

The small set of standardized elements and relationships made effective comparison of multiple lightweight design concepts possible. Clients were able to focus on identifying the content needed (for their internal clients, the actual end users of the new US Portal), while our team addressed questions of structure, interaction, and technology. After extensive but substantially faster iteration of design concepts, we launched the first version of the US Portal. Figure 1 shows an early production version of the home page.

Figure 1. US portal home page

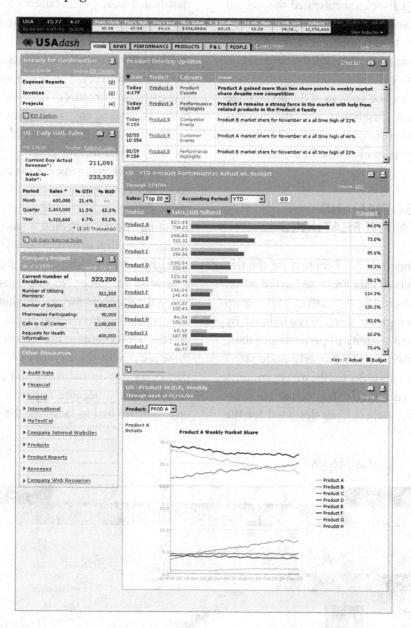

THE REGIONAL DASHBOARD

The next portal in the lineage, called the Caribbean Dashboard, was regionally focused. Intended to show financial performance for a geographic perspective, the Caribbean Dashboard borrowed new map-based visualizations from the growing library of shared enterprise assets. The heat-maps allowed users to visually compare data, activity, and the status of a group of related countries, to a fine level of granularity. While the map visualizations were new, the data sources were the same as those offered within the US Portal, filtered for the different geography. The structure of the Caribbean Dashboard closely echoed the structure of the US Portal, largely because this portal directly reused many of US Building Block assets created for the US Portal.

The Building Blocks accelerated the design portions of the Caribbean Dashboard effort, allowing a small team to generate and refine detailed design concepts and initial design documentation in less than a week.

Figure 2 shows one version of the home page for the Caribbean Dashboard, with the new visualizations, and reuse of the existing US Portal information architecture visible in the tabs.

EVOLVING SOCIAL AND COLLABORATIVE FEATURES

Shortly after launch, lack of context for the tremendous amounts of data presented in the portal became a problem. The executives making up the primary user group were overwhelmed by the new depth and quantity of performance data, and needed perspective to properly understand the information. This reflected the transformation from paper-based to digital information sharing. Many of the earliest Tiles designed for the dashboard were portal-based versions of reports that executives used to consume via paper. Staff prepared these reports in advance, and then briefed the executives on their contents and meaning at the time of delivery. The new portal environment presented rich streams of data literally around the clock, bypassing any distillation and synthesis.

The Building Blocks served as effective basis for re-establishing context, and supporting the social mechanisms people rely on to make sense of events and information. The addition of many Enterprise 2.0 style social features to the Building Blocks reflected a shift from seeing a business intelligence portal as a sort of distributed spreadsheet, to a collaborative socially enhanced enterprise resource. No one asks a spreadsheet 'what the numbers mean', or what it thinks about the connections between changes in performance and the latest events in the industry. But of course these are exactly the sorts of interactions that happen every day in hallways and meeting rooms, and it quickly became apparent that the portal environment had to facilitate them.

Figure 2. The regional dashboard

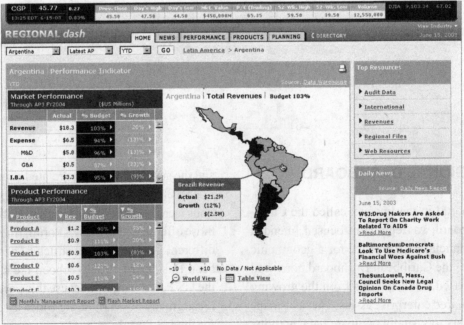

The first step was to make the contents of Tiles and other blocks in the framework sharable via email, the most common enterprise productivity tool. This first convenience function allowed portal users to export an image of the current Tile contents (built on the fly, reflecting any custom combination of filters / parameters applied in the Tile) to their preferred email program for despatch to colleagues. Emailing capability included a link to the source within the portal, to indicate the origin of the data shown in the exported image of the Tile.

We then added a commentary capability allowing people to write explanations to accompany a feed of numeric data, chart, or other report element. The combination created a package of qualitative and quantitative information. In the first stages of commentary use, interpretive or explanatory commentary typically flowed 'upwards' from line managers to senior managers and executives,

Figure 3. Commentary elements

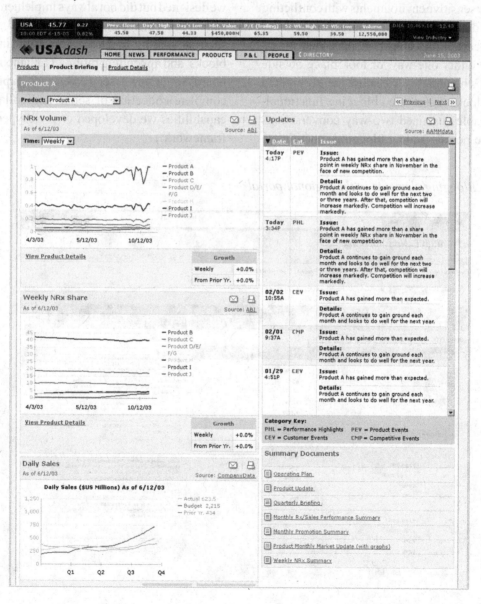

mirroring existing reporting structures. Figure 3 shows one version of this commentary function, collecting all the individual 'Updates' created by managers for a single product into a common feed.

As the social interactions taking place within the portal increased in volume and complexity, we distinguished the capability to append qualitative "annotations" to data at the source, from "commentary" on data originating from elsewhere. Separating annotation and commentary addressed the very different perspectives of context of origin vs. context of use, a very important distinction in politically sensitive environments with conflicting pieces of data about the same subject.

These capabilities supported social interactions that were either one-way, or took place outside the portal's boundaries. We subsequently created a set of blocks that offered blogging functionality, to enable sustained two-way conversations within the portal. Adding blogging functions to

existing content instantly created a conversational interaction layer for the original asset, as well as introducing the attributes of history and searchability into the conversation. Figure 4 shows a later stage rendering of some of the blogging elements added to the Caribbean Dashboard. Figure 4 also includes the Utility Functionality created for the second release of the Executive Dashboard (visible on the far right of the screen), which became part of the blocks framework and was retrofitted to other portals.

Over the course of the full set of portal projects, we designed but did not always implement tagging and many other now-common social features, such as sharing and recommending individual blocks, and appending ratings. (Enhancing Dashboard Value and User Experience explores the complete collection of social and collaborative capabilities we developed or prototyped for the framework.)

Figure 4. Blogging elements in the regional portal

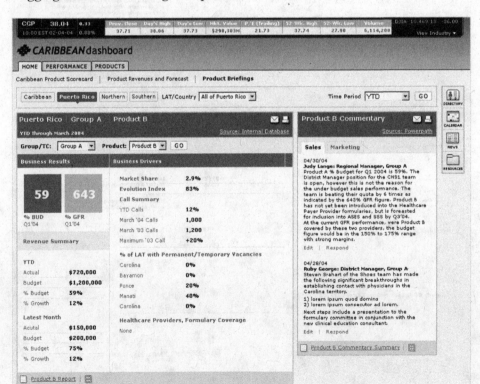

EVOLVING CONTENT AND STRUCTURAL CHANGES

The next major revision of the US Portal included substantial new amounts of content. Incorporating these new resources necessitated changes to the Building Blocks framework, resulting in the definition the View and Section Container blocks, and the addition of the Page Connector.

At this time, I saw two clear indicators that the framework itself was both recognizable and valuable. First, sales and project management members of our team used the constructs in the Building blocks to make estimates about effort, time, and cost of proposed projects. They crafted reporting documents, status communica-

tions, resource forecasts, and in some instances even contracts and statements of work using the language and concepts of the building blocks to specify deliverables and milestones.

Second, our team's technical architects sought out direct involvement in the definition of new Containers, Connectors, and Convenience Functionality. The framework became a natural common ground for the user experience and technical leadership to discuss the long-term aspects of the suite of portals. The technical architects wanted to influence the evolution of the framework in order to increase its utility and relevance, as it made their lives easier.

Figure 5 shows one of the Pages in the new Customers Section of the US Portal.

Figure 5. Structural changes

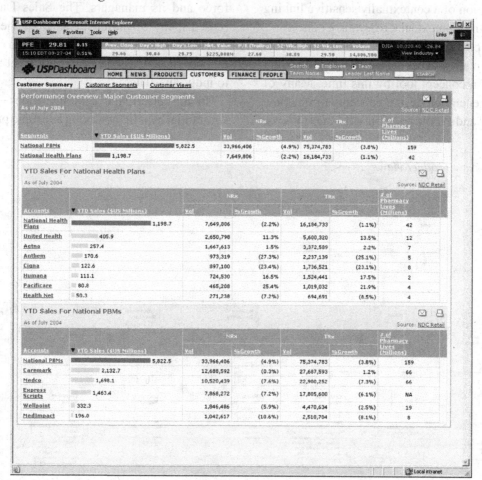

The definition of the View as a standard Container block inspired the creation of many additional types of View within the original Products Section of the portal. These new Views addressed more specific needs than the typical Products overview page created for the first launch of the USA Dashboard. They included a much greater amount of content. The need to provide effective navigation to this group of closely related but still distinct Views drove the definition of the View Selector.

Common practice before the introduction of the Views was to link any mention of a major entity such as a product, place, or competitor to its corresponding dedicated overview Page. The rapidly increasing set of Product Views required designers to choose from more than one possible destination for linked product names, which drove the definition of a contextually sensitive linking element, the Contextual Crosswalk Connector.

I was pleasantly surprised to see that clients had begun to independently use the Building blocks as a concept tool by this time. Many of the first generation design concepts for the new Customer and Product content offerings (Views, Pages, Tiles) were created and then substantially refined by clients without involving us, but integrated smoothly into the architecture of the user experience.

Figure 6 shows a rendering of the site map for the USA Dashboard that includes the new Customers Section and associated content, as well as three of the new Views for an individual Product that became part of the expanded Products Section. The new Contextual Crosswalk links that pointed to the various Product Views are not marked on this map.

THE SALES DASHBOARD

The next portal in the USA Dashboard lineage addressed the operational needs of the field sales force and its managers. The Sales Dashboard reused many of the elements from the current USA Dashboard, but drove the creation of a large number of new assets, from high level Sections to individual Tiles.

In this effort, the Building Blocks yielded substantial benefit by serving as a rapid prototype

Figure 6. New product views

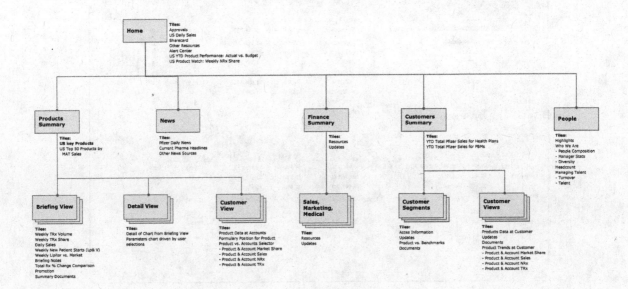

tool that made it easy and cost-effective to test proposed user experience structures and interactions for usability and value.

Figure 7 shows some of the major structural changes that the Sales Dashboard required, identifying new and modified Tiles, Sections, Pages, Views, and Connectors.

Figure 8 shows the home page of the Sales Dashboard

INTEGRATING PORTALS

The final phase of development for the USA Dashboard was the integration of all the concurrently active portals in the lineage into a single portal platform and technology base, and user experience. Driven by dramatic organizational changes in the structure of the enterprise itself, integration required combining the very different audiences, content, functionality, perspectives, and structures of the four existing portals into a coherent offering.

The integrated USP Leadership Dashboard included all of the relevant content of the pre-

ceding portals; the Executive Dashboard, USA Dashboard, the Caribbean Dashboard, the Sales Dashboard, as well as a dedicated administrative Section built to serve the needs the of the various support staff who curated the portal on a daily basis, visible only to designated users.

Befitting the politics of most enterprise efforts, the process was......somewhat acrimonious. But because the majority of the assets involved were designed using the Building Blocks at many layers of the information stack, the questions were straightforward compared to other similar portal and custom application integration efforts.

Figure 9 shows the overview page of the Sales Section in the integrated USP.

The user experience of the integrated US Leadership Dashboard offered a deep set of powerful data and functional content to a diverse set of audiences, ranging from executives to managers operational staff. The value and context of this substantial pool of shared content was enhanced by social mechanisms that spanned the boundaries of the portal suite. The Leadership Dashboard reused assets form or connected directly to a set of other portals, serving specialized purposes.

Figure 7. Sales dashboard structure

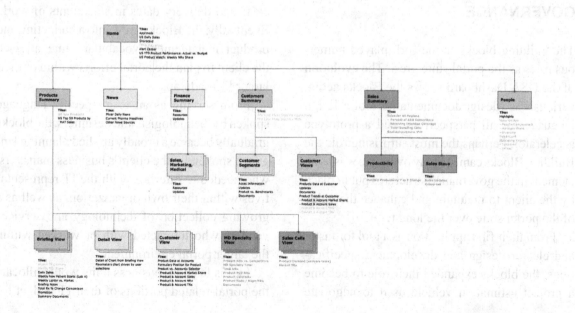

Figure 8. Sales dashboard home page

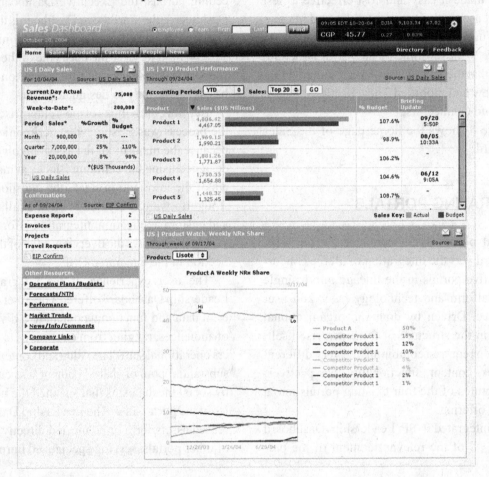

GOVERNANCE

The building blocks framework played numerous roles as the portal suite grew. The evolution of the USA Dashboard shows the Blocks acting variously as a design documentation tool, a design language for all perspectives, and a prototype accelerator. Perhaps the most surprising role the Building Blocks came to play over time was as an element in the governance structures put in place by the client to maintain and enhance the value of the portal suite over the long term.

From their first application as a tool for faster and clearer design and development specifications, the blocks expanded their role to become a project estimation vehicle used to negotiate

costs and delivery dates in statements of work. Eventually, the Blocks grew into a budgeting and product management vocabulary that allowed the client to plan the portal efforts within of their larger IT roadmaps.

From serving as an team-specific language spoken by technologists and designers, the blocks gradually became a broadly applied planning language spoken by the client's business managers, who needed to interface with the IT representatives within their own organization, as well as a growing collection of technology and services vendors who interacted with or worked within the larger portal environment.

In this fashion, business units would allocate the portal-related portions of their IT budget for

Figure 9. Integrated US leadership

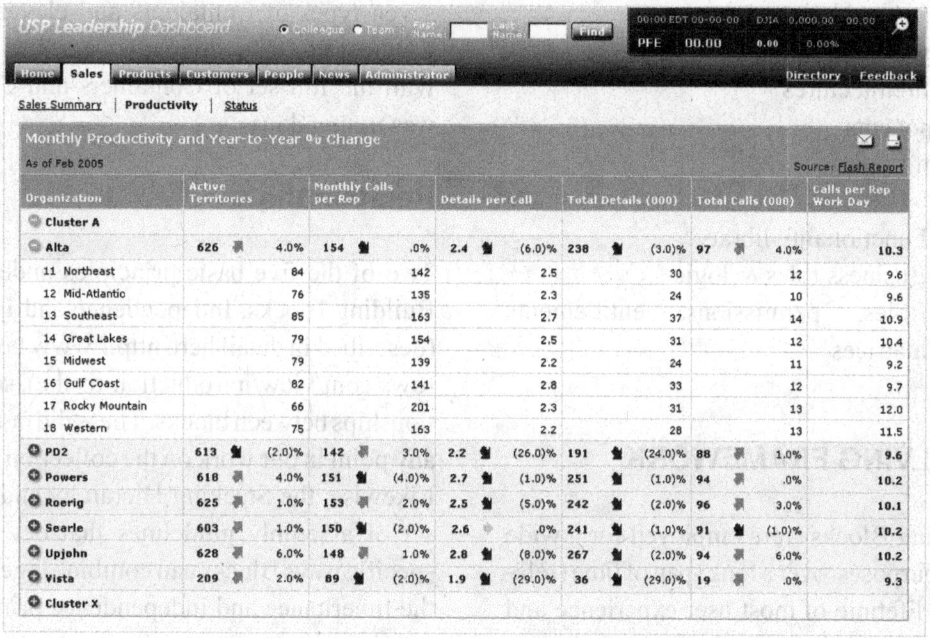

USP Leadership Dashboard

Monthly Productivity and Year-to-Year % Change

As of Feb 2005 — Source: Flash Report

Organization	Active Territories		Monthly Calls per Rep		Details per Call		Total Details (000)		Total Calls (000)		Calls per Rep Work Day
Cluster A											
Alta	626	4.0%	154	.0%	2.4	(6.0)%	238	(3.0)%	97	4.0%	10.3
11 Northeast			84		142		2.5		30	12	9.6
12 Mid-Atlantic			76		135		2.3		24	10	9.6
13 Southeast			85		163		2.7		37	14	10.9
14 Great Lakes			79		154		2.5		31	12	10.4
15 Midwest			79		139		2.2		24	11	9.2
16 Gulf Coast			82		141		2.8		33	12	9.7
17 Rocky Mountain			66		201		2.3		31	13	12.0
18 Western			75		163		2.2		28	13	11.5
PD2	613	(2.0)%	142	3.0%	2.2	(26.0)%	191	(24.0)%	88	1.0%	9.6
Powers	618	4.0%	151	(4.0)%	2.7	(1.0)%	251	(1.0)%	94	.0%	10.2
Roerig	625	1.0%	153	2.0%	2.5	(5.0)%	242	(2.0)%	96	3.0%	10.1
Searle	603	1.0%	150	(2.0)%	2.6	.0%	241	(1.0)%	91	(1.0)%	10.2
Upjohn	628	6.0%	148	1.0%	2.8	(8.0)%	267	(2.0)%	94	6.0%	10.2
Vista	209	2.0%	89	(2.0)%	1.9	(29.0)%	36	(29.0)%	19	.0%	9.3
Cluster X											

the upcoming quarter or year (time horizons varied) in terms of creating or updating Portals or other smaller Building Blocks, such as Sections, Views, and Tiles. Budget commitments for new or modified functionality and audiences were made according to requests and priorities from their internal customers, the end users. These longer range forecasts and decisions about what to build or re-use and modify were based on standardized estimates for the complexity, cost and time to implement common combinations of Building Block functionality within the client's well-known enterprise environment.

Managing the Portal Suite involved many different stakeholders, from data owners and business users, to the teams responsible for enterprise IT infrastructure and the creation of new assets for syndication. The client also needed tools that would allow their own staff and other vendors to effectively maintain and expand the Portal Suite without our involvement. As a governance apparatus was established, the neutral Building Blocks constructs and ideas were used to communicate many of the details of the business, technology, and user experience aspects for the Portal Suite to all the interested parties.

To support this effort, we created a detailed collection of architecture, design, and development documentation that described every aspect of the portals, from the database structures, to the code behind the library of Tiles, and the user experience. (Many of the examples used throughout this series of articles have been drawn from this collection.) We also created a set of planning and project management tools meant to act as 'accelerators' for portal efforts using the Building Blocks.

Below is a list of the assets we created in support of the client's governance effort.

Planning & Project Management
Estimation Tools
Portal Roadmaps & Project plans
Build & Deployment Plans Dependencies
User Experience
Information Architecture elements
Interaction Design flows and standards

Information Design patterns
Visual Design guidelines
Technology
Reference architectures
Code components
Application Logic
Business
- ◦ Functionality library
- ◦ Business rules & logic
- ◦ Roles, permissions, entitlements matrices

AN EVOLVING FRAMEWORK

The Building Blocks were employed for a wide variety of purposes, over a long span of time (relative to the lifetime of most user experience and information architecture designs), by a diverse audience. Did these changes in use lead to changes in the design of the framework itself?

To understand how a framework evolves, we have to consider the pieces that make up the framework. At the most fundamental level, all frameworks are made up of a set of defined components, and the relationships that determine how those components interact. A chosen scope determines what falls within the framework, and boundaries indicate how the framework relates to the world 'outside'. (More on these ideas is available from my IA Summit Workshop "Succeeding With Frameworks" http://www.slideshare.net/moJoe/designing-frameworks-for-interaction-and-user-experience).

How did the four parts of the Building Blocks framework change?

Components

In response to the many new design challenges that arose from new audiences and new business needs, the number and types of blocks defined in the framework grew. When first defined, we needed only 3 types of Containers and 2 kinds of Connectors. Eventually, the framework included seven types of Containers and eleven kinds of Connectors. The diversity of content created with the full set of Containers and Connectors was tremendous.

Relationships

Two of the five basic principles underlying the Building Blocks, Independence and Inheritance (described in detail here http://www.boxesandarrows.com/view/introduction-to-the), set the relationships between blocks. These did not change at any point in our work on the collection of portals. Likewise, the Stacking Hierarchy and the small set of assembly guidelines that determine the specific ways Blocks can combine together under the Inheritance and Independence principles did not change.

Scope

The scope of the Building Blocks framework, as set by the Layering principle, did not *directly* change. The blocks did become part of broader perspectives, such as project planning and governance, but this reflects a shift in usage (by whom, and in what contexts), rather than in what the framework itself addressed. The blocks were concerned with the structure of portals and other modular information environments from the beginning, and this did not change.

Boundaries

The boundaries of the Building Blocks, as set by the Openness and Portability principles, also did not change. The system began as an open framework, intended for to facilitate sharing and reuse of assets within the enterprise in social and technical sense, and remained open for the duration of our work.

In retrospect, altering the fundamental principles behind the framework was unnecessary, since there was no substantial change in the overall operating environment the Building Blocks were designed to address.

From an architectural perspective, we knew that changing any of the basic principles, or even the assembly rules based on them, would result in a very different framework, bringing on large scale questions of compatibility and integration with the existing set of portals, user experience disruptions, and increased costs. Beyond adding to the collection of defined components, the framework remained unchanged.

CONCLUSION

It's been a long journey, but we've (almost) reached the end.

Looking around and ahead, we can see that the decentralized model underlying Web 2.0 reflects (or is driving, or both?) a fundamental structural shift; the information realm is ever more modular and granular. Consequently, the digital world is evolving complex structure at all levels of scale, and across all layers, from the organization of busi-

nesses into networks of operating units collaborating within and across corporate boundaries, to the structured data powering so many experiences.

In fact, the digital / information realm (public, private, commercial, etc.) is rapidly coming to resemble the enterprise environments that encouraged the creation and use of the Building Blocks, and shaped their evolution as a design tool.

It is a world made up of syndicated streams of modular content and functionality, contextualized by tangible social structures such as networks and communities, supported by services that answer essential questions like identity and security.

This is true in every sense - witness the rise of widgets and micromedia - and will have especially far reaching implications as it affects our digital identities and their accompanying digitized social relationships.

I hope the ideas, concepts, examples, and experience communicated in this series of articles has helped others confronting similar design challenges to those my team faced, and will continue to help more people in the future, as the digital world changes around us.

This work was previously published in the International Journal of Web Portals 2(3), edited by Greg Adamson and Jana Polgar, pp. 43-55, copyright 2010 by Information Science Publishing (an imprint of IGI Global).

Compilation of References

Adajian, T. (2007). *The Definition of Art*. Stanford Encyclopedia of Philosophy.

Adamson, G. (2004). *The mixed experience of achieving business benefit from the Internet: A multi-disciplinary study*. Retrieved April 18, 2010, from http://adt.lib.rmit.edu.au/adt/public/adt-VIT20041105.112155/index.html.

Adamson, G. (2009). Portals and the challenge of simplifying Internet business use. *International Journal of Web Portals, 1*(1).

Adamson, G., & Wong, K. (2010). Case study: SOA, part of the tool-kit. *International Journal of Web Portals, 2*(1).

Adobe Systems. (n.d.). *Adobe flex 3 developer guide*. Retrieved from http://www.faqs.org/rfcs/ rfc2068.html

Afuah, A., & Tucci, C. (2001). *Internet Business Models and Strategies*. Boston: Harvard.

Agarwal, V., Chafle, G., Mittal, S., & Srivastava, B. (2008). Understanding approaches for web service composition and execution. In *Compute '08: Proceedings of the 1st Bangalore Annual Compute Conference* (pp. 1–8). New York: ACM.

Agrawal, M., Kishore, R., & Rao, H. R. (2006). Market reactions to e-business outsourcing announcements: An event study. *Information & Management, 43*(7), 861–873. doi:10.1016/j.im.2006.08.002

Agre, P. E. (1999, September). *The fall of Babbage's theology*. Paper presented to People and Computers seminar, University of Newcastle upon Tyne, Newcastle upon Tyne, UK.

Aickelin, U. (2002). An Indirect Genetic Algorithm for Set Covering Problems. *The Journal of the Operational Research Society, 53*(10), 1118–1126. doi:10.1057/palgrave.jors.2601317

Akkiraju, R., Goodwin, R., Doshi, P., & Roeder, S. (2003, August). A Method for Semantically Enhancing the Service Discovery Capabilities of UDDI. *In Proceedings of the IJCAI Information Integration on the Web Workshop*, Acapulco, Mexico. Retrieved from www.isi.edu/info-agents/workshops/ijcai03/papers/Akkiraju-SemanticUDDI-IJCA%202003.pdf

Aladwania, A. M., & Palvia, P. C. (2002). Developing and validating an instrument for measuring user-perceived Web quality. *Information & Management, 39*(6), 467–476. doi:10.1016/S0378-7206(01)00113-6

Almaer, D., & Galbraith, B. (n.d.). *Robot replay: Watch your users via ajax*. Retrieved from http://ajaxian.com/archives/ robot-replay-watch-your-users-via-ajax

Amazon. (2009). *Amazon Elastic Compute Cloud (Amazon EC2)*. Retrieved from http://aws.amazon.com/ec2/

Aoyama, M. (2002). Metrics and analysis of software architecture evolution with discontinuity. In Proceedings of the International Workshop on Principles of Software Evolution (p. 107). New York: ACM.

Armitage, S. (1995). Event study methods and evidence on their performance. *Journal of Economic Surveys, 9*(1), 25–52. doi:10.1111/j.1467-6419.1995.tb00109.x

Ball, R., & Brown, P. (1968). An empirical evaluation of accounting income numbers. *Journal of Accounting Research, 6*(2), 159–178. doi:10.2307/2490232

Barais, O., Meur, A., Duchien, L., & Lawall, J. (2008). Software architecture evolution. *Software Evolution,* 233-262.

Barron, M. (2002). *Retail web-based self-serve isn't just for customers, it's for employees.* Chicago: Internet Retailer.

Barua, A., & Whinston, A. (2001). *Measuring the Internet economy.* Paper presented at the Cisco Systems/Center for Research in Electronic Commerce, University of Texas, Austin, Texas.

Barua, A., Kriebel, C. H., & Mukhopadhyay, T. (1995). Information technologies and business value: An analytic and empirical investigation. *Information Systems Research, 6*(1), 3–23. doi:10.1287/isre.6.1.3

Bass, T., & Gruber, D. (2005, August 18). A glimpse into the future of id. *Usenix.* Retrieved from http://www.usenix.org/publications/login/1999-9/features/future.html

Bass, L., Clements, P., & Kazman, R. (2003). *Software architecture in practice.* Reading, MA: Addison-Wesley Professional.

Bauer, H. H., & Hammerschmidt, M. (2002). Financial portals in the internet. In *Proceedings of the WSEAS Conference on E-Commerce,* Athens, Greece.

Behl, S., & Hesmer, S. (2007). *Refreshing individual portlets and preferences using Single Portlet Refresh in WebSphere Portal V6.0.1.* Retrieved from http://www.ibm.com/developerworks/websphere/library/techarticles/0712_behl/0712_behl.html

Behl, S., Hesmer, S., Koch, S., & Steinbach, D. (2006). *Leveraging WebSphere Portal V6 programming model: Part 2. Advanced URL generation in themes and portlets.* Retrieved from http://www.ibm.com/developerworks/websphere/library/techarticles/0612_behl/0612_behl.html

Bell, H., & Tang, N. K. H. (1998). The effectiveness of commercial internet Web sites: a user's perspective. *Internet Research: Electronic Networking Applications and Policy, 8*(3).

Bendjebbour, A., & Delignon, Y. (2001, August). Multisensor Image Segmentation Using Dempster-Shafer Fusion in Markov Fields Context. *IEEE Transaction on GeoScience and Remote Sensing, 39*(8), 1–10. doi:10.1109/36.942557

Berners-Lee, T., & Fischetti, M. (2000). *Weaving the Web.* New York: HarperBusiness.

Bharadwaj, A. S. (2000). A resource-based perspective on information technology capability and firm performance: An empirical investigation. *Management Information Systems Quarterly, 24*(1), 169–197. doi:10.2307/3250983

Bishop, K., & Phillips, D. (2006). *Using Ajax with WebSphere Portal.* Retrieved from http://www.ibm.com/developerworks/websphere/library/techarticles/0606_bishop/0606_bishop.html

Blackboard Inc. (n.d.). *Blackboard.* Retrieved from http://www.blackboard.com/

Booch, G. (2006). *Software architecture.* IBM Rational Software Group Presentation.

Booch, G., Rumbaugh, J., & Jacobson, I. (2005). *Unified Modeling Language User Guide.* Reading, MA: Addison-Wesley Professional.

Boston, J. R. (2000, February). A Signal Detection System Based on Dempster-Shafer Theory and Comparison to Fuzzy Detection. *IEEE Transactions on Systems, Man and Cybernetics. Part C, Applications and Reviews, 30*(1), 45–51. doi:10.1109/5326.827453

Bowman, D., & Gatignon, H. (1995). Determinants of competitor response time to a new product introduction. *JMR, Journal of Marketing Research, 32*(1), 42–53. doi:10.2307/3152109

Boye, J. (2006). *The enterprise portals report.* Olney, MD: CMS Watch.

Brandic, I. (in press). Towards self-manageable cloud services. In *Proceedings of Second International Workshop of Real-Time Service-Oriented Arachitecture and Applications.*

Braun, J. (2000). Dempster-Shafer theory and Bayesian reasoning in multisensor data fusion, Sensor Fusion: Architectures, Algorithms and Applications IV. *Proceedings of the Society for Photo-Instrumentation Engineers, 4051,* 255–266.

Bredemeyer, D., & Malan, R. (2002). *The Role of the Architect.* Resources for Software Architects.

Brown, J. S. (1997). *Seeing differently: insights on innovation*. Boston: Harvard Business School Press.

Brown, S. J., & Warner, J. B. (1985). Using daily stock returns: The case of event studies. *Journal of Financial Economics, 14*(1), 3–31. doi:10.1016/0304-405X(85)90042-X

Brugger, S. T. (2004). *Data Mining for Network Intrusion Detection* (pp. 8–55). Retrieved from www.bruggerink.com/~zow/papers/dmnid_qualpres.pdf

Burroughs, J., Wilson, L. F., & George, V. (2002). *Analysis of Distributed Intrusion Detection Systems Using Bayesian Methods*. Paper presented at IPCCC 2002 (pp. 142-147).

Bush, V. (1996). As we may think. In Stefik, M. (Ed.), *Internet dreams: archetypes, myths, and metaphors* (pp. 15–22). Cambridge, MA: MIT Press.

Buyya, R., Yeoa, C. S., Venugopala, S., Broberg, J., & Brandic, I. (2009). Cloud computing and emerging it platforms: Vision, hype, and reality for delivering computing as the 5th utility. *Future Generation Computer Systems, 25*, 599–616. doi:10.1016/j.future.2008.12.001

Campbell, N. (2009). *What is science? BiblioBazaar*. LLC.

Cannon, R. (2000, September 23-25). *Where Internet service providers and telephone companies compete: a guide to the Computer Inquiries, enhanced services providers and information service providers*. Paper presented to TPRC Research Conference on Communication, Information and Internet Policy, Alexandria, VA.

Capra, L., Emmerich, W., & Mascolo, C. (n.d.). *Middleware for mobile computing*.

Cardoso, J., Busslerand, C., Shethand, A., & Fensel, D. (2002). *Semantic web services and processes: Semantic composition and quality of service*. Paper presented at the Federated Conferences on the Move to Meaningful Internet Computing and Ubiquitous Computer, Irvine, CA.

Carr, N. G. (2003). IT doesn't matter. *Harvard Business Review, 81*(5), 41–49.

Castells, M. (2000). *The rise of the network society* (2nd ed., *Vol. 1*). Oxford, UK: Blackwell.

Castells, M. (2001). *The Internet galaxy: reflections on the Internet, business, and society*. Oxford, UK: Oxford University Press.

Chaney, P. K., Devinney, T. M., & Winer, R. S. (1991). The impact of new product introductions on the market value of firms. *The Journal of Business, 64*(4), 573–610. doi:10.1086/296552

Chang, K. C., Jackson, J., & Grover, V. (2003). E-commerce and corporate strategy: an executive perspective. *Information & Management, 40*(7), 663–675. doi:10.1016/S0378-7206(02)00095-2

Chapman, S. (n.d.). *Using window.onload*. Retrieved from http://javascript.about.com/library/blonload.htm

Chatterjee, D., Pacini, C., & Sambamurthy, V. (2002). The shareholder-wealth and trading-volume effects of information-technology infrastructure investments. *Journal of Management Information Systems, 19*(2), 7–42.

Chatzigiannakis, V., Lenis, A., Siaterlis, C., Grammatikou, M., Kalogeras, D., Papavassiliou, S., & Maglaris, V. (2002). *Distributed Network Monitoring and anomaly Detection as a Grid Application* (pp. 1-13).

Cho, N., & Park, S. (2001). Development of electronic commerce user consumer satisfaction index (ECUSI) for internet shopping. *Industrial Management & Data Systems, 101*(8), 400–405. doi:10.1108/EUM0000000006170

Clements, P. (1996). A survey of architecture description languages. In P*roceedings of the 8th International Workshop on Software Specification and Design* (p. 16). Washington, DC: IEEE Computer Society.

Collins, H. (2001). *Corporate portal definition and features*. AMACOM.

Comer, D. E. (2000). *Internetworking with TCP/IP: principles, protocols, and architectures* (4th ed., *Vol. 1*). Upper Saddle River, NJ: Prentice Hall.

Computer Society Institute. (2002, April). *Cyber crime bleeds U.S. corporations, survey shows*. Retrieved January 16, 2003, from http://www.gocsi.com/press/20020407.html

Coplien, J. (2006). Organizational Patterns. *Enterprise Information Systems, 6*, 43–52.

Crazy Egg. (n.d.). *See where people click: Visualise the user experience on your website*. Retrieved from http://crazyegg.com/

Cross, J., Hartley, S. W., Rudelius, W., & Vassey, M. J. (2001). Sales force activities and marketing strategies in industrial firms: relationships and implications. *Journal of Personal Selling & Sales Management, 21*(3), 199–206.

Dardan, S., Stylianou, A., & Kumar, R. (2006). The impact of custmer-related IT investment on custmer satisfaction and shareholder returns. *Journal of Computer Information Systems, 47*(2), 100–111.

Das, A. S., Chaudhuri, A. P., & Chawla, M. (2006). *Point of view for WSRP compliant portal technologies*. Retrieved from http://searchsoa.techtarget.com/tip/0,289483,sid26_gci1186223,00.html

Degabriele, J. P., & Pym, D. (2007). *Economic aspects of a utility computing service* (Tech. Rep. HPL-2007-101). Palo Alto, CA: HP Laboratories.

Dehning, B., Richardson, V. J., & Stratopoulos, T. (2005). Information technology investment and firm value. *Information & Management, 42*(7), 989–1008. doi:10.1016/j.im.2004.11.003

Dehning, B., Richardson, V. J., Urbaczewski, A., & Wells, J. D. (2004). Reexamining the value relevance of E-commerce initiatives. *Journal of Management Information Systems, 21*(1), 55–82.

Dehning, B., Richardson, V. J., & Zmud, R. W. (2003). The value relevance of announcements of transformational information technology investments. *Management Information Systems Quarterly, 27*(4), 637–656.

Denton, T. M., Menard, F., & Isenberg, D. (2000). *Netheads versus Bellheads*. Ottawa, Canada: Federal Department of Industry.

Deokar Amit, V., & El-Gayar Omar, F. (2008). A semantic web services-based architecture for model management systems. In *HICSS '08: Proceedings of the 41st Annual Hawaii International Conference on System Sciences*, Washington, DC: IEEE Computer Society.

Department of Justice. (2009). *Former Enron Broadband Co-Chief Executive Officer Sentenced for Wire Fraud*. Retrieved October 15, 2009, from http://houston.fbi.gov/dojpressrel/pressrel09/ho092809.htm

Dewan, S., & Ren, F. (2007). Risk and return of information technology initiatives: Evidence from electronic commerce announcements. *Information Systems Research, 18*(4), 370–394. doi:10.1287/isre.1070.0120

Dewar, J. A. (2000). *The information age and the printing press: looking backward to see ahead*. New York: ACM. Retrieved October 15, 2009 from http://portal.acm.org/citation.cfm?id=347634.348784&coll=GUIDE&dl=GUIDE&CFID=56515123&CFTOKEN=92433459

DiMaggio, P., Hargittai, E., Neuman, W. R., & Robinson, J. P. (2001). Social implications of the Internet. *Annual Review of Sociology, 27*, 307–336. doi:10.1146/annurev.soc.27.1.307

Dong, & Deborah. (2005). *Alert Confidence Fusion in Intrusion Detection Systems with Extended Dempster-Shafer Theory* (pp. 142-147). New York: ACM.

Donthu, N. (2001). Does your Web site measure up? *Marketing Management, 10*(4), 29.

Dos Santos, B. L., Peffers, K., & Mauer, D. C. (1993). The impact of information technology investment announcements on the market value of the firm. *Information Systems Research, 4*(1), 1–23. doi:10.1287/isre.4.1.1

Drake, S. (2009). *App store mania will further delay growth of browser-based applications*. Retrieved October 2009, from http://www.fiercemobilecontent.com/story/app-store-mania-will-further-delay-growth-browser-based-applications/2009-08-04

Dyson, E. (1998). *Release 2.1: a design for living in the digital age*. London: Penguin.

Edmonds, A. (2003). A new tool for web usability testing. In *Proceedings of Behavior Research Methods, Instruments and Computers*. Uzilla.

Eisenmann, T., & Pothen, S. T. (2000). *Online portals* (Case No. 9-801-305) (pp. 1-29). Boston: Harvard Business School.

Evans, R. J. (1997). *In defence of history*. London: Granta Books.

Falcarin, P., & Alonso, G. (2004). Software architecture evolution through dynamic aop. *Software Architecture*, 57-73.

Federal Networking Council. (1995). *Definition of 'Internet'*. Retrieved October 15, 2009, from http://www.itrd.gov/fnc/Internet_res.html

Feiler, P., Gluch, D., Hudak, J., & INST, C.-M. U. P. P. S. E. (2006). *The architecture analysis & design language (AADL): An introduction.*

Fensel, D. (2003). The unified problem-solving method development language UPML. *Knowledge and Information Systems, 5*(1), 83–131. doi:10.1007/s10115-002-0074-5

Ferguson, C., Finn, F., & Hall, J. (2005). Electronic commerce investments, the resource-based view of the firm, and firm market value. *International Journal of Accounting Information Systems, 6*, 5–29. doi:10.1016/j.accinf.2004.08.001

Fielding, R., Gettys, J., Mogul, J., Frystyk, H., & Berners-Lee, T. (2008). *Rfc2068 -hypertext transfer protocol.* Retrieved from http://www.faqs.org/rfcs/rfc2068.html

Fischer, D. H. (1970). *Historians' fallacies: toward a logic of historical thought.* New York: HarperPerennial.

Garlan, D., & Schmerl, B. (2009). Ævol: A tool for defining and planning architecture evolution. In *Proceedings of the 2009 IEEE 31st International Conference on Software Engineering* (pp. 591-594). Washington, DC: IEEE Computer Society.

Garlan, D., & Shaw, M. (1993). An introduction to software architecture. In *Proceedings of the Advances in software engineering and knowledge engineering* (Vol. 1, pp. 1-40).

Garlan, D., Barnes, J., Schmerl, B., & Celiku, O. (2009). Evolution Styles: Foundations and Tool Support for Software Architecture Evolution. In *Proceedings of the Joint Working IEEE/IFIP Conference on Software Architecture 2009, European Conference on Software Architecture.*

Garlan, D., Monroe, R., & Wile, D. (1997). Acme: An architecture description interchange language. In *Proceedings of the 1997 conference of the Centre for Advanced Studies on Collaborative research* (p. 7). IBM Press.

Gehrke, D., & Turban, E. (2000). Determinants of successful web-site design: relative importance and recommendations for effectiveness. In *Proceedings of the 32nd Hawaii International Conference on System Sciences,* HI.

Genachowski, J. (2009). *Improving broadband and mobile communications.* Washington, DC: Brookings Institution. Retrieved October 15, 2009 from http://www.brookings.edu/~/media/Files/events/2009/0921_broadband_communications/20090921_broadband.pdf

Geyl, P. (1958). *Debates with historians.* Glasgow, UK: Fontana/Collins.

Geyskens, I., Gielens, K., & Dekimpe, M. G. (2002). The market valuation of internet channel additions. *Journal of Marketing, 66*(2), 102–119. doi:10.1509/jmkg.66.2.102.18478

Gillies, J., & Cailliau, R. (2000). *How the web was born.* Oxford, UK: Oxford University Press.

Glushko, R. J. (2009). Seven Contexts for Service System Design. In *Handbook of Service.*

Goel, A., Schmidt, H., & Gilbert, D. (2010). Formal Models of Virtual Enterprise Architecture: Motivations and Approaches. In *Proceedings of 14th Pacific Asia Conference on Information Systems (PACIS).* Association for Information Systems.

Goldstein, P. (2009). *Handset requirements outpacing battery life.* Retrieved October 2009, from http://www.fiercewireless.com/story/report-handset-requirements-outpacing-battery-life/2009-09-29

Google Analytics Official Site. (n.d.). Retrieved from http://www.google.com/analytics/

Google. (2009). *Google App Engine.* Retrieved from http://code.google.com/appengine/

Gorodetski, V., Karsaev, O., Kotenko, I., & Khabalov, A. (2002). Software Development Kit for Multi-agent Systems Design and Implementation. In B. Dunin-Keplicz & E. Nawareski (Eds.), *From Theory to Practice in Multi- agent Systems* (LNAI 2296, pp. 121-130). New York: Springer Verlag.

Gounaris, S., & Dimitriadis, S. (2003). Assessing service quality on the web: evidence from business-to-consumer portals. *Journal of Services Marketing, 17*(5), 529–548. doi:10.1108/08876040310486302

Grocholsky, B., Makarenko, A., & Durrant-Whyte, H. F. (2003). *Information-theoretic coordinated control of multiple sensor platforms* (pp. 1521–1526). ICRA.

Haas, H. P. L. H., Moreau, J.-J., Orchard, D., Schlimmer, J., & Weerawarana, S. (2004). *Web Services Description Language (WSDL) Version 2.0 Part 3: Bindings. W3C.* Retrieved from http://www.w3.org/TR/2004/WD-wsdl20-bindings-20040803

Habib, A., Hefeeda, M., & Bhargava, B. (2003). Detecting service violations and DoS attacks. In *Proceedings of the NDSS Conference* (pp. 439-446). Reston, VA: Internet Society.

Haenel, W. (2004). Multi Device Portals (Multi Device Portals). *it - Information Technology, 46*(5), 245-254.

Hafner, K., & Lyon, M. (1998). *Where wizards stay up late: the origins of the Internet.* New York: Touchstone.

Hall, D. (1992). *Mathematical Techniques in Multisensor Data Fusion* (pp. 99–105). Norwood, MA: Artech House.

Hamel, G., & Sampler, J. (1998). The e-corporation (cover story). *Fortune, 138*(11), 80–87.

Hawking, P., Stein, A., & Foster, S. (2004). e-HR and Employee Self Service: A Case Study of a Victorian Public Sector Organisation. *Issues in Informing Science and Information Technology, 1.*

Hayes, D. C., Hunton, J. E., & Reck, J. L. (2000). Information systems outsourcing announcement: Investigating the impact on the market value of contract-granting firm. *Journal of Information Systems, 17*(2), 109–125. doi:10.2308/jis.2000.14.2.109

Hayes, D. C., Hunton, J. E., & Reck, J. L. (2001). Market reaction to ERP implementation announcements. *Journal of Information Systems, 15*(1), 3–18. doi:10.2308/jis.2001.15.1.3

Hayes-Roth, F. (1994). *Architecture-based acquisition and development of software: Guidelines and recommendations from the ARPA domain-specific software architecture (DSSA) program. Teknowledge Federal Systems (Version 1). ISO/IEC/(IEEE) 2007ISO/IEC/(IEEE). (2007). ISO/IEC 42010 (IEEE Std) 1471-2000: Systems and Software engineering - Recommended practice for architectural description of software-intensive systems.* Washington, DC: IEEE.

Hayward, B. (2002). *The impact of IT investment on the Australian economy.* Stamford, CT: Gartner Group.

Hepper, S. (2003). Comparing the JSR 168 Java Portlet Specification with the IBM Portlet API. Retrieved May 11, 2005, from http://www-128.ibm.com/developerworks/websphere/library/techarticles/0312_hepper/hepper.html

Hepper, S. (2004). *Portlet API Comparison white paper: JSR 168 Java Portlet Specification compared to the IBM Portlet API.* Retrieved May 11, 2005, from http://www-128.ibm.com/developerworks/websphere/library/techarticles/0406_hepper/0406_hepper.html

Hepper, S., & Hesmer, S. (2003). *Introducing the Portlet Specification, JavaWorld.* Retrieved from http://www-106.ibm.com/developerworks/websphere/library/techarticles/0312_hepper/hepper.html

Herman, E. S., & McChesney, R. W. (1997). *The global media: the new missionaries of corporate capitalism.* London: Cassell.

Herssens, C., Faulkner, S., & Jureta, I. (2008a). Context-driven autonomic adaptation of sla. In Bouguettaya, A., Krger, I., Margaria, T., eds. ICSOC. Volume 5364 of Lecture Notes in Computer Science. 362–377

Herssens, C., Faulkner, S., & Jureta, I. (2008b, June 23-26). Cloud computing: Issues, research and implementations. In *Proceedings of Information Technology Interfaces* (pp. 31-40).

Holdener, A. T. (2008). *Ajax: The Definitive Guide.* New York: O'Reilly.

Hugh, F. (2005). *Durrant-Whyte: Data fusion in sensor networks* (pp. 545–565). IPSN.

Huizingh, E. K. R. E. (2002). The antecedents of web site performance. *European Journal of Marketing, 36,* 1225–1248. doi:10.1108/03090560210445155

Hundt, R. E. (2000). *You say you want a revolution: a story of information age politics.* New Haven, CT: Yale University Press.

Huston, G. (1999). *ISP survival guide: strategies for running a competitive ISP.* New York: Wiley Computer Publishing.

IBM. (2009a). *IBM Application Services for SAP.* Retrieved from http://www-935.ibm.com/services/us/index.wss/offerfamily/gbs/a1030831

IBM. (2009b). *IBM Perspective on Cloud Computing*. Retrieved from http://www.ibm.com/cloud/

ICL. (2010). *Academic and corporate e-learning in a global context*. Retrieved April 18, 2010, from http://www.icl-conference.org/icl2010/index.htm

IETF. (2005). *The Atom Syndication Format*. Retrieved from http://www.ietf.org/rfc/rfc4287.txt

Im, K. S., Dow, K. E., & Grover, V. (2001). A reexamination of IT investment and the market value of the firm: an event study methodology. *Information Systems Research, 12*(1), 103–117. doi:10.1287/isre.12.1.103.9718

Infocetner. (2010) *Portal configuration service*. Retrieved from http://publib.boulder.ibm.com /infocenter/wpdoc /v6r1/topic/com.ibm.wp.ent.doc_v6101/admin/srvc fgref.html #srvcfgref_state_manager

Ivar Jorstad, D. V. T., & Dustdar, S. (n.d.). *Personalisation of next generation mobile services*.

Java Community Process. (2004). *JSR-000154 Java servlets specification 2.4*. Retrieved from http://www.jcp.org/aboutJava/communityprocess/final/jsr154

Java Community Process. (2005). *JSR 168. Portlet specification*. Retrieved from http://www.jcp.org/en/jsr/detail?id=168

Java Community Process. (2008). *JSR 286 JSR-000286 portlet specification 2.0*. http://jcp.org/aboutJava/communityprocess/final/jsr286/index.html

Java Community Process. (n.d.). *JSR 188: CC/PP Processing*. Retrieved from http://www.jcp.org/en/jsr/summary?id=188

Johnson, J. (2010). *CHAOS Chronicles III*. Retrieved April 16, 2010, from http://www.standishgroup.com/chaos/

JSR 168. (2005). *Portlet Specification*. Retrieved from http://www.jcp.org/en/jsr/detail?id=168

Kahn, R. E. (1994). *The role of government in the evolution of the Internet*. Paper presented to Revolution in the U.S. Information Infrastructure, Washington DC.

Kalakota, R., & Whinston, A. (1996). *Frontiers of Electronic Commerce*. Reading, MA: Addison Wesley.

Keown, A., Martin, J., Petty, J., & Scott, D. (2004). *Financial Management: Principles and Applications*. Upper Saddle River, NJ: Prentice Hall.

Khallaf, A., & Skantz, T. R. (2007). The effects of information technology expertise on the market value of a firm. *Journal of Information Systems, 21*(1), 83–105. doi:10.2308/jis.2007.21.1.83

Khemakhem, S., Drira, K., & Jmaiel, M. (2006). SEC: A search engine for component based software development. In *SAC '06: Proceedings of the 2006 ACM Symposium on Applied Computing* (pp. 1745–1750). New York: ACM.

Khemakhem, S., Drira, K., & Jmaiel, M. (2007). SEC+: an enhanced search engine for component-based software development. *SIGSOFT Softw. Eng. Notes, 32*(4).

Khemakhem, S., Jmaiel, M., Hamadou, B. A., & Drira, K. (2002, May). *Un environnement de recherche et d'intégration de composant logiciel*. Paper presented at the Seventh Conference on Computer Sciences, Annaba, Algeria.

Khemakhem, S., Drira, K., Khemakhem, E., & Jmaiel, M. (2008). An experimental evaluation of SEC+, an enhanced search engine for component-based software development. *SIGSOFT Softw. Eng. Notes, 33*(4), 1–3. doi:10.1145/1384139.1384143

Kim, H. M., Sengupta, A., Fox, M. S., Dalkilic, M. M. (2007). A measurement ontology generalizable for emerging domain applications on the semantic web. *Database Manag., 18*(1).

Kitchenham, B. (2004). *Procedures for Performing Systematic Reviews* (Tech. Rep. No. SE0401). Newcastle-under-Lyme, UK: Keele University.

Klein, L. A. (1999). *Sensor and Data Fusion Concepts and Applications* (2nd ed., pp. 1-252). Melville, NY: SPIE Optical Engineering Press. ISBN 0-8194-3231-8

Kleppe, A., Warmer, J., & Bast, W. (2003). *MDA explained: the model driven architecture: practice and promise*. Reading, MA: Addison-Wesley.

Knorr, E., & Gruman, G. (2009). *What cloud computing really means*. Retrieved from http://www-935.ibm.com/services/us/index.wss/offerfamily/gbs/a1030831

Koh, J., & Venkatraman, N. (1991). Joint venture formations and stock market reactions: an assessment in the information technology sector. *Academy of Management Journal, 34*(4), 869–892. doi:10.2307/256393

Kohler, A. (2002). Access to Foxtel network may be a dog of a deal. *Australian Financial Review, 72.*

Koks, D., & Challa, S. (2005). *An Introduction to Bayesian and Dempster-Shefer Data Fusion* (pp. 1-52)

Koller, M. (2001). Tool offers personalization on the fly. *Internet Week, 857*(16), 15.

Krugman, P. (1997). How fast can the U.S. economy grow? Not as fast as "new economy" pundits would like to think. *Harvard Business Review, 75*(4), 123–129.

Kumar, K. S. (2000). *Intrusion Detection and Analysis.* Vancouver, Canada: University of British Columbia.

Landrum, V. (2009, October). *Mobile Portal Accelerator.* Paper presented at Portal Excellence Conference, San Diego, CA.

Lee, H. G., Cho, D. H., & Lee, S. C. (2002). Impact of e-business initiatives on firm value. *Electronic Commerce Research and Applications, 1*(1), 41–56. doi:10.1016/S1567-4223(02)00005-4

Lessig, L. (1999). *Code and other laws of cyberspace.* New York: Basic Books.

Leue, C. (2009). *What you always wanted to know about URIs in WebSphere Portal v6 – or more than that ....* Retrieved from http://www-10.lotus.com /ldd/portalwiki. nsf/dx /what-you-always-wanted- to-know-about-uris-in- websphere-portal-%E2%80%93- or-more-than-that-%E2%80%A6

Li, X., Madnick, S., Zhu, H., & Fan, Y. (2009). An approach to composing web services with context heterogeneity. In *ICWS '09: Proceedings of the 2009 IEEE International Conference on Web Services* (pp. 695–702). Washington, DC: IEEE Computer Society.

Liesche, S., & Uhlig, S. (2006). *IBM WebSphere Developer Technical Journal: Using portal analytics with open-source reporting tools.* Retrieved from http://www.ibm.com/developerworks/websphere/techjournal/0609_liesche/0609_liesche.html

Lin, J. C., Jang, W., & Chen, K. (2007). Assessing the market valuation of e-service initiatives. *International Journal of Service Industry Management, 18*(3), 224–245. doi:10.1108/09564230710751460

Liu, C., & Arnett, K. P. (2000). Exploring the factors associated with Web site success in the context of electronic commerce. *Information & Management, 38,* 23–34. doi:10.1016/S0378-7206(00)00049-5

Liu, C., Dub, T. C., & Tsai, H. (2009). A study of the service quality of general portals. *Information & Management, 46,* 52–56. doi:10.1016/j.im.2008.11.003

Livingstone, S. (1999). New media, new audiences? *New Media & Society, 1,* 59–66. doi:10.1177/1461444899001001010

Loiacono, E. T., Watson, R. T., & Goodhue, D. L. (2002). WebQual: a measure of Website quality. In *Proceedings of the Marketing Educators' Conference: Marketing Theory and Applications* (Vol. 13, pp. 432-437).

Lotus®, is a trademark or registered trademark of IBM Corporation and/or Lotus Development Corporation in the United States, other countries, or both.

Loucopoulos, P., & Zicari, R. (1992). *Conceptual Modeling, Databases, and Case: An Integrated View of Information Systems Development.* New York: John Wiley & Sons.

Luna, L. (2009). *Finally, a mobile enterprise app store.* Retrieved October 2009, from http://www.fiercemobileit.com/story/finally-mobile-enterprise-app-store/2009-09-16

Ma, B. (2001). Parametric and Non Parametric Approaches for Multisensor Data Fusion (pp. 1-212). Unpublished PhD thesis, University Of Michigan, Michigan.

Ma, Y., Ma, X., Liu, S., & Jin, B. (2009). A proposal for stable semantic metrics based on evolving ontologies. In *Proceedings of the International Joint Conference on Artificial Intelligence* (pp. 136–139).

MacDonald, T. (1986). *Making a new people.* Vancouver, BC, Canada: New Star Books.

Maclaurin, W. R. (1971). *1947). Invention and innovation in the radio industry.* New York: Arno Press.

Mahdavi, M., Shepherd, J., & Benatallah, B. (2004). A collaborative approach for caching dynamic data in portal applications. In *Proceedings of the fifteenth conference on Australian database* (Vol. 27, pp. 181-188).

Marler, J. H., & Dulebohn, J. H. (2005). A Model of Employee Self-Service Technology Acceptance. *Research in Personnel and Human Resources Management, 24,* 137–180. doi:10.1016/S0742-7301(05)24004-5

Marvin, C. (1988). *When old technologies were new: thinking about electric communication in the late nineteenth century*. New York: Oxford University Press.

Mazzoleni, P., & Srivastava, B. (2008). Business driven SOA customization. In A. Bouguetaya, I. Krger, & T. Margaria (Eds.), *Proceedings of International Conference on Service-Oriented Computing (ICSOC)* (LNCS 5364, pp. 286-301).

McKinsey Global Institute. (2001). *US productivity growth 1995-2000: understanding the contribution of information technology relative to other factors*. Washington, DC: McKinsey & Company.

McKinsey Global Institute. (2002). *Whatever happened to the new economy?* San Francisco, CA: McKinsey & Company.

McLuhan, M. (1994). *Understanding media: The extensions of man*. Boston: MIT Press.

McPhail, T. L. (1989). Inquiry in international communication. In Asante, M. K., Gudykunst, W. B., & Newmark, E. (Eds.), *Handbook of international and intercultural communication* (pp. 47–66). Newbury Park, CA: Sage Publications.

McWilliams, A., & Siegel, D. (1997). Event studies in management research: Theoretical and empirical issues. *Academy of Management Journal, 40*(3), 626–657. doi:10.2307/257056

Medvidovic, N., & Taylor, R. (1997). A framework for classifying and comparing architecture description languages. In *Proceedings of the ACM SIGSOFT Software Engineering Notes* (Vol. 22, No. 6, p. 76).

Medvidovic, N., Rosenblum, D., Redmiles, D., & Robbins, J. (2002). Modeling software architectures in the Unified Modeling Language. *ACM Transactions on Software Engineering and Methodology, 11*(1), 57.

Medvidovic, N., & Taylor, R. (2000). A classification and comparison framework for software architecture description languages. *IEEE Transactions on Software Engineering, 26*(1), 70–93.

Meng, Z. L., & Lee, S. Y. (2007). The value of IT to firms in a developing country in the catch-up process: An empirical comparison of China and the United States. *Decision Support Systems, 43*(3), 737–745. doi:10.1016/j.dss.2006.12.007

Metzger, A., & Pohl, K. (2007, May 20-26). M variability management in software product line engineering. In *Proceedings of 29th International Conference on Software Engineering* (pp. 186-187).

Mika, P., Oberle, D., Gangemi, A., & Sabou, M. (2004). Foundations for service ontologies: aligning OWL-S to dolce. In *WWW '04: Proceedings of the 13th International Conference on World Wide Web* (pp. 563–572). New York: ACM.

Mishina, Y., Pollock, T. G., & Porac, J. F. (2004). Are more resources always better for growth? Resource stickiness in market and product expansion. *Strategic Management Journal, 25*(12), 1179–1197. doi:10.1002/smj.424

Mishra, P., & Dutt, N. (2006). Architecture Description Languages. In Ienne, P., & Leupers, R. (Eds.), *Customizable and Configurable Embedded Processors*. San Francisco: Morgan Kaufmann Publishers.

Mobiles, W. A. P. (2009). *WAP review*. Retrieved from http://wapreview.com/?id=134

Moodle Trust. (n.d.). *Moodle*. Retrieved from http://moodle.org/

Mullen, T., & Wellman, M. P. (1995, June). A simple computational market for network information services. In *Proceedings of the First International Conference on Multiagent Systems* (pp. 283-289). Washington, DC: IEEE Computer Society.

Nabrzyski, J., Schoof, J. M., & Weglarz, J. (Eds.). (2003). *Grid Resource Management: State of the Art and Future Trends*. Dordrecht, The Netherlands: Kluwer Academic Publishers.

Negroponte, N. (1995). *Being digital*. London: Coronet.

Nielsen, J. (2000). *Designing web usability: The practice of simplicity*. Indianapolis, IN: New Riders Publishing.

Nigam, A., & Caswell, N. S. (2003). Business artifacts: An approach to operational specification. *IBM Systems Journal, 3*, 428–445.

Ning, P., Xu, D., Healey, C., & Amant, R. (2004). Building Attack Scenarios through Integration of Complementary Alert Correlation Methods. In *Proceedings of the 11th Annual Network and Distributed System Security Symposium* (pp. 97-111).

Nyquist, H. (1928). Certain topics in telegraph transmission theory. *Trans. AIEE, 47*(2).

OASIS. (2003). *WSRP specification version 1*. Retrieved from http://www.oasis-open.org/committees/download.php/3343/oasis-200304-wsrp-specification-1.0.pdf

OASIS. (2005). *Web Services for Interactive Applications specification – WSIA*. Retrieved from http://www.oasis-open.org/committees/wsia

OASIS. (2009). *Web Services for Remote Portlets Specification v2.0*. Retrieved from http://docs.oasis-open.org/wsrp/v2/wsrp-2.0-spec.html

Oh, W., Gallivan, M. J., & Kim, J. W. (2006). The market's perception of the transactional risks of information technology outsourcing announcements. *Journal of Management Information Systems, 22*(4), 271–303. doi:10.2753/MIS0742-1222220410

O'Reilly, T. (2005). *What is Web 2.0?* Retrieved October 15, 2009, from http://oreilly.com/web2/archive/what-is-web-20.html

Pacific Bell. (1994). *The Information Superhighway*. Retrieved October 15, 2009, from http://www.youtube.com/watch?v=QQS6gTdbOsk

Parasuraman, A., Zeithaml, V. A., & Berry, L. L. (1988). SERVQUAL: a multiple-item scale for measuring consumer perceptions of service quality. *Journal of Retailing, 64*(1), 12–40.

Parasuraman, A., Zeithaml, V. A., & Berry, L. L. (1994). Alternative scale for measuring service quality: A comparative assessment based on psychometric and diagnostic criteria. *Journal of Retailing, 70*(3), 201–230. doi:10.1016/0022-4359(94)90033-7

Patterson, E. (2004). *Web Analytics Demystified: A Marketer's Guide to Understanding How Your Web Site Affects Your Business*. New York: Celilo Group media and Cafe Press.

Paulin, M., & Perrien, J. (1996). Measurement of service quality: the effect of contextuality. In Kunst, P., & Lemmink, J. (Eds.), *Managing Service Quality* (3rd ed., pp. 257–273). London: Chapman.

Payne, A., & Holt, S. (2001). Diagnosing customer value. *British Journal of Management, 12*, 159–182. doi:10.1111/1467-8551.00192

Peak, D., Windsor, J., & Conover, J. (2002). Risks and effects of IS/IT outsourcing: a securities market assessment. *Journal of Information Technology Cases and Applications, 4*(1), 6–33.

Perry, D., & Wolf, A. (1992). Foundations for the study of software architecture. *ACM SIGSOFT Software Engineering Notes, 17*(4), 40–52.

Peterson, E. (2004). *Web analytics demystified: A marketer's guide to understanding how your web site affects your business*. Portland, OR: Celilo Group Media and CafePress.

Peterson, E. (2009). *The truth about mobile analytics*. Retrieved from http://www.nedstat.com/white-paper/uk.html

Polgar, P., Bram, R., & Polgar, T. (2004). Building and Managing Enterprise Wide Web. In *Proceedings of the 2004 Informing Science and IT Education Joint Conference, Portals – Tutorial*, Monash University, Melbourne, Australia.

Polgar, J. (2009). Using WSRP 2.0 with JSR 168 and 286 Portlets. *International Journal of Web Portals, 2*(2).

Polgar, J., & Polgar, T. (2007). WSRP Relationship to UDDI. In Tatnall, A. (Ed.), *Encyclopaedia of Portal Technology and Applications* (Vol. 1, pp. 1210–1216). Hershey, PA: IGI Global.

Polgar, J., & Polgar, T. (2009). Building Portal Applications. *International Journal of Web Portals, 1*(1), 47–67.

Portal Catalog. (2009). *IBM Lotus Web Content Management Rendering Portlet*. Retrieved from http://www-01.ibm.com/software/brandcatalog/portal/portal/details?catalog.label=1WP1001S6

Porter, M. E. (1985). *Competitive advantage*. New York: Free Press.

Porter, M. E. (1990). *The competitive advantage of nations*. New York: Free Press.

Porter, M. E. (2001). Strategy and the Internet. *Harvard Business Review, 79*(3), 62–78.

Prokoph, A. (2007). *Help Web crawlers efficiently crawl your portal sites and Web sites*. Retrieved from http://www.ibm.com/developerworks/library/x-sitemaps/

Rahim, M. M. (2006). *Understanding Apdotion and Impact of B2E E-Business Systems: Lessons Learned from the experience of an Australian University*. Melbourne, Victoria, Australia: Monash Univesity. 5 Trademarks Trademark information is provided to identify terms that are exclusively reserved for use by the owner.

Ranganathan, C., & Brown, C. V. (2006). ERP investment and the market value of firms: Toward an understanding of influential ERP project variables. *Information Systems Research, 17*(2), 145–161. doi:10.1287/isre.1060.0084

Rehman, R. (2003). *Intrusion Detection System with SNORT* (pp. 1-288). Retrieved from http://www.snort.org/

Richardson, V. J., & Zmud, R. W. (2002). The Value Relevance of Information Technology Investments Announcements: Incorporating Industry Strategic IT Role. In *Proceedings of the 35th Hawaii International Conference on System Science,* HI.

Rindsberg, S. (n.d.). *Make your vba code in powerpoint respond to events*. Retrieved from http://www.pptfaq.com/FAQ00004.htm

Roach, S. (1987). America's technology dilemma: a profile of the information economy. *Special Economic Study*.

Robertson, J. (2009). *Custom code, CMS and portals*. Retrieved from http://www.steptwo.com.au/papers/kmc_customcode/index.html

Sabherwal, R., & Sabherwal, S. (2005). Knowledge Management Using Information Technology: Determinants of Short-Term Impact on Firm Value. *Decision Sciences, 36*(4), 531–568. doi:10.1111/j.1540-5414.2005.00102.x

Saltzer, J. H., Reed, D. P., & Clarke, D. (1984). End-to-end arguments in system design. *ACM Transactions on Computer Systems, 2*(4), 277–288. doi:10.1145/357401.357402

Sam. (2008). *COST OF SMS v Cost of ISP analysis*. Retrieved October 2009, from http://gthing.net/the-true-price-of-sms-messages/

Schiller, D. (1999). *Digital capitalism: networking the global market system*. Cambridge, MA: MIT Press.

Schluting, C. (n.d.). *Analyzing web server logs*. Retrieved from http://www.serverwatch.com/tutorials/article.php/3518061/Analyzing-Web-Server-Logs.htm

Schumpeter, J. A. (1934). *The theory of economic development: an inquiry into profits, capital, credit, interest, and the business cycle*. Cambridge, MA: Harvard University Press.

Schumpeter, J. A. (1939). *Business cycles: a theoretical, historical and statistical analysis of the capitalist process (Vol. 1)*. New York: McGraw-Hill.

Servlets Specification 2.4. (2004). Retrieved November 2005 from http://www.jcp.org/aboutJava/community-process/final/jsr154

Shapiro, E. (2009). *Making content searchable anywhere using IBM WebSphere Portal's publishing Seedlist Framework*. Retrieved from http://www.ibm.com/developerworks /websphere/zones /portal/proddoc/dw-w-seedlist/

Shapiro, E., & Ben-Nahum, B. (2008). *Customizing and extending the functionality of the IBM WebSphere Portal 6.1 Search Center portlet*. Retrieved from http://www.ibm.com/developerworks /websphere/library /techarticles/0809_shapiro/0809_shapiro.html

Shen, J., Yang, Y., & Lalwani, B. (2004). Mapping web services specifications to process ontology: Opportunities and limitations. In *FTDCS '04: Proceedings of the 10th IEEE International Workshop on Future Trends of Distributed Computing Systems* (pp. 229–235). Washington, DC: IEEE Computer Society.

Shilakes, C. C., & Tylman, J. (1998). *Enterprise information portals*. New York: Merril Lynch. Retrieved from http://www.sagemaker.com/home.asp?id=500&file=Company/WhitePapers/lynch.htm

Shiller, R. J. (2001). *Irrational exuberance*. Princeton, NJ: Princeton University Press.

Shuler, J. (2002). Of Web Portals, E-Gov, and the Public's Prints. *Information Policy the Journal of Academic Librarianship, 28*(6), 410–413.

Siaterlis, C., & Maglaris, B. (2004). Towards Multisensor Data Fusion for DoS detection. In *Proceedings of the 2004 ACM symposium on Applied Computing* (pp. 1-8).

Sieber, S., & Volor-Sabatier, J. (2005). Competitive dynamics of general portals. In Tatnall, A. (Ed.), *Web portals: The new gateways to Internet information and services* (pp. 64–79). Hershey, PA: IGI Global.

Silverstone, R., Hirsch, E., & Morley, D. (1991). Listening to a long conversation: an ethnographic approach to the study of information and communication technologies in the home. *Cultural Studies, 5*(2), 204–227. doi:10.1080/09502389100490171

Singh, S. (2001). Studying the user: a matter of perspective. *Media International Australia*, (98), 113-128.

Singh, S. (2000). *User-centred design of smart Internet technologies*. Melbourne, Australia: Smart Internet Technology CRC.

Spafford, E. H. (1991). *The Internet worm incident* (Tech. Rep. No. CSD-TR-933). West Lafayette, IN: Purdue University, Department of Computer Science. LEM OS, R. (1991). *Counting the cost of slammer* (pp. 1-19).

Specifications, U. D. D. I. (2005). *Universal Description, Discovery and Integration v2 and v3*. Retrieved November 2005, from http://www.uddi.org/specification.html

Spencer, J. (2004). *Togaf* (enterprise ed., version 8.1).

Spinellis, D. (2003). The decay and failures of web references. *Communications of the ACM, 46*(1), 71–77. doi:10.1145/602421.602422

Staeding, A. (n.d.). *List of user-agents (spiders, robots, crawler, browser)*. Retrieved from http://user-agents.org

Stefik, M. (1996). *Internet dreams: archetypes, myths, and metaphors*. Cambridge, MA: MIT Press.

Subramani, M., & Walden, E. (2001). The impact of e-commerce announcements on the market value of firms. *Information Systems Research, 12*(2), 135–154. doi:10.1287/isre.12.2.135.9698

Sultan, Z. (2009). Multiple Simultaneous Threat detection System in UNIX. *IJCSNS, 9*(1), 56–66.

Sun MicroSystems. (n.d.). *Virtualbox*. Retrieved from http://www.virtualbox.org/

Tapscott, D. (2000). Rethinking strategy in a networked world: or why Michael Porter is wrong about the Internet. *Strategy+Business, 24*. Retrieved October 15, 2009 from http://www.theecademy.com/downloads/Strategy+Business.pdf

Tatnall, A. (2005). *Web Portals: from the General to the Specific*. In *Proceedings of the 6th International Working for E-Business (We-B) Conference*, Victoria University, Melbourne, Australia.

Thiagarajan, R., & Stumptner, M. (2006). A native ontology approach for semantic service descriptions. In *AOW '06: Proceedings of the Second Australasian Workshop on Advances in Ontologies* (pp. 85–90) Darlinghurst, Australia: Australian Computer Society, Inc.

Tivoli®, and WebSphere®, are trademarks of the IBM Corporation in the United States, other countries, or both.

Tolstoy, C., & Tolstoy, L. (2009). *What is art? Biblio-Bazaar*. LLC.

Tran, L. (2002). Authoring Device Independent Portal Content. In *Proceedings of W3C Workshop on Device Independent Authoring Techniques: Authoring Device Independent Portal Content*. Retrieved from http://www.w3.org/2002/07/DIAT/posn/sun-portal.html

Trinca, H. (2002, September). Absolute Porter. *Australian Financial Review: Boss magazine*, pp. 34-39.

Turner, R. M. (1993). Context-sensitive reasoning for autonomous agents and cooperative distributed problem solving. In *Proceedings of the IJCAI Workshop on Using Knowledge in its Context* (pp. 141-151).

Van Riel, A. C. R., Liljander, V., Lemmink, J., & Streukens, S. (2002). *Boost customer loyalty with online support: the case of mobile telecomms providers*. Retrieved from http://www.fdewb.unimaas.nl/blokken/9010/documents/onlinesup.pdf

Velayathan, G., & Yamada, S. (2006). Behavior-based web page evaluation. In *Proceedings of the Web Intelligence and Intelligent Agent Technology Workshops. WWW Consortium*. (n.d.a). *Common* logfile *format*. Retrieved from http://www.w3.org/Daemon/User/Config/Logging.html#common-logfile-format

Venugopal, S., Buyya, R., & Winton, L. J. (2004). A grid service broker for scheduling dis- tributed data-oriented applications on global grids. In *Proceedings of the 2nd Wordshop on Middleware for Grid Computing* (pp. 75-80).

VMWare. (2009). *VMWare Mobile Virtualization Platform (MVP)*. Retrieved November 2009, from http://www.vmware.com/technology/mobile/

W3C. (n.d.). Mobile Web Best Practices 1.0: Basic Guidelines. Part 5.1.2 Exploit Device Capabilities. Retrieved from http://www.w3.org/TR/mobile-bp/

W3C. (n.d.). *Standard RFC-1738*. Retrieved from http://tools.ietf.org/html/rfc1738

W3C. (n.d.). *W3C Device Description Repository Simple API*. Retrieved from http://www.w3.org/TR/DDR-Simple-API/

Wachowski, L., & Wachowski, A. (1999). *The Matrix*. Retrieved April 18, 2010, from http://www.screenplay.com/downloads/scripts/The%20Matrix.pdf.

Wang, Y.-S., Tang, T.-I., & Tang, J.-T. E. (2001). An instrument for measuring customer satisfaction toward Web sites that market digital products and services. *Journal of Electronic Commerce Research, 2*(3), 1–14.

Web Services Description Language (WSDL). An Intuitive View. (n.d.). Retrieved from http://java.sun.com/dev/evangcentral/totallytech/wsdl.html

Webb, H. W., & Webb, L. A. (2004). SiteQual: An integrated measure of Web site quality. *The Journal of enterprise information management, 18*(4).

Webopedia. (2010). Retrieved from http://webopedia.com/TERM/P/portal.html

Wellman, M. P. (1994). Market-Oriented Programming: Some Early Lessons. In *Market- Based Control: A Paradigm for Distributed Resource Allocation* (pp. 74-95).

Wikipedia. (n.d.). *URL normalization*. Retrieved from http://en.wikipedia.org/wiki/URL_normalization

Winchester House. (2010). *Winchester Mystery House Homepage*. Retrieved from http://www.winchestermysteryhouse.com/

Winner, L. (1978). *Autonomous technology: technics-out-of-control as a theme in political thought*. Cambridge, MA: MIT Press.

Winston, B. (1998). *Media technology and society: a history from the telegraph to the Internet*. London: Routledge.

Wolfinbarger, M. F., & Gilly, M. C. (2002). *comQ: dimensionalizing, measuring and predicting quality of the e-tailing experience* (Tech. Rep. No. 02-100). MSI.

WSRP 2.0 Portlet Specification. (2006). Retrieved November 2009 from http://www.oasis-open.org/committees/download.php/18617/wsrp-2.0-spec-pr-01.html

WSRP specification version 1. (2003). *Web Services for Remote Portlets, OASIS*. Retrieved in 2005 from

Wu, H., Siegel, M., Stiefelhagen, R., & Yang, J. (2002). Sensor fusion using Dempster-Shafer theory. In *Proceedings of IEEE Instrumentation and Measurement Technology Conference*, Anchorage, AK (pp. 1-6).

WWW Consortium. (n.d.b). *Document object model (dom) level 2 events* specification. Retrieved from http://www.w3.org/TR/2000/REC-DOM-Level-2-Events-20001113/

WWW Consortium. (n.d.c). *A vocabulary and associated apis for html and xhtml*. Retrieved from http://dev.w3.org/html5/spec/Overview.html

Yang, Z., Cai, S., Zhou, Z., & Zhou, N. (2005). Development and validation of an instrument to measure user perceived service quality of information presenting Web portals. *Information & Management, 42*(4), 575–589. doi:10.1016/S0378-7206(04)00073-4

Yang, Z., Peterson, R. T., & Huang, L. (2001). Taking the pulse of internet pharmacies: online consumers speak out on pharmacy services. *Marketing Health Services, 21*, 4–10.

Yen, V. (2008). Business Process and Workflow Modeling in Web Services. In *Electronic Commerce: Concepts, Methodologies, Tools, and Applications* (pp. 202–208). Hershey: Idea Group.

Yeo, C. S., & Buyya, R. (2006). A taxonomy of market-based resource management systems for utility-driven cluster computing. *Software, Practice & Experience, 36*(13), 1381–1419. doi:10.1002/spe.725

Yoo, B., & Donthu, N. (2001). Developing a scale to measure the perceived quality of internet shopping sites (SITEQUAL). *Quarterly Journal of Electronic Commerce, 2*(1), 31–47.

Young, A. (in press). Mobilizing the enterprise. *International Journal of Web Portals*.

Young, A. E. (2009). Service Oriented Architecture Conceptual Landscape PART II. *International Journal of Web Portals*3.

Young, A. E. (2009a). Mobilising the Enterprise. *International Journal of Web Portals*, , 6.

Zakas, N. C. (n.d.). *History of the user-agent string*. Retrieved from http://www.nczonline.net/blog/2010/01/12/history-of-the-user-agent-string/

Zakas, N. C., McPeak, J., & Fawcett, J. (2006). *Professional Ajax*. New York: Willey Publishing.

Zakon, R. H. (2010). *Hobbes' Internet timeline, version 10.* Retrieved April 20, 2010, from http://www.zakon.org/robert/internet/timeline/

Zamboni, D. (2000, October). *Doing intrusion detection using embedded sensors* (Tech. Rep. No. 2000-21, pp. 1-9). West Lafayette, IN: Purdue University, CERIAS.

Zeithaml, V. A., Parasuraman, A., & Malhotra, A. (2001). *A conceptual framework for understanding e-service quality: implications for future research and managerial practice* (Tech. Rep. No. 00-115, pp. 1-49). Cambridge, MA: MSI.

Zeithaml, V. A., Parasuraman, A., & Malhotra, A. (2002). Service quality delivery through Web sites: a critical review of extant knowledge. *Journal of the Academy of Marketing Science, 30*(4), 362–375. doi:10.1177/009207002236911

Zhang, P., & Von Dran, G. (2001). Expectations and rankings of Website quality features: Results of two studies. In *Proceedings of the 34th Hawaii International Conference on System Sciences*.

Zhang, P., & Von Dran, G. (2002). User expectations and rankings of quality factors in different Web site domains. *International Journal of Electronic Commerce, 6*(2), 9–33.

About the Contributors

Greg Adamson currently works as a portal project manager in the financial services industry. He has worked with Internet-based services as a consultant and in delivery in Australia, Asia and Europe since 1991. He has experience in the media, banking, health insurance, government, trade and telecommunications sectors among others. Greg has a PhD in the field of e-business from RMIT in Melbourne. This was undertaken from a multidisciplinary approach involving business, technical, regulatory, media and historical perspectives. He has a Bachelor in Technology (Engineering) from the University of Southern Queensland.

Jana Polgar worked as a lecturer at Monash University in Melbourne, Australia where she was teaching subjects focusing on web services, SOA and portal design and implementation in postgraduate courses at the Faculty of Information Technology. .Her research interests include web services, SOA and portal applications. She has also extensive industry experience in various roles ranging from software development to management and666 consulting positions. She holds master degree in Electrical Engineering from VUT Brno (Czech Republic) and PhD from RMIT Melbourne.

* * *

Ajay Mohindra works for IBM Research Division, Thomas J. Watson Research Center, 19 Skyline Drive, Hawthorne, New York 10598. Dr. Mohindra has been a research staff member at IBM since 1993. For his technical contributions to IBM, he has been received one Outstanding Innovation Achievement Award, one Outstanding Technical Achievement Award, two Research Division Awards, and one Technical Group Award. He also holds 16 patents. He holds a PhD in computer science from the Georgia Institute of Technology. His research interests include distributed systems management and cloud computing.

Amit Goel is a research scholar at RMIT University, Melbourne, Australia. He brings more than 20 years of experience in Information Technology Industry. His main areas of interest are Enterprise Architecture and Strategy, Enterprise Integration and Services Oriented Computing, Software Architecture and Formal Methods. Amit has worked with large and medium enterprises including AT&T, IBM, Keane, Sapient, Globallogic and NetAcross. Amit is a Senior Member of IEEE, Member of ACM and Life Member of IoD (Institute of Directors). Amit holds Bachelors and Master Degrees in Computer Applications, Certified Enterprise Architect from Carnegie Mellon University (USA) and TOGAF Certified Enterprise Architect from The Open Group, apart from various other certifications such as PMP, CISSP and CISM. Amit also holds Certified Corporate Director certificate from Institute of Directors and Diploma in Management. Amit enjoys travelling, long drives and watching movies. He recently developed a passion for healthy eating for healthy living.

Andreas Prokoph has been working at IBM in the field of text search and information retrieval for the past 18 years. Various positions as technical lead and architect for search solutions scaling from Intranet to client-side embedded. Some projects: NetQuestion (which was the core search engine of IBM's Intranet and www.ibm.com search service in 1996), GTR/GT9 search engine (Domino and DB2 Extenders), Text Search Engine (TSE), Portal Search (today). In addition spending time with IBM Research and various boards within IBM to discuss strategies and prepare new technologies to move into text search offerings: categorization/taxonomies, spell-checking, text analytics, etc.. Also consulting and supporting IBM teams cross brand on search topics, such as OmniFind enterprise search. Currently lead software architect overseeing search integration in WebSphere Portal and IBM Web Content Management as well as consulting and service engagements for Portal customers on the topics of content and search integration projects.

Don Naro is an Information Developer for IBM and has worked on several different projects for WebSphere Portal as well as other Lotus branded products. He has worked as a writer for several different education and technology companies throughout the USA, Asia, and Europe. Don holds post graduate qualifications in Education and Technical Communication from the University of Cambridge and the University of Limerick.

Ed Young is currently a consultant with Young Consulting, Chief Technology Officer of Sportsbet Pty Ltd and researching Information Systems at Victoria University, Australia. His research interests include Enterprise Architecture (EA), Service-Oriented Architecture (SOA) specialising in architectures for mobile platforms, and ethics. He holds post-graduate degrees in mathematics and object-oriented software technology, is a chartered scientist and mathematician, and an active member of the Australian Computer Society. Ed is Associate Editor of International Journal of Web Portals (IJWP).

Henry Chang (hychang@us.ibm.com) is a senior technical staff member and a research manager at the IBM T.J. Watson Research Center. He leads the research effort in smarter living services on Cloud, business performance monitoring and management framework and innovation leadership to IBM Websphere BPM suits and IBM internal supply chain visibility initiatives. He received an IBM Innovate Award for his work on B2B collaboration solutions. Before joining IBM at the Thomas J. Watson Research Center, he received PhD in computer sciences from U. Wisconsin-Madison at 1987 and a BS in electrical engineering from National Taiwan University. He is a member of ACM and IEEE.

Jaye Fitzgerald is Architect for IBM Mobile Portals Accelerator and a software industry veteran at Lotus Development, OneSource Information Systems, Wall Data and Iris Associates. He has worked at IBM for over 12 years. Prior to his current role, he provided consulting services to IBM customers in the lab services organization. He has presented at Lotusphere and the Portal Excellence Conferences.

Jeaha Yang is an advisory software engineer in the Business Informatics Department. He has a BS degree from Polytechnic Institute of Technology of New York and an MS degree from Syracuse University. His recent work has involved the service cloud and business performance monitoring and analytics.

Jeremiah (Jerh.) O'Connor is a software architect at IBM Ireland. His professional interests include information retrieval and data privacy. He is an engineer at heart and holds a bachelors degree in Computer Engineering from University of Limerick and an MSc. in Computer Systems from Dublin City University.

Joe Lamantia has been a designer, consultant, and thought leader in the Internet and user experience communities since the middle 90's. An accomplished leader and former entrepreneur, his clients range from global Fortune 100 enterprises in diverse industries, to community focused non-profits. Lamantia contributes regularly to leading professional publications including Boxes and Arrows, UXmatters, and Intranets Today, and recently launched a column exploring the intersection of ubiquitous computing and experience design. He speaks frequently at design and technology conferences in North America and Europe on current topics, as well as the future of the user experience discipline. Lamantia enjoys creating and sharing design and research tools for the user experience community; most recently, the Building Blocks design framework for portals. Following a stint in management consulting and enterprise IT strategy, Lamantia recently took the plunge into expat life by moving to Amsterdam, where he works as a strategist and experience architect at Webby award winning digital interactive agency MediaCatalyst BV.

Jun-Jang Jeng is a research staff member in the Business Informatics Department at the Thomas J. Watson Research Center. He received a BS degree in chemical engineering from National Taiwan University, and MS and PhD degrees in computer science from the Michigan State University. He has been associated with IBM Research since 1999. His research interests include business process & performance management, formal discipline of software and system engineering, real-time enterprise computing & SOA, sense-and-respond systems, and software agents. He has published more than 80 conference and journal papers in these areas. Before joining IBM, Dr. Jeng served as a senior member of technical staff at AT&T Labs, Middletown, New Jersey. He also taught in several universities, including The George Washington University, Rutgers University and NJIT, as a visiting professor. Dr. Jeng is a senior member of the Institute of Electrical and Electronics Engineers and the Computer Society.

Manish Gupta is a PhD candidate at State University of New York at Buffalo. He also works full-time as an information security professional at a northeast US based bank. He received an MBA from SUNY-Buffalo (USA)and a bachelor's degree in mechanical engineering from I.E.T, Lucknow (India). He has more than a decade of industry experience in information systems security, policies and technologies. He has published 3 books in the area of information security and assurance. He has published more than 50 research articles in leading journals, conference proceedings and books including DSS, ACM Transactions, IEEE and JOEUC. He serves in editorial boards of 7 International Journals and has served in program committees of several international conferences. He holds several professional designations including CISSP, CISA, CISM, ISSPCS and PMP.

Michael Jessopp is a Lead Consultant for Object Consulting, Australia specialising in content applications. He attended Monash University, Australia and is a regular at Australian Computer Society Special Interest and Enterprise Java events. Michael is the proud father of two; Caitlin and Indiana.

Neil Richardson has worked for several major European/Global companies in a managing consultant role and specialises in managing and delivering complex programmes of technology and business change, often from an initial need to rescue or create pragmatic, yet strategic solutions. He has many years experience in leadership positions selling, delivering (and training) within top tier consultancy firms. In recent years Neil has undertaken numerous assurance roles managing significant risk in complex programmes enabling successful delivery - from both client and supplier-side. Neil has much experience/expertise managing suppliers including offshore outsourcing. He operates at board level with multi-national clients with a wide range of senior industry relationships in the UK and overseas across financial services, defence, utilities and logistics (amongst others). Neil also provides advanced/bespoke training, ad hoc master-class consultancy and individual coaching to a number of blue-chip project management communities and teaches independent contract programme & project managers the pragmatic and theoretical aspects of how to deliver project success.

Raj Sharman is an Associate Professor in the Management Science and Systems Department at SUNY, Buffalo, NY. He received his B. Tech and M. Tech degree from IIT Bombay, India and his M.S degree in Industrial Engineering and PhD in Computer Science from Louisiana State University. His research streams include Information Assurance, and Disaster Response Management, Business Value of IT, Decision Support Systems, Conceptual Modeling and Distributed Computing. His papers have been published in a number of national and international journals. He is also the recipient of several grants from the university as well as external agencies.

Ronan Dalton is a Software Development Manager at IBM's Ireland Development Lab. Ronan has worked with IBM in a number of technical positions prior to working in management. Most recently, Ronan held the position of technical team lead in the Lotus Workforce Management development team.

Tony Polgar works as a Portal development manager. Tony has first hand experience with the software life cycle, development methodology and use of various Web/Portal technologies in a large retail organisation. Over more than 30 years' career, Tony started as a software developer, worked in management appointments, and also spent 7 years in various IBM development labs in Australia and USA. He went on managing multiple client server, Web and Portal software projects. He is a certified project manager with interest in software quality, programming methods and future technologies. Tony has degrees in Mechanical Engineering, Mathematics, and Computing, as well as interest in classical music and photography.

Van W Landrum is a Certified Consulting IT Specialist who has worked for IBM for almost 19 years and has been working in the mobile arena for the past 9 years. He currently is the Technical Sales Lead for Mobile Portal Accelerator in North America. He has delivered presentations at Lotusphere, Impact, The Portal Excellence Conferences, eBusiness University, and others. He has helped many companies with their mobile strategies. Van co-authored an IBM Redbook on IBM's Commerce product which he supported for several years. He was also the Business Manager of IBM's Personal Systems and /AIXtra magazines.

Index